William Howitt

The History of the Supernatural

William Howitt

The History of the Supernatural

ISBN/EAN: 9783743382732

Manufactured in Europe, USA, Canada, Australia, Japa

Cover: Foto ©Lupo / pixelio.de

Manufactured and distributed by brebook publishing software (www.brebook.com)

William Howitt

The History of the Supernatural

THE HISTORY OF
THE SUPERNATURAL

IN ALL AGES AND NATIONS, AND
IN ALL CHURCHES, CHRISTIAN AND PAGAN:
DEMONSTRATING A UNIVERSAL FAITH.

BY WILLIAM HOWITT.

'Die Geisterwelt ist nicht verschlossen,
Dein Sinn ist zu, bein Herz ist todt.'
GOETHE, *Faust.*
'There are two courses of Nature—the ordinary and the extraordinary.'
BUTLER'S *Analogy.*
'Thou canst not call that madness of which thou art proved to know nothing.'
TERTULLIAN, *Apology I.*

IN TWO VOLUMES.

VOLUME THE SECOND.

LONDON:
LONGMAN, GREEN, LONGMAN, ROBERTS, & GREEN.
1863.

The right of translation is reserved.

CONTENTS

OF

THE SECOND VOLUME.

CHAPTER I.

MAGIC IN ITS RELATION TO THE SUPERNATURAL.

Magic in general—Found in the most ancient Nations—Chaldeans, Chinese, Indians, Phœnicians—Magic of the Greeks and Romans—Of the Scythians, Germans, Sclaves, Celts, Gauls—Dualism—Magic of the Hebrews—The Cabbalah—Its elementary Spirits—Magic amongst the Natives of America, Greenland, Kamtschatka, Siberia, Africa, California, &c.—Query as to who was the original Inventor of it—The two Kinds of Magic, Black and White—Magic as it existed in Egypt—Mode of exorcising—Formulas of Invocation—Black Magic—Forms of Conjuration—Professors of Magic; Albertus Magnus, Paracelsus, Agrippa—Learned Authorities on the Art . PAGE 1

CHAPTER II.

THE SUPERNATURAL IN THE GREEK AND OTHER EASTERN CHURCHES.

The Historians of the Church for the first six Centuries, all Greek or Syrian—Eusebius, Socrates, Sozomen, Theodoret, and Evagrius—The Doctrines of the Greek, Syrian, and Roman Churches during that time Identical—Faith in the Supernatural in the Syrian Church shown by their Liturgies—Prayers for Protection against evil Spirits—The Spiritualism of the ancient Syrian Saints and Fathers—This Faith still retained by the Greek and Russian Churches—Miraculous Greek and Russian Pictures—Notice of one by Miss Bremer in Greece—Exorcism as practised in Palestine, seen by Dr.

Thompson—The Practice called Dousch—Form of Invocation used by Abdel Kader el Mugraby—Universal Prevalence of Magic in the East—Belief that Jins watch over hidden treasure—Destruction of Aleppo predicted by M. Lustenau, and witnessed by Dr. Wolff—Predicted Death of Ezra de Piccitto—Silence of Church of England Writers on the East on this Subject—Dr. Stanley, Etheridge, Appleyard—Circumstances in the Life of the Russian Patriarch, Nicon—Instances of the Miraculous in the Russian Histories of the Church—Platon and Mouravieff—The Rev. R. W. Blackmore confirmatory of Mouravieff—The holy Icons—Warnings and miraculous Cures   PAGE 21

CHAPTER III.

SUPERNATURAL IN THE WALDENSIAN CHURCH.

Separated from the Roman Church in the fourth Century—Protested against Romish Corruptions—So called from their Valleys—Waldenses the earliest Protestants—Their Persecutions by the Princes of Savoy—MSS. of their History brought to England by Sir Samuel Morland—Historians of the Waldenses, Morland, Perrin, Brez, Leger, and Arnaud—Peter Waldo of Lyons conveys the Faith to France—Continued Persecutions by the Popes and the Savoyard and French Princes—Cromwell's Intervention—Marvellous Events in their Wars against their Oppressors—March of Henry Arnaud—Waldensian Colonies settle in Germany—Annual Allowance to them by William III. of England—Wonderful Deliverances—Opinion of Bernard of Clairvaux of the Waldenses—The 'Nobla Leyçon'—Account of them by the Rev. W. S. Gilly   32

CHAPTER IV.

THE SUPERNATURAL AMONGST THE SO-CALLED HERETICS AND MYSTICS OF THE MIDDLE AGES.

The so-called Heretics of all Ages, Manichæans, Pelagians, Montanists, Flagellants, Anabaptists, &c., all had Faith in the Miraculous—Instances of Fools predicting—Basilicus—Claus at Weimar—Bodin Angevin's Account of a Priest announcing a distant Battle in his Sermon at Perouse—Similar Occurrence to Apollonius at Ephesus during a Lecture—Prophetic Woman during the Persecution of A.D. 260—The Shepherdess of Cret—Account by Fernelius of a young Nobleman during Convulsions speaking Greek, though he had never learned it—Mode of accounting for such Phenomena by Magnetism, Hallucination, and Illusion—These Reasoners recommended to try Hallucination and Illusion for the teaching of Greek—Cures and Prescience resulting from apparently inadequate Causes, as the Cure of Mademoiselle Perrier, and Aspasia in ancient Greece—Singular Facts from Cotton Mather and Olaus Magnus—The real operative Principle to be sought deeper—This Principle

CONTENTS. vii

a Lex Magna of the Universe—It is Universal and Irresistible—Its Appearances in Churches and Heresies—We must choose the Good or Evil of it—The Albigenses and other Sects—The Apostolikers, Beghards, and Beguines—Brethren of the Full Spirit and Brethren of the Free Spirit—Persecuted by the Roman Church—Bulls issued by the Popes against them—Many of them burnt in Germany, the Netherlands, France, and Savoy—Swestronæ Conventualæ—Luciferists, Adamites, Turlupins, Lollards—The Cruciferi, Flagellants, Pusserer, and Dancers—Eckardt's Doctrines and Death—The Friends of God, Suso, Tauler, Rulman Merswin, Heinrich of Nördlingen, Nicolas of Basle, Berthold of Rohrbach—The Winkelers—Nicolas predicts the Schism in the Popedom, and Death of Gregory XI.—Nicolas put to Death—Corruption of the Church—Approach of the Reformation PAGE 41

CHAPTER V.

THE SPIRITUALISM OF LUTHER AND THE EARLY REFORMERS.

Rejection of Miracles by Protestantism — A Recent Discovery of a Copy of the Gospel — Popish False Miracles, the cause of the Rejection of the True — Luther admitted apparitions chiefly in connection with the Devil — His supposed View of one in the guise of Christ — His belief in Guardian Angels, and also in Inspiration — Luther afraid of Exorcising lest the Papists should say it was by the Devil — His Ideas of Possession, and of Exorcism — Expels a Demon from two Women — Madame Luther's Vision before the Death of her Daughter — Luther's Vision of the Rainbow Bridge — He saw the Devil everywhere, in Winds, Storms, Plagues, and noxious Reptiles, &c. — Idiots, the Lame, Blind, and Insane, Possessed by Devils — The Devils in Pilate's Pond — The Devil, he thought, tried to kill an Abbot — The Devil at the Wartburg — The Inkstand — The Bag of Nuts — Mrs. Berblibs heard Infernal Noises at the Wartburg — The Devil helping Suicides — The Devil hates God's Word, Prayers, and Ridicule — Bossuet's Remarks on Luther — The Devil's Arguments with Luther on the Mass — Luther, a great Medium, open to good and bad Spirits — Melancthon — An Apparition to warn Grynæus — Melancthon recalled from the Verge of Death by Luther's Prayers — So also Myconius — Calvin, a Spirit-Medium — Heard the Sounds of a distant Battle — Belief of Beza and Wolfgang Musculus in Possession — The Faith of John Knox in Spiritual Revelations to himself — Instances given by McCrie and Boys — The same in Grindal and Wishart — Wishart's Spiritual Warning against Cardinal Beatoun — Wishart's Prophecy of Beatoun's Death 66

CHAPTER VI.

THE SUPERNATURAL AND THE CHURCH OF ENGLAND.

Progress in Material Science, but none in Psychology — Recognition of Spiritualism in the Homilies; but denied in the Practical Belief of Clergymen — The Prelates of the Anglican Church have from the beginning for the most part held a Faith in Spiritual matters in opposition to the Prayer-Book — They contend that Miracles have ceased, yet acknowledge them in their Lives — Declarations of Cranmer, Latimer, Hooker, Bishop Hall of Norwich — Hooker and Hall avowed Spiritualists — Hall's 'Invisible World' — Providences in his Life — Lilly the Euphuist — Tillotson, Stillingfleet, Beveridge, Butler, Sherlock — Butler maintains that there are two Orders of Nature, the Ordinary and the Extraordinary — Beveridge and Sherlock Spiritualists — Milton, Bacon, Sir Thomas Browne, and Cudworth, wholly Spiritualists — Proofs from their Works — Proofs of Raphael, Guido, Dannecker, and other Artists being Spiritualists — Lucretius, Tasso, Coleridge, Schiller, Goethe, Mozart, their Opinions — Opinions of John Locke, Sir Matthew Hale, a Bishop of Gloucester, De Foe, and Blackstone, all avowed Spiritualists — The Period of Sceptical Writers, Hobbes, Toland, Collins, Wallaston, Bolingbroke, and Hume — Addison, Steele, Dr. Johnson, and Dr. Goldsmith, believed in Apparitions — A further race of Sceptics — Douglas, Farmer, Middleton, &c. . . . . PAGE 86

CHAPTER VII.

PRESENT MATERIALISED CONDITION OF THE CHURCH OF ENGLAND AND OF GENERAL OPINION.

Middleton's 'Free Enquiry into Miraculous Powers' — Farmers on the 'Credibility of Miracles'— Deny all Miracles out of the Bible — Deny that Spirits or Demons can do Miracles — Treat the performances of the Egyptian Magicians and of the Witch of Endor as Illusions — Douglas, Bishop of Salisbury, follows in the same course — His Rules for testing true Miracles — These Rules shown to equally explode Scriptural Miracles — Their Effect as applied to the Gospels — Douglas denies Miracles as existing amongst the Fathers — Proofs from many of these to the contrary — Origen and Athanagoras affirmed the Miracles of the Pagans — Irenæus mentions the raising of the Dead in his time — Attack of Douglas on the Miracles at the Tomb of the Abbé Paris — His mode of treating them — The Evidences of their Truth from Montgeron an Eyewitness 116

CHAPTER VIII.

THE MIRACLES IN THE CHURCHYARD IN PARIS IN 1731 AND SUBSEQUENTLY.

Youth and Conversion of Carré de Montgeron — Scenes in the Churchyard of St. Mèdard — The Abbé Paris a Jansenist — Miracles at his Tomb — Montgeron writes an Account of them — Presents his Book to Louis XIV. — Thrown into the Bastile for it — Nine Cases of the Miraculous fully described — The Opposition of the Jesuits, and of the Archbishops of Paris and Sens, and others — Proofs of the Reality of the Cases given by Montgeron from Public Documents — Testimonies of eminent Medical Men and distinguished Men of Science and of the Church — Cavillings of Douglas, Bishop of Salisbury, on those Cases — His false and dangerous Reasonings in his 'Criterion' — The Convulsionaires — Proofs of the Reality of the Marvels attending them.

PAGE 132

CHAPTER IX.

THE SUPERNATURAL AND THE CHURCH OF ENGLAND CONTINUED.

Wonderful Cures by Valentine Greatrakes — Commenced these Cures in Ireland — Came to England at the instance of the Earl of Orrery — Sojourn at Lord Conway's — Came to Court — Abode in Lincoln's Inn Fields — Testimonies of the Royal and other Physicians, and of Bishops and Noblemen to his Miraculous Cures — Cavils of Bishop Douglas against him — His Arguments those now used by Strauss and the Rationalists — Paley's Notions — His Blunder regarding Mesmerism corrected by Archbishop Whateley — Douglas on Methodism made ludicrous by Time — Milman's 'History of the Jews' — Dr. Hook of Chichester says he would reject Miracles if sent — The Protestant Church now isolated from all others on the subject of the Supernatural — Consequently a Fragment and an Abortion — Opposed to the Testimony of all Time — State Churches, what is to become of them? — Symptoms of Reaction — Penrose and Le Bas on present Miracles — Le Bas considers Scepticism a Disease — Spiritual Tendency of Dr. Goddard in the Bampton Lectures and of the present Bishop of London — Dr. Maitland's Satire on Farraday and Brewster — High time to protest against Protestantism . . . 150

CHAPTER X.

SPIRITUALISM IN NORTH AMERICA.

Works in which the History of Spiritualism in America is contained — Appeared first at Hydesville in 1848 — Phenomena in the Fox Family — Knocking in former Times in various Places — At Rushton Hall, at Tedworth, Oppenheim, in Lincolnshire — At the Wesleys at Epworth — Answering Questions by Knocks — The use of the Alphabet suggested by Isaac Post, a Friend — This used under the Emperor Valens — The Spirit Pendulum known to the Romans, recently used in France by Dr. Eymard, and in London by Mr. Welton — Phenomena at Dr. Phelps's in Connecticut, also at Mr. Grainger's at Rochester — The Phenomena increase in Power and Variety — Vast Extension of Spirit-Circles — American Spiritualists in 1855 amounted to 2,500,000 — Conversions at the rate of 300,000 Annually — Convincement of Judge Edmonds, Professors Hare, Bush, Mapes, and others — Trance-Speakers, Mrs. Hatch, Mrs. Henderson, Miss Hardinge — Speak on Sundays to 500,000 Hearers — Theory of the Phenomena by Dr. Rogers — Professor Mahan a Disciple of Rogers — The Experiments of Dr. Hare and Judge Edmonds — Mediums using Languages unknown to them — Governor Tallmadge — Opponents at Buffalo, Boston, Harvard College, &c. — Defence by Dr. Gardner of Boston — Report on Spiritualism by the Rev. Charles Beecher — Avowal of the Rev. Henry Ward Beecher — Mr. Coleman's Report on American Spiritualism — Spirit-Painting witnesssed by him — Koons' Rooms in Ohio — The Davenport Boys — Accounts of these by various Persons of Credit — The Kentucky Jerks — The Shakers Spiritualists — Their Views on Spiritualism — Letter of F. W. Evans — Mormonism a Phase of Spiritualism — Remarks of Mr. Orson Pratt — Spiritual Therapeutics — Madame Saint-Amour in France — Her wonderful Cures at Nantes — Madame Ehrenborg's account of Madame Saint-Amour — Vast growth of Mormonism Supernatural — Typal Mediums from America — Home, Jackson Davis, and Harris — Their several Characteristics — Some account of them — Condition of the United States prior to Spiritualism — Account of it by W. Robson — Harris warned of the coming Civil War — Effects of Spiritualism on the American Mind . . . . PAGE 168

CHAPTER XI.

SPIRITUALISM IN ENGLAND.

Spiritualism in England a weaker Reproduction of that in America — Its most prominent Phenomena — Perhaps the greatest Exhibition of Power the Destruction of Dr. ——'s Table in Kent — The chief Public Mediums from America, Mrs. Hayden, Mr. Home, Mr. Squire, Dr. Randolph, Dr. Redman, Mr. T. L. Harris — Probable Causes of the Difference of Intensity in the two Countries — Ignorance of the American Facts by English Opponents — Remark of Judge Edmonds on this Circumstance — The English Opponents merely going over the old Ground — Many of their Arguments borrowed from the first Opponents of Christianity — Examples from Julian the Apostate, and from the Writings of Tertullian and Lactantius — Rapid Progress of Belief in the midst of Opposition — Private Mediums most Satisfactory — The great Cry of the Human Heart after Certainty of a Spirit World — Apparition to Lord Chedworth — Expression of the Rev. J. H. Tuttle —

CONTENTS. xi

Shelley's early longing to see a Ghost—Such seen by him in After-life—
Instances from Lady Shelley's Memorials and Williams's Diary—Apparition
of Shelley seen by Lord Byron—Aspirations after Spiritual Certainty by
Bishop Heber and Robert Burns—Condemnation of Scepticism by the Author
of the 'Apocatastasis'—The Mission of Spiritualism to destroy Materialism
—Spirit Drawings in England by Lady Ellis, Mrs. W. Wilkinson and Mrs.
Watts—Ladies who see Spirits habitually—Mrs. N——, who saw the Appa-
rition of Captain Wheatcroft; Miss. A—— who saw that of Squire and Dame
Children at Ramhurst, as mentioned in Mr. Dale Owen's 'Footfalls'—The
Case of Elizabeth Squirrell—Literature of English Spiritualism—Mrs.
Crowe's 'Night-Side of Nature'—The 'Seeress of Prevorst'—Rymer's Lec-
tures—Leighton's Edition of Adin Ballou—Newton Crosland's 'New Theory
of Apparitions' — Mrs. Crosland's 'Light in the Valley'—Wilkinson's
'Spirit Drawings' and 'Revivals'—Coleman's 'Spiritualism in America'—
Fawcett's 'Angel Visits'—'The Confessions of a Truth-Seeker'—Jones's
'Natural and Supernatural'—Owen's 'Footfalls'—Barkas on Spiritualism
—'The Yorkshire Spiritual Telegraph'—'The British Spiritual Telegraph'
—'The Spiritual Magazine'—Nicodemeans, or Seekers to Spiritualism by
Candle-light—Involuntary Tributes to Spiritualism by the Bishop of London,
the Rev. E. Bickersteth, Hallam the Historian, Dean Trench, the Rev. Pro-
fessor Kingsley, the Rev. F. D. Maurice, &c.—Note on Spirit Photo-
graphs . . . . PAGE 214

CHAPTER XII.

OPPOSITION TO NEW FACTS.

The inevitable Destiny of new Truths to go out as Lambs amongst Wolves—
This experienced in the earliest Times, by Socrates, Pythagoras, Moses,
Christ, &c.—The early Christians suffered from it, and yet Ridiculed new
Truths themselves—Lactantius's Ridicule of Antipodes—Such the Fate of
Truth also in Huss, Jerome of Prague, the Lollards, Waldenses, Huguenots, in
Fox, Wesley, and all Reformers, in Galileo, Harvey, and Jenner —Solomon
de Caus imprisoned for advocating Steam—Thomas Gray treated as Insane,
for advocating Railways; Gall for Phrenology—Many other such Cases in
the Course of Medical Discovery—The Treatment of Columbus, Franklin,
and Perdonnet — The Steam Ship ridiculed by the French Academy, as
Franklin's Lightning Conductor by the Royal Society—Franklin treated
Mesmer as an Impostor—Hahnemann and Reichenbach persecuted for the
Discovery of Homœopathy and Odyle—Microscopes and Telescopes originally
denounced as Perverters of Sight — The Vaccination Society as Introducer of
an impious Tyranny—Winnowing Machines as Ungodly—Mause Headrigg
in 'Old Mortality'—Forks and the Route across Panama denounced as
equally Impious 235

CHAPTER XIII.

THE PHILADELPHIAN BRETHREN.

Dr. Pordage and the Philadelphian Society — The Will-power of Spirits — Conflicts of Pordage with them — Demon Processions — Their offensive Effluvia — They painted Scenes indelibly on Glass and Tiles — These Phenomena confirmed by Phenomena of to-day — Similar Effects in the Case of Mary Jobson — Spirit-writing and Spirit-drawings of this Period — Baron Guldenstubbe — Jane Leade — Her Description of Christian Magic — The Exercise of it obtained through the New-birth and Faith — The Works of Jane Leade — Antoinette Bourignon — Early Initiation into Religious Spiritualism — Obliged to fly from Flanders through the Malice of her Enemies — Her Residence in Holland and Germany — Her numerous Works — Her Admirers — Poiret, Swammerdam, &c. — Her Persecutions — Her Views of Christian Truth — Christina Poniatowski and Anna Maria Fleischer — Many Prophetic Mediums appeared during the Thirty Years' War—Margaret Frölich—Christina Poniatowski predicts the Death of Wallenstein, with peculiar Circumstances — Anna Maria Fleischer used to float in the Air — Predicts War, Pestilence, and great Religious Revolutions — These were laughed at, but came all to pass. . . . . . . PAGE 243

CHAPTER XIV.

SPIRITUALISM AMONGST THE DISSENTERS.

The Dissenters, like the Church, imbibed Scepticism — The importance of the Phenomena of Spiritualism in destroying this Scepticism — Professor Hare on Comte's Philosophy — This he declares instead of a Positive Philosophy, essentially a Negative one— Richard Baxter a decided Spiritualist — His 'Saint's Everlasting Rest '— Knockings noticed by him —Sees in Apparitions a proof of the Immortality of the Soul — Quotes Zanchius 'De Potentia Dæmonum;' Lavater de Spectris; Alexander ab Alexandro; Fulgatius; Ludovicus Vives; Olaus Magnus ; Cardan ; Manlius ; and Melancthon — Various Characteristics of Apparitions noticed by Baxter — Clement Writer preceded Hume in denying any Amount of Evidence sufficient to establish the Supernatural — John Bunyan — Many Pilgrim's Progresses— His the best— Bunyan's early Spiritual Conflicts — His Belief in the actual Operations of the Divine Spirit, and of the Devil— His Belief in Divine Judgements — Apparitions in Wales, mentioned by Edward Jones, an Independent Minister —The Sheepfold seen by him — Dr. Doddridge's Vision — Dr. Isaac Watts defends Belief in Apparitions — Thinks them a Proof of an Intermediate State—The Countess of Huntingdon—Her Husband's Vision of his Death—

Becomes the great Friend of Whitefield—Sudden Deaths at one of Whitefield's Meetings — Singular Dream, by a Lady of Brighton, concerning the Countess — Spiritual Intimations regarding the Death of her Daughter, Lady Selina Hastings—Mr. Berridge and the *Sortes Biblicæ* — The Countess providentially prevented from taking a fatal Journey—Providential Gifts of Money—Similar Experiences of Lady Anne Erskine, the Successor of Lady Huntingdon—The Colleges and Preachers of Lady Huntingdon — Introduces Religion to the Aristocracy — The first to commence the Enquiry into the Abuses of School Charities —William Huntington, the Coal-heaver, who lived by Faith — His Book 'The Bank of Faith'—Special Providences in his Case —The Rev. Isaac Taylor on Apparitions and Demoniac Possession — Dr. Campbell's Defence of Spiritualism in the 'British Banner'— Mrs. Schimmelpenninck's Faith in Spiritual Intercourse — Case of her Aunt, Lady Watson — Her Reasons for Belief in the Supernatural — Relates the Appearance of the Spirit of Mr. Petty — Sentiments of Theodore Parker . . . . PAGE 252

CHAPTER XV.

GEORGE FOX AND THE FRIENDS.

Ridicule of Fox for his Doctrine of immediate Inspiration — Dead state of Religion in his time — Richard Baxter's account of this State — A Hundred Years of Political Churchism had destroyed Christianity — Birth, youth, and spiritual Trials of George Fox — His strange Interviews with Parish Clergymen — Driven by these 'empty Casks' to his Bible — Adopts the literal Doctrines of the New Testament, and preaches them — Macaulay's Remarks on Fox — Fox an Idiot to Macaulay, and Macaulay an Idiot to Fox — Fox travels—His interviews with the Seekers — Stirring effect of his Preaching — Men of all Classes and Creeds flock to him — His Persecutions and Imprisonments — General Persecutions of the Friends — The Oxford Students — Spirit Manifestations through Fox — Heals the Sick and Crippled — Banishes an Evil Spirit — Is healed marvellously himself — Prophetic Visions — Cruelties practised on his Followers— Fox and Cromwell — Fox and Nayler — Opinions of Robert Barclay — His Vision of the Death of Archbishop Sharpe — Spiritual Manifestations to the Wife of Miles Halhead — Female Quakers in the Inquisition — Spiritual Assurances of their Deliverance — Vision of Daniel Baker — George Fox foretells the Repulse of the Turks from Vienna — Advises Friends to try the Spirits — Judgements on the Persecutors — Prophecies of Friends — Of the Destruction of Cromwell's Government — Of the Fire and Plague of London — The Persecutions of Friends in New England — Judgements on the Persecutors — Muggleton and Reeves — Fall and Repentance of James Nayler — Nayler misrepresented — His beautiful Description of the Spiritual Life — Mistaken notion that Quakerism is dying out—Evidences of Spiritualism in all the Writings of Friends, and in the Lives of their Ministers. 276

CHAPTER XVI.

MADAME GUYON AND FENELON.

Madame Guyon's Spiritualism that of the Fathers and Saints of the Catholic Church — The Offence of Madame Guyon was that she made hers independent of the Church — The Incidents of her Youth — Resigns her Children to her Relatives — Publishes Spiritual Works — Patronised by Madame Maintenon and then persecuted by her — The Persecutions of Bossuet — Her Imprisonment — Defended by Fenelon — His Persecutions on her account — Father Lacombe — Controversy betwixt Bossuet and Fenelon — Fenelon banished to Cambray — His Book condemned by the Pope — Fenelon publishes 'Telemachus' — Venerated by all Europe — His Diocese protected by Marlborough and Prince Eugene — Madame Guyon's Doctrines the Doctrines of Friends — Her Description of Spiritual Conversation without Words — This the Doctrine of the Early Church, of Michael Molinos, and others. . . . . PAGE 311

CHAPTER XVII.

THE PROPHETS OF THE CEVENNES.

Slight Notices of the Cevennois in English History — English Misrepresentations of them — Defended by Bishop Burnet, Dr. Woodward, Sir Richard Bulkeley, and others—Their true History to be found in French Authorities —Their terrible Persecutions by Louis XIV. — The Attempt to exterminate them — Banishment of their Pastors — Emigration of their Flocks — Montrevel sent with an Army to exterminate them — They rise on their Destroyers — Miracles which attended their Resistance — Victories over the Royal Troops — Cavallier, Rowland, and their other Leaders — Marshal Villars sent against them — Imposes on Cavallier, and induces him to lay down his Arms—The Fall of the Camisards — After-fates of their Heroes — Continued Persecutions till the French Revolution — Horrors revealed on opening their Prisons — Peyrat's Visit to the Cevennes in 1840 — The Descendants of the Camisard Heroes —The *Athenæum* in favour of Spiritual Views — Peyrat on the Influence of the Hebrew Literature and Inspiration.
322

CHAPTER XVIII.

THE WESLEYS, WHITEFIELD, AND FLETCHER OF MADELEY.

Dearth of Religion in the Days of Wesley and Whitefield — Statement of Watson on this Head — All Attempts to break up such Religious Torpor violently opposed — Phenomena at the Parsonage of Wesley's Father —

Dissolute State of the Universities —Wesley and Whitefield commence their Reforms — Fierce Persecutions — Characters of Wesley and Whitefield — Connection of Wesley with Count Zinzendorf and the Moravians — Southey's Ideas of Wesley's Faith in the Supernatural — Corrected by Coleridge — Violent Agitations of the Converted — Mr. Watson's Defence of Wesley's Belief — Whitefield's Assertion of direct Divine Inspiration — Expulsion of Students from Oxford for Praying — Fletcher of Madeley records direct Acts of Providence on his Behalf — Mrs. Fletcher's Vision — Mr. Fletcher foretells his own Death — Wonderful Success and Effects of Methodism.

PAGE 349

CHAPTER XIX.

BÖHME, SWEDENBORG, AND IRVING.

Sentiments of Michelet and Vinet on the Introduction of New Truths — Böhme's Youth and Spiritual Revelations — Prediction of his Future Eminence — Is shown the Inner Nature of Things — His chief Works — Persecuted by the Clergyman of his Parish — Banished from his Native Town — His Works read over all Europe — Much esteemed by Charles I., Sir Isaac Newton, &c. — Translation and Advocacy of his Works by William Law — Characteristics of Böhme and some of his Views — Specimens of his Style — Emanuel Swedenborg — Present Influence of his Doctrines — These Revolutionising the Popular Faith — Laying the Foundation of a Practical Psychology — His Scientific Works — These preparatory to his theologic ones — The Spiritual World opened up to him more extensively than to Epimenides and Hermotimus — His Spiritual Works — His Predictions in Physical Science now being successively realised — Translations of his Works — Lives of him by Dr. Wilkinson and Mr. White — Notices of Swedenborg's Doctrines by Dr. Wilkinson — Repugnance of Science to the Spiritual — Edward Irving — Early History — His great Popularity in London — Accepts the Truth of Inspiration in his Audience — The Unknown Tongues — Prophetic Inspirations — Cures by Prayer — Irving Persecuted by his own Church — His Death 377

CHAPTER XX.

THE MORAVIAN BRETHREN OR UNITAS FRATRUM.

Origin of this Society — Received by Count Zinzendorf at Herrnhut — Their firm Faith in Spiritual Agency and Phenomena — Examples of such Phenomena — Herrnhut described — Its Silence — The Missions of the Moravians — Calumnies by their Enemies — The Burial-place of the Zinzendorf Family and of the Founders of Herrnhut 403

CHAPTER XXI.

A CHAPTER OF POETS.

All Poets Spiritualists in their Writings—Artists the same—Raphael, Michael Angelo, Benvenuto Cellini—Dickens—Miss Brontë, Miss Mulock, Sir Edward Bulwer Lytton the same—Dante's 'Divina Commedia' a Spiritual Poem—The Spiritual Views in his 'Convito,' 'Monarchia,' and 'Vita Nuova'—Boccaccio's Account of the Vision of Dante's Mother—Dante's Vision of Beatrice—Dante's Revelation of the lost Cantos of the 'Divina Commedia' to his Son—Boccaccio a profound Believer in Spiritualism—The 'Decameron' full of its Evidences—Petrarch commissioned by Pietro Petroni on his Deathbed to warn Boccaccio of his approaching Death—His Reform in consequence—Petrarch's Faith in the Spiritual Powers of the Church—The Poems of Ariosto and Tasso full of Spiritualism—Evidences of it in the 'Jerusalem Delivered'—Tasso falsely declared mad—His Converse with Spirits—His Attempt to introduce the Marquis Manso to an Interview with them—Persecution of Tasso by Spirits in his Prison—The Improvisatori—Spiritualism of Milton — Proofs from 'Paradise Lost'— Proofs of Spiritualism found in Quarles, Herbert, Herrick, Cowper, Keble, Tennyson, Browning, Philip Bailey, &c.—Proofs from Young and Mrs. Hemans — From Byron, Shelley, and Coleridge — Sir Walter Scott — From Wordsworth's 'Peter Bell,' and other Poems—Anecdote by Wordsworth of Haunted Rooms at Cambridge.

PAGE 412

CHAPTER XXII.

MISCELLANEOUS MATTERS.

Review of the Spiritualism in History — The great Extent of the Department of Apparitions — Many Cases enumerated — Apparition of Captain Wheatcroft—Colonel Swift's Account of the Apparition in the Tower—Clamps-in-the-wood — The Cambridge Ghost Club — Two Thousand Cases of Apparitions collected by a Clergyman —Cases related by Dr. Kerner in Germany—Cock-lane Ghost— Drummer of Tedworth — Knocking in many Times and Places noticed—At Oppenheim — By Calmet— By Mr. Sargent in the Rocky Mountains— By Beaumont, in 1724 — By Glanville, in 1677— In the Minories, in 1679— Strange Phenomena at a Camp-fire in the Prairies — Experience of Mr. Wolf at Athens, United States — The Hauntings at Willington Mill— This Case recently confirmed by Mr. Procter—Heaton's Account of the Possession of a Boy — A Nun, in 1858, prophesied at Rome — Vision of the Troubles in America, by Joseph Hoag — Second Sight — The 'Secret Commonwealth,' written by Mr. Kirk, Minister of Aberfoil — His Ideas of Spirits, that they are the Ancestors of the People of each particular Country

CONTENTS. xvii

— Tract by Theophilus Insulanus — Vision of Robert Barclay — Insulanus defends the Power of Spiritual Vision — Facts of Second Sight seen by Lord Tarbot — The Preaching Epidemic — Bealings Bells — Mysterious Ringing of Bells in many Places referred to — Strange Phenomena at Sydersterne Parsonage — Case of Mary Jobson of Sunderland — Healing by Spiritual Means — Sleeping Preachers — Direct Spirit-writing by Baron Guldenstubbe — Witnessed by various Distinguished Persons — Instances of Spirit-writing in Scripture — The Law of Moses — The Hand at Belteshazzar's Feast — Case mentioned by Dr. Moore, as occurring to a Country Clergyman, to reveal a Murder — The case of the Laird of Redcastle — Wonderful Cure related by two Members of the Society of Friends a few Years ago.
PAGE 429

CHAPTER XXIII.

CONCLUSION.

Fresh difficulties for the Scientific — Cases of Toads, Frogs, &c., living in Blocks of Stone, Coal, &c., denied as possible by Captain Buckland and Professor Owen — Numerous recent Cases of such proved by direct Evidence — A Toad found in a Block of Stone sawn asunder for a Plinth of Birmingham Town-hall — Toad in Marble Chimney-piece at Chillingham — Toad in the Rock at Little Gonerby Brewery in October, 1862 — Great Experiment on Toads inclosed in Blocks of Gypsum by M. Seguin — The Winter Sleep of Snakes, Toads, Frogs, Lizards, and innumerable Insects — Serpents seen by Dr. Shaw in Egypt living in closely Corked Bottles — Frogs at Farnsfield — Hair Worms kept dry by Dr. Valentine, and reviving after Three Years — Similar Evidence by Dr. Braid regarding Animals in Torrid Climates — Similar Evidence by Humboldt — Lizard found alive by Dr. Clarke of Cambridge in Chalk Rock Forty-five Fathoms deep — The Ignis Fatuus denied by Y. in the 'Times' — Proved to exist by the Naturalists Gosse and Phipson — Also by Beccaria, Humboldt, and others — These all Proofs of Scepticism advancing in the Department of Physics — General Concluding Reflections . . 460

HISTORY OF THE SUPERNATURAL.

CHAPTER I.

MAGIC IN ITS RELATION TO THE SUPERNATURAL.

> The awful shadow of some unseen Power
> Floats, though unseen, among us ; visiting
> This various world with as inconstant wing
> As summer winds that creep from flower to flower.
> Like moonbeams that behind some piny mountain shower,
> It visits with inconstant glance
> Each human heart and countenance ;
> Like hues and harmonies of evening,
> Like clouds in starlight widely spread,
> Like memory of music fled,
> Like aught that for its grace may be
> Dear, and yet dearer for its mystery.— SHELLEY.

AS the belief in the supernatural, or spiritualism, has, from the earliest ages, had a constant tendency to degenerate into magic, because human nature has that downward bias, it is very desirable to have a clear notion of what magic is, that we may the more sacredly guard the great gift of spiritual life, which, more or less, is conferred on us, from everything but its own holy uses and objects. For this purpose I here take a summary view of magic, that it may also save me the necessity of farther extended reference to it in the course of this history.

Magic in General.

Magic, in the highest sense of the word, and in its construction into an art, is clearly traceable to high Asia, and to its south-eastern regions. The most ancient accounts of it, if we except Egypt, which may almost be said to belong to that quarter of the globe, are altogether from Asia. The books of Moses make us acquainted with several distinct, artistic, and highly perfected kinds of conjuration, and certain positive laws against it. The same is the case with the Indian Law Book of Menu, who, according to Sir William Jones, lived about 300 years before Christ. We say nothing of the Persians and their Magi. We find the same traces of magic as an art amongst the most ancient Chinese. Amongst the Chaldeans and Babylonians magical astrology and soothsaying are as old as the history of these people, and the same is the case with the Phœnicians.

If we turn from eastern, central, and northern Asia to high Asia, we find Prometheus paying on Caucasus the penalty of endeavouring to make man independent of the gods. Prometheus and Sisyphus are, as far as magic power is concerned, the Fausts of the ancient world. It is in the vicinity of the Caucasus, too, that we find the notorious magic family, which come before us so frequently in Homer and the later writers of Greece and Rome—Æetes, Pasiphae, Circe, and Medea. Homer shows distinctly that magic is not of European, expressly not of Grecian growth. Wachsmuth thinks that the whole family, by a visible syncretism in the early ages of Greece, were deduced from Helios in order to bring them nearer to the national and mythologic sphere, and thence to introduce their magic mysteries into the Greek literature. Circe herself was a goddess, sister to Æetes, both the children of Helios and of Perseis, the daughter of Oceanos. Their magic art is not Greek, but points to Asia; as they, to effect their metamorphoses, were obliged to mix φάρμακα λυγρὰ (Odyssey x. 236; Pindar, Pyth. iv. 415), and touch the Grecians with a magic rod.

Even the latter and very characteristic magic term θέλγειν does not appear in Circe's first conjuration, and she does not use the magic formulæ. In order to defeat her sorcery, human science is not sufficient, but Hermes, a god, is sent to find the μῶλυ, Moly. Men cannot easily pluck it — θεοὶ δέ τε πάντα δύνανται! The gods can do all things; and hence we see the reason for their constant invocation in all such magic processes. Let the reader clearly understand this. Notwithstanding this later developement of magic in Greece, this foreign art brought from Asia, which strove to make itself independent of the higher gods of the country, the oldest popular faith of Greece, as Hesiod shows, had its under-world, and its good and bad subterranean gods and demons, and along with it, as in all other nations, an original belief in magic power; but this expanded and perfected itself, through the later influence of the East, into an artistic system. The old national under-world was drawn into the sphere of the new magic; the machinery and operations of the arts of sorcery were attached to it, and men sought through the dark and destruction-pregnant powers of fate, what could not be accomplished by the gods of the country. The best commentary on this is in Virgil:—

> Flectere si nequeo Superos, Acheronta movebo.

The under-world, before the importation of the new Asiatic doctrines of magic amongst the Greeks, was detested, as everywhere else, by both gods and men (Hesiod, Theog. 743; Homer ii. 4, 157). Terrific monsters haunted it; the hostile races of giants and Titans were banished thither; there stagnated the mysterious Stygian flood. Hence in Lucan vi. 432, 'Ille supernis detestanda Deis noverat:' hence Erechtho, the celebrated Thessalian sorceress, 'grata Diis Erebi arcana Ditis operti,' &c. Hence in the later Greek and Roman magic eras, the original powers of the under-world, Pluto, Proserpine, &c., are not the masters and protectors of the new foreign art, but it is Hecate. This power, who in Hesiod had been placed over the elements, in this later mythology is transferred to the under-world with Selene — no doubt, because adjurations, magic arts, and offerings were made by night — Artemis, Persephone, &c., and a whole infernal court and environment of spectres, phantasms, dogs, serpents, &c., being made obedient to the great queen of sorcery.

This includes a complete outline of the origin of magic in Greece and Rome, and of its main features to the latest period. We may now take a hasty glance at it in other regions. Turn again to the East. The belief in good and bad spirits prevailed universally amongst the Chaldeans, Persians, Egyptians, Phœnicians, Indians, Carthaginians, Canaanites, &c.; and everywhere the idea of magic was associated with it. Amongst the greater part of the Asiatics and Africans there could be no conflict betwixt their mythology and this art; for their gods were of the class of powers invoked. As for the Scythians, Germans, Sclaves, Celts, Gauls, &c., from the meagre knowledge that we have of their mythologies, the same ideas appeared to prevail as amongst all other people in the same degree of cultivation. Pliny (H. N.) tells us, 'Britannia hodieque attonita Magiam celebrat tantis ceremoniis, ut dedisse Persis videri possit.' Helmont shows us that the Sclaves had their Zerne-Bog, their black, bad god; and the very name reveals a dualism, for Bog is yet in Polish God, and Zerne black. Thus, amid all these people, and still more distinctly amongst the Scandinavians — see the Eddas — the faith in magic was universal.

The religion of most of these nations consisted chiefly in a corrupted star and fire worship. The Persians alone appear to have preserved this in any degree of purity. Over the whole East extended the intellectual system, but under the most varied forms, and everywhere connected with dualism. Wherever the Greeks and Romans planted colonies their mythology soon received the Oriental inoculation of the dark and hostile powers. Thus the magic of the Romans and

Greeks, carried back to those regions, naturally coalesced with the Asiatic ideas and became doubly strong. In Persia, Egypt, and Carthage, this was the case. But it was in the system of Zoroaster that the dual strife assumed the most positive form. Ormuzd and Ahriman stand as the representatives of the two principles in perpetual conflict. In a less distant degree the same is the case in the teachings regarding Osiris, Isis, and Typhon. In the mythologies of both these peoples, prevails the demon system, the good and the bad principle, and each has its subordinate powers. The dualism of the Chaldeans is less known, but Plutarch says that they had two good and two bad gods, and numerous neutral ones.

Dualism lies equally at the foundation of the Indian mythologies. They have whole troops of contending demons or Dews, which do not confine themselves to the theology, but spread through all their poetry, dramas, and tales, as in Sacontala, &c. Sir William Jones, in the Asiatic Researches, (ii. 49), points out the relationship of the language of the Zend Avesta to that of the Sanscrit; and Ammianus Marcellinus tells us that Zoroaster made acquaintance with the Brahmins; and Arrian in the Indian expedition of Alexander, and Strabo, also tell us abundance of things about Indian magic, and about the little men three spans high, which proclaim their kinship to our fairies.

The Jews brought back from the Babylonian captivity all the ideas of the Persian dualism, and they accused our Saviour and the Apostles of performing all their miracles by magic, and the great master of sorcery, the devil. Horst, in his 'Zauber Bibliothek,' in quoting a long list of instances from the Gospel narratives, says, 'It is in vain to attempt to clear away from these Gospel narratives the devil and his demons. Such an exegesis is opposed to the whole faith of the world at that time. If we are to make these statements now mean just what we please, why did no single man in the ancient world understand them so? Are we become wiser? Then let us congratulate ourselves on our good fortune: but we cannot, on that account, compel those venerable writers to say what they, in their own time, neither could nor would say' (vol. ii. 31).

The Cabbalah contains a most comprehensive account of the magic of the Jews. Of the Kischuph or higher magic; the Monen, the astrological; and the Nischusch, or prophetic department.

'According to the Cabbalah, there is, besides the angels, a middle race of beings, which men usually call the elementary spirits, but known to the Jews under the general name of Schedim (the male being called Ruchin, the female Lilin), and described as the dregs or lowest of the spiritual orders. These spirits of the elements, the head of whom is the better Asmodeus, are divided into four principal classes. The first, which consist of the element of fire, and therefore cannot be seen with the eye, are well disposed to the good. They willingly help and support men. They are white, and understand the Thorah or law, since they stand in connection with the angel-world. They possess many secrets of nature. Solomon made use of them, and addressed himself to their king. The second class, formed out of fire and air, is lower, but yet good and wise, but invisible to human eyes. Both classes inhabit the upper regions. The third class consist of fire, air, and water, and are sometimes apparent to the senses. Their soul, according to Loriah, is of the vegetable nature. The fourth class, besides the former elements, has a component of fine earth, and their soul is of the mineral nature, and can be fully perceived by the senses. All these spirits of the elements eat and drink, propagate, and are subject to dissolution. The greater part of the two last kinds are of wicked disposition, mock, and deceive men, and are glad to do them mischief. Therefore they are under the authority of the evil Asmodeus, who is on the side of Smaëls, the devil. Whence they are called, like the dark satanic spirits, Masikim and M'chablim. There are amongst them some individuals of a more friendly nature, who mean well to men, and employ themselves in all sorts of domestic services. These two classes divide into different sorts; some live amongst men, others in the waters, a third kind in filthy places, and a fourth in mountains and deserts; each loves that element out of which it had its origin. Some called Jemim are of hideous aspect, and appear bodily in the open day, amongst the mountains.

'The two higher orders of these elementary spirits, who form the transition link betwixt the visible and invisible, stand bodily next to man, and are very dangerous, being endowed with various extraordinary powers, and having great insight into the hidden kingdoms of the lower nature; and, through their connection with the spirit-world, have some knowledge of the future, but chiefly in natural things. Hence men so soon began to worship them, and make offerings to them.

'Some of these answer to our Hobthrushes and Brownies, others to the gods of the heathen and the oracles. The higher these spirits, says the Cabbalah, though they can predict something of the future, are not much to be depended upon, because they are more connected with the natural than the spiritual world, and see only through such media. The lower of these natures are still less trustworthy; since, from their lower position, their vision is more obscure, and they often seek to deceive men by lies. These spirits of the elements live in the birds both of the upper and lower air, in beasts, and in the earth and its minerals. Hence the augurs obtained instructions from them through birds of prey, and magicians through stones, metals, and crystals.

'Maimonides says that it was not only allowed the Jews by their traditions, but commanded them to maintain an intimate connection with their departed friends, not out of curiosity or selfish purposes, but for fellowship in and through God. Therefore the Israelite was bound to pray for his brother who was yet in the region of purification; but only in cases of the highest necessity, and for the good of those left behind, was it permitted to enquire of the dead. They had a feast of blood on such occasions. A hole was dug, blood poured in, and over it a table was set at which they ate, and the Schedim or spirits of a middle nature appeared and answered their questions, even about the future. The Jews had the practice of tattooing certain names or pictures on their hands by which they came into rapport with these spirits, and they used many magic ceremonies for the same purposes. They put to flight fierce beasts by the utterance of the sacred name, and cured many hurts and diseases by means of magic.' (Maimonides in Abodah sarah 12, Absch: 11 Abth.)

By the Monen, they produced what the Scotch call glamour, making imaginary things appear real; but this delusion would not bear the test of water. (Trakt. Sanhedrin, fol. 65).

In the Sohar it is taught that, in the hour of death, a higher Ruach or spirit is imparted to men than what they had in life, by which they see what they never saw before; see their departed friends and relations. (Maichi, fol. 218.; Trumah, fol. 141). The Jews, however, believed that the soul was not wholly sundered from all connection with the body, but that the Habal de Garmin, the elementary body, or what the Germans call the Nerve-spirit, remained in the grave incorruptible, till the resurrection, when it was reunited to the soul. That this Habal de Garmin had all the form of the body, and was the real resurrection body. That it had a certain consciousness, and passed the time in pleasant dreams, unless disturbed by the nearness to some wicked or hostile body. Hence the necessity of burying friends together, and enemies far apart. Hence the desire of those who love each other to rest together in the earth. (Nakanti, fol. 66).

The soul, in the other world, is held in connection with this elementary body in the grave by the Zelem or shade in which it is wrapped, the vehicle of the Greek philosophers. All souls must pass through a condition of purgation; when the purer souls passed into the Gan Edin or subterranean paradise, till the general resurrection, and the impure into the place of farther purgation and punishment. In the middle, betwixt the outer world and G'hinham or hell, lies the region of the spirits of the elements, or of nature (Sepher Makiäl, fol. 12).

To these spirits of the elements, or Schedim, no doubt St. Paul alludes where, in our vague translation of the passage, speaking of the spiritual powers against which we have to contend, he names amongst them spiritual wickedness in high places, 'but which should be rendered the spiritualities or spirits of wickedness in the upper regions τὰ πνευματικὰ τῆς πονηρίας ἐν τοῖς ἐπουρανίοις: which the French have more correctly rendered, ' les esprits malins *qui sont* dans les airs,' and Luther ' den bösen Geistern unter dem Himmel.'

As it was in the ancient world both amongst cultivated and uncultivated nations, so it is in the present age. We find the same faith in both classes of spirit-power, in good and bad, and in magic arts everywhere, and even amongst nations who seem to have had, for ages, no intercourse with the Old World—namely, those of America. Locke says, 'We find, everywhere, no other ideas of the powers and operations of what we term spirits than those which we draw from the idea of our own spirits, as we reflect on the operations of our own souls, and carefully note them. Without doubt, the spirits which animate our bodies possess a very inferior rank; whence the belief in higher and more powerful, better or worse spiritual natures operating on the earth, is very natural to the human soul.'

We find these ideas in Greenland, where, according to the missionaries, Kranz and Egede, the inhabitants pay little regard to the good Pirksama; meaning, in their language, He above there; because they know that he will do them no harm, but they zealously worship the evil power, Angekok, from whom their priests, medicine-men, and conjurors are also named; and all the operations of the magicians are supposed to become effectual from the cooperation of Angekok and his inferior spirits. So in Greenland, too, that widely diffused dualism exists. We find, again, very much the same class of ideas and practices in Kamtschatka, according to Pallas, Kraschininikow, and others. So, also, amongst the Samojedes and Siberians. Herr von Matjuschkin, who accompanied Colonel Wrangel on the North-pole expedition in 1820, gives us a remarkable account of the incantations of the Schamans in northern Asia. These men enter into a wild dance, in which they throw their heads about in a wonderful manner, every now and then pausing to take some stupifying drink. They finally fall into unconsciousness, followed by convulsions and groans, and wild howls. The Schamans then stare wildly and terribly, and in this state questions are put to them. Matjuschkin says that at Alar Süüt, a day's journey from Werschojansk, he saw a Schaman who, in this state, answered him questions regarding his far-distant friends, which he afterwards found to be quite true. The Schaman could possibly have known nothing of him or his friends. On awaking, like all the clairvoyants, he knew nothing of what had passed.

In Loskiel's 'History of the Missions of the Evangelical Brethren amongst the Delaware and Iroquois Indians,' we learn that these as well as the Illinois tribes and Hurons, and other North American natives, not only believed in good and bad spirits, but in the operations on man through magical and therapeutic arts. In another part of these volumes I have given particular relations of such things amongst the Ojibbeways, from Schoolcraft and Kohl; others from the Mexicans, Peruvians, Caribs, &c. Such is the faith in magic and demon-power also, according to Father Antonio Zuchelli, and other writers, amongst the Africans of Congo and Loango, who pay particular reverence to a black goat; such also amongst the Mandingo negroes; according to Campbell and other missionary travellers, amongst those of South Africa, the Bushmans, the Namaquas, &c. In Dutch Guiana, says Howe, the natives believe in the existence of a host of subordinate evil spirits who produce thunder, storms, earthquakes, and diseases. These they name Yowahoos (probably the origin of Swift's name, Yahoos), and seek, by magic, to win them over, so as to render them innocuous to them.

The natives of California hold the same faith. The Koschimer, in the north of California, declared to the missionaries that the highest good God, he who lives, created a great number of subordinate spirits who fell away from him, and are now in hostility to him, and torment us. In a word, the faith is universal, and Home, Lord Kaimes, says truly, in his 'Sketches of the History of Man,' that the faith in mingled good and evil spirits amongst savage and uncultivated peoples, is one and the same with their faith in magic.

A celebrated German poet has equally well expressed this great fact:—

> Ein alter Stamm mit tausend Aesten,
> Die Wurzeln in der Ewigkeit,
> Neigt sich von Osten hin nach Westen
> In mancher Bildung weit und breit.
> Kein Baum kann blüthenreicher werden,
> Und keines Frucht kann edler seyn,
> Doch auch das 'Dunkelste' auf Erden—
> Es reift auf seinem Zweig allein.

On this cosmopolitan and ineradical persuasion was gradually erected the artistic system of magic, which has not yet lost its hold even on the most cultivated nations. Who was the original discoverer of it? Adam, Enoch, Seth, Abraham, Solomon, Zoroaster, Hermes Trismegistus, or some other more remote and mysterious personage according to Egyptian or Indian theories? To all these has the science been attributed, and Pliny tells us that a certain great magician, Osthanes, brought it from Asia into Greece. But to none of these does it owe its origin; it lies in the very foundations of the human mind. Given a conviction of the existence of spiritual and mighty powers exerting their influence over men, the attempt to find means of propitiating those powers, and of cooperating with them for the restraint and subjection of one section or the other of them, is a certainty.

As there are good and evil spiritual powers, so the art of invoking them soon naturally directed itself into the good and the evil; the μαγεία and the γοητεία. Cicero derives the name of magic from the Persians. 'Magi augurantur atque divinant. Sapientum et doctorum genus Magorum habebatur in Persis' (De Div. i. 41, 46). So too Apuleius. 'Si quidem Magia id est, quod Plato interpretatur θεῶν θεραπείαν, si, quod apud plurimos lego, Persarum lingua Magus est, qui nostra sacerdos; sin vero more vulgari eum isti proprium Magum existimant, qui communione loquendi cum diis immortalibus ad omnia, quæ velit, incredibili quodam vi cantaminum polleat' (De Magia, 30). Suidas tells us the difference exactly betwixt μαγεία and γοητεία. Undoubtedly, the word is of Median, or old Persian origin; Meh, or Megh, meaning something great, excellent, and revered; and the Magi of the Persians, Medes, Chaldeans, and Indians, being their highest class of religious philosophers. Mog is still the Persian word, and Mogbed, their high priest, as the high priest of the Parsees at Surat is called Mobed.

When magic arrived in Greece, it found a mythology essentially built on the elements of nature, and, therefore, essentially congenial to it. In Chaldea it had already been combined with astrology, or with the powers supposed to preside over the stars. The Greeks had already discovered more of those secret powers of nature, electricity, magnetism, mesmerism, clairvoyance through means of particular vapours or manipulations, which we suppose the moderns only to have discovered, and thus gave a significance and a strength to their ideas of magic, which carried it to its highest perfection. (See 'Ennemoser's History of Magic'). The Greeks conveyed it to the Romans. Let anyone refer to the passages in Homer and the Greek tragedians, in Virgil, Horace, Ovid, Propertius and others, where magic is mentioned, and to their celebrated enchantresses, Medea, Circe, Erechtho, Canidia, &c.; and then they at least see what was the popular opinion of the art, and of those women as commanders and compellers of the gods, as rulers over fate and men.

We see in the Bible striking examples of the art as it existed in ancient Egypt; and even after the Christian era, the Neo-Platonists, and, indeed, some classes of Christians, were deeply devoted to it. Christianity, on the whole, from its higher and purer knowledge, must necessarily reject it; yet it found its way into the church through the practice of exorcism, employed in imitation of Christ, to cast out devils. The formulas of the church, as time advanced, became more and more ceremonious, and approaching in character, at least to White Magic, in opposition to Black Magic, or Black Art, in which appeal was made to demons to assist in obtaining hidden treasures, acquiring honours, wealth, and other worldly advantages, or in which the sacred names of God and Christ were blasphemously used for the same base ends.

In what came to be called Pneumatologia Occulta et Vera, all the forms of adjuration and conjuration were laid down. The exorcist was, in a well-washed and cleansed room, or under the open sky, having the preceding morning well-washed his body all over, to enter a circle, but not before midnight. He must be newly and purely clad in a sort of surplice, having a consecrated band falling in front, hanging from the neck, and written over with sacred characters. He must wear on his head a tall, pointed cap of fine linen, on the front of which is attached a paper label, having written upon it in Hebrew the holy name TETRAGRAMMATON: a name not to be spoken. The ground must be purified from all uncleanness, and well fumigated. He must fumigate the sacred name on his cap, the letters of which must be written with a never-before-used pen, dipped in the blood of a white dove.

When the exorcist wishes to release a miserable spirit which haunts some spot on account of its hidden treasure, he is recommended to take one or two other persons, properly purified, into the circle with him; so that, whilst he exorcises the spirit, the others may make two different kinds of smoke, one to allure the spirit, and the other to drive it, or any evil spirits, away when necessary. They are to carry each a piece of chalk, and on the four outsides of the circle draw as many pentacles. One of the associates must hold in one hand a glass of holy water, in the other a cup containing the mixed blood of a black lamb, not a year old, and of a white pigeon, not two months old. The exorcist must hold in his right hand a crucifix, and four wax-lights must be lit within the circle; the staff Caroli standing in the centre. They must then sprinkle the mingled blood and water all round the circle, and, kneeling down, each must cross himself on the forehead, the mouth, and the heart, in the name of the Father, of the Son, and the Holy Ghost. The exorcist then makes a prayer for the success of their attempt. Scarcely shall this be done when the wicked spirits will begin to torment the unhappy soul which they seek to release; and the adjuration must recommence, saying, 'All good spirits, praise the Lord with us.' At this the poor soul will sigh and complain, and say, ' With me too.' The incense is at the same time to be waved, and the associates to repeat, 'Amen!' to all the prayers of the exorcist, which are made in succession. The poor soul reaches the outside of the circle, but its gaolers hold it fast, and when the exorcist bids it depart to its eternal rest, in the name of the Father, the Son, and the Holy Ghost, the devils set up a horrible raven-cry, croak like frogs, and fly like ravens around the exorcists' heads, but they must trust in God's name and presence. The devils will try all kinds of illusions to put them off their guard, but they must not be alarmed. They must have three bits of bread, and three bits of paper, on which the name of Jesus is written, and the instant the demons are compelled to deliver into the circle the treasure, the exorcist must lay a piece of bread and the inscribed paper upon it, that it may not be whisked away again, or changed for something else, as will be the case if this be not promptly done.

Then the exorcist must abjure the evil spirits and princes of hell, Acheront, Ashteroth, Magoth, Asmodi, Beelzebub, Belial, Armagmon, Paymon, Eggson, with their subordinates and aiders, and all present spirits, keepers, and damned souls, in the all-sacred mighty name Jehovah, Adonay, Elohah, Saday, and Sabaioth, which is and was the God of Abraham, Isaac, and Jacob, who appeared face to face with Moses on Mount Sinai, who dwelt in the Urim and Thummim—to depart, and that in the strength of Tu Hagiu, Hagiotatu, which the holy angels adore in heaven with singing and cries of ' Holy! holy! holy! Lord God of Sabaioth!' And as the rebellious spirits left their seats in heaven, never to return, so shall these evil ones evacuate the earth in the name of Jesus, Amen!

Then the damned souls will fling in the face of the exorcist that he is a sinner, and in no condition to force the treasure from them, and will mock and insult him; but he shall answer that all his sins are washed out in the blood of Christ, and he shall bid them depart as cursed ghosts and damned flies, and, though they shall still resist, the exorcist shall utter fresh prayers and bannings in all the holy names, cross himself and his companions, who shall, during the same, make fresh consecrated smoke, and he shall point to the pentacles and extacles described on paper with various sacred characters, and shall add the last adjuration in the sacred names:—Hel, Heloym, Sotter, Emmanuel, Sabaioth, Agla, Tetragrammaton, Agyros, Otheos, Ischyros, Athanatos, Jehovah, Va, Adonai, Saday, Homousion, Messias, Eschereheye, Uncreated Father, Uncreated Son, Uncreated Holy Ghost, Christ conquers, Christ rules, Christ triumphs.

Still fresh adjurations and prayers are necessary before the cursed spirits will relinquish the poor soul and depart; but the exorcist adds fresh and more terrible adjurations, and banishes them, as cursed hell-hounds, into dark woods and fetid pools, and into the raging floods of hell, by the name of Christ and all the Evangelists. He holds up the cross before them, and fresh and stronger fumigations are made till they are compelled to depart, and the poor tormented soul is comforted in the name of the Saviour, and consigned to the care of good angels, and the rescued treasure, of course, is secured for the church, and then all is concluded by hymns of praise and the singing of Psalm xci.

Certain days are laid down in the calendar of the church

as most favourable for the practice of exorcism; and, if the devils are difficult to drive, a fume of sulphur, assafœtida, bear's gall, and rue, is recommended, which, it was presumed, would outstench even devils.

BLACK MAGIC.

As its name imports, Black Magic, or the Black Art, was a machinery constructed for compelling the devils, by the power of the divine names, to submit to the magician, and do his will for all or any of his earthly purposes; to bring him money, render him successful in love or war, or in any other ambition. It is a most blasphemous art, presuming to use the most holy names for the most unholy purposes. That the divine names ever did convey any such power, it is absurd to suppose; but it is certain that the devils, under appearance of compulsion, are only too ready to anwer such summonses, and that infernal magic is a real power, and has done strange things.

The magician and his companions, if he took any, entered a circle nine feet wide, inscribed round with the names and intervening crosses—Elohim + Adonay + El Zebaoth + Agla + Jehovah + Alpha + Omega + On. On means the word Oum, said in the Talmud to be the omnipotent word, by the pronunciation of which God created the world. The magician clad as the exorcist, in pointed cap and long robe, with magic signs on the cap, and a scapulary thrown over the robe, bearing also magic characters, holds a rod of peeled hazel, on which are written, in the blood of a white pigeon, Jesus Nazarenus Rex Judeorum. The conjuration must not take place before midnight, and if in a house, the doors or windows must stand open, with no more persons in the house than are engaged in the business. It is most securely performed in the open air, in solitary woods, fields, or meadows. The smoke used must be from poppy, hemlock, coriander, parsley, and crocus seeds. The conjuration must take place on a Wednesday or Friday, and in a house sacred to Mercury or Venus.

The magician takes with him the signs and seals of the spirits he wishes to command, for the seals and signs of all of them are drawn. These he lays close to the fire which he makes in the circle, and strikes them with his hazel rod; and, if they do not appear, he begins to burn them, on which they become obedient. As he and his assistants enter the circle, they say;—Harim, Karis, Astecas, Enet, Miram, Baal, Alisa, Namutai, Arista, Kappi, Megrarat, Sogisia, Suratbala. Then the signs of the spirits called upon are exhibited, and their names pronounced. But not the names of the summoned spirits alone, but all sacred names are invoked. Here is a conjuration of the spirit-prince Aziel— 'I conjure thee, Aziel, by these words of power—Mongrad, Gratiel, Lalelai, Emanuel, Magod, Vagod, Saboles, Sadai, Ai, Sadoch, Oseoth, Mayne, Lalli, that thou bringest me as much money as I desire, in good coin and unchangeable gold; and I command thee to do this in the power of Tetragrammaton, Agla, Ephbiliaon, Sia, Osion, Zellianole, Elion, and, descend to me: appear to me in friendly guise before my circle, and bring what I demand from thee, Azil, in the name of Jesus. Amen!'

When the conjuration has succeeded, praises are sung to God, equally impious. The most frightful curses were heaped on the head of Lucifer, the prince of the devils, if he did not compel Aziel to appear in the shape of a boy twelve years old, and do all that was required of him, bringing a specific sum, 299,000 ducats, in payable coin but unchangeable gold. If the last condition was not imposed, the gold would, the next morning, be found dissolved into withered leaves, or even horse-dung. The magician, bearding the devil, said that he set his foot on the threshold of hell, and would compel him by the name of Christ and the seal of Solomon to obey, or would heap upon him the most unimaginable pangs and torments to which the hottest hell should seem mild.

This specimen of the infernal art may suffice. Whole volumes, almost libraries, exist of it in all the ancient languages, but especially in Arabic and Latin, as well as in all the modern languages. Amongst the most celebrated professors of the art, many of whom have left treatises of it, more or less white or black, are Herpentil, Cormeyther, Psellus, Albertus Magnus, Roger Bacon, Tritthemius, Cardan, Pomponazzi, Cæsalpinus, Campanella, Gaffarelli, Pignatelli, Robert Fludd, Casper Pucer, John Dee, Ægidius Gutmann, Heinrich Runath, Jacob Horst, Paracelsus, Cornelius Agrippa of Rhettersheim, Dr. Faustus, etc., etc.

In the various departments of magic, astrology was deeply interwoven; great power was attributed to amulets, seals, astral and other diagrams; magic roots, or the spring-root, or mandrake, out of which little images were made, and were pretended to have grown so naturally, which were called Alrunes or Alrouns. In ancient times, the herb moly, snakes, hyænas, etc., played a great part; and in later times, the hearts of moles and of black dogs were supposed to possess great magic virtues. In the witch times, a white otter played a great part. This white otter could, however, only be obtained by pronouncing thirteen words:—Studi, Hadi, Hanadmæ, Comdardne, Kuker, Lice, Unhollzæ, Erns, Lucan, Curide, Sagina, Sagine, Kati, Ecknealy, Trinery; which the devil said he had rather be in the hottest hell than hear. The words, indeed, are almost as barbarous as those which Suidas tells us the Milesian women and children sang to their goddess to get rid of the plague:—Bedu, Zaps, Chthon, Plectron, Sphinks, Knaxzbi, Clithüptäs, Phlegmos, Dro-o-ops!

Having obtained the white otter, you can go about invisibly on foot or horseback, pass through closed doors; you shall have all the world in your power; magistrates and judges shall decide in your favour: and you have only to desire wealth, honour, or anything else, to have it. The Hypericum, or St. John's wort possessed wonderful powers, like the ancient Aglaophtis, whatever that might be, and the Osyris herb mentioned by Pliny, Ælian, and others. With the wonderful story of the beautiful gardens raised by magic by Albertus Magnus, for the entertainment of William Earl of Holland at Cologne, with wonderful fruits and tropical flowers, scenery and climate in the midst of winter, the reader is familiar. Such were the notions of magic power in that age!

The professors of the occult sciences, as Albertus Magnus, Paracelsus, Agrippa, &c., not only believed in astral influences operating on the earth, but they had a perception of secret potencies in physical nature, which have since been proved realities by the discoveries of electricity, magnetism, the odylic force, mesmerism, &c. The astrologists and alchemists were foster-fathers of the more actual sciences, astronomy and chemistry. In both of these, as in the moon's influence on the tides, in the recent discoveries in the properties of the solar rays, and the varied developements of chemistry, they were already in contact with facts which they had not the instruments and the modern science to bring forth to the light of demonstration.

I have thus sketched at once an outline of magic, the shadow haunting the course of spiritualism, that I may have no farther occasion to dwell upon it, except it may be in a mere passing reference. Those who would inform themselves farther of Jewish magic, may consult the Talmud and the Cabbalah, with the book Shemhamphorash founded on the latter, printed in 1686 by Andreas Luppius of Wesel; the Shemhamphorash being not the sacred name, but the description and meaning of it. (See Rosenroth's 'Kabbalah,' and the Introduction to Budeus's 'History of the Hebrew Philosophy;' Paxtorf's Biblioth. Ratlin. p. 48; or Hottinger's Biblioth. Orient. i. 33).

In contemplating even the less offensive magic, even that so much used by the Catholic Church in the middle ages in cases of exorcism, we are struck with the awful fall from the simple sublimity of the theurgy of the Gospel times, when Christ and his apostles 'commanded the unclean spirits and they came out of' their victims. In its best shape magic is a revolting invasion of the sacred power of the supernatural in the church; in its darkest form it is concretely devilish. Yet there have not been wanting journals which have been repeatedly inviting spiritualists to this prostitution of a divine power, to predict the winner of the Derby, or to enable sordid speculators to make profitable transactions on the stock exchange.

CHAPTER II.

THE SUPERNATURAL IN THE GREEK AND OTHER EASTERN CHURCHES.

> Perhaps, with the exception of Protestantism, there is not a faith recorded in the world's history, which has leant not upon supernatural revelations, and these the most bright and frequent in proportion as we approach the primitive ages.—Dr. J. J. GARTH WILKINSON.

> There is a great difference betwixt philosophy and other arts; and a greater yet betwixt that philosophy itself which is of divine contemplation, and that which has a regard to things here below. Divine philosophy is much higher and braver; it seeks a larger scope, and being unsatisfied with what it sees, it aspires to the knowledge of something greater and fairer, and which nature has placed out of our view. The one only teaches us what is done upon the earth; the other reveals to us that which is actually done in heaven.
> SENECA'S *Morals*.

IT is scarcely necessary to produce evidence of the spiritualism of the Greek Church; for it was for six centuries identical with the Roman Church, and on separating, did so politically and not polemically. The tenets of the Greek Church continued, and still continue, the same in all essentials except with regard to the procedure of the Holy Ghost, and in rejecting purgatory—without, however, expressly rejecting the intermediate state. All the historians of the first six centuries are the historians of the Church at large, up to that time including both Rome, Greece, and Syria; all were Syrians or Greeks. Eusebius was the Bishop of Cæsarea in Syria. Socrates was a native of Constantinople; he was educated at Constantinople; commenced his career there as a special pleader, and, on retiring from practice, employed himself in writing his history. Sozomen was a Syrian, born in Palestine, educated at Berytus, the modern Beyrout; and afterwards removed to Constantinople. Theodoret was a Syrian; was educated under the celebrated Chrysostom, Patriarch of Constantinople, and himself lived most of his life at Antioch. Evagrius also was a Syrian of Antioch.

Thus, for the first six centuries the doctrine and practice of the Roman, Greek, and Syrian Churches were identical. Their historians were, as I have observed, Syrian or Greek, and are all redolent of miracle. Without encumbering my page with voluminous examples of the continuance of this faith both in the Greek and Syrian Churches, I may refer to the works of recent travellers, where the same belief and practice are shown to remain. In the Syrian Churches, whether Nestorian, Maronite, or Jacobite (the latter professing to be the church of the primitive Jews at the time of our Saviour), we find the liturgies full of the expressions of the presence and action of spiritual beings, both good and bad. In the Jacobite liturgy we find the deacon saying, 'The gates of heaven are opened, and the Holy Spirit descends upon these mysteries to overspread them. We stand in the dreadful place, with cherubim and seraphim surrounded! Brethren and companions are we made in the watches and services of angels and spirits, who are flames of fire' (Etheridge's 'Syrian Churches,' p. 202).

Like the Roman Church, this Church prays to the 'Holy Virgin,' the 'Mother of God,' and for her intercessions. Unlike the Protestant Churches, it and the other Syrian Churches preserve distinct in their gospel, the *sheul* and the *gihana*, the scheol and gehenna of the original Hebrew and Greek Scriptures, the hades, or intermediate state and hell. In the passage in the Gospels where our Saviour comes walking on the water, Mr. Etheridge has truly translated the word $\phi\acute{a}\nu\tau a\sigma\mu a$, a *spectre*, and not a spirit, as our translators have done; the term showing that the Jews at that time perfectly understood the theory of ghosts.

The priest prays for 'Those who by evil spirits are persecuted and troubled.' 'To be defended from every attack and violence of demons' (*Ibid.* p. 208). He prays for the 'exorcists' and others who have fallen asleep. The Nestorian liturgy represents the people as drawing near, 'with thousands of cherubims and myriads of seraphims to sanctify, adore, confess, and glorify the Lord of all' (*Ibid.* p. 222). He calls on the people to join their voices to those of seraphim and archangels, and glorifies God because, through His mercies, 'the earth-born have communion with the spiritual' (p. 227). He prays to be delivered from the evil one and his hosts; and gives thanks that 'mortal men, weak by nature, are enabled to sanctify His name with the heavenly hosts.' The Maronite liturgy approximates still more to the Roman Catholic, as does their system in the multitude of monasteries. (See Jowett's 'Christian Researches.')

This is, as it might be expected in churches founded by Thomas the Apostle; Thaddeus, who 'performed signs and wonders amongst them;' St. Peter, Chrysostom, Jerome, Leo, Innocent, and other founders and builders of the church at Antioch; Nestorius, Ignatius, Serapion, Babylas the Martyr, and Jacob Zanzala, the consolidator of the Jacobite Church. It is what might be expected of churches which had Eusebius, Sozomen, and Theodoret for historians; which had Ephrem of Edessa, the famous Solitary, Joseph the Seer, of Nisibis, in the sixth century; Gregory Bar-Hebræus, the chronicler of saints and patriarchs, in the thirteenth century, and from which proceeded Simeon the Stylite, and Cosma his biographer.

The same causes render our dwelling on the spiritualism of the Greek Church unnecessary. It preserves all its faith in miracles derived from its common origin with the Roman Church. The works of travellers show this amply, and the 'Travels in Greece' of Miss Bremer, just published, record her attendance at a Greek Church festival, where a miraculous picture, found by miraculous means, was exhibiting. This was in the island of Tenos. The church had been built in 1821, in consequence of the dream of a drunken schoolmaster, who declared that the Pan-Hagia, or Holy Virgin, had appeared to him in a dream, and revealed to him that, if they would dig into the foundations of the ancient temple of Poseidon, they would find a picture of her. Nobody took any notice of the man or his dream till a contagious disease broke out in 1821, when they began in earnest to delve for this promised picture. They soon came to a half-ruinous vault of a Christian church, and, on removing the rubbish, discovered a small picture of the Annunciation of the Virgin. The picture was carried in solemn procession through the island, and it is asserted that the pestilence was forthwith stayed. It is farther affirmed that the discovery of the picture took place on the very day that the Greek independence was achieved, thus elevating the banner of the Cross over the Crescent. A church was, therefore, raised on the spot where the picture was found, and the anniversary was instituted for the Christians of both the Eastern and Western Churches to meet there, and every year celebrate the event. Miss Bremer saw the priests touching the eyes of a young nobleman with the picture, which, she said, was evidently an ancient one. The young man was quite blind, and had come very far in hopes of restoration of his sight by the operation, but that it did not take effect. Numbers of other persons afflicted with divers complaints were crowding to the church to seek relief from the picture, and the people asserted that many cures were done through its means. She met, however, with a priest who expressed disbelief in any miracles, and in such hands no miracles were very likely to be performed. Still, the mode of the picture's discovery, and the use made of it, testify to the professed belief of the Greek Church in its ancient doctrine of miraculous powers.

Dr. Thompson, who was American Missionary in Palestine for twenty-five years, says, ' Exorcism of demons and evil spirits is still practised, and with many superstitious rites and magical powers; but this is so common in all the ancient churches that it needs no illustration.' . . . ' There are many who pretend to discover thieves and stolen goods by incantations and other means.' We have seen how Mr. Salt of Cario recovered his plate. He says what the means are by which serpent-charmers act with impunity, and by which persons handle live scorpions, and even put them into their bosoms without fear or injury, are yet a secret. He adds that he has often seen small boys even put scorpions into their bosoms, notwithstanding that they are the most malignant and irascible of all reptiles. He notices the riding of dervishes over boys laid side by side flat on the ground, without their receiving any material injury; and the practice is called Dousch, and is accompanied by a multitude of magical ceremonies. He quotes the account of seeing into the ink in boys' hands in Egypt as given by Lane; says he has met with English and other gentlemen who witnessed things equally astonishing through the same celebrated magician, Abd el Kader el Mugraby, and he gives us Mugraby's formula of invocation:—

>Turshoon, Turyooshoon, come down,
>Come down; be present. Whither are gone
>The prince and his troops? Where are el Ahhmar,
>The prince and his troops ? Be present,
>   Ye servants of these names. And this is the removal ; and we have removed from thee the veil, and thy sight to-day is piercing : *correct, correct.*

Dr. Thompson asked a magician in Sidon whether Turshoon and Turyooshoon were known to him and employed by him; and he said they were; and Dr. Thompson adds: —'In short, this whole subject is involved in no small mystery. It exercises a prodigious influence on Oriental society, and always has done, and merits a thorough examination. The boys evidently see just such scenes as are depicted in the wildest stories in the "Thousand Nights;" and I expect that this very art was in greater perfection then than now, and that the gorgeous creations of that work were, in many cases, mere verbal pictures taken from the mirror of ink' ('The Land and the Book,' pp. 157-159).

Dr. Thompson also says that the people of the East believe that spirits or jins watch over treasures hidden in the earth. Numbers of people are continually employed in seeking hidden treasures, and many spend their last farthing in the search. They have a notion that people of the Western nations have a knowledge of the signs by which these treasures are discovered, and the spells by which the spirits who guard them are overcome; and they, therefore, follow Englishmen who visit the remains of old cities and buildings, believing that they are seeking hidden treasures, and no arguments can convince them to the contrary. They will frequently offer to go partners with them in the pursuit.

I will here give a remarkable instance of prophecy taking place, not precisely in the Greek Church, but in the region of its prevalence. Dr. Wolff mentions in his travels that being at Aleppo in 1822, at the house of John Barker, Esq., British Consul-general of Aleppo and Antioch, he was enquiring after Lady Esther Stanhope. 'She is crazy undoubtedly,' said Mr. Barker; and he told him, in proof of it, that she kept in her house a French gentleman of the name of Lustenau, who had formerly been a general of Tippoo Sahib in India, and who was deemed a prophet. He had declared to Lady Esther the precise day and hour of Napoleon's escape from Elba. Mr. Barker then, in the presence of M. Lesseps, M. Derche, his interpreter, and M. Maseyk, the Dutch Consul, read a letter of Lady Esther's, dated April 1821, begging him not to go to Aleppo or Antioch; as M. Lustenau declared that both those places would be destroyed by an earthquake in about a year. The time had nearly arrived, and M. Derche said that she had recently warned him not to go to Aleppo, for that it would be destroyed by an earthquake in less than a fortnight.

These gentlemen made themselves very merry over the prophecy at dinner. A few days afterwards Wolff quitted Aleppo in the afternoon, and encamped that evening on the road to Latakia in the desert, near the village of Juseea. As the people of Juseea were talking with Wolff and the people of his little camp, they felt the first motions of an earthquake. In another instant the village of Juseea disappeared, being swallowed up by the gaping earth, and the thunder as of cannon came from a distance. Shock after shock succeeded, and presently came troops of wild Arabs and Bedouins, flying over the plains on their terrified horses, and with the hoods of their burnouses drawn down, crying, as they fled past one after another, 'This is of God! this is of God!' For, says Dr. Wolff, the people of the East always come to the primal cause in everything—to God Himself. They do not, as Europeans do, invariably dwell upon the second causes, but refer everything at once to the Governor of the world.

Wolff immediately sent an express messenger to Aleppo to Mr. Barker. He found the whole of Aleppo, Antioch, Latakia, Hums, and Haina had been destroyed by the earthquake, with all the villages for twenty miles round, and that 60,000 people had been plunged at once into an awful eternity! Mr. Barker himself had escaped marvellously by creeping, with his wife and child of six years old, from beneath the ruins of their house!

Amongst those who perished in the ruins of Aleppo was Ezra de Piccitto, a Spanish Jew, the Austrian Consul-general of Syria. He was a man detested for his tyrannies by the inhabitants of all nations. A hundred days before the earthquake he had sent an Austrian subject out of the town in irons. A Turk who had heard of it coolly asked M. Maseyk to count a hundred upon the beads which he held; for, said he, 'on the hundredth day from this act of his tyranny Ezra de Piccitto will die.' This, in fact, was the hundredth day, and, as M. Maseyk had counted the ninety-ninth bead, the earthquake came, and Piccitto was killed. This M. Maseyk told Dr. Wolff himself.

Very little can be found in Church of England writers on the Eastern Churches regarding their belief in the miraculous. They pass it over, as they do not themselves believe in it, as matter that no one cares to know of. Without this, however, no work on these churches is really of much value, and, therefore, the volumes of Etheridge, Appleyard, &c., are of little use in endeavouring to arrive at a sound view of the Greek, Syrian, and Russian Churches. In Dr. Stanley's 'Lectures on the Eastern Church,' you find a few slight allusions to the subject; but it is to native writers that we must go for real information. In the native historians we have already found abundant matter on this head. We may now glean the few light ears of fact which Stanley affords us. He assures us, however (and this includes all the rest), that 'the theology of the East has undergone no systematising process. Its doctrines remain in the same rigid yet undefined state as that in which they were left by Constantine and Justinian' (p. 35). They are, in fact, the same as we have seen them in Eusebius, Socrates, Sozomen, and Evagrius. 'A general expectation,' he says, 'prevails, that, by some unknown process, the souls of the simple will be purified before they pass into the Divine presence; but this has never been consolidated into a doctrine of purgatory.' No: the belief of the middle state, as we see in the Syrian gospel, has been left as it existed there and amongst the Jews. Hades has not been converted into Gehenna, nor metamorphosed into a paying purgatory. At p. 46, Dr. Stanley passingly says, 'Remember that Athos can boast its miraculous pictures and springs, no less than Rimini or Assissi.' Speaking of the Moslem faith, he says, 'The sanctity of the dead man is attested by the same means as in the Eastern Churches generally, the supposed incorruptibility of the corpse. The intercession of a well-known saint is invested with peculiar potency' (p. 278).

'The frantic excitement of the old Oriental religions,' says Stanley, 'still lingers in their modern representatives. The mad gambols of the Greek and Syrian pilgrims have been sufficiently told.' That is, there are more life and active faith in these religions than in modern Protestantism. They, he tells you, assert that St. Andrew first planted the cross on the hills of Kieff, and foretold that a great city and many churches should arise there. Dr. Stanley quotes Sir Jerome Horsey, who wrote in 1570. 'I saw this impostor or magician, Nicolas of Rokoff, a foul creature; went naked both in winter and summer. He endured both extreme heat and frost; did many things through the magical illusions of the devil; much followed, praised, and renowned both by prince and people. *He did much good*,' &c. (p. 333).

Speaking of the siege of the Troitza Monastery near Moscow, in 1613, he says, 'rude pictures still represent, in strange confusion, the mixture of artillery and apparitions, fighting monks and fighting ghosts, which drove back the Polish assailants from the walls of the beleaguered fortress' (p. 342). In the story of the Russian Patriarch, Nicon, in 1667 (chiefly drawn from Mouravieff), in his banishment to the monastery of Therapontoff, on the shores of the White Lake, when shut up at night in an empty house in the depth of a Russian winter, an old woman came up through a trap-door, and assured him that she had been shown his coming in a dream, and ordered to provide all things necessary for his comfort. By such repeated interpositions his fearful journey was made tolerably easy. When he was about to die, one of his worst enemies, the Archimandrite Sergius was warned of it in a dream, and led to meet him, and implore his forgiveness (p. 377). Peter the Great, in his reforming career, declared that he would have no false miracles ascribed to holy pictures (p. 407).

These slight passages show that Dr. Stanley could have told us more than he has done both of the faith of the Russian and Eastern Churches in the miraculous, and of the abuses of this faith which priestcraft has introduced into the Greek as well as into the Latin Church; for in both there is the true and the false, as in everything else on earth.

Turn now to the native historians of the Greek Church, and you find in full what Stanley and other Anglican Church writers only hint at. The assertions of the miraculous stand on almost every page. Of the Greek Church as it still exists in the East, I have given as many of these proofs as my space allows. In Platon and Mouravieff, the historians of the Russian Church, a patriarchate of the Greek, they are so abundant, that I shall confine myself to Mouravieff, as he is of

our own time. He says,' When the Church of (
only a short time back, became an integral p
Russian Church and empire, after having stood
and isolated from all other churches ever sinc
century, there was not found to have arisen in
fifteen hundred years the slightest difference b
in doctrine—no, nor even in ceremonies ; but tl
all points with us and with the other œcumenic
Constantinople, Alexandria, Antioch, and Je
with the other churches dependent upon the fir:
Moldavia, Wallachia, Servia, Montenegria, '
Illyria, and in a word, throughout all Sclavonia' (

This is decisive as to the continued belief i
which I have quoted from their ancient histori:
down not to the fourth century, as here notec
seventh. This may save us much farther quoi
assertion is fully supported by the Rev. R. W
the translator of Mouravieff, graduate of Mer
Oxford, and chaplain in Cronstadt to the Russi;
In his preface, he says, ' This history exhibits tł
spectacle of a church, which, ever since her firs
has faithfully retained that creed which was
delivered to her ; which has not altered her doc
services, her rites, ceremonies, or discipline, and
her internal government (and that more in f
spirit), for nearly nine hundred years, during
period, both clergy and laity have enjoyed free ;
sublime liturgies of St. Basil and St. Chrysosi
native tongue. Her apostolic hierarchy and
first received from Greece, she has venerated
the periods of her history alike, and has pr(
the utmost care in all their integrity. She
founded on her unbroken succession from th(
throne of Constantinople and from the apostles
her claim to divine authority in teaching and a
the sacrament,' &c. (Translator's Preface, p. xi

Accordingly throughout his history, we fin

ravieff and his church acknowledging the metropolitans Peter, Alexis, and Jonah, as 'wonder-workers' (p. 303). He tells us that his or her 'angel' is the customary phrase in Russia for the patron saint after whom anyone is named; but that they also believe in guardian angels appointed to each baptised person (p. 360). The church counts, as its chief guardians and intercessors, a considerable number of saints (p. 81). The Russian Church believes firmly in 'the doctrines of the holy Icons (pictures of saints and the Virgin), in relics, the sign of the venerable cross, of tradition, of the mystery of the most pure blood and body of Christ, of the invocation of saints and angels, of the state of souls after death, and of prayers for the departed' (p. 273). In the time of Peter the Great, the Anglican Church made application to be admitted to unity with the Œcumenical Church, and desired the Russian patriarch to transmit their prayer to Constantinople; but the Russian prelates, having consulted, declined, because the Anglican Church had heretically renounced the traditions of the Fathers, the invocation of saints, and the reverencing of Icons—sacred pictures (p. 287). Warnings received in divine and prophetic declarations by eminent prelates, as well as cases of miraculous cure at the tombs, or from the prayers of holy men, the successful drawing of lots laid on the altar, and like proofs of spiritual intervention, will be found numerously throughout Mouravieff; and with this I may conclude the ample substantiation of my assertion of the universal credence by the Christian church of the divine and imperishable powers of that church—Protestantism alone having fallen from that faith. Who must not lament that a church which has done so much to purify Christianity from the falses and corruptions which have crept into it, should have been led by the arch-enemy to run into an error which has done far more than neutralising these great benefits, has laid the foundation of an incredulity, which, under the name of philosophy, is going like a dry rot through the timbers of the whole temple of religious faith?

CHAPTER III.

SUPERNATURALISM IN THE WALDENSIAN CHURCH.

> Moti milhier d'angels seren en sa compagnia ;
> Tuit faren festa e auren grant alegria
> Del cavalier vittorios, compli de vigoria,
> Que vence lo demoni cum tota sa baglia.
> *Lo novel Confort.* Old Waldensian Poem, A.D. 1100.

THE Vaudois or Waldenses have furnished a topic of much contention to the ecclesiastical writers. Some have asserted that they have been a church from the days of the apostles, continuing pure in doctrine and in constant opposition to Rome; others that they date only from the twelfth century, and originated with a certain Peter Waldo of Lyons. Some have stated that they were only a branch of the Albigenses, and descended from the Manichæans, who appeared at Albi, near Toulouse in Provence, in the twelfth century; but the simple truth seems to be that they were from the time of Pope Silvester, about A. D. 314, when the corruptions of the church became obvious, through its being constituted a state church. At that period being pure members of the church, they became a protesting party; but were not for a long time afterwards absolutely separated from the Roman Church, and thus forming a separate church or sect. They protested against the assumption of worldly power by the Pope; declared Rome the true Babylon, and the Pope Anti-Christ; declared that those only who read and followed the Gospel were the true Church of Christ; that there were no ranks in the church except bishops, priests, and deacons. They protested against the mass and its ceremonies as damnable, and against all the tribes of monks and nuns; against benedictions and consecrations; against all oaths and pilgrimages; against purgatory, which they declared an invention for gain; against confession to priests; against all pictures and images in churches; against the forty days' fast, and fasts in general; against extreme unction; against invocations of saints, and prayers for the dead. In fact, they were in their creed and practice strictly primitive. Being violently persecuted by the Papal Church in consequence, they retired into the fastnesses of the Piedmontese Alps, and there maintained themselves against their enemies. In the early part of the twelfth century, they became conspicuous by the simple fact that Popery had then become powerful and extremely domineering, and was determined to crush all who differed from it, wherever they could be found. Hence the terrible persecutions which continued, not only against them, but against the Albigenses in France, the Cevennois, the Huguenots, and the Lollards, and succeeding Reformers in England and everywhere.

The Waldenses drew their name from the valleys in which they lived; they were first called Vallenses, or Valdesi, or Vaudés, according to the French or Italian prevalence of pronunciation. The Papal Church endeavoured to heap upon them, according to its custom towards all which it deemed heretics, the most base calumnies. They were represented as monsters, having four rows of teeth, hair like wild beasts, as being addicted to the most vile habits, and rebels against the magistracy and the holy church. Numerous authorities, however, both of friends and enemies, as those of De Thou, Claudius, Scyssel, Coggeshall, Gerard, and others having opportunities of personal knowledge, pronounce their character for piety and purity of the most admirable kind. They were, in fact, amongst the earliest Protestants, far prior to the times of Huss, Wycliffe, and Luther, and continue so to this day. During the Protectorate, Cromwell interfered to check the terrible persecutions of them by their ruler, the Duke of Savoy; and Milton not only wrote flaming letters in Cromwell's name to the Duke of Savoy, to Louis XIV. of France, and to the States of Holland; but also penned that noble sonnet on their behalf, commencing—

> Avenge, O Lord, Thy slaughtered saints, whose bones
> Lie bleaching on the Alpine mountains cold.

Cromwell did not satisfy himself with writing and threatening, but he sent Sir Samuel Morland to Piedmont to use personal exertions in favour of the Waldenses, and to relieve their necessities. Morland collected one-and-twenty volumes of MSS. regarding the history and doctrines of this 'Israel of the Alps,' which were deposited in the University of Cambridge; but of these, seven of the most important volumes were abstracted by the Catholics during the reign of James II., and are lost for ever. Morland, however, had made good use of them in his 'History of the Church in Piedmont,' and from him, Perrin, Brez, Leger (who was a pastor in the valleys in the seventeenth century), from Henry Arnaud (who also died the pastor of the Würtemburg colony of the Waldenses in 1721), we derive a striking history of this noble people, whose characteristics and condition have been made more recently familiar to the British public by the Rev. Prebendary Gilly of Durham, and to foreigners by Hahn's 'Geschichte der Ketzer,' and Muston's 'Histoire des Vaudois.' Peter Waldo, who has been vainly advanced to the honour of being the founder of this people in the twelfth century, was, no doubt, a man who had visited the Waldensian mountains and brought thence the faith to his native place, Lyons—whence he, of course, obtained the surname Waldo or Waldensis, and whence the doctrines of his alpine Protestantism spread through the south of France. In the writings of the Waldenses, we find little mention of miracles. They were too much opposed to the teaching of Rome, too much afraid of its dogmas to touch much on miracle, knowing that Rome was, by that time, too apt to mingle fable with the truth. It is not, therefore, in their writings that we are to look for miracle, so much as in their history. That history was one of continued persecution for four long centuries, and of frequent deliverances of so striking a kind that the narrators of them are compelled to exclaim that they are divine.

The persecutions, which had paused for some time, were renewed in 1400 with increased fury. In 1487 Pope Innocent VIII. issued a bull against them, and his legate with 18,000 men, supplied by the Duke of Savoy and the King of France, committed many horrible atrocities in the valleys of Lucerne, Angrogne, and other places. In 1550 the Marchioness of Saluzzo, Magaret de Foix, perpetrated a monstrous amount of devil work in her territories. Francis I. of France, making himself master of Piedmont in 1534, continued this devil work in God's name. This was perpetrated on his own subjects when Duke Emmanuel Philibert regained his estates, under a certain Earl of the Trinity—of all men; and raged on under the instigations of the Pope, and of a society founded in 1650 for the propagation of the faith and extirpation of heresy, till 1658, under such horrors of extermination; their valleys desolated with fire and sword, women dishonoured, ripped up with swords, children stuck on spears and hurled down rocks, &c., that Cromwell and other Protestant princes were compelled to interfere. These interventions, however, produced little effect. Victor Amadeus II., their sovereign, incited by Louis XIV. of France, pursued them still with horrible ferocity.

In these wars of extermination, this Christian people performed deeds which resemble nothing but the marvellous acts of the Jews under the direct guidance of God. On one occasion, only seventeen men, of whom six only were armed with slings, drove before them enemies fifty times more numerous. They defended the little hamlet of Rora, consisting of but fifty houses, for some time against the combined attack of 10,000 men, and, when no longer able to resist this overwhelming force, made good their retreat. At another time, being compelled to march in the night, they had to wrap their guides in white sheets that they might discern them, and in this manner they proceeded along the faces of the most frightful precipices, and carrying their wounded on horseback along this terrific path; yet all escaped in safety. When, by daylight, they saw over what awful places they had passed, they were terrified at the view, and Leger, their pastor, says, anyone who had not been in the transit would treat the whole recital as a fiction.

Frequently they succeeded in sallying from the rocks and caverns in which their enemies were endeavouring to suffocate them with smoke of burning wet straw or brushwood, or to burn them alive in their retreats, and chased them down headlong into the plains, till the French and Savoyard troops declared they must be aided by God. But in April 1686, the united power of France and Savoy made a tremendous onset on the unhappy people, and so completely conquered them that, after two days' hard and unequal contest, the Waldenses laid down their arms and sued for mercy. Fourteen thousand of them, says Arnaud, their gallant leader and pastor, were thrust into the prisons, which were glutted with them, and there, he asserts, that no fewer than 11,000 perished of cold, of heat, of hunger, of thirst, and all the miseries accompanying them. Only 3,000 of the 14,000 issued out alive. Those who had refused to submit dispersed themselves into Switzerland and the Protestant states of Germany—Wurtemberg, Durlach, Hesse Darmstadt, and Brandenburg.

There was one little band of less than nine hundred men which determined to return and fight their way into their own mountains—this was headed by Henri Arnaud, their pastor. In the night betwixt August 16 and 17, 1689, they crossed the lake of Geneva in boats, and commenced a march which, to all human calculation, could be only one to certain destruction. They had to cross snow-capped mountains, and thread passes through a country swarming with hostile troops, French, Swiss and Savoyard

Catholics. Did they escape, there was at least a fifteen days' probable march, and a host of inveterate enemies to receive them. Arnaud, in reviewing this wonderful march, as admirable, though not so long, as the retreat of Xenophon, cannot help exclaiming in wonder, 'L'Éternel s'est servi, non pas d'un homme versé dans l'art de la guerre, mais d'un pauvre ministre qui n'avait jamais fait de la guerre qu'à Satan, pour faire paraître d'autant mieux sa force et sa puissance. Et cependant, vous avez vu cet homme, sous les étendards célestes, s'ouvrir son passage partout, faire prisonniers comtes, barons, gentilshommes, avocats, syndics, châtelains, moines, prêtres et autres, presqu'au nombre de 67, qu'il menait avec lui pour contempler les merveilles que la véritable foi est capable d'opérer, et pour être au même temps les témoins oculaires du bon ordre qu'il maintenait dans sa troupe, n'ayant rien pris partout où il a passé qu'il ne l'eut payé ; et enfin, avec dix pistoles seulement, il pénètre avec toute sa troupe jusque dans les vallées, dans le Chanaan qu'il cherchait, et où en arrivant, il ne lui restait plus qu'un demi-louis.'

He expresses his wonder that he did not fall into the hands of the Catholic Swiss, who were on the look-out to seize and carry him to Constance, to burn him as the Austrians had burnt Huss and Jerome of Prague. Equal wonder how they managed to force passes against countless enemies where a few hundred men might have defied thousands. How, with a little band, covered only with rags, and subsisting on the most scanty and wretched fare, he cut his way through the lately victorious bands of France, Switzerland, and Savoy. 'Is it not wonderful,' he asks, 'that such a handful of starving men, few of whom had ever handled a musket, forced the passage of the bridge of Sababertran against 2,500 well-entrenched men, killing 600 of them, and losing only fourteen or fifteen, of whom more than eight were shot through the inexperience of their comrades? Who is so dull,' he asks, 'as not to see that God alone could give victory to a mere parcel of men, without money and almost without arms, against the King of France, before whom all

Europe trembled, and whose banner the Pope had blessed in certain assurance of triumph? Who could be stupid enough to ascribe it to nature, and not to a divine providence, that the people of the valleys had not in summer reaped their crops, but found, on their return to the valley of St. Martin, bread, wine, meat, rice, legumes, flour, corn, cut and uncut, their gardens in fine condition, and a plentiful gathering of chestnuts and grapes; and, moreover, that the corn which they were not able to cut in time, was preserved under the snow, through a long and hard winter, till the following January, February, and even May, without being spoiled? Can anyone believe that about 367 people of the valley of Balsill had been able, on a diet of herbs, beans, and water, and lying on straw, to resist 10,000 French and 12,000 Piedmontese, who had besieged them, not only with abundance of arms, ammunition, provisions, and everything, and who had brought mules loaded with ropes to hang them with, and had done this by any other power than the direct power of God, who is the King of kings, and jealous of His honour? That the Waldenses fought more than eighteen battles against these swarming hosts which had penetrated into their valleys, and destroyed above 10,000 of them in their march of nine days, yet lost only about seventy of themselves? And that, at length, their unnatural ruler should be compelled to seek the aid of the very men whom he had thus hunted down, whose fields and houses he had burnt, and whom he had given up as prey to the French and papal commissioners?'

This last event was occasioned by the French and Amadeus II. coming to open feud and war. Thus the miserable duke sought humbly to these his outraged subjects to save him from the very hell-hounds that he had turned loose on them. Thus this despicable duke published in all haste an edict in May 1694, by which he restored the Waldenses to all their property and rights, and gave them full freedom of religion. Then he whiningly told them that, if they would be true to their duke as they had been to their God, he would love and cherish them as dear children. The loyal people joined his standard, helped him to beat back his most formidable foe, and were immediately rewarded for their gallant conduct by being deprived again of all rights; and all who were not born in the valleys were ordered, on pain of death, to quit them within two months. The number of these amounted to 3,000. They were driven away in the most destitute condition, and the noble Arnaud volunteered to lead them into Protestant countries. They marched to Geneva, and thence into Prussia, Hesse Cassel, Hesse Darmstadt, Würtemberg, and other states, where lands and villages were assigned them, and there they remain, as Waldensian colonies, to this day. For many years they received a considerable money allowance from England, the English Government also paying annually 250*l*. for the support of thirteen pastors in the valleys of Piedmont. Arnaud received a pension from England, and was made a colonel of the British army by William III. He died the head of the Würtemberg colony in 1721. It is only in very recent times that the Waldenses have received decent treatment from their own Government, but their faith is now rapidly revolutionising the north of Italy.

Such was the spiritualism of the Waldenses. Well might Arnaud declare that the interpositions of God on their behalf were 'non seulement extraordinaires, mais même surnaturels.' Well may Leger, their historian (Histoire des Eglises Evangéliques Vaudoises) declare their deliverances as 'most miraculous.' On one occasion he says, they were carried off in great numbers from their harvest fields, and cast into different prisons, but their enemies, to their unbounded astonishment, soon found them all at liberty again, equally to the amazement of the captives themselves, who knew nothing of the arrest of their fellows in different places at the same time, and were set free again 'miraculously,' and in a wonderful manner.

It was of this miraculously preserved church that even the venerable St. Bernard, of Clairvaux, in 1140, said,

'There is a sect which calls itself after no man's name, which affects to be in the direct line of apostolic succession, and rustic and unlearned though it is, yet it contends that we are wrong and that it is only right;' and he adds in the true spirit of Catholic priests of to-day, as expressed towards spiritualism, 'It must derive its origin from the devil, since there is no other extraction which we can assign to it' (Sermo sup. Cant. 66). What their faith was the great Bernard might have read in the 'Nobla Leyçon,' the poem expounding their doctrines, and extant at least forty years before. This people, whose origin was thus charitably ascribed to Satan, is now being held as especial favourites of the Church of England, and has wrung from one of its members William Stephen Gilly, Prebendary of Durham, otherwise so incognisant of the miraculous, this sentence, 'It was the will of God that they should be left as a remnant, because it was written in the counsels of heaven that they should continue *as a miracle* of divine grace and providence' ('Waldensian Researches,' p. 289).

CHAPTER IV.

THE SUPERNATURAL AMONGST THE SO-CALLED HERETICS
AND MYSTICS OF THE MIDDLE AGES.

That effect, that sanguinary struggle with which humanity wrestling, so to speak, against itself, seizes one by one the most necessary truths, the bad grace with which it is done, and the incapacity of not doing otherwise, indicate two things at once ; the first, that man cannot do without the truth ; the second, that he is not in fellowship with the truth. But truth is one, and all those truths successively discovered are only parts, or diverse applications of it.
VINET's *Vital Christianity*, p. 72.

Spricht man aber, wie jetzt die Zeiten laufen, solche Worte aus, sogleich wird aus der Ferne dumpfer, immer näher kommender Schall der Lärmtrommel vernommen; wie der Staub auf den Wegen, so wird ein zahlreich Volk vom geschlagenen Wirbel aufgerührt; Väter und Älterväter und ihre Kinder und Kinders Kinder kommen in Hast herbeigelaufen, alle rufend: Mystik, Aberglauben, Pfaffentrug, Mönchbethörung, nieder mit der Mystik.
Die Christliche Mystik von J. GÖRRES, i. 1.

But if, as the times go, one but utter such words, immediately we hear from a distance the dull, but ever-approaching sound of the alarmdrum. Like the dust on the roads, a swarm of people are roused into a furious whirlwind ; father and grandfather, and their children and children's children, come running in hot haste, all shrieking, 'Mysticism ! Superstition ! Priestcraft ! Monkscheatery ! down with Mysticism !'

BESIDES the Waldenses there were numbers of other socalled heretics, so called by the Roman Church. In every age of the church these so-called heretics have abounded, from the earliest Manichæans, Pelagians, and Montanists to the Flagellants and the Anabaptists of Westphalia. The idea which numbers of writers have employed to account for these manifestations, that they result from mere delusion, from excited imaginations, and hallucinations, is the shallowest of ideas; the result of the profoundest ignorance of the human soul. The cause assumed is utterly inadequate to the production of the effects; it is an attempt to raise a fountain higher than the spring-head. In the worst of these demonstrations things have been done and prophecies enunciated which nothing but a spiritual power, seeing farther than man sees, could originate. It is not the property of disease and delusion to strike out truths, and truths lying often buried in the depth of years and distances. I have produced too many instances of such things arising out of the most disorderly spiritualism in every age and in every country, to make it requisite to reproduce them here. Even fools, so called, have often astonished the so-called wisest and soberest men by their flashes of superhuman knowledge. Take ancient or modern times, we find it the same. Nicetas Goniates relates in his life of Isaac Angelus that, when the emperor was at Rodostes, he paid a visit to a man called Basilicus, who had the reputation of possessing the faculty of seeing into futurity, but who was otherwise regarded by all sensible persons as a fool. Basilicus received the emperor without any particular marks of respect, and returned no answer to his questions. Instead of doing so, he walked towards the emperor's picture, which hung in the apartment, scratched out the eyes with his staff, and attempted to strike the hat from his head. The emperor took his leave, setting him down as a perfect fool. Nevertheless, all that Basilicus intimated came to pass. The emperor was deposed in a rebellion, and his brother Alexis, being placed on the throne, put out his eyes.

Claus, the court-fool at Weimar, rushed into the council-room on one occasion, as the council was sitting, exclaiming, 'There you all are, consulting, no doubt, about very important matters; but nobody gives a thought about the fire at Colmar, nor how it is to be extinguished!' On the arrival of the mail it was found that at that moment an alarming fire was raging at Colmar.

How did these fools come at knowledge which none of the wise could pretend to? To say that it was the result of their foolishness would be to confound all human ideas; it was clearly no delusion in either case, it was no hallucination, but a reception of a fact from some spiritual source, is certain as that of the most orthodox prophecy. And what is curious, the sane and the learned receive precisely the same sudden and unerring oracles. At Perouse in 1616, says Bodin Angevin in his 'Démonomanie des Sorciers,' a priest of the name of Jacques, one day, while celebrating mass, turned round to the people, and instead of saying, 'Orate, fratres!' he exclaimed, 'Orate pro castris ecclesiæ, quæ laborant in extremis.' 'Pray for the army of the church, which is in extreme peril.' And, at the moment that he was speaking, the army in question was defeated about twenty-five leagues from Perouse.

It was under similar circumstances that Apollonius of Tyana, in the midst of a lecture at Ephesus, announced the death of Domitian at Rome.

Even in what appears as disease, the patients speak things that no *disease* can teach. In St. Cyprian's Epistles we find Fermilianus writing to him that, when all the faithful took to flight in the persecution A.D. 260, a woman suddenly appeared who fell into fits of ecstasy, in which she showed herself a wonderful prophetess. She not only foretold extraordinary things which came true, but she did marvellous things, and performed real miracles. But these Fathers did not foolishly imagine that her abnormal state was mere disease, or that miracles done and true prophecies made could result from hallucination, that illusion could be the parent of truth. They were incapable of any such shallow logic; they at once attributed the effects to spirits, and the woman asserted the same thing.

In the 'Pastoral Letters' of Jurieu, we have an extraordinary account of a young girl amongst the Protestants of the south of France, who was about seventeen years of age, and was known by the name of the Shepherdess of Cret.

She fell frequently into ecstasies and convulsions, and a deep accompanying sleep, in which she uttered the most striking and real predictions; and though she was ill-educated and spoke a wretched patois in her waking state, in these sleeps she spoke excellent French. She recollected nothing of what she had said after being awoke. She was a clairvoyant, exhibiting the exact phenomena of clairvoyants of to-day. She was a mystic, according to Görres's classification, of the lower or natural order, as distinguished from the higher class of mysticism, the spiritual revelation which ascends above all natural causes, and is in communion with purified spirits, not with lower spirits, but with God Himself, or the highest and holiest of His angels.

Fernelius gives the account of a young gentleman who was attacked by convulsions which came on him several times a-day. As these fits proceeded, he became very clairvoyant in them; began to speak in Latin and Greek, though he was thoroughly ignorant of Greek. He read the thoughts of everyone about him, and rallied the physicians on their ignorance of his complaint and their absurd remedies. He asserted that a spirit gave him the knowledge and language which he clearly had not from any natural source; yet the magnetists satisfy themselves that magnetism will explain all. In fact that magnetism can teach a man in a moment not only to understand, but to *speak* Latin and Greek. In scores of cases such patients have spoken learned languages; in the Witch cases there were abundance of such instances. If this explanation be true, why do not the magnetists introduce magnetism at once into our classical schools, and save our poor lads a world of crucifying labour? If illusion can teach languages, why not our wise literary and scientific men introduce illusion to the schools, which is obviously a much more efficient teacher than all the ordinary masters put together? What matters it by what means our children are endowed with the full mastery of the classics, whether it be by magnetism or illusion, or hallucination, if *these* can give that in one hour which Dr. Birch and the Rev. Prosody

Long Labour take seven years to do at Harrow or Eton? It is amazing to find people, who have such glib and off-hand explanations of wonderful effects, taking no pains to give us the practical advantage of their discoveries.

We find the apparently most ridiculous means producing most astonishing ends. The niece of Pascal was undoubtedly cured of an otherwise incurable disease by the touch of a thorn called holy; some of the most otherwise incurable cases were cured at once by the wiping with a napkin brought from the tomb of the Abbé Paris, as people were cured by napkins and handkerchiefs taken from the body of St. Paul. Cotton Mather in his 'Magnalia Christi Amicana,' says nothing was so common for the old set of Quakers as to proselyte people by merely stroking or breathing upon them. It was the same in the pagan world; causes as apparently trivial or foolish produced effects out of all proportion to them. Laplanders, according to Olaus Magnus, fell asleep after certain ceremonies, when required to obtain exact information from far-distant places, or countries, and, after perhaps twenty-four hours of such profound sleep, woke up, assured the enquirers that they had been at the place, seen the persons required, and brought certain information, which rarely, if ever, was found to be untrue.

Elian, in his 'Variæ Historiæ,' &c., says that the celebrated Aspasia had, when very young, a tumour on the face which extended below the chin, and thoroughly disfigured her. Her father refused to pay the sum demanded by the physicians for her cure, and Aspasia, in an agony of distress, retired to her room, bewailing her fate; there fell asleep, and dreamed that a dove appeared to her, gradually assuming the form of a woman, who bade her to be of good courage: to despise the physicians, and pulverise and apply the powder of the roses in one of the wreaths hung on the statue of Venus, and she should be cured. She did so, and was not only cured, but became gradually so beautiful that she enchanted all men, and became Queen of Persia.

What shall we say, then, to all these things which are

scattered thickly over the whole mass of history and literature, sacred and profane, Christian and Pagan? If, I repeat, the theory of their being illusions, or that diseases can do these wonders and inspire prophecies; if imagination, that darling resource of so many *soi-disant* philosophers, can effect them, in the name of common sense, why do they not abandon science and physic and hard years of study, and betake themselves to imagination, and illusion and disease, which, according to their own showing, are far more potent than health and reason, philosophy and science? But they do not resort to these agencies, so promptly and continually invoked, to help them out of their difficulties; and never will, simply because they know, in their own souls, that they are mere shams brought forward to conceal their ignorance. We must, therefore, look to some other and really adequate cause of the ever-recurring, ever-extending phenomena called miraculous. And this brings us back to the old and only paramount cause—spirit operating on spirit encased in matter. 'That which is born of the spirit is spirit: that which is born of the flesh is flesh,' Christ said to Nicodemus; but that great master in Israel found it hard to understand this. 'Like the fathers of Israel,' says Dr. Ennemoser, ' the new fathers do not willingly take cognisance of things which are not a part of their faith, and which are out of their horizon, whether temporal or heavenly things be in question.' We must, therefore, leave the new fathers, the Nicodemuses of to-day, and draw from all history a cause more potent than their causes to unlock the mystery of miracle which arises again and again in the successive generations as surely as the sun rises and the winds blow.

We find, then, a great spiritual power, the Lex magna of the universe, as fixed, and permanent, and omnipotent as the law of specific gravity itself, operating on the human mind in every age and country, and under every variety of circumstance. No human force can suppress it, though it may distort it. It comes forth like light and darkness, with features of good and evil. It stands forward in prophets and inspired warriors, sublime, clear as the sun, and irresistible as its beams. It speaks, and distant ages hear it; it acts and nature takes the impression of its blows. God descends and wields infinite power, apostles and martyrs follow and triumph over kings and hierarchies, over mind and matter, even in subjection and in death. Churches arise, and even in their corruption and inhuman pride work signs and wonders. They stamp on pure spirit and pure conscience; they endeavour to crush out all opposition to their boasted self-will by fire and dungeons and desolating arms; and the same spiritual potence bursts forth in the varied shapes of heresy, of damnable doctrines and even of devilry confessed. The great spiritual power is a power residing in good and evil agents, in God and His hierarchies, in the devil and his legions. The combat of sin and soul are going on for ever, and exhibit their effects over all this beautiful but serpent-haunted and blood-stained earth. Where faith and religion triumph, the malignant and envious spirits of darkness seek to undermine and corrupt. They push prosperity into pride and despotism, into sensuality and voluptuousness, tending to rottenness. They rouse the venom of vengeance in the powers which have changed from holy to unholy, to stamp out the fires of denunciation and reform, which begin to kindle under their feet, to crush the purer souls who cry for God and truth. Hence arise sects and heresies; hence the mystic incensed by outrageous denunciation rushes forward into dangerous utterances, into paradoxes from which develope licentious falsities as surely as fungus is developed from the fermentation of decaying wood.

You cannot check the invincible operation of this Lex magna of the universe. It will burst up ever and anon, through the dry crust of petrified society, as underswelling floods burst up the ice-cover of frozen rivers. It will burst up in good or evil, in truth or fanaticism. It is there, mighty, vast, untameable, diffused through all things, through mind and matter as universally as the electric principle. Whether you notice it or notice it not; whether you repudiate it, ignore it, or treat it as disease and delusion, it will appear amongst you as an inevitable apparition, laughing at your theories, throwing down your philosophies, and shattering your churches. It must and will exert itself in utter contempt of learned dogmas, of church creeds; it recks not whether it be denied or admitted; but, in proportion as it is coerced or recognised, it will produce blessings or monstrosities.

Like the pent-up gases of the world's interior, it will make itself felt in moral earthquakes, or show itself in blazing volcanoes of crime and fanaticism, if it cannot steal freely through fissures and earth-pores, and fructify the roots of tree and herb. Thus it has ever been, from the days of the Manicheans to those of the Mormons. Whether it be good or evil, it is all spiritualism, and it is most important that men should recognise its real nature; and, instead of mocking at it, endeavour to open the eyes of the multitude to discern that nature too; to teach them that it is about them as sure as God and the devil exist, and operate unperceived around us and within us; that we may open up our souls to one or the other to our infinite hurt or advantange; but that, whether we cultivate or reject, this great eternal principle in its conflicting elements will operate upon us whether we will or not. We may turn our backs on the sun — that will not prevent his shining: we may shut our eyes to the tempest, but that will not chain the winds or arrest the forked lightning. Good and evil are set before us, we may choose which we will; spiritualism is upon us, we may have *its* good or evil; we cannot, by any abjuration of it, exempt ourselves from its influences, any more than we can from that of time bringing age and death.

Let us now notice the progress of this great power in and around the churches during the ages preceding the Reformation. Besides the Albigenses, who were so fearfully persecuted and exterminated in the twelfth and thirteenth centuries, the south of France had also its Waldenses, or Poor Men of Lyons, the followers of Peter Waldo; called also Insabbatati, or people wearing sabots or wooden shoes, on which they are said to have had the sign of the cross to distinguish them from other peasants, not of their faith. These also had their plentiful persecutions. These had been preceded by the sects of Peter de Bruys, of Heinrich, of Eudo de Stella of Brittany, and Tranchelin of Utrecht in the Netherlands, in the twelfth century. All these sects were equally opposed to the corruptions of the Church of Rome, though differing in many points one from another. They most of them rejected fasts, priestly confessions, oaths, purgatory, priestly absolution, the authority of the pope, the celibacy of the clergy, the extreme unction. Many of them denied the lawfulness of capital punishments and of war by Christians. All were spiritualists, holding that the ancient power of Christianity remained amongst true disciples.

Of this character especially were the Apostolikers, who may be regarded as a section of the French Waldenses, though arising in Italy. The founder of this sect was Gerhard Segarelli of Parma, who instituted it in 1260, which thence spread into France, Spain, Germany, and England. Segarelli was burnt for his heresy in 1300; but his place was supplied by his disciple Tode Dolcino of Novara, who spread the faith in the Tyrol and Dalmatia, and was also put to death by the papal authorities in 1307. In their doctrines they condemned the corruptions of the Church of Rome, and declared that the Church of Christ in its purity possessed the power of the apostles, and the spirit of prophecy and of revelation. That oaths, persecutions, and papal assumptions, are deadly sins; the Gospel is the only creed of true believers.

Allied to the Apostolikers are the Beghards and Beguinen, who, however, took their rise in the eleventh century, and spread through the Netherlands, Germany, France, and other countries. They were so called from the old Saxon term *beggen*, the same as the German *beten*, to pray; they were thus literally praying brethren. They lived in large houses called *beguinages*, though not bound together by any oath, or belonging to any particular monkish order. There were also associations of women who lived together in the same manner. Some of these remained in the Romish Church, and continue to the present day; others were pronounced heretical, and were exterminated or dispersed. From these sprang two great sects, the Brothers and Sisters of the Full Spirit or Fratricelli, and the Brethren and Sisters of the Free Spirit, of whom the Lollards were an off-shoot. The Brethren of the Full Spirit prevailed chiefly in the south of France, Italy, and Sicily. They seem to have amalgamated themselves in a great degree with the Tertianis, or Franciscans. Like the Franciscans, they bound themselves to obedience, chastity, and poverty. They denied that the pope, or any other power of the church had any right to interfere with their ordinances, or to absolve any of them from their oaths. They believed that the reform of the church must proceed from them; that a new outpouring of the Holy Ghost would take place on them, as great and abundant as the first; and that through them the world would be eventually converted, and so filled with love that the faithful would exceed even the apostles in virtue and grace. That they had ere this, however, to fight the great fight with Anti-Christ, as it had been revealed to St. Francis.

The Brethren and Sisters of the Free Spirit appear to have arisen at Cologne in 1210. Amalrich von Bena has been named as their founder by Gieseler; but Hahn thinks this improbable and not demonstrated. Amalrich, however, held the mystical pantheistic notions afterwards ascribed to Eckhardt, who unquestionably belonged to this body. He believed in the perfectability of man by the union with God and the Spirit of Christ, and that no happiness was possible except through this union—a genuine Christian Buddhism, which he partook with the ancient anchorites, and also with St. Paul. But this doctrine was not held by him, as by too many of the Brethren and Sisters of the Free Spirit, as a warrant for all sorts of licentiousness. This sect became more prominent nearly thirty years later—namely, in 1238, when Albertus Magnus noticed it in Cologne. In 1261 they excited several convents and monasteries in Swabia to break their rules, as inconsistent with spiritual freedom. In 1292, under the general name of Beghardos and Beghardas, their proceedings were condemned, and in 1306 the Archbishop of Cologne issued an edict against them. He charged them with preaching that God Himself would, some day, cease to exist; that anyone was at liberty to abandon his wife in order to follow God more strictly; but that, as those who were blest by the Spirit of God were no longer under the law, they were at liberty to indulge their appetites as they pleased, or as Hudibras expresses it:—

> For saints may do the same things by
> The spirit in sincerity,
> Which other men are tempted to,
> And at the devil's instance do;
> And yet the actions be contrary,
> Just as the saints and wicked vary.

They begged 'bread in the name of God,' and were, therefore, nicknamed 'Bread-through-God.' They wore a particular dress and had a particular system of associated life. Whether they carried their licentiousness so far as their papal enemies asserted, may, in many cases, be well doubted. But it is probable that there were some of them who used their Christian liberty in a genuine sense as a liberty in God; a freedom, through the power of His Spirit, from vice and the temptations to vice; and another and a large section who were led by their lusts to wrest the doctrine of St. Paul, that they who are in Christ are no longer under the law, into an assumed charter for the commission of any crime whatever. These declared that man, becoming perfect, could do anything without doing it sinfully—a sophism which only the devil and the flesh could make possible. A great deal of licentiousness would have passed in that corrupt age with the church, but as these Beghards and Brethren of the Free Bands set themselves to denounce the sacraments of Romanism, they were fiercely assaulted by its authorities, and many of them were burnt in the different countries into which they had spread themselves—Saxony, Hesse, Thuringia, the

Netherlands, &c. They appealed to the pope at Avignon, John XXII., but he confirmed the decrees against them, and condemned twenty-six articles of opinion of the famous Master Eckhardt of Cologne. Eckhardt will claim our attention again particularly, but just now we may follow the disorderly spiritualism of this sect to its farther issues.

The great head-quarters of the sect remained in Cologne, but its archbishops continued such a war upon them that, about 1357, they fled from that city and spread themselves over the north of Germany. There, at Constance and in the Netherlands, in France and Savoy, they were persecuted, and many famous men and professors burnt. Bulls were issued by Pope Urban V., Boniface IX., and Gregory XI., against them, on which both Beghards and Beghins or Swestronæ Conventualæ, Conventual Sisters, were painted in blackest colours. Still more heretical sects sprang out of them, as the Luciferists, Adamites, Turlupins, &c. The Luciferists maintained that Lucifer, after his battle with Michael the archangel, was restored to heaven and all his glory: the Adamites held the same doctrine, and all these sects held that the Virgin Mary was not an object of worship, and that the Church of Rome was a fallen church. The Lollards were frequently confounded with these, but unjustly. They acquired the name of Lollards from the Flemish word *lollen* or *lullen*, to sing in a muffled undertone, as they did in burying those who died of the plague in Antwerp, in 1300.

Licence having been carried to its extreme by the wild section of the Brethren of the Free Spirit, there arose another fashion of people, the Penitents, who declared that God was angered at the sins of the world, and must be appeased. To effect this object they commenced a system of the most astonishing self-chastisements. They regarded the great plague which ravaged both Europe and Asia in 1348, as the manifest sign of God's wrath, and from this date they commenced their fearful discipline. They went about naked to the waist, cutting themselves with wire-lashed scourges till they ran down with blood, and at the same time singing the hymn of the last judgment, 'Dies iræ, dies illa;' weeping and groaning piteously at the same time. They obtained the names of Cruciferi, Crucifratres, Flagellatores, Verberantes, Pusserer, or Büsser. They declared that an angel had brought them a letter commanding these self-inflictions, and they published this letter, one of a considerable length. An army of Flagellants made their appearance at Avignon, and called on Pope Clement VI. to submit himself to the same discipline; but he not only refused, but commanded them to cease their processions under pain of excommunication. But the papal bull did not stop the Flagellants, nor could all the severity of the Inquisition. They spread into Italy, where 70,000 at one time appeared, including in their ranks princes, bishops, clergy of various ranks, and monks. Boniface IX. caused their leader to be seized and burnt alive, and they were scattered by main force. But other armies appeared in Germany, where other burnings took place, and fresh dispersions by military. In the beginning of the fifteenth century, Vincent Ferreri, a Spanish Dominican of great popularity, led a great troop of Flagellants through Spain, France, and Upper Italy, nor did this extraordinary manifestation totally disappear from Europe till 1481, having lasted 132 years.

Contemporary with the Flagellants, were the Dancers. They appeared in 1374 on the Rhine and in the Netherlands, and continued till 1418 or the greater part of half-a-century. They appeared like the ancient Bacchanti, half-naked, and with garlands on their heads—driven, say the old writers, and plagued by demons. Not only in the open air, but in churches and houses, they danced their wild dances, men and women; and in their hymns used the names of hitherto unheard-of demons. Enormous licentiousness resulted from this dancing mania, and, as it was attributed to possession by demons, exorcism was diligently applied, and the aid of St. Vitus, famous for dancing, was, on the homœopathic principle, invoked to put it down. The dancers, like the other sects, called loudly for a new church, a church of the spirit. Other sects, as the Pastorells, which lasted seventy years or more of the same era, joined in the cry for the removal of the corrupt church and for a new one; and they did their best to put the Roman Church down by killing the priests and plundering the monasteries, and were only subdued by the soldiery.

In the meantime, whilst the demon powers were thus taking advantage of the condition and the coercive domination of the church, to urge men into a delirium of sin and blasphemy, mingled with cries for a new order of things; a new order was silently springing up in the souls of men who were seeking for the kingdom of heaven, not from without, but, as Christ had taught them to seek it, within. The papal hierarchy was seized suddenly with consternation by learning that the renowned Master Eckardt had joined the sect of the Brothers of the Free Spirit—was become, in the words of Schmidt, in his 'Studien und Kritiken,' their amicus et patronus. Eckardt, the celebrated teacher of Aristotle and Plato, doctor of theology, formerly professor of this science in Paris, and now Provincial of the Dominicans at Cologne, had not only joined this heretical sect, but had put forth six-and-twenty propositions, not only asserting, but farther developing their doctrines. These Henry, the Archbishop of Cologne, condemned; and, on the Brethren appealing to Pope John XXII., then at Avignon, he confirmed the condemnation, by an edict in A.D. 1330, of the first fifteen as heretical, and of two others beyond the six-and-twenty, also ascribed to Eckardt. Before the issue of this edict, Eckardt had recalled his propositions, and was dead. The propositions, nevertheless, were accepted by the Brethren, and, as we have seen, some of them wrested to their own corrupt purposes by the wild and sensual.

Master Eckardt's propositions were, in substance, as follows:—Being asked why God did not create the world sooner, he replied, 'God could not produce the world at first because a thing cannot act until it is; whence, no sooner was

God, than He created the world; and hence we may infer that the world was eternal. God cannot be without the world: it is His other self, and eternal with Him. God brings forth His Son continually, for the producing His Son is the speaking forth His creative power; and He speaks all things in Him. All created entities, from the highest angel to the humblest spider, are one in the first origin of things. They who love not honour, nor usefulness, nor inward devotion, nor reward, nor the kingdom of heaven—they out of whom all these things are gone—yet of these people God still has honour, and they pay Him what is His own. I thought lately whether it were good to desire or accept anything from God; and I am anxious still to deliberate earnestly on this; because, if I accept from God, I place myself under Him as a servant or a slave, and He Himself becomes a Lord over me by the very act of giving; and thus we ought not to be in the eternal life. As in the sacrament the bread is wholly changed into the body of our Lord, so shall I be changed into Him, as He operates in me His own being, the same and not merely like. Whatever God the Father has given to His only-begotten Son in human nature, he has given as fully to me; whatever the sacred Scriptures say of Christ, they say of every good and divine man. Men ask, How can man work with God the works which He did thousands of years ago? and they understand not that in eternity there is neither before nor after; and therefore, all that God worked thousands of years ago, and is yet working, is nothing but a work in eternity; and so the man who is in eternity works all these works, for he is one with God and the same. I am in God; therefore, he who takes not these works from God, takes them not from me. I cannot be shut out from them; or God, with whom I am one, must be shut out. The Father rests not, therefore it is of necessity that the Son is born in me; He operates and strives in me at all times, that I may be as the Son to Him. The man who exists in God conforms himself to the will of God; he will not have it otherwise, since what is of God is the will of God.

Some people fast, others eat; some watch, others sleep; some pray, others are silent; but they who practise internal devotion derive more advantage in a moment than through all the outer works that they can work. Quod bonus homo est unigenitus Filius Dei. Homo nobilis est ille unigenitus Filius Dei, quem Pater eternaliter genuit. Or, as God produces his Son in me, I myself am that Son and no other. God begets the Son in the soul in the same manner as He begat Him in eternity, and not otherwise. God is one in all modes and according to all reason, and without distinction; for he who sees things sees not God. God is one, without number and above number, without intellect and above intellect. No distinction can possibly be comprehended in God. All creatures are absolutely nothing. I say not that they are small, or that they are not, but they are an absolute nothing. There is something in the mind which is uncreated and uncreatable; if the whole mind were such, it would be altogether uncreated and uncreatable, and this is intellect. God is neither good, nor better, nor best. He who says that God is good, does him as much injustice as to say that white is black.'

I give these propositions because, not only a great theological school was based on them, called the Friends of God, but because they have had, and continue to have, a deep influence on theological metaphysics. Hegel has asserted in his ' Lectures on Religion,' that Master Eckardt had penetrated to the very depths of religious philosophy; and Martensen, in his Works, and Baur, in the ' Tübingen Year-Book ' of 1843, declared that he was not only the father of German mysticism, but by anticipation, of modern theologic speculation.

From these propositions we see at once that Eckardt's was a mind of the intensest metaphysical nature; and such minds love to push profound psychologic propositions into utter paradox; and, in seeking to sound the abysses of thought, emerge at the antipodes, wrapped in the cobwebs of the incomprehensible, and swart with the nether flames of blasphemy. So, at least, Eckardt will appear to the general religious mind. Yet in his sermons he explained these propositions so as to deprive them of much of their startling audacity; and it will be observed that he limited their operation by declaring that whoever becomes one with God, conforms, by consequence, his will to the will of God. It suited the sensual to overleap this limitation, and hence the worst portion of the Brethren of the Free Spirit rendered Eckardt's doctrines thus: — Becoming one with God, we are invested with the liberty of God. To God all things are lawful, and, therefore, to us who are in God and one with Him, all things are lawful. Master Eckardt says, there can be no distinction or difference of things to God, all are one; therefore, there is no distinction or difference of things to us, all are one to us. And there were three or four propositions included amongst those condemned by the pope, so outrageous, that Martensen and others imagine them to have been foisted in by enemies who regarded them as the legitimate results of his propositions. Namely, articles fourth, fifth, and sixth, which assert, in every work, whether good or bad, God is equally glorified. That whoever vituperates God praises Him; and the more he vituperates, and the greater the sin, the more he praises God. And again, the fifteenth, sixteenth, and seventeenth, which assert, that if a man commit a thousand sins, if such a man were rightly disposed, he ought not to desire not to have committed them, and that this is true repentance. That God does not particularly regard outward actions. That an outward act is not properly good, nor divine; nor is it, properly speaking, originated by God.

Whether, however, these propositions are really part of those of Eckardt, as Mosheim, Ullmann, Hase, Gieseler, Baur, Schmidt, Thomson, and other German theologians contend they are, the rest are sufficiently daring and dangerous to repel the generality of readers from his teaching. Yet, stripped of their more extravagant dialecticisms, they probably meant no more, in the mind of Eckardt, than that Christian Buddhism common to all mystics, and which, in

fact, is founded in the teaching of Christ and of St. Paul:—
That the soul may become so purified that it shall retain
nothing but what is absolutely divine, absolutely that which
it brought from God, and carries back to Him. That in
this pure and perfect unity of nature with God, it acquires
the perfect liberty of God. That this liberty is not a liberty
to commit sin, as the sensual interpret it, but is a perfect
liberty and freedom from all sin and power of sin. That it
can do nothing but what is pure and holy, because it has
nothing left in it but what is pure and holy. It is in that
state to which the Buddhist aspires, and to which the solitaries
of the early church aspired, and for which their victories
over all fleshly tendency were the preparation and the
avenues. That state which Christ described when He said
the Father was in Him, and He in the Father; and in which
the disciples should also be in Him and in the Father, and
He and the Father should be in them, and that they should
be all one. In which St. Paul said that when Christ had
put all things under His feet, including death and sin, He
should render up the kingdom to God, and God should 'be
all in all.' It is this state in which the nature of God becomes the nature of all living souls, from which all sin and
frailty and tendency to sin and frailty are purged out; a condition of perfect and boundless holiness, power and perfection,
towards which all earnest aspirants, Pagan or Christian, a
Socrates, a Plato, a Buddha, St. John, a Simon Stylites, a
Fénelon, a Fox, a Wesley, or a Swedenborg, have, in all ages
and regions, striven and suffered, walking the rugged paths
of life in tears, in daily martyrdom, in shame and persecution; but at the same time in joy and triumph, far beyond
the conception of the rejoicing and the triumphs of the world
—seeing before them, and above them, and within them that
Paradise of God long since shut out from our vision by the
clouds of mortal passion, but never lost from the memory
and the hopes of the most abject—that home-land in which
God had walked with Adam, and is still walking with
the saints — the land of divine liberty, which is divinest

love; it is this state which Master Eckardt really sought to designate, though his speculative genius led him into tropes and figures made unbefitting by his intensest yearnings.

So Suso, his admiring disciple, read him; so Tauler of Strasburg, Heinrich of Nördlingen, Rulman Merswin of Strasburg, and others, read him; and on these purified interpretations arose, with these great men, the Society of the Friends of God. These Friends of God, like the Methodists of the present day, did not abandon their union with the church to which they belonged; they sought only to organise an association for mutual comfort and strength, not to found a new heretical sect. They sought to imitate Christ, and to restore the original purity of the church. Their opposition was not to the church itself, but to the corruption of its doctrines and the immorality of the clergy. Their zeal was not to throw down the organic constitution of Catholicism, but for the purification of it and for comfort for the people at large. They stood as a middle link betwixt the church and the Waldenses, and in the bosom of the Waldenses also arose another Society of the Friends of God, at the head of whom stood Nicolas of Basle, who was eventually burnt as a heretic at Vienne; Berthold von Rohrbach, put to death at Speir; and Martin of Mayence, who also was burnt at Cologne in 1393.

None of these wholly rejected the doctrines of Catholicism. They honoured the Virgin highly, but rejected the worship of images; some of them frequented mass, but contended that the laity might perform it as lawfully as the clergy. They preached and wrote books in the mother-tongue, and thus vastly extended the circle of their operations. In close connection with these associations, was another called the Brotherhood of the Winkelers, a German word indicating workers in corners, or in secret places. Röhrich, in his 'Friends of God,' says, that these Winkelers, or confessors of the people, were not located merely in Strasburg, or were the leaders of the association there merely; but they were missionaries, leading a wandering life, instructing individuals as they met with them, and confirming in the faith those already converted. They were men of blameless life and strict morals, remaining single not from a notion of the sanctity of celibacy, but to enable them to devote themselves more entirely to their duties. From the impression of a direct divine call, they endured the hardships of a self-denying life, which frequently was terminated by a violent death. They were twelve, after the number of the Apostles, and they were regarded by their followers as the only genuine priests. They were supported by the contributions of the association; and when they came amongst the believing brethren, they were received as guests by those of property. Others gave them money, which they distributed. When a new Master was needed, he was elected from youths of pure morals. For this solemn choice the whole community came together, and seating themselves in a circle around the proposed Master, each one gave his judgement whether he was of a pure life, and worthy of becoming a Master. After proper enquiries and satisfactory answers, the young man was desired to stand up, and was exhorted to lead a chaste life and to remain voluntarily poor; whereupon he solemnly pledged himself never to forsake the faith. So he became Master, and was greeted as such. From this time he must prosecute no other business, nor follow any trade; he must live exclusively the life of a teacher; and possess no property, but subsist on the offerings of the brethren and sisters. There were not only Masters but Mistresses, who were chosen in the same manner; but of their particular duties we have no certain information. In the absence of a Master, one of the community offered exhortations; and meetings were much oftener held when Masters were absent than when present, but when a Master arrived amongst them, the occasion was celebrated by a general feast and rejoicing.

The Winkelers kept no sacred holiday, except Christmas, Easter and Whitsuntide; as to Mary's days and Apostles' days, they regarded them not. They had no faith in purgatory. They took the sacrament in the churches; but they held that a material church was no church, and that they could confess to one another, and that wherever they were, they could pray and be heard of God. As for masses, public almsgivings, prayers and singing for the dead, they regarded them as of no real avail; nor did they put faith in holy water, nor the blessing of meats, cakes, candles, &c. Of these Winkelers, who were regular Protestants, no fewer than eighty were condemned to death at the stake in Strasburg in 1222, together with their Master, Johannes.

But, before closing this chapter, we must take a nearer view of the Friends of God, and especially of Tauler, Nicolas of Basle, and Rulman Merswin. Much light has been thrown upon the lives and characters of these great men by the discovery of a large folio volume found in the archives of Strasburg, and formerly belonging to the convent of the Knights of St. John in that city. The English reader has been made acquainted with the contents of this volume by Miss Susannah Winckworth in her 'Life and Sermons of Dr. John Tauler.' The discovered folio contains the correspondence of Nicolas of Basle with Rulman Merswin, who established a company of Friends of God in the convent of the Knights of St. John on an island in the Rhine, called the Gruenen-Woerth or Green Meadow. In it were found the letters and religious experiences of Tauler, Nicolas, and Merswin up to 1382. And most remarkable they are. The central figure is Nicolas of Basle, who, though only a layman, had, with his pious friends, entered on a course of religious reform which threatened to revolutionise the whole of the Popedom. It was, therefore, necessary that this work should be carried on with all possible secrecy, or their lives would have been cut very short. They attacked the rank corruptions of the church, and even its learning, if unbased on the direct teachings of the Divine Spirit. Nicolas, therefore, comes forth, ever and anon, like an apparition from some hidden scene, whence he sees the movements of the world. He bears no name on such occasions but the 'Man from the Oberland,' and, his mission accomplished, he retires again to his invisible abode, which is known only to his four intimate friends. Thus we have him suddenly appearing in Strasburg for the conversion of Tauler.

Dr. John Tauler was a learned and eloquent preacher of that city. His preaching excited the wonder of the country far round. Nicolas of Basle came to hear him. Having heard him, he desired to confess to him; but in his confession Tauler is struck with astonishment at his words. He tells Tauler that he is really come, not so much to hear him as to show him that he has not yet qualified himself to preach. That to do that effectually and acceptably to God he must first empty himself of all his mere human learning and self-knowledge, and, like a child, sit down and learn of God, whose Spirit in one hour will teach him more than all the schools in a whole life. Tauler is struck with the truth of this; he desires Nicolas to put him in the way of this new teaching, and here the Man began to teach the Master. It is soon seen which is the real master in God; and Tauler, in amazement and humility, flings himself at the foot of the cross, and for two years, renouncing all preaching, submits to the tuition of the Holy Spirit in solitude, reading of the Gospel, and prayer. Once more he comes forth a new and far more wonderful man. His sermons have a life and fire in them such as had never been witnessed by any of that time. Men and women were struck down under his ministry by scores, and lay for hours as dead, but only to revive to a more genuine life. From that day John Tauler became a great name in the church of Christ, and remains so at this age.

Rulman Merswin was a wealthy merchant of Strasburg who retired from a mercantile life to a religious one. He, too, became acquainted with the 'Man from the Oberland,' and, as to Tauler, it was a new era to him. He became inspired with the true spirit of that real and interior religion which at once reduces all worldly wealth to its proper place, that of making men not nominal, but real Christians. He founded the convent of the Order of St. John, as an asylum for pious persons like himself, who were not bound by any oath, but lived together for the benefit of mutual edification; seeking not counsel from men, but from the Spirit of God; and, so long as they had it, indifferent whether it flowed through priest or layman. In fact, a society of the Friends of God, based on the declaration of Christ, that they who were His genuine disciples were no longer His servants, but His friends. Rulman, like Tauler, remained in close but secret correspondence with the 'Man from the Oberland' till his death; no doubt actively engaged with these great and mysterious men in spreading the knowledge of Gospel truth through countries far and wide.

Nicolas of Basle and his friends predicted the death of Gregory XI., which took place at the time foretold—namely, in the fourth week in Lent, 1378. They foresaw also the grand schism in the Popedom, which commenced in the following year. So deeply was Nicolas concerned for the shameful corruptions of the church and of the papal court, that in his seventieth year, in the year 1376, taking a trusty 'Friend of God' with him, he went to Rome, and, in a personal interview with Gregory, warned him of the troubles coming, and of his own death, if he did not commence a real and sweeping reform. The pope received this mission kindly, but did not profit by it, and died as they had foreshown. Many wonderful spiritual phenomena and revelations are related as attending the meetings of these Friends of God, who, after this, set out different ways into France, Germany, Italy, Hungary, and other countries to prosecute the work of Gospel reform. They fell in honoured martyrdom in different places; Nicolas himself at Vienne, in France, as already stated, when he was about ninety years of age. Many ladies were distinguished members of the Society of the Friends of God, and amongst them preeminent Agnes, Queen of Hungary, the widow of King Andrew; and the sisters Christina and Margaretta Ebner, both nuns.

For a very interesting account of the 'Friends of God,' see the 'Spiritual Magazine' for 1862, Nos. for May and August.

Such were the various sects heralding the downfall of corrupt

Catholicity; good and bad, all were crying for a new order of things. The good were entering deep into the arcana of the Christian life in the soul; the bad were driven, as by disorderly and sensual spirits, into crimes and rabid heresies. The true and the false equally maintained the doctrine of spiritual agency, and both good and bad exemplified it in their actions. There were a rabies and an orgasm running through all mortal affairs clearly drawing fire from deeper sources than mere mortal passions. The power of God, long neglected and outraged in the Roman Church, had departed and left it open to vice, luxury, libertinism, and a terrible lust of dominion and destruction. Rome had scourged, martyred, and calumniated the faithful. The devil had shown to the Saviour all the kingdoms of the world, and offered them if He would bow down and worship him. The offer was declined. But it was again made to the Saviour's professed vicars on earth, and the fatal gift had been accepted. The church abandoned Christ and his poverty, and accepted temporal power, and regal instead of apostolic state. The demon virus in the gift soon operated. The church became secularised. Instead of poverty, wealth; instead of nowhere to lay their heads, the pontiffs and cardinals, and many a proud prelate and mitred abbot, laid theirs on silken pillows in palaces. Instead of being summoned before kings and magistrates for Christ's sake, they sate as kings and judged His honest followers. By the very places the two parties occupied, was plainly indicated which of them were the disciples to whom Christ had promised the kingdom of heaven with persecutions. Instead of fasts there came feastings, instead of being surrounded by the sick seeking to be healed, they were surrounded by martial guards, and sate at banquets on the right hand of kings. In spite of all Christ's warnings, the world had got them and the devil. They sent out their armies and exterminated whole peoples who demanded to serve God in the ancient simplicity. Under Simon de Montfort, the papal legate, they ravaged Provence, drove out Raymond, the rightful sovereign, usurped his lands, and murdered his subjects. They exterminated the whole of Christian Bohemia, by the hand of their gloomy agent, Ferdinand II. of Austria. They laid waste the mountains of the Cevennes with fire and sword, and their Inquisition in Italy, Spain, and other countries, made hell and Romanism synonymous. Everywhere the flames of burning martyrs, everywhere their instruments of torture, everywhere their arrogance, and insolence, and sensuality, proclaimed that the gift of the devil had done its work, and that Satan reigned in the outraged name of Christ. The very cells of nuns, awful witnesses of the insurrection of nature against spurious religionism, were declared to be paved with the skeletons of murdered children. Luther, in his 'Table-Talk,' p. 307, says Pope Gregory, who confirmed celibacy, ordered a fish-pond at Rome, hard by a convent of nuns, to be cleared out. The water being let off, there were found at the bottom more than six thousand skulls of children, that had been cast into the pond and drowned. He adds, that in his own time, the foundations of a nunnery being removed at Neinburg in Austria, similar revelations were made.

The work of the devil's gift of temporal dominion was equally efficacious on the people at large. Thrust out from all personal knowledge of the gospel, they were grown brutish as the beasts they tended. The spiritualism of the church had become the spiritualism of devils, and rioted in lying miracles, and forced, by its iron repression of conscience, a plentiful crop of heresies and a sanguinary harvest of martyrdom. Millions of groaning souls cried, ' How long, O Lord!' The times were ripe, and men's violated hearts were ripe for the great catastrophe of retribution. The avatar of reformation came at length by the natural weight of rottenness in the apostolical hierarchy, and by the mingled efforts of Huss and Wycliffe, of Luther and the crowned Balaam of reform—Henry VIII. of England, who meaning the work of the devils of lust and murder, did the work of God. It was the era of revival, the memorable sixteenth century. The Reformation was come.

CHAPTER V.

THE SPIRITUALISM OF LUTHER AND THE EARLY REFORMERS.

The Christian system of the spiritual and material world stood for 1500 years unshaken. All at once, the monk Copernicus stood forth! With a mighty hand he pushed away the globe from the centre of creation, fixed the sun in its place, and bade the former make the circuit of the latter in a year, and revolve upon its axis in twenty-four hours. By this fortunate discovery much that was incomprehensible became intelligible, and much that was inexplicable, demonstrable. The pope and the clergy were struck with consternation at it. They threatened curse and excommunication; but Copernicus had already made his escape from them, the earth was now in motion, and no anathema was able to arrest its progress.

But Protestantism was not satisfied with this; it went farther. It promulgated the dogma that there were no such things as apparitions or a middle state. Luther and his confederates renounced all claim to the government of the invisible world; they extinguished the fires of purgatory, and *enlarged the bounds of Hell by adding Hades to it.* No middle state of purification was any longer believed in, but every departed soul entered upon its place of destination, either heaven or hell. Presentiments, visions and apparitions, were regarded either as deception, delusion and imagination ; or, where the facts could not be denied, as the work of the devil and his angels. By their decree that the pious were immediately after death received into heaven, and the impious plunged into hell, the gate was closed against the return of departed spirits to this world.

Encouraged by this, the physical philosophers very soon promulgated the doctrine that there was nothing in the world but matter, and its properties. They delved in matter, and, finding nothing by their tests but matter, they declared that there were no powers but such as were material. But Leibnitz was a stumbling-block to the physical philosophers ; for he insisted on such things as principles of 'indivisibility' and 'predetermined harmony,' etc.

STILLING's Pneumatology, p. 15 to 22.

IN the above extract Stilling has correctly described the progress of modern infidelity and materialism from the act of Protestantism at the Reformation. Finding the Lord's heritage overrun with a rampant growth of the devil's tares in the shape of fictitious miracle, they forgot to consult the Lord's recommendation so conspicuously given in the Gospel, to let the tares grow with the wheat till the final harvest, lest they should pull up the wheat along with them. To get rid of false miracles, they plucked up the true; and to prevent the return of the false, they determined to root up the very principle of faith in the miraculous, in spite of the whole world, with its five thousand five hundred years of miraculous facts, protesting against so insane a rejection of its laws. In spite of the plain words of Christ and His apostles, that miracle was the patrimony of the Christian church; and that the mark of the true disciple should be that 'these signs should follow them that believe. In my name shall they cast out devils; they shall speak with new tongues; they shall take up deadly serpents, and, if they drink any deadly thing, it shall not hurt them; they shall lay hands on the sick, and they shall recover' (Mark xvi. 17, 18). (I am aware that a recently discovered copy of the Gospel of St. Mark was found destitute of these words; but is it any wonder that a scroll of parchment so rotten as to resemble an old cigar should want a verse or two at the very end of it? Even had this copy been in good condition, it could not set aside the evidence of copies equally ancient and authentic. The Syrian Gospel, which has been in the hands of the Syrian Church since the time of the apostles, has the passage complete.) In spite of volumes of authentic history by men of undoubted character narrating ages of such facts, prior to the corruptions of Rome. It was a fatal act, and being in open opposition to nature and history, was certain to produce the most deplorable consequences.

But Protestantism does not bear alone the blame; the Church of Rome, by its shameless traffic in miracles and in the fires of purgatory in later ages, led the Protestants into this overstrained reaction. Rome caused the damage which Protestantism, in its righteous but ill-considered indignation, perpetrated. When the devil's rule is in danger, he rarely fails to find a trap for his opponents. In this case they thought to clip his wings by cutting off miracle, and he recommended them, as an admirable and infallible measure, to cut off the very roots of faith in it, and they fell into the satanic snare. It is not for nothing, says Luther, that the devil has been ranging about these thousands of years.

So profoundly was Luther himself frightened at the very name of miracle, that he would not admit it, or even talk of it as existing in the church, if he could avoid it. 'Luther,' says Michelet, 'did not love to hear anyone insist on the miracles. He looked upon them as a very secondary class of proofs.' Yet he was continually admitting them, if they were only connected with the devil. He observed that 'Christ once appeared on earth visibly, showed His glory, and, according to the divine purpose of God, finished the work of redemption and the deliverance of mankind. I do not desire He should come once more in the same manner, neither would I that He should send an angel to me.' He added, that he desired no 'visions or revelations.' And here we have that mistaken idea adopted so generally by Protestantism, and which has proved, indeed, 'a most deadly error,' namely, that miracles and revelations once made, would serve for ever. That evidence given in one age will serve for a very distant age. Time has shown the fallacy of this idea. It has shown that evidence, like all other things on earth, wears out, and loses its life. It is precisely on this ground that the erroneous materialism of the present day rests. The evidence of the ancient miracles is so far off that people deny that it ever existed, and nothing but new miracles, those miracles which Christ promised to the end of the world, and which would have been the constant attendant of the church, if men had retained their faith, can renew that faith. But more of this anon.

Luther, however, was forced to admit that angels were 'watching and protecting;' but he desired his followers not to trouble themselves about the manner in which it was done: God having said it, it was sure. 'The angels, he said, are all up in arms, are putting on their armour, and girding their swords about them.' Desiring no outward gifts of miracles himself, he yet added, 'Not, however, that I derogate from the gifts of others, if haply to anyone, over and above Scripture, God should reveal aught by dreams, by visions, or by angels.' He, moreover, firmly believed that he was incited to his attack on the Papacy, by direct divine inspiration, and he often spoke things prophetically concerning Charles V., concerning the affairs of Germany and of Protestantism, and he said, 'I certainly am of opinion that I speak these things in the Spirit.'

Believing, then, in direct spiritual inspiration, in the probability that spirits, visions, and angels might appear to others, why did not Luther wish them to appear unto himself? It was because this stout-hearted man, who did not fear the devil, like too many of to-day, was afraid of ridicule and criticism. He confessed that if God gave him the grace to work miracles, the Papists would immediately say that the devil did them by him. He had so bitterly ridiculed, and so heartily abused the Catholics for their manufactured miracles, that he was now afraid to have the power of working true ones, lest they should retort. We have a striking example of this given by Seckendorf in his 'Comment. de Lutheranismo.' Certain persons had brought to Luther a girl eighteen years of age, said to be possessed of the devil. Now Luther believed firmly in possession, but had a fear of using exorcism for the reason just given. He says, 'Men are possessed two ways, corporally and spiritually. Those possessed corporally are mad people, whom he has permission to vex and agitate, but he has no power over their souls. The impious, who persecute the divine truth, are possessed spiritually.' Such men as Annas, Caiaphas, Julian the Apostate; the pope, his cardinals, bishops, and priests who persecuted Protestantism, he believed were possessed spiritually, and would not be delivered by any human means. He had a notion too, that 'we cannot expel demons with certain ceremonies and words as Jesus Christ, the prophets, and apostles did. All we can do is, in the name of Jesus Christ, to pray the Lord God, of His infinite mercy, to deliver the possessed persons.' And he adds that, if this was done in faith, it will be efficacious. 'But we cannot of ourselves expel the evil spirits, nor must we even attempt it.' In these remarks the great Reformer, so far as the apostles were concerned, makes a distinction without a difference; for the apostles were assured by Christ that the devils did not go out without prayer and fasting. The apostles never pretended to cast out devils of themselves, but by the conferred power of God. But Luther was, no doubt, thinking of the wordy forms of exorcism employed by the Romanists.

The young girl in question being brought before him, he ordered her to repeat the Apostles' Creed, but she stopped at the name of Jesus Christ and could not pronounce it. Upon this Luther said, 'I know thee, Satan; thou wouldst have one begin exorcising with great parade; but I will do no such thing.' On the following day she was brought into the church whilst Luther was preaching, and after the service into a small chapel. She was thrown upon the floor in convulsions, and Luther laid his hand on her head, and repeated over her the Creed, the Lord's Prayer, and the words of John, 'He that believeth in me, the works that I do he shall do also, and greater works than these shall he do.'

These words, one would have thought, might have inspired Luther with a bolder faith in the delegated power of Christ; and had they done so, he would have saved Protestantism a fearful loss of divine potency, and from a long dark reign of rationalistic barrenness. However, he prayed to God with the rest of the ministers of the church, that for Christ's sake He would cast the devil out of the girl. He then touched her with his foot, saying, 'Proud devil, thou wouldst indeed that I should now proceed against thee with great parade, but I will do no such thing. I know that thy head is crushed, and that thou liest prostrate at and under the feet of our Lord Jesus Christ!' He then went away, and the girl was taken home to her friends, who afterwards wrote that she was no more troubled by the spirit.

On another occasion at Eisenach, a woman was the victim of horrible convulsions, of which no doctors could cure her; for, says Luther in his 'Table-Talk,' it was the direct work of the devil. Her hands and feet were bent into the form of horns, her tongue was dry and rough, and her body much swollen. Luther visited her, and said, 'God rebuke thee, Satan, and command thee, that thou suffer this, His divine creature, to be at peace.' He then prayed for her release from the demon, and the woman said, 'Amen.' That night, for the first time for a long period, she enjoyed refreshing sleep, and awoke in the morning perfectly well.

Thus, it is clear, that Luther was a genuine spiritualist, not ignoring the divine side of it, as our clergy and literati do now-a-days, but was only afraid of throwing himself boldly into its practice from fear of that bugbear, criticism. His wife occasionally saw visions, and Luther fully believed in them. In the night preceding the death of their daughter Magdalen, who died at the age of fourteen, Madame Luther in a dream saw two beautiful youths come to her and ask her daughter in marriage. On telling the dream to Melancthon in the morning, he said, the youths were the angels coming to carry the dear virgin to the true nuptials of the heavenly kingdom. Magdalen died that afternoon. Luther, too, had his own visions. He says that, on one occasion, he saw two signs in heaven. One was the arch of heaven resting without any visible support; and the men of to-day, he said, were trying in vain to find out where the supports were, and to grapple them with their hands, if they could: but he felt a conviction that they never would be able to do it. Then he saw beneath him a rainbow bridge bearing up the heavens, and he saw that God could make even a slight aërial line do His will, and support the whole firmament if necessary. On another occasion, he says, 'On Good Friday last, being in my chamber in fervent prayer, contemplating with myself how Christ my Saviour on the cross suffered and died for my sins, there suddenly appeared upon the wall a bright vision of our Saviour Christ, with the five wounds, steadfastly looking upon me, as if it had been Christ Himself corporeally. At first sight I thought it had been some celestial vision, but I reflected that it must needs be an illusion and juggling of the devil, for Christ appeared to us in His word, and in a meaner and more humble form; therefore, I spoke to the vision thus, "Avoid thee, confounded devil! I know no other Christ than He who was crucified, and who in His word is pictured and presented to us." Wherefore the image vanished, clearly showing of whence it came.'

It is pretty apparent that Luther was so possessed of the idea of the devil that, had Christ appeared to him, as He did to St. Paul, or to St. John in the Revelations, he would have said, 'Avaunt thee, Satan!' and lost the benefit of the vision. This was the weak side of Luther. The devil, he imagined, was so outrageous at his war on the Papacy, that he haunted him day and night in a most vindictive manner. In the 'Tischreden' or 'Table-Talk' of Luther, written down and published by his friends, we have some scores of pages relating the personal appearances of the devil to Luther, and of his conversations with him, and the Reformer's defiances of him. Luther saw devils in everything. He saw them in tempests, in diseases, in calamities. 'Many devils are in the woods, in waters, in wildernesses, and in dark poolly places, ready to hurt and prejudice people; some are also in the thick, black clouds, which cause hail, lightnings and thunderings, and poison the air, the pastures, and the grounds. When these things happen, then the philosophers say it is natural, ascribing it to the planets, and showing, I know not what reasons for such misfortunes and plagues as ensue.'
. . . 'I see him there, not very far off, puffing out his cheeks till they are all red, blowing, and blowing, and blow-

ing against the light: furious, mad; but our Lord Jesus Christ, who, in the outset, gave him a good blow on his inflated cheek, still combats him vigorously, and will combat him till the end of things.' One day when there was a great storm abroad, Luther said, ' It is the devil who does this; the winds are nothing else but good or bad spirits. Hark how the devil is puffing and blowing!' (' Tischreden,' 219.) ' The devil harasses the workmen in the mines, and often makes them think they have found new veins, and they labour and labour, and it turns out all a delusion.' Luther taking up a caterpillar, said, ' 'Tis an emblem of the devil in its crawling walk, and bears his colours in its changing hue. I maintain,' he said, ' that Satan produces all the maladies which afflict mankind, for he is the prince of death.' He had absolute belief in the reality of witchcraft. ' Witchcraft is the devil's proper work, wherewith, when God permits, he not only hurts people, but makes away with them; for in this world we are as guests and strangers, body and soul cast under the devil. He is god of this world,' &c. ' Idiots, the lame, the blind, the dumb, are men in whom ignorant devils have established themselves; and all the physicians who attempt to heal these infirmities, as though they proceeded from natural causes, are ignorant blockheads, who know nothing about the power of the demon.' . . ' In many countries there are particular places to which devils more especially resort. In Prussia there is an infinite number of evil spirits. In Switzerland, on a high mountain, not far from Lucerne, there is a lake they call Pilate's Pond, which the devil has fixed upon as one of the chief residences of his evil spirits, and they are there in awful numbers. In Poltersberg, there is a lake similarly cursed. If you throw a stone into it, a dreadful storm immediately arises, and the whole neighbouring district quakes to its centre. 'Tis the devils kept there prisoners, who occasion this' (' Tischreden,' 212). Luther attributed direct acts of violence and abduction to the devils. ' Satan once tried to kill our prior, by throwing down a piece of wall upon him, but God miraculously saved him.'

'At Sassen, the devil carried off, last Good Friday, three grooms who had impudently devoted themselves to him.' &c. &c.

Now nobody now-a-days need be told that Luther was attributing to the devil on many occasions the simple operations of nature, and nobody is called on to believe that the devil threw down walls, rotten probably by time, or flew away with impious grooms. The fact was, that Luther's openness to spiritual influences was made one-sided by his horror of being charged by the Papists with doing the sacred miracles, which in them he had charged to diabolism or trick. The whole weight of his spiritualism was thus thrown to the demoniac side, and on that side became exaggerated. He saw where devils were so frequently, that he at length saw them in appearances and causes where they were not. He is one of the greatest warnings against rejecting phenomena from prejudice, and not weighing well both sides, and thus arriving at a well-balanced cognisance of things. Shutting his mind against the fair side of spiritualism, he opened it not only to the palpably evil near him, but to the vague and dark beyond. There was, undoubtedly, in Luther's experience, a mixture of the real and the unreal, the unreal arising from this fixed one-sidedness.

The palpable personal appearances of the devil to Luther are amongst the most curious passages of his life. Everyone is familiar with the fact of his throwing the inkstand at the devil's head as he interrupted his translation of the Bible in the castle of Wartburg, and many, like myself, have seen the reputed mark on the wall. The matter-of-fact manner in which he relates these occurrences is amusing. 'When, in 1521, on my quitting Worms, I was taken prisoner near Eisenach, and conducted to my Patmos, the castle of Wartburg, I dwelt far apart from the world in my chamber, and no one could come to me, but two youths, sons of noblemen, who waited on me with my meals twice a-day. Among other things, they had brought me a bag of nuts, which I had put in a chest in my sitting-room. One evening, after

I had retired to my chamber, which adjoined the sitting-room, had put out the light and got into bed, it seemed to me all at once that the nuts had put themselves in motion, and jumping about in the sack, and knocking violently against each other, came to the side of my bed to make noises at me. However, this did not harm me, and I went to sleep. By and by I was wakened up by a great noise on the stairs, which sounded as though somebody was tumbling down them a hundred barrels one after another. Yet I knew very well that the door at the bottom of the stairs was fastened with chains, and that the door itself was of iron, so that no one could enter. I rose immediately to see what it was, exclaiming, " Is it thou ? Well be it so ! " (meaning the devil) and I recommended myself to our Lord Jesus Christ, and returned to bed. The wife of John Berblibs came to Eisenach. She suspected where I was, and insisted upon seeing me ; but the thing was impossible. To satisfy her, they removed me to another part of the castle, and allowed her to sleep in the apartment I had occupied. In the night, she heard such an uproar that she thought there were a thousand devils in the place ' (' Tischreden,' 208).

' Once,' he says, ' in our monastery at Wittenberg, I distinctly heard the devil making a noise. I was beginning to read the Psalms, after having celebrated matins, when interrupting my studies, the devil came into my cell, and there made a noise behind the stove, just as though he was dragging some wooden measure along the floor. As I found that he was going to begin again, I gathered together my books and got into bed. . . . Another time in the night, I heard him above my cell, walking in the cloister, but as I knew it was the devil, I paid no attention to him, and went to sleep.'

' It is very certain,' says Luther, ' that as to all persons who have hanged themselves or killed themselves in any other way, 'tis the devil who has put the cord round their necks, or the knife to their throats.' ' If we could see for how many angels one devil makes work, we should despair.' There are, according to Luther, three things that he is afraid of, ridicule,

God's word, and sacred songs. He says he has often made him fly by calling him 'Saint Satan!' and telling him that, if Christ's blood shed for man be not sufficient, he had better pray for us. Our songs and psalms sore vex and grieve him. Yet Luther had the profoundest idea of the devil's intellect and power of reason. 'The devil, it is true, is not exactly a doctor who has taken his degrees, but he is very learned, very expert for all that. He has not been carrying on his business during thousands of years for nothing' ('Tischreden,' 224). 'I know the devil thoroughly well; he has over and over pressed me so close that I scarcely knew whether I was alive or dead. Sometimes he has thrown me into such despair that I even knew not that there was a God, and had great doubts about our dear Lord Christ. But the word of God has speedily restored me' ('Tischreden,' 12).

''Tis marvellous,' says Bossuet, 'to see how gravely and vividly he describes the devil coming to him in the middle of the night, and awakening him to have a dispute with him: how closely he describes the fear which seized upon him; the perspiration which covered him; his trembling, the horrible feeling of his heart throughout the dispute; the pressing arguments of the devil, leaving no repose to his mind; the sound of the evil one's powerful voice, and his overwhelming method of disputation, wherever question and answer came immediately one upon the other. "I felt," he tells you, "I felt how it is people so often die suddenly towards the morning. It is that the devil can come and strangle men, if not with his claws, at all events with his pressing arguments"' ('Variations de l'Eglise,' ii. 206).

The case immediately referred to is the grand argument given by Luther in his treatise 'De Missâ Privatâ et Unctione Sacerdotum,' and quoted at length in Audin's 'Vie de Martin Luther.' Luther, according to this famous colloquy, had celebrated private mass nearly every day for fifteen years. The devil, as Luther supposed the spirit to be, commenced by throwing in a doubt whether the wafer and the wine were really the body and blood of Christ, and whether he had not all that time been worshipping merely bread and wine. He upbraided him with putting the Virgin Mary and the saints before Christ, and thus degrading and dishonouring Christ. In the second place, that he had abused the institution of the mass by using it privately, contrary to its ordained purpose, and thus committed sacrilege as a consecrated priest. He supported his arguments by the most apposite references to Scripture. He reprehended him for depriving the people of the sacrament, taking the elements only himself; whereas it was clear that Christ meant all His followers to partake of His sacrament. He called in question his very consecration as a priest, as having done contrary to the institution of Christ, and, telling him that, in that case, he had performed mass without due authority, and at the same time withheld the sacrament from the people. He upbraided him as impious on this account; that in the mass there was wanting the end, the design, the fruit, the uses for which Jesus Christ established the sacrament—that it should be eaten and drunk by the whole flock. That it was not there that Jesus Christ was Himself taken in the sacrament, but that it was not intended that a priest should take the sacrament himself, but take it with the whole church. With these and many other arguments the spirit pressed home the matter on Luther, threw him into the deepest distress, and so completely convinced him of the sinfulness of private masses, that he never again practised them.

And here we may ask whether this powerful spirit was, as Luther supposed it, the devil, or a devil? Is it likely that the devil, if Luther was in the practice of an iniquity, would come and reason him out of it? All the spirit's arguments are sound and scriptural, and convince the Reformer. Is that the language or the object of a devil? On the contrary, the whole scene, and the whole of the sentiments, go to prove that the spirit was a great as well as a powerful spirit; but which Luther, from his crotchet that all spirits appearing to him were devils, could believe nothing else. Many readers, however, will move the previous question, and doubt whether Luther really saw and conversed with spirits at all; whether he were not under a mere delusion of his excited imagination. On that point I should myself have doubted too, had I not seen so many things of a like nature of late years, and that only in common with some millions of people. Luther, no doubt, was a great and open medium. This was essential to his great mission. To call a man a great religious reformer is the same as calling him a great spiritual medium. Without this mediumship this communication, intimate and enduring, with the spiritual world, with the Holy Spirit and His holy angels, a man can reform nothing; he is a dead thing, and cannot emit new life and sentiment to the world. That Luther saw and conversed with spirits, good and bad, there can be no doubt; but there can be as little that he received stories of such things from other people too credulously. As little can there be any doubt that his horror of falling into the practices which he had condemned in the Romanists had so completely usurped his mind that to him all spirits who came were devils to his imagination, though they, as in the mass case, convicted him of error, and converted him to the truth. But if Luther, heart of oak as he was, could not see in spirits manifesting themselves to him aught but demons, he was a thorough spiritualist, not only in a most positive faith in them, but also in the power of Christian ministers to cast them out, in the truth of witchcraft, and in the sensible inspiration of the Holy Spirit in true preachers of the gospel.

His contemporaries and coadjutors, if they had not more vigorous convictions than himself in spiritual agencies, had a more equably balanced faith in them. Melancthon, as we have seen, believed in Madame Luther's dream of the angels coming for her daughter's soul. He showed his firm belief in angelic interpositions on various other occasions. He relates a case in which he was an eyewitness. A learned and holy man, named Simon Grynæus, going from Heidelberg to Speir, was desirous to hear a certain preacher in that city, who, in his sermon, did let fall some erroneous propositions of Popish doctrine, much derogatory to the majesty and truth of the Son of God; wherewith Grynæus, being not a little offended, craved speedy conference with the preacher, and, laying before him the falsehood and the danger of his doctrines, exhorted him to an abandonment of these misopinions. The preacher gave good words and fair semblance to Grynæus, and desiring farther and more particular conference with him, each imparted to the other their names and lodgings.

Grynæus, upon his return to his lodgings, reported the conference to those who sate at table with him—Melancthon was one. Presently Melancthon was called out of the room to speak to a stranger, who had just arrived. A grave old man of a good countenance, and richly attired, in a friend's manner, told him that within one hour would come certain officers as from the King of the Romans, to attach Grynæus, and carry him to prison: wishing Melancthon to charge Grynæus with all possible speed to flee out of Speir. This said, the old man vanished out of his sight. Melancthon returned to his companions, and related to them what he had seen and heard. He hastened the departure of Grynæus, who had no sooner boated himself on the Rhine, than he was eagerly sought for at his lodgings by Roman officers. This worthy divine, as he is styled by Bishop Hall, in his Commentary on Daniel, relates these facts, and acknowledges God's providence in sending His angel to rescue His faithful subject.

It is related by Leckendoye, on the authority of Solomon Glasse, Superintendent-general of Gotha, that Melancthon was recalled from the verge of death by Luther's prayers. 'Luther arrived, and found Philip about to give up the ghost. His eyes were set, his understanding was almost gone, his speech had failed, and also his hearing; his face had fallen; he knew no one, and had ceased to take either solids or liquids. At this spectacle Luther is filled with the utmost consternation — turning away towards the window, he called most devoutly upon God. After this, taking the hand of Philip, and well knowing what was the anxiety of his heart and conscience, he said, " Be of good courage, Philip ; thou shalt not die." While he utters these things, Philip begins, as it were, to revive and to breathe, and, gradually recovering his strength, is at last restored to health.' Melancthon writing to a friend said, ' I should have been a dead man, had I not been recalled from death by the coming of Luther.' A similar detention in life of Myconius by Luther's prayers is recorded, and that six years afterwards Myconius, being again at the point of death, sent a message to Luther desiring him this time not to detain him by his prayers. Melancthon fully recognises the reality of apparitions, and mentions a case occurring in his own family. He says his father's sister appeared to her husband after death, and earnestly conjured him to pray for her.

John Calvin was not of a temperament to imagine groundless or merely airy things. His stern mind bent on establishing the sternest doctrines even by the application of fire, to recalcitrant theologians, as in the case of Servetus, was not one to originate or indulge in dreams of mere spiritual fantasies, yet Beza, than whom no man knew him better, being his colleague at Geneva, both in the church and the university, tells us that ' he regarded satanic wonders as supernatural and real, not mere slights.' He says that he had a genuine spirit of prophecy, and predicted events which came wholly to pass. He had his spiritual ear open to hear sounds quite beyond the reach of the outward sense. ' One thing,' says Beza, ' must not be omitted. On December 19, 1562, Calvin, lying in bed sick of the gout, it being the Sabbath day, and the north wind having blown two days strongly, he said to many who were present, " Truly, I know not what is the matter, but I thought this night I heard warlike drums beating very loud, and I could not persuade myself that it was so. Let us, therefore, go to prayer; for surely some great business is in hand." And this day there was a great battle fought between the Guisians and the Protestants, not far from Paris, news whereof came to Geneva within a day or two.' For abundant evidence of a like kind see Audin's 'Histoire de la Vie, &c., de Calvin,' and Dr. Paul Henry's 'Leben Johann Calvins.'

As to Beza himself, he gives us his own opinion on these subjects: 'According as God in His righteous judgment grants liberty to the spirit, it is not difficult to evil spirits to misemploy a corpse; and for the purpose of deceiving some one, to speak in it, exactly as he uses the tongues of living demoniacs. . . . So also it often occurs in profane histories that brutes, and even idols, have spoken; which, indeed, is by no means to be rejected as false.' And in his Notes on the New Testament (Matthew iv. 24), he says, 'There are not wanting persons with whom demon or devil means nothing more than madness; that is to say, a natural malady, and one which may be cured by physic. Such persons, however, are refuted both by sacred and profane histories, and by *frequent experience*.' Wolfgang Musculus, one of the stanchest of the continental Reformers, originally a monk of Lorraine, but afterwards professor of divinity at Berne, and a great disciple of Luther's, in his Commentaries on the Scriptures, maintains the spiritual character of Christianity unflinchingly. Speaking of demons, he says, 'These malignant spirits lurk in statues and images, inspire soothsayers, compose oracles, influence the flight of birds, trouble life, disquiet sleep, distort the members, break down the health, harass with diseases.' In fact, he believed both the histories of all the Gentile nations, and those of the Jews and of Christianity too.

Coming nearer home and opening the life of the great Reformer of Scotland, we find the sternest of all stern religionists, John Knox, avowing, 'I dare not deny, lest I be injurious to the giver, that God hath revealed unto me secrets unknown to the world; yea, certain great revelations of mutations and changes where no such things were feared, nor yet were appearing. Notwithstanding these revelations I did abstain to commit anything to writing, contented only to have obeyed the charge of Him who commanded me to cry.' The 'Truth-seeker,' in the 'Spiritual Telegraph,' has called our attention to the following passage in Mc Crie's 'Life of Knox:'—' It cannot be denied that the contemporaries of John Knox considered these revelations as proceeding from a prophetic spirit, and have attested that they received an exact accomplishment.

' The most easy way of getting out of this delicate subject is, to dismiss it at once, and summarily to pronounce that all pretensions to extraordinary premonitions, since the completion of the canon of inspiration, are unwarranted, and that they ought, without examination, to be discarded, and treated as fanciful and visionary. But I doubt much if this mode of determining the question would be doing justice to the subject. A prudent enquirer will not be disposed to acknowledge as preternatural whatever was formerly regarded in this light, and will be on his guard against the illusions of imagination as to the impressions which may be made on his own mind. But, on the other hand, there is danger of running into scepticism, and of laying down general principles which may lead us obstinately to contest the truth of the best authenticated facts, and to limit the operations of divine providence. That there have been instances of persons having had presentiments as to events which afterwards did happen to themselves and others, there is, I think, the best reason to believe. The *esprits forts* who laugh at vulgar credulity, and exert their ingenuity in accounting for such phenomena on ordinary principles, have been exceedingly puzzled with some of these facts—*a great deal more puzzled than they have confessed*—and the solutions which they have given, are, in some instances, as mysterious as anything included in the intervention of inferior spirits, or in preternatural and divine intimations.'

These passages in the Scotch Reformers and theologians are most important. They show us that the easy mode of whisking away all belief in modern spiritual phenomena,— that of accepting it as a fact, in the very teeth of the most enormous piles of evidence, that miracles ceased with the apostolic age, and had done the work of Christian credence for ever,—had been applied to these colossal and logical North British heads, and had failed to impress them. With the natural caution of Scotchmen, they were ready to weigh and examine scrupulously all extraordinary things presented to their attention, but they were not ready to toss to the winds the solemn assurance of the most able and conscientious man, the leader and remodeller of their age, at the request of every shallow sceptic. John Knox, sparing no custom, no prejudice, no work of man, that he deemed not based in truth or wisdom, who knocked down steeples as he knocked down Popish mummeries, yet spared the facts and intimations that came to him as they had come to the prophets and martyrs before him; and he not only boldly assumed inspiration in his own case, but in the case of his predecessor George Wishart and of others. 'Orthodox, orthodox, who believe in John Knox,' says the acute 'Truth-seeker,' 'and all others whom it may concern, lay these words to heart, and ponder them well.'

Knox, says Mr. Boys, in his 'Proofs of the Miraculous Faith and Experience of the Church of Christ in all Ages,' delivered predictions so particular in their details, and even regarding particular persons, that they could not be resolved upon any principle into mere inferences or sagacious prognostications. Of this Mr. Boys gives various instances, adding that Knox declared that Wishart, Grindal, and other godly men amongst the Reformers, spoke by special revelations things that were to happen. He asserted, too, that even that 'blinded prince,' James of Scotland, had certain spiritual visions that 'men of good credit can yet report.' The following passages in Knox's history, also brought forward by the 'Truth-seeker,' are extremely striking and impressive:—

'Whilst George Wishart was so occupied with his God in preaching and meditation, the Cardinal (Beatoun) drew a secret draucht. He caused write unto him a letter, as it had been from his most familiar friend, the Laird of Kinnyc, desiring him with all possible diligence to come unto him, for he was struck with a sudden illness. In the meantime had the traitor provided three-score men with jackis and spears, to lie in wait within a mile and a half of the town of Montrois for his dispatch. The letter coming to his hand he made haste at the first, for the boy had brought a horse, and so with some honest men he passed forth of the town. But suddenly he stayed, and moving a space, returned back; whereat they wondering, he said, "I will not go, *I am forbidden of God, I am assured there is treason.* Let some of you go to yon place and tell me what they find." Diligence made, they found the treason as it was; which being shown with expedition to Mr. George, he remarked, "I know that I shall end my life in that blood-thirsty man's hands; but it will not be of this manner."

'Subsequently Wishart was apprehended and put to death by the machinations of his enemy, the cardinal, according to his own prophecy. The cardinal was present at the martyr's death, reposing leisurely, with other prelates, on rich cushions, laid for their accommodation in the window of a tower, from which the execution might be seen. The following is the account of it from the "Biographia Scotiana:"—"Being raised up from his knees, he was bound to the stake, crying with a loud voice, 'O Saviour of the world, have mercy upon me! Father of Heaven, I commend my spirit into Thy holy hands.' Whereupon the executioner kindled the fire, and the powder that was fastened to his body blew up. The captain of the castle perceiving that he was still alive, drew near, and bade him be of good courage; whereupon Mr. Wishart said, 'This flame hath reached my body, yet it hath not daunted my spirit; but he who from yonder place beholdeth me with such pride, shall within a few days lie in the same as ignominiously as he is now seen proudly to rest himself."'

'A few weeks after this the castle was surprised, and the cardinal put to death, and his body was suspended from the window whence he had witnessed the martyrdom of Wishart, whose prediction was thus fulfilled.'

Thus the chief heads of Protestantism abroad, and even in Scotland, though protesting against the corruptions and the abuse of the doctrine of the supernatural by Rome, seem far from having abandoned their faith in it, and were still found exercising the spirit of prophecy, the spirit of exorcism, and receiving continued inspiration from the Divine Head of the Christian church.

CHAPTER VI.

THE SUPERNATURAL AND THE CHURCH OF ENGLAND.

A certain class adhere firmly to the articles of faith of the Protestant Church, and while they believe all the appearances from the invisible world which are related in the Bible, reject everything of this nature subsequent to the times of the Apostles ; and when undeniable facts are adduced, ascribe them to a delusion of Satan and his angels, rather than detract anything from their system.

STILLING's *Pneumatology*, Introduction, p. 3.

Ich bin der Geist der stets verneint.
I am the spirit which still denies.

Mephistophiles in *Faust*.

It now appeareth clearly in the light of Christ, that the man of the earth has totally lost his divine instinct, his sensible feeling knowledge of the Deity, as well as that of his own natural humanity; living solely to the vain imagination of his natural reason.—HIEL, old German writer.

This contempt prior to examination, is an intellectual vice, from which the greatest faculties of mind are not free. I know not, indeed, whether men of the greatest faculties are not the most subject to it.

PALEY's *Evidences*, p. 357.

FROM what has preceded, it appears that the great actors in the Reformation in all other countries, though protesting against the abuses of the doctrine of the supernatural in the church, did not pretend to deny its existence. It remained for the Church of England to take this step in opposition to the universal evidence and practice of man in all countries and all time. It assumed the character which Goethe has conferred on Mephistophiles, that of the spirit which for ever denies. It was a deed as opposed to all philo-

sophy as to all history. To destroy the faith in the perpetual and sensible intercourse of spirit with spirit, whether in the body or out of the body, was to give the lie to a host of great and good men through fifteen hundred years; to undermine all historic credit, and to enthrone that sneering and impotent materialism, which has, in consequence, overspread the world, and infected all science, all sentiment, all religion with dry rot of the soul, from which the pulpit cannot free itself any more than the mere scientific chair. We do wonders in material discovery; we do none in psychology, because we hardly believe in soul at all. We hear in sermons sounding phrases about the operations of the Divine Spirit, and we hear still in the Homilies of the Church of England such words as these at Whitsuntide:—
'The Holy Ghost doth always declare Himself, by His *fruitful* and gracious gifts—namely, by the word of wisdom, by the word of knowledge, which is the understanding of the Scriptures; by faith *in doing of miracles*, by *healing them that are diseased*, by *prophecy*, which is the distribution of God's mysteries; by *discerning of spirits, diversities of tongues*, and so forth. All which gifts, as they proceed from one Spirit, and *are severally given to man* according to the measurable distribution of the Holy Ghost; even so do they bring men, and not without good cause, into a wonderful admiration of God's power.'

Similar avowals are made in the second part of this Homily, and in the Homily for Rogation Sunday. In the early copies of the *unabridged* Prayer-book, previous to 1721, still more distinct recognition of miraculous gifts is found. Such words, indeed, are to be found in that book: but when do we see them realised? when do they bring us to this wonderful admiration of God's power? How long is it since these miracles were done by the church which professes belief in them in its Book of Common Prayer? How long since the gifts of healing were exercised apostolically by its ministers? How long since they cast out evil spirits? How long since they prophesied as a function of the Christian faith, or practised the discernment of spirits? Never as a church, in most of these departments, since it was a church. How, then, is this? All other branches of the Christian church, save Protestantism, have ever done, and still do profess to believe and practise these gifts of the Holy Spirit, but the Church of England,—and the same deadness has passed by prestige and contact on to the Dissenters, has had a spiritual creed but no spiritual practice since it assumed the position of a church. Hence it is that the Catholics have ever declared that the Protestant faith is no true faith; for it is destitute of God's great criterion, the existence of miracle in it. Hence the Catholics have always declared that Protestantism 'is but a slippery highway to Deism,' and Protestantism has but too fully proved the truth of the accusation.

Look up! cast your eyes abroad over Protestantism, and behold the swarms of rationalists who believe little, and of materialists who believe nothing! See clergymen, who read the Homilies about miracles and healing of sickness by laying on of apostolic hands, and who write in 'Essays and Reviews' to assure you that they think all this nonsense, and impossible from the fixed natural order of things. Ask the *most believing* of clergymen when they have been reading such words, as soon as they have got outside their church-doors, if they believe them, and they will smile at your simplicity. What then? Is this a solemn national hoax? Must we apply to Anglicism the epithet of a stately and expensive sham? And yet between the non-belief in actual and practical supernatural life in the church, and this harsh phraseology, where is the refuge?

Look abroad still, over millions of Protestants, Church and Dissenting, who have weekly drawn their spiritual pabulum from the dry spiritual larders of these pulpits;—are they alive, or are they walking automata of dead morals and deader faith? If they believe in the existence of miracles, and the discerning of spirits, and the healing of sickness by spiritual means, and the revelations of spiritual messages from the sacred dead, why do they persecute or sneer at those whose vital faith and creed this is? Look onward still, and behold the learned professors of arts and sciences with their souls all shrivelled up by the exsiccating process of this Anglican drying-house, and whose looks and words are of the purest dryasdust order, capites-mortuum men—of the earth, earthy. Yet all, or many of these men, profess to believe in the Gospel, and in the Homilies of the church, and think themselves cognisant of the requirements of logic, and yet declare positively in the world their disbelief of doctrines out of the hour of church-service which they solemnly assert in it. Such are the fungus-growths of systems which assert and deny alternately on Sundays and on week-days.

But in this depth of inconsistency there is yet a lower depth. The English Church retains in its formulas of worship sundry traces of the Gospel truth of miracle; but its bishops have systematically disclaimed the creed they were appointed to teach, and some of them, to whom I shall immediately come, have written against all miracle since the days of the apostles with a zeal and a success which have done marvels of spiritual desolation, and have forged the most trenchant weapons of the unbeliever. From the very earliest days of the Anglican Church its great dignitaries and great theological writers have taken up the maxim that all miracles have ceased; and they have followed one another in this parrot-rote with a most wonderful and most infidel fidelity. And in saying this let me add, that it is uttered in no spirit of hostility to these prelates and other writers. They were men profoundly sincere in their views; many of them great and good men; men ready to lay down their lives for their faith, and some of whom did lay down their lives for it. Their error on this head was, therefore, the more to be lamented; and in speaking of such men and doctrines the plainness of our words must be excused for the sacred interests of truth.

ARCHBISHOP CRANMER at the very foundation of the English Reformed Church, took up the cry of the non-necessity of farther miracle. 'Some there be now-a-days that ask why men work no miracles now?' And he answers, 'If thou be faithful, as thou oughtest to be; if thou love Christ as He should be loved, thou needest no miracles, for signs are given to unbelievers, and not to the faithful.'

But we say precisely so; and why are not signs then given to unbelievers? Christ gave them to the unbelievers of His time, and so made believers of them. He was not sent, He said, to those who were whole, but to those who were sick; and the sick of these days, the unbelievers, ask for signs, and why shall they not get them, as the unbelievers of old did? Is God a respecter of persons? But Cranmer was not yet so thoroughly hardened into the non-miracle creed as his followers. He had full faith in miracles worked by the devil. He quotes a great deal from the Fathers—Lactantius, Chrysostom, Cyril, Irenæus, Cyprian, Augustine, Jerome, Scapulensis, etc.—to show what they did amongst them and amongst the heathen, in the oracles, and in performing many wonders. Ghosts also, he says, appeared; but that he thinks with Chrysostom that the devil's innumerable deceits brought so much fraud into the life of man that, for that cause, God hath shut up the way; neither doth He suffer any of the dead to come again hither, to tell what is done there, lest by that means he should bring in all his wiles and subtelties' ('Unwritten Verities,' vol. iv. of Cranmer's Works, p. 203).

Accordingly, he says, when you hear a dead man's soul cry 'I am the soul of such an one,' you are not to believe it the soul of that man, but of a devil. He does not, however, tell us why God should allow the devil to deceive us, when ghosts are not allowed to do it. He afterwards relaxes a little, and after giving us some 'sham' Popish miracles, gives us what he believes to be 'real.' 'A strange thing it is to hear of the wonderful trances and visions of Mistress Ann Wentworth of Suffolk, which told many men the secrets of their hearts, which they thought no man could have told them, but God only. She cut stomachers in pieces, and made them whole again, and caused divers men who spoke against her delusions, to go stark mad. All which things were proved, and openly by her confessed to be done by necromancy and the deceit of the devil.'

From all this it would appear that Cranmer thought that God had ceased to work miracles to convince and save men, but that He allowed the devil to work them to deceive and destroy men. Yet, like others of our old divines, he must have had better notions when he got out of his ecclesiastical dogmas; for in a letter written from Austria to Henry VIII., he speaks of having seen a great blazing star, called cometa. This was in October, 1532. Others, he says, report having seen other strange phenomena, but he had only seen the 'cometa;' and he adds, that 'God knows what these tokens foretell, for they do not lightly appear, but against some great mutation.' So that, after all, he did believe in God sending wonderful tokens, which is but another phrase for believing in miracles.

Cranmer's contemporary, that good, simple-hearted, honest-souled BISHOP LATIMER, at whose name every heart kindles with a glow of warm affection, what a beautifully and quaintly consistent inconsistent old patriarch he was! He had got his non-miracle theory as glibly as Cranmer, and held it with the same charming inconsequence. 'And peradventure some one will say, " How happeneth it that there are no miracles done in these days, by such as are preachers of the word of God?" I answer, the word of God is already confirmed by miracles: partly by Christ Himself, and partly by the apostles and saints. Therefore they which now preach the same word need no miracles for the confirmation thereof; for the same is sufficiently confirmed already' (vol. i. 161).

Thus, these two great founders of the Reformed Church of England, because the Papists taunted them with having no miracles, and being therefore a mere heretical schism, instead of seeking to the Divine Founder of Christianity to confirm to them His favour of miraculous powers, adopted the convenient but deadly theory, that miracles had ceased. It would have been in vain to have asked them exactly *when* they ceased, or where was the authority of the Gospels for their ceasing at all; they had got their easy-going answer, and you find most of the old divines repeating it. But what is most singular, and what they do not appear to have seen, is, that most of them at the same time that they held this theoretic notion, held the practical one of believing in miraculous interferences on their own behalf. The proceeding was inconsistent, but their private experience was much nearer the truth, than their public or ecclesiastical creed. Let us, therefore, turn to Latimer's Life. His biographer says—

'During the reign of Edward VI. God not only gave unto him plenteously of His Spirit, but also by the same Spirit he did most ardently prophesy of all those kinds of plagues which afterwards ensued; so plainly, that if England ever had a prophet, he might seem to be one' (p. xxi). Thus, according to his biographer, he was miraculously endowed at the moment that he was denying miracles. He adds, that he always prophesied his own death by martyrdom. In his sermons the good bishop is continually quoting miracles, and he dwells with great gusto on the fact that the Jews were driven away by arms by the Emperor Adrian, when, in defiance of prophecy, they assembled from all countries to reseat themselves at Jerusalem. He quotes, at length, and comments zealously on the miraculous dispersion of the Jews again by fire and earthquake, when Julian the Apostate had summoned them to rebuild the temple at Jerusalem. He was fond of introducing stories in his sermons of the personal appearances of the devil. On one occasion he slapped a man in the face for not having bowed at the name of Jesus, saying, if Christ had taken upon Him the nature of devils as He had done that of man, they would have revered Him more than men do. On another occasion he related this anecdote:—The devil came to take a German's soul on its departing from the body, and, pulling out a book, began to make a catalogue of his sins, commanding the sick man to confess them; but the man replied that God had promised that, if his sins were as scarlet, He would make them white as snow. The devil passed that over, and bade him go on. On this the man said, that " the Son of God appeared that He might destroy the works of the devil," and at this the devil vanished, and the soul of the man escaped to God.' It is clear that honest Latimer's creed about miracles was a new one, and that he altogether forgot it when he became warm in his sermons, or praised God in his private life for His miraculous interference on man's behalf.

The JUDICIOUS HOOKER was more judicious than these two noble old martyrs in his creed, and more scriptural. His colossal mind could not be wrapped up in the new cobwebs of the new Protestant theory about miracles. He admits the permanent continuance of their working in Christ's church. ' Men may be extraordinarily, yet allowably, two ways admitted with spiritual functions in the church. One is, when God Himself doth of Himself raise up any whose labour He useth without requiring that man should authorise them; but then He doth ratify their calling by manifest signs and tokens Himself from heaven; and thus, such even as believed not our Saviour's teaching, do yet acknowledge Him a lawful teacher sent from God. " Thou art a teacher sent from God, otherwise none could do those things which thou doest" (John iii. 2). Luther did but reasonably, therefore, in declaring that the Senate of Müllhouse should do well to ask of Muncer, from whence he received power to teach, who it was that had called him; and, if his answer were that God had given him his charge, then to require, at his hands, some evident sign thereof for man's satisfaction, because so God is wont, when He Himself is the author of any extraordinary calling.' (' Ecclesiastical Polity,' iii. 23.)

Speaking of St. Augustine's saying, that ' such gifts were not permitted to last always lest men should grow cold with their commonness,' he contends that the words of Augustine, declaring that the vulgar use of those miracles was then expired, are no prejudice to the like extraordinary graces more rarely observed in some, either then or of later times' (ii. 340).

He says, 'The angels resemble God in their unweariable and even insatiable longing to do all manner of good to men by all means.' 'The paynims,' he says, 'had arrived at the same knowledge of the nature of angels; Orpheus confessing that the fiery throne of God is surrounded by those most industrious angels, careful how all things are performed amongst men.'

Σῷ δὲ θρόνῳ πυρόεντι παρεστᾶσιν πολυμόχθοι
Ἄγγελοι, οἷσι μέμηλε βροτοῖς ὡς πάντα τέλειται.

The fallen angels, he says, 'are dispersed, some in the air, some on the earth, some in the water, some among the minerals, in dens and caves that are under the earth, labouring to obstruct, and, if possible, destroy the works of God. That they were the *dii inferi* of the heathen, worshipped in oracles, in idols, some as household gods, some as nymphs,' &c.

'Angels,' says Hooker in another place, 'are spirits immaterial and intellectual. In number and order they are large, mighty, and royal armies, desiring good unto all the creatures of God, but especially unto the children of men; in the countenance of whose nature, looking downward, they behold themselves beneath themselves; besides which, the *angels have with us that communion* which the Apostle to the Hebrews noteth, and in regard whereof they disdain not to profess themselves our fellow-servants. And from hence there springeth up another law, which bindeth them to works of *ministerial employment*.'

BISHOP HALL OF NORWICH, that excellent poet, like Hooker, vindicated the existence of miracle in the Protestant Church. He wrote an express treatise on 'The Invisible World,' in which he maintains all the doctrines of the primitive times. In his section on 'Apparitions and the Assumed Shapes of Evil Spirits,' he says that, though much fraud has been mixed up both in the acting and the relating of such things, yet to deny the truth of all would be as foolish as to deny that men were living in those ages before us. He adds that, 'by applying active powers to passive subjects, they can produce wonderful effects, as were easy to show in whole volumes, if it were needful, out of history and experience.' 'So sure as we see men, so sure we are that holy men have seen angels.' He invokes the guardian angels in various places most feelingly, and says that knowing their eyes are on him, he walks carefully but confidently. 'Have we been raised up,' he continues, 'from deadly sickness, when all natural helps have given us up? God's angels have been our secret physicians. Have we had intuitive intimations of the death of absent friends, which no human intelligence had bidden us to suspect, who but our angels have wrought it? Have we been preserved from mortal danger, which we could not tell how by our providence to have evaded, our invisible guardians have done it.'

Father Costerus, whom he saw at Brussels, he said had a dispute with him, and charged the Anglican Church with not possessing one miracle. 'When,' he says, 'I answered that in our church we had manifest proofs of the ejection of devils by fasting and prayer.' Is there a single bishop or priest of the Church of England who would dare now to say as much? Certainly Dr. Hook, present Dean of Chichester, is not such a man; for in his 'Lives of the Archbishops of Canterbury,' he says, 'So far from expecting a miracle, we are bound to reject it if offered.'

In his own Life, Bishop Hall notes sundry miraculous or providential interventions. His mother, whom for piety he compares to Monica, the mother of St. Augustine, and other as famously good women, 'had,' he says, 'much affliction of a weak body and of a wounded spirit; the agonies whereof she would oft recount with much passion, professing that the greatest bodily sicknesses were but as flea-bites to those scorpions.' But she had a dream, in which a physician appeared and assured her that she should be immediately healed, and that she had now the last fit of it. This dream she that very day related to Dr. Gilby, her parish minister, who replied that he believed the dream to be divinely sent, and would prove true; which, says the bishop, was the case. ' For God,' he adds, ' though ordinarily He keeps the common road of His proceedings, yet sometimes, in the distresses of His servants, He goes unusual ways to their relief.'

Bishop Hall considered that God continually ordered the events of his life, contrary to the determinations of himself and others. He believed his wife to have been pointed out to him by the instrumentality of God. His father, spite of his remonstrances, destined to bind him for some years to a certain schoolmaster instead of letting him go to college. He threw himself in earnest prayer on God, and at the last moment, contrary to all expectations, his father's plans were broken up, and he went to the university. ' Certainly never did I in all my life,' he says, ' more clearly roll myself on the divine providence than I did in this business. And it succeeded accordingly' (vol. i. 14).

When he was given the living of Halstead in Suffolk, he found there John Lilly, supposed to be the dramatist, and author of ' Euphues, the Anatomy of Wit.' ' Euphues and his England,' &c., made so much use of by Walter Scott in his novel ' The Monastery,' and parodied also by Shakspeare in ' Love's Labour Lost,' &c. This Lilly was an atheist, was very witty, and not only annoyed Mr. Hall, but did him much mischief with Sir Robert Drury, his patron. He prayed God earnestly to have him by some means removed, and, contrary to all appearances, this soon took place. In his journey to the Netherlands, he says, he was delivered from robbers by the manifest hand of God. In fact, the good bishop, and as good a poet, all his life through believed in the immediate protection and guidance of Providence, and that by this he was led from small beginnings to his final station of influence and importance. Nothing can be more diametrically opposed than the cold, hard disbelief in the supernatural of the church of to-day, and the cordial living faith of such men as Hall, Hooker, and Butler in his 'Analogy.'

ARCHBISHOP TILLOTSON in his sermon on 'The Trial of the Spirits,' says, miracles are owned by all mankind to be a sufficient testimony to any person or doctrine that they are from God, providing that the doctrine sought is not contrary to those of the gospel or to the common sense and moral sense of mankind. He does not argue, like Farmer and others, that the Egyptian magicians performed only *seeming* miracles. He believes that God permits the devil to do miracles up to a certain point, and quotes those cases where both Christ and the apostles suppose a false Christ, or false prophet working true miracles to give credit to his doctrines. The apostles in their epistles abound with the assertion of supernatural powers of the devil; thus fully confirming the dark as well as the light side of spiritualism. In his sermons on the joy in heaven over the repentance of a sinner (Luke xv. 7), and in another on the nature and employment of angels (Heb. i. 14), he speaks most fully of the continual intercourse of angels with men for their protection and advantage. That they are God's great ministers here below, he says has been the constant tradition of all ages, and is plainly asserted by Scripture. They are no more dead or idle than they were in Jacob's time, or in our Saviour's, and both good and bad spirits are each in their way busy about us.

BISHOP STILLINGFLEET in his 'Origines Sacræ,' says, 'I lay down this as a certain foundation that a power of miracles is not constantly and perpetually necessary in all who may manage the affairs of heaven here upon earth, or that act in the name of God in the world. When the doctrine of faith is once settled in sacred records, and the divine revelation of that doctrine sufficiently attested by a power of miracles in the revelators of it, what imaginary necessity or pretext can there be conceived for a power of miracles, especially amongst such as already own the divine revelation of the Scripture?' (vol. i. 109).

This is the old song, introduced at the English Reformation, with which the prelates sought to evade the objections of Rome, and which has proved so fatal a doctrine to the church. What of those who *do not* already own the divine authority of the Scriptures? As to the imaginary necessity or pretext for a power of miracles, that, as I have said, exists in the millions who have abandoned Christianity expressly because it no longer works those miracles which it represents its founders to have wrought 1860 years ago.

Stillingfleet goes on to say, ' To make a power of working miracles to be constantly resident in the church of God, is to put God upon that necessity which common nature is freed from—namely, of multiplying things without sufficient cause to be given for them, and to leave man's faith at a stand when God hath given sufficient testimony for it to rely upon.'

The test whether it be sufficient, and whether it is multiplying things without sufficient cause, however, is just whether the causes given do produce the effects required. In this case the effect required is the faith of men in Christianity, and the answer is obvious that this effect is not produced by the record of miracles said to have occurred nearly 2,000 years ago. Stillingfleet argues at great length on these premises; but the premises themselves being unsound, the reasoning is of no value. He contends that, if miracles were a standing order in the church, there would be no faith. But I say, on the contrary, they could not be wrought without faith; and it does not follow that miracles should be commonised, but, existing in the church, should, from time to time, on great occasions, in eras of great scepticism, be renewed to the renewal of faith. He says that, if miracles were a permanent rule for a long time, whenever they happened to cease, ' men would throw off their faith concerning the Gospel.' This is precisely what they have done. Miracles, according to the Scripture history, were the rule from the foundation of the world till the establishment of Christianity: and, according to the Catholic Church, ever since; but Protestants having cast off belief in them, hundreds of thousands—nay, millions—have cast off all faith in Christianity and in the Bible, declaring that all the miracles of the Bible are myths, or mere natural occurrences metamorphosed in the description of them. He says that the false miracles of Rome have produced atheism. Most true—the *false* miracles, but that is no argument against true ones. What has the renunciation of all miracles by the Protestant Church produced? The rankest and most wide-spread scepticism and rationalism, as the last eighty years of Germany, and the German poison now revended in England as new, too well testify. To spiritualists who see miracles every day, what simpletons do these Essayists and Reviewers appear!

BISHOP BEVERIDGE in his sermons supports all said by the prelates already quoted on the reality of ministering angels and ministering devils being perpetually about us; and that the devils can do miracles, contrary to the opinion of Farmer, Douglas, and others. No one, he says, who believes the word of God can doubt but that the false Christs and false prophets were to perform actual and not merely apparent signs and wonders. He asserts that we may see spirits by a strong faith spiritually. 'And though we can never see them with our bodily eyes, except they assume, *as they sometimes do, a bodily shape,* yet they are always as evident to our faith as anything can be to our sight. Inasmuch,' he adds, 'as we have more cause to believe the word of God than we have our bodily eyes.' Nothing can be more explicit than this. This is precisely the doctrine of the spiritualists, confirmed by the fact of spirits having, in numerous instances, assumed a bodily shape, or equally tangible objectiveness to the senses.

The bishop fully believes that miracles may be performed to introduce false doctrines, and justly observes that Christ has warned us on this head; and no warning can be more important; for the recent manifestations show nothing more strongly than that evil spirits are exceeding prompt to introduce themselves and their lies into real spiritual manifestations, and to inculcate pernicious notions. Being warned, however, all Christian spiritualists will say with St. Paul, 'Though an angel from heaven should preach any other gospel than that which Christ and His apostles have preached, let him be accursed.' It is the concern of the spiritualists to embrace all the advantages of the communion, teachings, and strengthening of good spirits, and to reject and despise all the endeavours of the evil.

BISHOP BUTLER, in his celebrated 'Analogy of Religion, Natural and Revealed,' &c., gives a luminous theory of miracles existing in nature:—' Take in the consideration of religion, or the moral system of the world, and then we see distinct particular reasons for miracles; to afford mankind instruction additional to that of nature, and to attest the truth of it. And this gives a real credibility to the supposition that it might be part of the original plan of things, that there should be miracular interpositions. Then miracles must not be compared to common natural events, or to the events which, though uncommon, are similar to what we daily experience, but to the *extraordinary* phenomena of nature. And then the comparison will be between the presumption against miracles, and the presumption against such uncommon experiences, suppose as comets, and against there being such powers in nature as magnetism and electricity, so contrary to the properties of other bodies not endued with these powers,' &c. (Part ii. c. ii. 366).

BISHOP SHERLOCK thinks the creation of the world, and its daily maintenance, the greatest of all miracles. Like Tillotson, he does not doubt but that miraculous powers are conferred on both good and evil spirits by God. In his tenth discourse he asserts that such powers are permitted to evil spirits for the punishment of men, to deceive bad men by false appearances; but that this power is controlled by the power of God according to His will. He has no doubt whatever that God, who appointed the laws of nature, can direct these laws as He pleases; and that by talking of 'a settled course of nature,' we cannot tie up His hands. In his twenty-first discourse he talks in a perfectly Catholic strain, and claims supernatural power for the real Christian. 'The Christian only of all men pretends to supernatural power and strength, and an intimate acquaintance with the Spirit of God.' He adds that, though the Christian 'boasts of more than human strength, yet how does he sometimes sink below the character and dignity of even a man!' He says the lives of Christians of our days do not answer to the manifold gifts and graces bestowed upon them.' That this has led unbelievers to treat spiritual gifts as no real gifts or powers; but he reasserts that the graces of the Spirit are the arms of the Christian, with which he is to enter the lists against the powers of darkness, and are a certain indication to us that God intends to call us to the proof and exercise of our virtue; why else does He give us this additional strength?

Probably Sherlock looked for no great outward exhibition of supernatural strength, but he fully believed in the existence of these supernatural powers as the inheritance of the Christian; and on his own ground could not deny that, on requisite occasions, these powers might be more remarkably called forth; for he considered the great modern stumbling-block—'the settled course of nature'—as no difficulty at all with Him who made that course.

These may serve as examples from our chief and earlier bishops and fathers of the Anglican Church, of the faith regarding the miracle-working power of Christianity. The extracts might be drawn from all the earlier prelates and theologians with the same result. Some of them, like Hall, Hooker, and Sherlock, would be found retaining the old Catholic faith on that head, though in a mild and subdued tone; but the greater part of them, like Cranmer and Latimer, repudiating all miracles since the apostolic age, though admitting them in their own lives and experience. Down to the time of Sherlock, the prelates and clergy of the Anglican Church occupied a sort of middle ground on the subject: all believed most firmly in the presence and services of ministering angels, and most of them of ministering devils in their actuality; all were, more or less, ready to receive spiritual demonstrations if they came, or to reiterate their assumed formula that miracles were needless, and their day over—if they did not come. It was a period when the great writers, not officially belonging to the church, still also retained a great conviction of the truth on this subject; nor did they think, like the *Times* of our day, which, in a review of Mrs. Oliphant's 'Life of Irving,' Oct. 14, 1862, asserted that ours being a *mechanical* age we require a *mechanical* religion! Milton, Bacon, Sir Thomas Browne, Cudworth, and other front-rank men, were avowed spiritualists. How often have Milton's lines been quoted, asserting that

> Millions of spiritual creatures walk the earth
> Unseen, both when we wake and when we sleep.

But it is not only in his poetry, of which 'Paradise Lost' and 'Paradise Regained' are substantially and essentially spiritual; in his prose works he avows the same belief, as I shall show in the chapter of Poets. Bacon, the great perspicuous mind of his time, and the father of modern practical philosophy, is most explicit in enunciating his spiritualism. In the preface to his 'Great Instauration,' which included both 'The Dignity and Advancement of Learning' and the 'Novum Organum,' he prays God that in his labours 'what is human may not clash with what is divine; and that when the ways of the senses are opened, and a greater natural light set up in the mind, nothing of incredulity and blindness towards divine mysteries may arise; but rather that the understanding now cleared up, and purged of all vanity and superstition, may remain entirely subject to the divine oracles, and yield to faith the things that are faith's' (Bohn's Edition, preface, p. 9).

As to the enquiry into the nature and being of spirits, and even of evil spirits, which in spiritualists is so often commented upon as dangerous and even impious, Bacon speaks very confidently and very differently:—' As to the nature of spirits and angels, this is neither unsearchable nor forbid, but in a great part level to the human mind, on account of their affinity. We are, indeed, forbid in Scripture to worship angels, or to entertain fantastical opinions of them so as to exalt them above the degree of creatures, or to think of them higher than we have reason; but the sober enquiry about them, which either ascends to a knowledge of their nature by the scale of corporeal beings, or views them in the mind, as in a glass, is by no means foolish. The same is to be understood of revolted or unclean spirits; conversation with them, or using their assistance, is unlawful; and much more in any manner to worship or adore them; but the contemplation and knowledge of their nature, power, and illusions, appears from Scripture, reason, and experience, to be no small part of spiritual wisdom. Thus says the apostle, " Strategematum ejus non ignari sumus" (2 Cor. ii. 11). And thus it is as lawful in natural theology to investigate the nature of evil spirits, as the nature of poisons in physics, or the nature of vice in morality' (' Advancement of Learning,' 121-2).

In rejecting the ' mere levities,' as he calls them, of Astrology, Bacon seems to infer the actual result occasionally from it of true predictions to the cause assigned by me in an earlier portion of this work. ' The celestial operations,' he says, ' affect not all kinds of bodies, but only the nonsensible, as humours, air, and spirits' (*Ibid.* p. 130). He warns us against allowing our senses to obstruct our spiritual perception. ' The sense,' he says, ' resembles the sun, which shows the terrestrial globe, but conceals the celestial; for thus sense discovers natural things, whilst it shuts up the divine' (p. 31). This should make mere physical philosophers more modest than they generally show themselves in dictating dogmatically on the spiritual; according to their own great leader, the divine being shut up in them as a natural consequence of their constant researches in the regions of sense. He gives them another warning that their dicta on spiritual matters are utterly worthless, and had better be omitted; for he says, ' If we have spoken the truth,

Non canimus surdis, respondent omnia sylvæ ;

the voice of nature will cry it up, though the voice of man should cry it down' (p. 149).

In his chapter on the 'use of reason in religion,' he not only recognises spiritual mysteries, but advises us how to act in regard to them. 'We find that God Himself condescends to the weakness of our capacity, and opens His mysteries so that they may be best understood by us, inoculating, as it were, His revelations into the notions and comprehensions of our reason, and accommodating His inspirations to the opening of our understanding, as a key fitted to open the lock. Though, in this respect, we should not be wanting to ourselves; for as God makes use of our reason in His illuminations, so ought we likewise to exercise it every way, in order to become more capable of receiving and imbibing mysteries, provided the mind be enlarged, according to its capacity, to the greatness of the mysteries, and not the mysteries contracted to the narrowness of the mind' (p. 371).

Thus is another useful hint for our present physical men, who are always endeavouring to reduce all mysteries to the miserable narrowness of their own minds. He asserts the reality of direct and immediate inspiration: 'The pure waters of divinity are drawn and employed nearly in the same manner as the natural waters of springs; namely, first, either received into cisterns, and thence derived through different pipes, for the more commodious use of men; or second, immediately poured into vessels for present occasions' (p. 373). In his 'Novum Organum,' he gives, by anticipation, an answer to those objectors who reject spiritualism because it has not come in a more bustling and noisy form. 'Now, in all divine works, the smallest beginnings lead assuredly to some result, and the remark in spiritual matters that "the kingdom of God cometh without observation," is also proved to be true in every great work of Divine Providence; so that everything glides quietly on without confusion or noise, and the matter is achieved before men either think or perceive that it is commenced' (p. 426). He at the same time recognises the efficacy of faith in enabling us to become cognisant of spiritual objects:—'For man, by the fall, lost at once his state of innocence, and his power over creation, both of which can be partially recovered even in this life, the first by religion and faith, the second by the arts and sciences' (p. 567).

The witlings, and *soi-disant* men of science of to-day, should either renounce the so-much boasted authority of Lord Bacon, or should pay some respect to his teachings.

Still more full and explicit was the belief in spiritualism of Sir Thomas Browne, who lived about half a century after Bacon, and was considered one of the ablest thinkers of his period. In his 'Religio Medici,' he says most wittily, 'Those that, to confute their incredulity, desire to see apparitions, shall questionless never behold any. The devil hath them already in a heresy as capital as witchcraft, and to appear to them were but to convert them' (p. 90).

'As for spirits, I am so far from denying their existence, that I could easily believe that not only whole countries, but particular persons, have their tutelary and guardian angels. It is not a new opinion of the Church of Rome, but an old one of Pythagoras and Plato. (See "Mede's Apostacy of the Latter Times.") There is no heresy in it, and if not manifestly defined in Scripture, yet is an opinion of a good and wholesome use in the course of and actions of a man's life, and would serve as a hypothesis to solve many doubts whereof common philosophy affordeth no solution. Now, if you demand my opinion and metaphysics of their natures, I confess them very shallow; most of them are in a negative way, like that of God; or in a comparative, between ourselves and fellow-creatures. For there is, in this, a universal stair, a manifest scale of creatures, rising not disorderly or in a confusion, but with a comely method and proportion' (p. 95).

He adds:—'I believe they have an extempore knowledge, and upon the first motion of their reason, do what we cannot without study and deliberation. That they know things by their forms, and define by special difference what we describe by accidents and properties, and therefore, probabilities, such as may be demonstrated unto them. That they have knowledge, not only of the specifical but numerical forms of individuals, and understand by what reserved difference each single hypostasis, besides the relation of its species, becomes its numerical self. That as the soul hath the power to move the body it informs, so there is a faculty to move anything though inform none, and upon restraint of time, place and distance; but that invisible hand that conveyed Habakkuk to the Lion's den, or Philip to Azotus, infringeth this rule, and hath a secret conveyance with which mortality is not acquainted. If they have that infinite knowledge whereby, as in reflection, they behold the thoughts of one another, I cannot peremptorily deny that they have a great part of ours. They that, to refute the invocation of saints, have denied that they have any knowledge of our affairs below, have proceeded too far, and must pardon my opinion till I can thoroughly answer that piece of Scripture, " At the conversion of a sinner the angels in heaven rejoice "' (p. 97).

Sir Thomas not only believed the angels intimately acquainted with our thoughts, but that we are greatly indebted to them for the communication of theirs :—' I could never pass that sentence of Paracelsus without an asterisk or annotation; *Our good angels reveal many things to those who seek into the works of nature.* I do think that many mysteries ascribed to our own inventions have been the courteous revelations of spirits ; for those noble essences in heaven bear a friendly regard unto their fellow-nature on earth, and, therefore, believe that those many prodigies and ominous prognostics which forerun the ruin of states, princes, and private persons, are the charitable premonitions of good angels, which more careless enquirers term but the effects of chance and nature' (p. 92).

Nor has Sir Thomas been singular in his belief. Colquhoun has called our attention to a number of such cases. One of the popes asked Guido Reni, ' Into what heaven didst thou look when thou paintedst this angel?'—the Madonna. Raphael said of himself and his productions, 'A certain idea arises in my mind; to this I hold fast, and endeavour to realise it, unconcerned about its artistic value.' In one of his letters he says, 'The world discovers many excellences in my pictures, so that I myself frequently smile when I find that I have succeeded so well in the realisation of my own casual conceptions. But my whole work has been accomplished, as it were, in a pleasant dream; and while composing it, I have always thought more of my object than of the manner of representing it. That I have a certain manner of painting, as every artist generally has his own. This seems to have been originally implanted in my nature; I have not attained it by means of severe toil, and such a thing cannot be acquired by study.'

Dannecker, the German sculptor, obtained his idea of his Christ in a dream after long and unsuccessful efforts to realise it in his waking hours. Lucretius and Tasso, as well as Lee the dramatist, Babœuf and many other poets, composed some of their finest pieces in what were called fits of insanity. Coleridge received 'Kubla Khan' in a dream. Plato in his 'Ion' says, 'True poets speak not by art, but as persons inspired and possessed. Kant, the great German metaphysician, in his 'Anthropology,' declares talent partly inborn, partly acquired by exercise, but genius altogether intuitive. Schiller declares in his Letters that his ideas were not his own; they flowed in upon him independent of his intellectual faculties, and came so powerfully and rapidly that his only difficulty was to seize them and write them down fast enough. Goethe has some similar assertions, and everyone will recollect the lines of Shakspeare concerning 'the poet's eye in a fine frenzy rolling,' and of Queen Mab running across the heads of mortals in their sleep.

Mozart says, speaking of his mode of composing his celebrated musical pieces, 'When I am in good spirits, and in the right trim—for example, when travelling in a carriage, or walking, perhaps during the night when unable to sleep, thoughts flow in upon me more readily, and, as it were, in a stream. Whence they come and, how, I know not, and I have no control over them. Those which come upon me I retain in my head, and hum them to myself, as others, at least, have told me. If I remain steady and uninterrupted, sometimes one thing, sometimes another, comes into my head to help to make a piece of confectionary, according to the rules of counterpoint, and the tone of the different musical instruments, &c. Now this warms my soul, provided I am not disturbed. Then my mental work gradually becomes more and more extended, and I spread it out farther and more clearly, until the piece really becomes in my head almost ready, even if it should be of considerable length; so that I can survey it in spirit with a glance, as if I saw before me a beautiful picture or a handsome person; and I hear it in imagination, not in detached portions, but, as it were, altogether as a whole. Now this is a feast. All my feelings and composition go on within me only as a lively and delightful dream. But to hear all this together is the best.'

The reader will recollect, in an earlier part of this work, the mention of a clergyman now living, who hears continually fine music, and has noted some of it down — often, like Mozart, when he is walking or travelling in carriages—whose wife hears it too, when he places himself in *rapport* with her by taking hold of her hand; two of his sisters also hear music continually, though living at a distance, and wholly different pieces. Nor are these altogether isolated instances. There are many recorded cases of spiritual music being heard, especially before death, both by the dying and others. 'Your father will die,' said an old nurse to a gentleman, visiting his father in extreme sickness; 'for I heard music proceeding from his body all yesterday. It was heavenly music; he is a good man, and will make a good end.' A very extraordinary case of music, played on a closed piano, and heard by a whole family, is related by a Dissenting minister of Yorkshire, in the 'British Spiritual Telegraph' (vol. iii. 281). Nothing is so common as to hear people say, 'An idea came into my head.' How or whence they don't know or trouble themselves to enquire; but many of the finest discoveries have come in this mysterious way; the only merit of the receiver being to have worked them out. To return, however, to Sir Thomas Browne.

He was of opinion that there was a universal Spirit, common to the whole world. It was the opinion of Plato and the hermetical philosophers. 'If there be,' he says, 'a common nature that unites and ties the scattered and divided individuals into one species, why may there not be one that unites them all? However, I am sure that there is a common spirit that plays within us, yet makes no part of us, and that is the Spirit of God, the fire and scintillation of that noble essence which is the life and radical heat of spirits, and those essences that know not the virtue of the sun, a fire quite contrary to the heat of hell. This is that gentle heat that brooded on the waters, and in six days hatched the world. This is that irradiation that dispels the mists of hell, the clouds of horror, fear, sorrow, despair; and preserves the region of the mind in serenity. Whatsoever feels not the warm gale, and gentle ventilation of this spirit, though I feel his pulse, I dare not say he lives; for truly without this to me there is no heat under the tropic, nor any light, though I dwelt in the body of the sun' (p. 93).

Sir Thomas avows his firm belief in miracles past and present. 'We cannot,' he says, 'deny it if we do not call in question those writers whose testimonies we do not controvert in points that make for our own opinions' (p. 81). So also at p. 83, and elsewhere. The devils, he avers, are not merely under the earth, but walk upon it, and are always seeking to invade 'that immutable essence, that translated divinity and colony of God, the soul.'

I have already quoted the firm belief of John Locke and Dr. Ralph Cudworth in miracles and spiritual phenomena. At the same period we had Sir Matthew Hale on the bench, a judge as full-length a spiritualist, noted for his belief in witchcraft. There was a Bishop of Gloucester who believed in and collected accounts of such things, and who has left us the extraordinary accounts of an intercourse with spirits furnished by the Rev. Arthur Bedford of Bristol, and of the apparition to Sir Charles Lee's daughter. There was the excellent Bishop Ken, who was driven from his bishopric for his conscientious scruples, who prayed:—

> O may thy angels while I sleep,
> Around my head their vigils keep:
> Their love angelical instil,
> Stop every avenue of ill.
> May they celestial joys rehearse,
> And thought to thought with me converse.'

Most prominently, too, at the end of the seventeenth and commencement of the eighteenth century stood forward the admirable author of 'Robinson Crusoe.' De Foe was as bold in the expression of the truth, however unpopular, as he was original in his conceptions. His opinions on all points of spiritualism were exactly such as the spiritualists hold now, or as really spiritual men in all ages have held. Mr. Forster, in his essay on this intrepid writer, has made a summary of them in the following passages:— ' Between our ancestors laying too much stress on supernatural evidence, and the present age endeavouring wholly to explode and despise them, the world seems hardly ever to have come to a right understanding. . . . Spirit is certainly something we do not understand in our present confined circumstances; and as we do not fully understand the thing, so neither can we distinguish its operation. Yet, notwithstanding all this, it converses here—it is with us and among us — corresponds, though unembodied, with our spirits: and this conversing is not only by an invisible, but to us an inconceivable way.' Such communication he believes to take place by two modes; first, 'by immediate personal and particular converse;' and, secondly, 'by those spirits acting at a distance rendering themselves visible, and their actions perceptible, on such occasions as they think fit, without any farther acquaintance with the person.' It was his conviction that God had posted an army of these ministering spirits round our globe 'to be ready at all events, to execute His orders, and to do His will; reserving still to Himself to send express messengers of superior rank on extraordinary occasions.' 'These,' he adds, 'may, without any absurdity, be supposed capable of assuming shapes, conversing with mankind by voice and sound, or by private notices of things, impulses, forebodings, misgivings, and other imperceptible communications to the minds of men, as God, their employer, may direct.' But upon the power of man to control, or communicate at his will, with such spiritual beings, he entertains doubts, and gravely protests against the acts of conjuration. I subjoin, also, the curious and somewhat touching passage in which De Foe accounts for the strength of these beliefs in him, by the ordinary amount of his daily experiences. 'I firmly believe,' he says, 'and have had such convincing testimonies of it, that I must be a confirmed atheist if I did not, that there is a converse of spirits—I mean those unembodied —and those that are encased in flesh. From whence come all those private notices, strong impulses, involuntary joy, sadness, and foreboding apprehensions of and about things immediately attending us, and this in the most important affairs of our lives? That there are such things, I think I need not go about to prove; and I believe they are, next to the Scriptures, some of the best and most undeniable evidences of a future existence. It would be endless to fill this paper with the testimonies of learned and pious men; and I could add to them a volume of my own experiences, some of them so strange as would shock your belief, though I could produce such proofs as would convince any man. I have had, perhaps, a greater variety of changes, accidents, and disasters in my short, unhappy life than any man, at least than most men alive; yet I never had any considerable mischief or disaster attending me but, sleeping or awaking, I have had notice of it beforehand, and, had I listened to these notices, I believe might have shunned the evil. Let no man think this a jest. I seriously acknowledge, and I do believe, my neglect of such notices has been my great injury; and since

I have ceased to neglect them I have been guided to avoid snares laid for my life, by no other knowledge of them than by such notices and warnings: and more than that, I have been guided by them to discover even the fact and the persons. I have living witnesses to produce to whom I have told the particulars in the very moment, and who have been so affected by them as that they have pressed me to avoid the danger, to retire, to keep myself up, and the like.'

These experiences of De Foe have been so much those of good men, in all times, and who have put them on record, that it is extraordinary that anyone is not so assured of their reality as to treat them as commonplaces. They abound not only in the history of Catholic saints, but in the memoirs of the Covenanters, the Friends, and the Methodists; and you can scarcely meet a sincere person of either sex, or of any country, who does not tell you something of the kind from their own experience.

Closing this period, and about half a century after De Foe, we have Sir William Blackstone, the great legal commentator, boldly asserting the like faith, and it was preeminently bold in him, for De Foe had noted the growing dispositions of the age to explode all such notions. He says, 'To deny the possibility, nay, the actual existence of witchcraft and sorcery, is at once flatly to contradict the revealed will of God in various passages of both the Old and New Testament;' adding 'the thing is in itself a truth to which every nation in the world hath borne testimony,' &c.

Such was the state of faith in the supernatural from the Reformation to the close of the seventeenth century, and even, in some instances, stretching to a considerable period after. In spite of the doctrine laid down by the fathers of the Anglican Church, many great minds clung fondly to the spiritual credence which was as old and as wide as the world. We have found it in the Church, we shall find it among the Nonconformists and Dissenters; we have found it also in the leading minds of philosophy, literature, and law. But this faith was fast dying out, and became faint and dilute in the eighteenth century. Hobbes, Toland, Collins, Wollaston, Bolingbroke, and Hume successively appeared, and the foundations of a new and soul-withering era were laid. The 'Leviathan' of Hobbes was published in 1650, the middle of the seventeenth, and the infidel essays of Hume appeared about the middle of the eighteenth, century. David Hume not only breathed upon us his spirit-benumbing virus in his 'Enquiry concerning Human Understanding,' 1752, and his 'Natural History of Religion' soon after, but he brought to bear upon his age that of Spinoza, by his translation of that great sceptic's 'Tractatus-theologico-politicus,' without either his own name or that of the author, in 1765. There were above a hundred years of steady attack on Christianity, and the public faith suffered a growing and most obvious eclipse. Some few of our great literary leaders made a sort of last stand in defence of the miraculous. Warburton, Douglas, and a host of others took the field against Hume, but it was only to defend miracles accepted because they were old. De Foe was amongst the earliest, and Blackstone amongst the latest, who took a broad stand. Sir Richard Steele, Addison, and Dr. Johnson gave their testimony; but it was only incidentally and regarding one single department of the marvellous — that of apparitions.

Addison's evidence occurs in the 'Spectator,' and after ridiculing some of the absurd omens of the day, he then says, 'At the same time, I think a person who is thus terrified with the imagination of ghosts and spectres much more reasonable than one who, contrary to the report of all historians, sacred and profane, ancient and modern, and to the traditions of all nations, thinks the appearance of spirits fabulous and groundless. Could I not give myself up to this general testimony of mankind, I should to the relations of particular persons who are now living, and whom I cannot distrust in other matters of fact. I might here add, that not only the historians, to whom we may join the poets, but likewise the philosophers of antiquity have favoured this opinion.'

Johnson was one of the few persons who were not persuaded that the Cock-Lane ghost was a clever trick, and the evidence shows that he was quite right. In his 'Rasselas,' he also ventilates his opinion that ghosts were substantive and a thousand-time proved facts: 'That the dead,' he says, 'are seen no more, I will not undertake to maintain against the concurrent and universal testimony of all ages and of all nations. There is no people, rude or learned, among whom apparitions of the dead are not related and believed. This opinion, which perhaps prevails, as far as human nature is diffused, could become universal only by its truth; those who never heard of one another, would not have agreed in a tale which nothing but experience could render credible. That it is doubted by single cavillers can very little weaken the general evidence; and some who deny it with their tongues confess it by their fears.'

Boswell, in his 'Life of Johnson,' also introduces the subject of apparitions on the occasion of a dinner at General Oglethorpe's, April 10, 1772, in which Johnson said that Mr. Cave, the publisher of the 'Gentleman's Magazine,' assured him that he had seen a ghost. Goldsmith, who was present, stated that his brother, the Rev. Mr. Goldsmith, had seen one, and General Oglethorpe, that Prendergast, an officer in the Duke of Marlborough's army, told his brother officers, that Sir John Friend, who was executed for high treason, had appeared to him, and told him that he would die on a certain day. On that day a battle took place, but when it was over and Prendergast was alive, his brother officers rallied him and asked him where was his prophecy now? Prendergast replied gravely, 'I shall die notwithstanding;' and soon after there came a shot from a French battery, to which the order for the cessation of firing had not reached, and killed him on the spot. Oglethorpe added that Colonel Cecil, who took possession of Prendergast's effects, found in his pocket-book a memorandum containing the particulars of the intimation of his death on the day specified, and that he was with Cecil when Pope came to enquire into the facts of the case, which had made a great noise, and that they were confirmed by the colonel.

To so fine a point had the belief in the miraculous, or supernatural, descended towards the end of the eighteenth century. Literary men could just, and upon instant and unquestionable evidence, conceive the actuality of a ghost. The poison of Spinoza, Hobbes, Toland, and Hume, had been, and was widely materializing the human mind, and there had arisen, or were about to arise, three Christian champions of the miraculous, so far as it was venerably old and mouldy, who, under the plea of defending this ancient faith, did more to destroy the faith in miracles altogether, than the whole one-eyed tribe of infidels whoever wrote. They welded weapons on the anvil of orthodoxy, which the infidels have wielded with many an exulting Io Pean! and dipped them in a poison bearing the name of a patent antidote to all former poisons, which has become the demon-life of that old monster infidelity in his new sleek skin of Rationalism. These three champions, dextrous in back strokes, were Middleton, Farmer, and Douglas, Bishop of Salisbury, who inaugurated the last and culminating period of disbelief in everything that cannot be felt and handled and carried to market — that in which we live.

CHAPTER VII.

PRESENT MATERIALISED CONDITION OF THE CHURCH OF ENGLAND AND OF GENERAL OPINION.

The Spirit of Truth, whom the world cannot receive, because it seeth Him not; neither knoweth Him.—*John* xiv. 57.

Wherefore? Because they sought it not by faith, but, as it were, by the works of the law; for they stumbled at that stumbling-block.
Romans ix. 32.

Au reste, c'est une grave erreur de croire que ces miracles bibliques sont des phénomènes tout à fait exceptionnels: les miracles ont eu lieu plus souvent qu'on ne pense; mais les hommes de nos jours, plongés dans le matérialisme, ont perdu le sens, la faculté de les observer.
LE BARON DE GULDENSTUBBE, *Pneumatologie Positive.*

In the sciences that also is looked upon as a property which has been handed down or taught at the universities, and if anyone advance anything new which contradicts, perhaps threatens to overturn, the creed which we for years respected, and have handed down to others, all passions are raised against him, and every effort is made to crush him. People resist with all their might; they act as if they neither heard nor could comprehend: they speak of the new view with contempt, as if it were not worth the trouble of even so much as an investigation or a regard; and thus a new truth may wait a long time before it can make its way.—GOETHE, *Conversations with Eckermann.*

THE 'Free Enquiry into the Miraculous Powers which are *supposed* to have subsisted in the Christian Church from the Earliest Ages through several centuries,' by Dr. Conyers Middleton, was published in 1749. Hume's 'Treatise of Human Nature' had preceded it eleven years, and may be supposed to have greatly influenced its tone. In this work Dr. Middleton undertakes what he justly calls an attempt, not only new, but contrary to the general opinion of the Christian world: namely, that miracles ceased with the apostles, and were only occasional amongst them. It was an attempt, in fact, not only in a single man to contradict the opinion of the Christian church in all ages, but the evidence of all mankind. It was, to say the least of it, an unrivalled specimen of human conceit. The declarations of Christ that His followers should do greater works than He did; that it should be the test of real belief in His church that signs should follow that belief; and that this His power and presence should attend His followers alway to the end of the world, went with this singular Christian for nothing. As to the universal testimony of the Fathers, and so downward of the different branches of the Christian church, Dr. Middleton at once and boldly declared all these Fathers, and all their successors who asserted the existence of miracles in their different ages, as downright liars. He declares the Fathers, one and all, to have been credulous, crafty, or designing men: men of such character, 'that nothing could be expected from them that was candid and impartial, nothing but what a crafty understanding could supply towards confirming those prejudices with which they happened to be possessed, especially when religion happened to be the subject.' As to all pagan nations, he included them in the same sweeping denunciation, and declared all the statements regarding the oracles, the prophecies, and miracles occurring amongst them, to have been forged, and imposed on the public! In a word, all mankind were declared liars, all the greatest philosophers, saints, martyrs, heroes, and worthies of every age and nation in the world—and Dr. Middleton was the only man deserving of belief. That was outspokenly his assertion. Many a madman has said as preposterous things before, but then they were treated as madmen. Middleton and Hume, who asserted the same thing—namely, that no amount of evidence would satisfy him of what he did not want to believe—alone were allowed, though holding the language of insanity, to pass for sane men. To such a pitch did Middleton carry his diseased conceit that, when reminded of the evidence for many of the miraculous events of the early ages of the church being of the most perfect kind, he cut the matter short in his vindication of his book by saying, 'To cut off, therefore, all reasonings and inferences about them, let it be understood that we deny the facts.' Here all reasonable and sane people should have left him. If Dr. Middleton chose to hold an opinion opposed to all history, and to libel all the greatest men of all ages as liars and crafty scoundrels, he should have been looked upon just as he was, gone mad with a crotchet. But his theory suited too well the growing materialism of the age. He himself died in the following year, but there were plenty of infidel spirits ready to seize on the nominally Christian theologian's doctrine to destroy Christianity altogether. If the doctor had really any faith in Christianity, which is greatly to be doubted, he must have been very blind not to see that the credence which he refused to all the world besides, others would, on equally good grounds, deny to Christ, the apostles, and to all the prophets before them. His example was a sound plea for any man whatever to set up himself as the only true man, and all the world besides as liars.

His case was quickly taken up by Hugh Farmer, and recommended to his friends the Dissenters. This Hugh Farmer, who was consulted by Dr. Doddridge, Dr. Lardner, and other Dissenting oracles on such points, wrote a work on the 'Credibility of Miracles,' in which he echoed the apology of Middleton for such a composition. 'Many,' he says, ' are ready to acknowledge that an opinion is not, therefore, false, because it contradicts received opinions.' And he adds, ' It is not the language of probity but of policy which has ever discouraged all enquiries after truth, and still continues to stop its progress in the world.'

Proceeding to exercise this undoubted right, Farmer commenced in a much more liberal strain than Middleton. He recognises miracles not as violations of the laws of nature, but as superseding, or controlling, certain known laws by higher laws. He denies that any ground can be shown for supposing that God is limited to a settled course of action and the present laws of nature (p. 26). He takes up Bishop Butler's idea that occasional interpositions might be designed from the beginning upon a foresight of a just occasion for them, and instead of arguing any change, or any inconsistency in the Almighty, be only the execution, at the preappointed season, of His eternal and immutable councils (p. 32). This is the idea so ably illustrated by Babbage by the operations and premeditated variations in the operations of his calculating machine. Rousseau, as well as Butler, however, in his ' Lettres écrites de la Montagne,' had said this more distinctly before Farmer—namely, ' That it might be in the power of an unknown law, in certain cases, to change the effect of such as were known.' And Dr. Watts in his ' Philosophical Essays on Various Subjects' (p. 132), though with a very different aim, asserts the like principle, that ' the Almighty Spirit who called the material universe into existence, can put the several parts of it into motion as He pleases; ' that is, that He has reserved certain laws to His own volition, to vary the ordinary course of nature as He sees fit, and for special purposes: and the great error of antimiracleists is that of supposing that they are acquainted with *all* God's laws, when they are utterly ignorant of thousands of them.

Farmer having taken up such liberal ground, began, however, speedily to narrow it to his real purposes. He showed himself as decided against any supernatural influence or phenomenon proceeding from any being except God, as Paley did after him. He will not allow that demons can produce any miraculous effects. He cuts away all the professed miracles of paganism, of the Fathers, and of the Roman Church, in the exact strain of Middleton. He goes upon the ground that, if spirits can perform miracles, and alter or impede the course of nature, they must be gods; as if God could not, and does not allow of a certain latitude of action, and a certain amount of power to both good and evil angels, yet all restrained within the circle of His own purposes. The plainest declarations of Scripture prove no obstacle to the over-riding sophisms of the worthy theologian. He treats the enactments of Moses against witchcraft as only directed against pretended witchcraft. The magicians who are positively declared to have done the like miracles with Moses, and to have produced frogs and serpents, and turned water into blood, are represented as only making the spectators believe so; and that they could not succeed with the lice because they were so small that it required such close looking to see them, that the imposture became evident! Never did a man with a hobby so completely ride it into the ridiculous. He treats the Witch of Endor, and all the lying spirits in the prophets, the demoniacs in the Gospel, and the declarations of the Saviour Himself concerning the false Christs and false prophets to come, and all the plain assertions of the apostles as to the existence and action of demons, in the same manner. In fact, what is there that a man bent on a purpose, will not explain away? He contends that the devils can do no such miracles on earth because they are all shut up in chains of darkness to the last day. On this point, however, it is plain that he has not convinced the preachers; for their great and perpetual theme is, that the devil and his angels are constantly going about the earth and tempting us.

To these insidious champions of miracle succeeded John Douglas, D.D., Lord Bishop of Salisbury, with his 'Criterion or Rules by which the True Miracles recorded in the New Testament, are distinguished from the Spurious Miracles of Pagans and Papists,' 1807. The infidel venom emitted in this country by the men already named, had now travelled into Germany and France. In Germany it had produced the Illuminati, and these through Mirabeau, on his visit as a government spy to Berlin, had communicated to the infidels of France what they called their system for the annihilation of Christianity. This system was adopted with avidity by the infidels of France, Voltaire and the Encyclopædists, who had before maintained only a sort of guerilla warfare upon it; and it had now travelled back to England from France with wonderfully augmented effect under the excitement of the French revolution. There was a new atmosphere for a new champion to work in, and Douglas therefore came out with a bolder and more dogmatic mien. He professed to combat David Hume, but in reality he fought most vigorously on his side. He laid down the following axioms:— 1. That we must suspect as false, asserted miracles which are not published at the time and in the place where they are said to have occurred. 2. That we must suspect them to be false, if, in the time when and at the place where they are said to have occurred, they might be supposed to pass without examination.

By his application of these dogmas, he thinks he gets rid of every miraculous circumstance except in the apostolic age. With those of the Old Testament he does not concern himself; he takes their authority for granted. He then endeavours to persuade the reader that, by these tests, he defends and strengthens the miracles of the apostolic age, whilst he destroys all others. But the reader is immediately struck with the obvious fallacy of these rules. He sees at once that they are two-edged swords, which, if allowed their legitimate operation, would shear away all the miracles of the Bible as perfectly as any others. We know that not a single Gospel was published at the time and in the place where the events which they celebrate are said to have occurred. The Gospel of St. Matthew is the only one which is said to have been written in Judea, and to have been published about eight years after the death of Christ, in the year forty-one. That is the earliest assumed date, but others fix the date much later. Thus, even the date of the only Gospel published in Judea, is a matter of uncertainty. St. Mark's is said to have appeared two years after St. Matthew's, and to have been published not at the place where the miracles were done, but at Rome. St. Luke is said to have written his Gospel in the year sixty-one — that is, twenty-seven years after the death of Christ—and that it was published at Rome or in Greece. Here, again, the place of publication is altogether uncertain. St. John's Gospel is said to have been published not earlier than the year ninety-seven, or sixty years after the death of the Saviour, and to have been published at Ephesus.

Thus, according to the bishop's rule, the Gospels have but a slender claim to credit; for none but St Matthew's were published in the place where the events took place, and none at all at the time. True, the events of the Gospel had a common notoriety at the time, sufficient to satisfy reasonable people, but the author does not allow such evidence in other cases. We must have all in black and white, and under these exact conditions, or we must reject the belief in whatever is miraculous. Now, as to the Gospels, the very dates assigned for their appearance are but presumptive. They are not attested on the positive evidence of contemporaries; they rest on the traditions of the church. But this kind of evidence he refuses to the Church of Rome, and to all the pagan world.

Still more thoroughly would Douglas's rules sweep through the Old Testament. For who shall say when and where many of the miraculous events which abound in its pages, were written or published? Who shall say when the early books were written which record the appearances of angels to Abraham, Isaac, and Jacob? Or the great miracle of the ark; when was it first written that the Lord put forth his hand, and shut Noah in? If Moses wrote these books, as is generally said, the record of these miracles must have taken place very long after their occurrence and in a very distant region. We might ask the same of Moses's own miracles in Egypt. Who shall say when he penned them down, or where? It would be equally difficult to assign the time, place, and author of most of the subsequent books of the Old Testament; and on the bishop's system of criticism, they must all pass for nothing.

Even where there is direct and immediate contemporary evidence of a miracle, and where, therefore, he ought, on his own grounds, to accept it, the slippery bishop finds some way out of the cleft stick. In fact, the only idea we can have of Bishop Douglas is that of a reasoning eel. Hume, amongst the few miraculous accounts which he admits to possess strong evidence, selects that of the Emperor Vespasian curing two people by miraculous agency. 'One of the best-attested miracles in all profane history,' says Hume, in his 'Essay on Miracles' (p. 192, 193), 'is that which Tacitus reports of Vespasian, who cured a blind man at Alexandria by means of his spittle, and a lame man by a mere touch of his foot, in obedience to a vision of the god Serapis, who had enjoined them to have recourse to the emperor for their miraculous and extraordinary cures. The story may be seen in that fine historian, where every circumstance seems to add weight to the testimony . . . The gravity, solidity, age and probity of so great an emperor, who, through the whole course of his life never affected those extraordinary airs of divinity assumed by Alexander and Demetrius. The historian, a contemporary writer, noted for candour and veracity, and withal the greatest and most penetrating genius perhaps of all antiquity, and so far from any tendency to superstition and credulity, that he lies under the contrary imputation of atheism and profaneness. The persons from whose testimony he related the miracles, of established character for judgment and veracity, as we may well suppose, eyewitnesses of the facts, and confirming their verdict after the Flavian family were despoiled of the empire and could no longer give any reward as the price of a lie.' Hume says truly, 'no evidence can be supposed stronger.' But as these miracles are contrary to Douglas's theory, though precisely according with his rules, he is at no loss for reasons for rejecting them. They might, he says, have been counterfeited; they were, probably, got up to favour an old superstition and to flatter the emperor; neither does it appear that the blind man's eyes were entirely destroyed.

The two-edged sword is here used most dangerously; for these are the very arguments advanced against the miracles of Christ by sceptics. We do not read that the man said to have been born blind, had *his* eyes totally destroyed; they might, say cavillers, have only been covered with a film which the clay might rub away; the whole might have been got up to favour the new religion. Nay, we are assured by the Jews that the resurrection of Lazarus was got up, and that Christ did never rise, but was stolen away by his disciples, &c. Such determined spirits 'who always deny,' are fatal champions of the cause they espouse. When the advocate of anything lays down his own rules of argument, and abandons them, he ruins his own cause. He ceases to be a reasoner; he becomes a mere sophist.

Dr. Douglas does not professedly deny every miracle subsequent to the apostles. On the contrary, he blames Dr. Church for asserting such an opinion; but he speedily proceeds to depreciate the miracles of the Fathers of the first three centuries, saying they were chiefly those of curing diseases which, perhaps, admitted of natural remedies, and of exorcising spirits which, probably, were no spirits at all; and he ends with reproducing the Protestant axiom, that miracles were given by Heaven to attest the authority of those first set apart for teaching that religion, and that once being taught, the purpose was answered, and they ceased to be necessary. He will not undertake to say that the miraculous ceased with the apostles, but he believes it ceased with the *immediate* disciples of Christ, which is precisely what he blames in Dr. Church. The facts appealed to as miracles, even during the two first ages, he says, 'are of so ambiguous a kind that, granting they *did* happen, it will remain to be decided by a consideration of the circumstances attending the performance of them, whether there was any miracle in the case at all.'

Now, we have seen the confidence with which Tertullian appealed to the public for proofs of the universal power of the Christians of his time — the third century — to cast out demons. He himself quotes similar instances from Justin Martyr towards the end of the second century (Cohortatio ad Græcos, p. 45). Two other passages of the same kind from 'Justin's Dialogues with Trypho,' pp. 247 and 311; from 'St. Cyprian's Appeal to Demetrianus, the Proconsul of Africa,' sec. 12, with a confidence equal to that of Tertullian; from Minutius Felix, p. 30 ('De Errore prophan. Relig.'); and from Lactantius, 'De Justitia,' lib. v. c. 12; where they all declare that the devils went forth with groans and cries of torment, confessing with human voices their nature. He quotes also from 'Origen's Defence of Christianity against Celsus,' where he says (p. 62, ed. sp.) that since Jesus came, the Jews ceased to have any prophets; but that the Christians continued to receive inspirations; that cures were performed in the name of Jesus (p. 80); that some Christians, by invoking the name of God and Jesus, were able to cure the sick (p. 124); and others cast out demons (p. 133); that they could always do this, even the most simple men, and that this power was chiefly exercised by laymen (p. 335). Nay, he quotes Origen to show that Æsculapius, a pagan, had done cures by appealing to his gods (p. 124); and also Athanagoras for the same purpose, who says that Christians generally admitted that such cures were done by appeal to pagan deities—that is, to demons.

Now, this is to confirm the assertions of both Christians and pagans in proof of miracles; a fact which, as I have amply shown, all nations and all ages claim. He then retreats into the denial that the Christians of the first three ages could perform the higher miracles of raising the dead, as the apostles did. But if they could perform miracles at all, the question is conceded of the power remaining during that period in the church. He notices, however, some claims to the highest degree of power, but only to reason them away, and we may select a case to show the manner in which the bishop could strain a point. He quotes Irenæus, as given by Eusebius (lib. v. c. 7. p. 127). 'The heretics are far from being able to raise the dead, as our Lord raised them, and as the apostles and many of the heathen raised them by their prayers. But frequently upon some necessary occasion, by the prayers of the whole church of the place, offered up with much fasting, has the spirit returned to the dead body, and a man has been given back to the prayers of the saints.'

Now this, in the end of the second and beginning of the third century, the bishop endeavours to persuade himself did not apply to the time of the writer, but to a past time. Nothing seems to me so positive as the matter referring to the writer's own experience. But again Eusebius quotes Irenæus in the same place. 'They who are the true disciples of Jesus do, in His name, confer blessings on others by a power received from Him; for some cast out demons, others have knowledge of futurity, and see visions; others, again, cure the sick by imposition of hands. Besides, I have observed already, the dead have been raised, and *have lived many years amongst us.*'

This surely is plain enough. Irenæus not only, speaking of what went on in his own time, says that the dead were then raised, but had lived many years *amongst us, καὶ νεκροὶ ἠγέρθησαν, καὶ παρέμειναν σὺν ἡμῖν ἱκανοῖς ἔτεσι.* But the bishop should not have paused there in his quotation; for Irenæus goes on, 'What should I say? The *gifts are innumerable* wherewith God hath enriched his church throughout the world, and by virtue whereof, in the name of Christ crucified under Pontius Pilate, the church *every day* doth many wonders for the good of the nations; neither fraudulently, nor in any respect of lucre and gain to herself, but as freely bestowing as God on her hath bestowed His divine graces.'

It is as clear from all this as any language can make it, that, in the second and third centuries, the church is declared by Irenæus to have possessed not only the abundant power of healing the sick and casting out demons, but of raising the dead. The Catholics, as we have seen, declare that these powers have never ceased; and there can be no doubt that they continued so long as there remained Christian faith and vital religion enough to command them; and that where these are they remain still.

But the bishop's practical renunciation of his own principle, that miracles may be tested at the time and place where they are exhibited, grows stronger as he descends towards our own times. Another case adduced by Hume, and declared by him to be equal in evidence to the miracles of Christianity, is that of the remarkable manifestations at the tomb of the Abbé Paris, in the churchyard of St. Médard in Paris. This Abbé Paris was a Jansenist. He died in 1727, and miracles were said to be performed at his grave. These grew so much that in 1731 the whole city of Paris was in a ferment about them. The churchyard was crowded from morning till night by sick praying for relief. To put an end to the concourse and tumult, the chief magistrate, probably at the instigation of the Jesuits, who were deeply exasperated at these successes of their rivals, the Jansenists, ordered all access to the tomb to be closed. Voltaire says he visited the place, and found inscribed by some wag on the churchyard wall,

De par le Roi,—defense à Dieu
De faire miracles en ce lieu.

And he adds, 'What is most astonishing is, that God obeyed!' But this, like many of Voltaire's assertions, was not true. Miracles continued to be performed near the tomb as much as ever for twenty years; and, in fact, more or less down to the time of the revolution. Bishop Douglas visited Paris in 1749 — that is, eighteen years afterwards, and was told they were still going on, especially amongst the *Convulsionaires*. The Jesuits omitted no exertions to cast discredit on these miracles; and the Archbishop of Sens wrote a work to disprove, or reason them away; but, when he and the whole body of Jesuits had done their best, they were compelled to confess that many of them were real, but proceeding from the devil. Hume, in his 'Philosophical Essays' (p. 195) says, 'There surely never was so great a number of miracles ascribed to one person, as those which were lately said to have been wrought in France upon the tomb of the Abbé Paris. The curing of the sick, giving hearing to the deaf, and sight to the blind, were everywhere talked of as the effects of the holy sepulchre. But, what is more extraordinary, many of the miracles were immediately proved upon the spot, before judges of unquestioned credit and distinction, in a learned age, and on the most eminent theatre that is now in the world. Nor is this all; a relation of them was published and dispersed everywhere; nor were the Jesuits, though a learned body, supported by the civil magistrates, and determined enemies to those opinions in whose favour the miracles were said to have been wrought, ever able distinctly to refute or detect them.' Of course Hume did not believe them, because he was committed to the 'absolute impossibility of miraculous events;' but such is, he admits, the historic evidence.

Dr. Middleton, the author of the 'Free Enquiry,' declares that the evidence of these miracles is fully as strong as that of the miracles recorded by the early Fathers of the church. He might have said immensely stronger, seeing that they were doing before all Paris at the very moment that he wrote his book, and had then been going on for eighteen years. Douglas was in Paris that very year (1749), and yet we do not find that he gave himself any trouble to see them himself. Middleton and Farmer might have gone over and examined them for themselves. But one of the most extraordinary phenomena in the world is, that the very men who most stoutly deny miracles, and who even write great books against them, never take a single step towards a personal enquiry into them. A celebrated caricaturist told me that he was going to write a book against spiritualism, and illustrate it. I said, 'Of course you have seen a good deal of it.' 'Oh no,' said he, 'nothing at all; and I won't see anything till I have done my book!'

'Let declaimers,' wrote Dr. Middleton, 'on the authority of the Fathers, produce, if they can, any evidence of the primitive miracles half so strong as what is alleged for the miracles of the Abbé Paris; or if they cannot do it, let them give us a reason why we must receive the one, and reject the other' (p. 226). And anyone might have retorted on him: ' The miracles at the tomb of the Abbé Paris are as fully and publicly attested as any of the miracles of Christianity; they have been as much tested and opposed, and are acting *now*—not 1749 years ago. Give us a reason why we must receive the one and reject the other.'

With such strong assertions of the excellence of the credence of these miracles, how then does the bishop act? His rules of test are all complied with. They are proved by thousands on the spot and at the time, and they have not passed without the utmost question and examination. Does he admit them, therefore? By no means. That would have put an end to his book, as my friend the caricaturist was afraid, if he examined spiritualism, *his* book would be put an end to. The object in both cases was to maintain blind theory and make a book, not to be convinced. Did the bishop venture to say that his rules had not been observed, and that these miracles were not sifted at the time and made known upon the spot? On the contrary, he reproves a writer for asserting that they were not examined at the time. Dr. Dodwell, in his ' Free Answer,' to the ' Free Enquiry,' asserted that these miracles were not enquired into at the time; that the Court of Paris and the Jesuits were afraid of a full enquiry. Yet Dodwell himself, who could have gone to Paris and settled the matter by ocular inspection, never seems to have thought of such a thing; so much easier is it to sit down and write without any enquiry into the statistics of your subject, but the bishop showed the absurdity of Dodwell's closet assertions. He says that ' Many free enquiries were made into them; as the pastoral letters of the Archbishops of Paris, of Embrun, of Sens, of many other bishops, an inundation of pamphlets of private ecclesiastics, and the repeated controversies in the " Journaux de Trevoux," and other periodical papers, sufficiently prove.' He shows that the Mayor of Paris and the Jesuits would only have been too glad to detect and expose them. How, then, did the bishop deal with them? In the first place, he endeavours to destroy the credit of the most distinguished historian of them, M. de Montgeron. He says, Montgeron, when he went to witness the miracles, was a confirmed infidel, and had been a very dissolute man. That, being greatly struck by the fervency of the prayers of the sick assembled there, he fell on his knees and prayed, that if the saint had influence with the Almighty, He would enlighten his understanding, and show him the truth. That immediately the strongest reasons for the truth of Christianity poured into his mind, and that, under the influence of those impressions, he remained on his knees for four hours, not in the least disturbed by all that was going on around him. This, the bishop thinks, is sufficient proof that Montgeron was an enthusiast, and that therefore his revelations are not worthy of credit. It is a singular thing that 'answer to prayer,' so much insisted on by all divines, should here, by an English prelate, be made sufficient cause for discrediting a man. What M. Montgeron really was we shall soon see.

But the bishop might have spared his attempt to remove the value of Montgeron's statements; for he had already assured us that the miracles rested not alone on his relation, but also on that of archbishops, bishops, clergymen, journalists, and innumerable pamphlets of the time. His next endeavour is to show that the cures might have been effected by natural means. That question, too, we shall soon see decided, though, had it been the fact that the cases were curable by natural means, and yet were cured instantly by prayer at the Abbé's tomb, the miracle is not the less a miracle. These cures at the tomb of the Abbé Paris were a very hard affair for the bishop; and he not only employed 120 pages of a volume of only 416 in earnest labour to disprove them, but he was so little satisfied with the result, that he returns again and again to the subject to the very end of the volume; and, after all, he passed with a mere allusion, perhaps, the most extraordinary cases, those of the Convulsionaires. We shall see that Paley does notice these, but satisfies himself with the slight remark that the nature of convulsive diseases was not then understood; nor are they now, if these were natural diseases.

But as the Bishop of Salisbury's endeavours to weaken the power of these miracles furnish the most daring and barefaced defiance of, perhaps, the most public and most complete evidence that is on record in all literature, I intend here to give a more entire view of the whole case than is to be met with, except in Montgeron's own voluminous work. It will present an ever-memorable example of the inveterate obstinacy and wrongheadedness which possess men determined not to be convinced. There is no similar example of it since the days of our Saviour, when He performed His magnificent wonders before the sealed ears and horny eyes of the scribes and Pharisees. ✶

✶ *Loquutus sum cum Paris, de cujus miraculis 2 Volumina constant, quomodo miracula sua fecit, quos per spiritus qui intrahant in hominis memoriam — sed usque ille in alicui religioni deditus est, et iste non aliquis Veri Ecclesiæ novit, quare hodie apud illos qui in inferno sunt. S. Sweden. Diar. p. VII. pp. 139, 141. Matth. VII. 22, 23. XI*

Quod miracula occludant internum hominem, et auferant omne liberum arbitrium per quod et in ipso homo regeneratur, et li num arbitrium est prorsus interni hominis quo occluso homo fit externus et natur qui non videt aliquod verum spirituale. Invitatio ad Novam Ecclesiam, p. N. b.

CHAPTER VIII.

THE MIRACLES IN THE CHURCHYARD IN PARIS IN 1731
AND SUBSEQUENTLY.

CARRÈ DE MONTGERON was the only son of Guy Carrè, Master of Requests under Louis XIV., and called Montgeron from his chief estate; his mother was a daughter of Field-marshal Diery. Being wealthy and indulged in everything, Carrè de Montgeron grew up a very dissipated man, indulging in all the sensuality of that court and time. To stifle the reproaches of his conscience, he assiduously endeavoured to convince himself of the infidel philosophy then coming fast into vogue, and succeeded in making himself at least a determined deist. Notwithstanding his licentious life, he stood well with the upper ranks, and became a member of Parliament. At this time the great feud between the Jesuits and Jansenists was raging. The Jesuits had long been all-powerful. They surrounded the throne of France in swarms, and Louis XIV. was completely their slave. By their influence, he was led to persecute every appearance of Protestantism, and every reform in the church. He was brought to destroy the flourishing convent and schools of Port Royal, whence much light under celebrated Jansenist teachers, was spreading throughout France. And he devastated the country of the Cevennes with fire and sword, to crush the Protestants. As the Jansenists preached and taught the necessity of divine grace for thorough conversion, and of purity of life and thought, they became intolerable to the Jesuits, who, on the contrary, taught the loosest and most accommodating principles. They appealed to Rome against the Jansenists as heretics, in the bosom of the church, and Rome, ever ready to crush heresy, issued bull after bull to serve the malignant purposes of the Jesuits. The Jesuits had drawn up a set of opinions from the posthumous work of Jansen, which they declared heretical, and all good Catholics were required to sign a condemnation of them. The Jansenists refused, and were therefore exposed to the most dreadful persecutions at the instigation of the Jesuits. The bull of Innocent X. of 1653, was brought into fresh operation by the celebrated work of Quesnel, in 1698, entitled 'Moral Observations on the New Testament,' which exposed the base doctrines of Jesuitism. In 1709, the Convent of Port Royal was destroyed, as I have said, with circumstances of unexampled horror, and the Jansenist teachers and nuns dispersed. In 1713, appeared the bull of Clement XI. called 'Unigenitus,' and from the despotic resolve of the Regent Orleans, that the bull should be obeyed, it was called also the 'Constitution.' And as the Jansenists appealed against it to a general council, though in vain, they were called Appellants. Many other Catholics, disgusted with this bull, refused submission as well, and the Catholics of France were divided into two great parties, Constitutionaires and Appellants. For awhile, the Jesuits triumphed by their influence both at Rome and at the Court of France, by their insidious arts and their relentless policy; but truth and power arose in the person of Blaise Pascal, and his 'Lettres Provinciales,' by their vein of wit and invincible reasoning, thoroughly unmasked them before the whole world, and never ceased in their operation till the suppression of the order was effected, and they were successively expelled from every country in Europe.

In 1713, M. de Montgeron says, that the appearance of the 'Constitution,' greatly delighted him. He was not, at that time, a very deep theologian, but he could perceive that this bull 'condemned the chief foundations of the Christian church; whence he drew the inference that those who issued it, secretly thought as he did; and that their religion was only a cloak of policy.' He assured himself that all the Constitutionaires were deists; and so he went on, confirmed in vice, till 1731. At that time he began to hear of the miracles performing in the cemetery of St. Mèdard ; for some time he laughed at them ; then he poohpoohed them, but they continued to come in such strength and from such quarters, that they startled him, and filled him with fear lest, after all, the Christian religion should be true. He resolved to go himself and see what really was taking place ; to consult at the same time the most celebrated medical men, and to spare no pains to discover whether truth or imposture were at the bottom of the matter.

The consequence was, he says, that on entering the churchyard, he was struck with a sentiment of respect on beholding the countenances of the afflicted people assembled there, never having before seen on any countenances such real devotion, compunction and fervour, nor having heard prayers uttered with such ardour. He soon fell on his knees on the edge of the tomb, covering his face with his hands, and prayed in these words, ' O thou by whose intercession it is published that miracles are performed, if it be true that a part of thee still survives thy death, and that thou hast influence with the Omnipotent, have pity on my blindness, and obtain for me, in mercy, the dissipation of my darkness.' From that moment, he says, a train of thought was developed in his mind, which kept him on his knees for four hours, though pressed and almost trodden on by the crowds around, but without being able to disturb his reflections. His whole life seemed to pass, things which he had utterly forgotten rose before him, and filled him with horror and astonishment. He had never, he says, lost the belief in the being of a God; but it was of a God who took no interest in men, whom he regarded but as machines, only organised for the present life. He now saw his folly, and the folly of imagining that the Jews would believe in historians and prophets, who had drawn a most unflattering character of them, had charged them with so many crimes, and denounced so many calamities upon them, if they had not known that the books in which they had recorded these things were true.

It appeared to him equally absurd to imagine that the apostles were not sincere, who recommended only to the early Christians simplicity, sincerity, and candour, and who forbade them, with awful severity, to indulge in falsehood. 'The portion of liars,' says St. John, in the Apocalypse, xxi. 8, 'shall be in the lake which burneth with fire and brimstone.' The sights which he beheld completed the effect of these new reflections. He went day after day, and convinced himself of the instantaneous, surprising, and perfect cures continually taking place at this tomb. All Paris, all France, was in an uproar with it. The Jesuits and the clergy in general were furious at the fact of miracles taking place at the tomb of a Jansenist, and exerted every means to throw ridicule and discredit on those wonders, but in vain. The cases were in hundreds; they took place in all ranks, even to those connected with the court, when the king, in the hands of the Jesuits, might at any moment crush with utter ruin those who avowed the truth of the miracles, much more those who sought to benefit by them. Nevertheless, people of all ranks were compelled to admit the truth of these things. The most celebrated doctors, who had pronounced the incurability of their patients, honourably gave certificates of the fact, and pronounced the cures not only beyond the reach of human aid, but, in many cases, the restoration of injured and decayed members, ' actual creations.'

It may seem to Protestants, hardened by a long course of education against miracles, extraordinary that such miracles should appear at the tomb of a Jansenist. The wind bloweth where it listeth, and God's providence is equally independent, though seldom without a meaning not far to seek. The Jesuits, grown by their acts to great power, wielded the very prerogatives of the throne; they had long sapped the foundation of all real religion by their rotten principles and their selfish ambition; the Jansenists were the proclaimers of pure morals, and of a vital life and love of God in the soul. The Popedom had set its stamp of sanction on the Jesuits, and God now came forward to unmask, to brand, and destroy them. Their rage and malice at the evidence of the divine power appearing amongst their opponents, carried them on to resist and decry what all the people, high and low, saw was real; and thus they destroyed their own prestige, and prepared the way for their own fall. The Abbé Paris had been confessedly a man of eminent and genuine piety and compassion to the poor and suffering, and it was, as it appeared, in testimony to his real Christianity, and to the pure faith and pure genuine love of his fellow professors, that the poor and the afflicted resorting to his tomb found the power of God proceeding from it.

Montgeron's conviction of his deism and of his sins at this tomb, produced by the sight of the suppliants and the result of their prayers, the English bishop, as we have observed, sets down to enthusiasm and the spirit of a visionary. On the very same principle, St. Paul, in his prostration by the light and form of Christ in the road to Damascus, must be pronounced an enthusiast and a visionary. On the same principle the apostles, who, when they had received the Holy Ghost, remained together in one place singing and praising God, were enthusiasts and visionaries. The English bishop at once placed himself on the side of the Jesuits — a singular spectacle for a Protestant prelate — and resolved to deny and decry these miracles; and his book has remained the great text-book of our universities on the subject, and all our national divines have been duly indoctrinated with it. I am bound to state and to show that the mildest term for Bishop Douglas's 'Criterion' is an infamous book, fraught with the most frightful falsehoods penned in the very face of the most remarkable, most irrefutable mass of official and other evidence, perhaps ever brought together.

M. de Montgeron, having watched with great interest the progress of the cures daily taking place at the cemetery of St. Médard, and having leisure, patience, and influence, though he was a member of Parliament, a privy councillor, and a magistrate, he did not dread any injury or disgrace which his testimony to their truth might occasion him. The Archbishop of Paris took the Jesuit side, and came out with a pastoral letter, in which he collected all the hearsay ridicule and denial of these miracles. Whoever reads the English bishop's ' Criterion,' may see the tortuous, indirect, and unfounded course which the French archbishop took; for the English bishop has servilely copied his stories and his arguments. Montgeron, however, did not let the archbishop and his zealous coadjutors, the Jesuits, escape. He selected from the hundreds of cases of cures through the mediumship of the Abbé Paris—some published, but more unpublished—nine cases in which the diseases or injuries had been of such an aggravated character, and had been so amply and undeniably attested by medical and other evidence, and had from these circumstances, or from the social position of the subjects, been made so universally known, that there could be no chance of the opponents escaping from the truth. Regarding these cases, Montgeron collected, with indefatigable industry, all the evidence from physicians and surgeons of the highest eminence, from magistrates, public notaries, clergymen, bishops, and archbishops, as well as from courtiers in the hostile court, and from the parties themselves and their friends. Whatever falsehoods and calumnies were issued by the Archbishop of Sens and his Jesuit allies regarding those cases, he hunted down and exposed on the most authentic and unopposable evidence. All this he carefully wrote in a thick quarto volume, entitled, ' La Vérité des Miracles opérés par l'Intercession de M. de Paris, demontrée contre M. l'Archevêque de Sens. Ouvrage dedié au Roi par M. de Montgeron, conseiller au Parlement.'

This book, afterwards successively enlarged, and continued from 1737 to 1741 in four quarto volumes, and containing a vast collection of official and personal testimonies to the truth of every case in every particular, he personally presented to the king, and after an apparently gracious reception of it, was seized the same night by lettre de cachet, and thrown attested, and that there is an abundance of others which have been performed under the eyes of all Paris. That there are numbers of atheists, deists, impious persons, and scandalous sinners, whose hearts were as obdurate and insensible as stones, who, from the miracles which they have witnessed, have been convinced, converted, and penetrated by the majesty of God, and who cannot cease, by tongue and pen, to publish what they have seen. He boldly accuses the leading clergy and those attached to the Pope's bull, who, finding that they could not deny the truth (having found that every time they attempted it they were contradicted by the notoriety of the circumstances) had exerted all their authority everywhere to destroy the *éclat* of the events, and had endeavoured by terror to suppress the proofs of them. That they had not hesitated to use his majesty's name to this end. That clergymen of the highest eminence and piety had been driven from their churches, and their parishioners left to ignorance and neglect, for their daring to assert the truth; whilst numbers of men, who disgraced their sacred office by their vices, remained in favour and peace. The cases brought forward by De Montgeron are the following :—

1. That of Dom Alphonse de Palacios.
2. That of Marguerite Thibault.
3. That of Marie Anne Couronneau.
4. That of Marguerite-Françoise du Chesne.
5. That of Philippe Sergent.
6. That of Pierre Gaultier de Pezenas.
7. That of Louise Coiren.
8. That of Marie Carteri.
9. That of Louise Hardouin.

Let us notice a few particulars of some of these cases. Dom Alphonse de Palacios was a young nobleman, the son of Dom Joseph de Palacios, councillor of state and of finance to the King of Spain. He was in Paris to obtain, if possible, relief for his right eye. His left eye he had lost, in 1725, entirely; the whole interior of it had been destroyed by a fluxion followed by inflammation. A blow received in the right eye in 1728 had rendered it blind for eight days, and it had remained ever since very weak, and he was menaced by its total loss by a cause which made constant progress. The optic nerve of the left eye being withered up, the nerve of the right, being connected with it, began to wither also. A fresh accident, in 1731, produced inflammation, which was checked for a time; but the sight of the eye now continued rapidly to disappear. After consulting in vain different oculists, he was taken to Auteuil, to the celebrated one, M. Gendron. That gentleman, after carefully examining him, pronounced the case utterly incurable, and that he must totally lose his sight. The young man, in a statement written by himself, describes his eye as resembling more a crushed mulberry than an eye. It was one piece of sanguine inflammation, and the least ray of light falling on it gave him the most intolerable agony; so that he was obliged to sit in darkened rooms with his eye carefully bandaged. For seven days preceding the miracle he had been wholly blind.

Hearing of the marvellous cures at the tomb of the Abbé Paris, he was anxious to try the effect of a visit; but the high office of his father in Spain, a country so under the influence of the terrible Inquisition, and the belief in that country that the Pope's bull against the Appellants was an infallible judgement, rendered it a very hazardous experiment. His agony and the loss of sight, however, drew his attendants and his tutor, the celebrated M. Rollin, to consent. The experiment was successful. He immediately received the perfect sight of the right eye, and could look with it full at the sun, and read with the most perfect comfort. Two days after, he went to Auteuil and presented himself to M. Gendron, who exclaimed, on seeing him, in the utmost astonishment, 'What has happened to you? Your eye appears perfectly well!' On hearing what had taken place, M. Gendron declared that M. Paris had done that which neither he nor any other man in the world could have done, that it was a genuine miracle. Dom Alphonse drew up, before his departure, a full statement of the facts, in Spanish, and also deposited with the public notary a French copy of it, made by himself in presence of the notary of the Sieur St. George and a dozen other persons. The notary entered it duly in his book, and twenty-two clergymen of Paris presented this statement to the Archbishop of Sens. That prelate, who might have informed himself of the whole affair from Dom Alphonse and everyone about him, but did not do it, declared the whole statement to be a tissue of falsehoods, of duplicity, imposture, and lying. He afterwards set it abroad that Dom Alphonse had signed this statement without reading it. He did not stop there, but he declared that there had been a defluxion on the eye of Dom Alphonse, but that it had been naturally cured, and that M. Jeoffroy had performed this cure. On this statement being communicated to M. Jeoffroy, he made the blunt reply in writing, ' I never knew M. de Palacios before his cure was talked of, and therefore he could not have been cured by me.' This statement was deposited with the public notary, M. Raymond.

Driven from this point, the Archbishop of Paris came to his aid, and in his last ordinance published against the miracles, made an extract from a pretended *procès verbal* made in Spain, which intimated that the poor young Dom Alphonso, at length succumbing to the menaces of the Inquisition, had signed a statement denying the miracle. It surprised the readers that such an act of the Inquisition should be in the hands of the Archbishop of Paris, as such acts remain in those of the secretary of the Inquisition. But as the archbishop stated that he had deposited the act in the hands of his registrar, application was made to him for a sight of it; but, to the still greater astonishment of the inquirers, he replied that no such act had ever been deposited with him, but that it might be with the secretary of the archbishop. Application being made to that gentleman, he replied he had it, but was not allowed to show it. The natural conclusion was that it did not exist.

But had it existed, it would only have proved that Dom Alphonse had signed a paper under compulsion. M. Rollin, the tutor of the young man in Paris, had received a letter from Dom Joseph, his father, expressing his unbounded joy and wonder at his cure. But it was known that, for some years, the Inquisition had menaced the ruin of the family if Dom Alphonse did not sign such a paper. His father, his mother, all his relatives, had urged it on him in the most vehement manner; yet he had resisted, and letters, during those years, had been received from him by M. Linguet, the Sub-regent of the College of Navarre, and other gentlemen, avowing how much he was persecuted on account of his refusal to deny the truth of his miraculous cure; how all worldly advantages were cut off from him by his persistence; but expressing his determination to maintain the truth, as he owed his cure to God. In September 1734, a letter also came to Dom Alphonse's friends in Paris, from M. Courcelles, of Rennes, who had seen him at Madrid, and found him in a sort of captivity in his father's house, but declaring that his cure was as permanent as it had been miraculous. Such was the spirit of vengeance in which the Archbishop of Sens prosecuted his opposition to these Jansenist miracles, that he expelled M. Linguet from his post of Sub-principal of the College of Navarre, for declaring this cure a miracle, and totally ruined him. Nevertheless M. Linguet not only continued to maintain this, but after his expulsion published an account of it. Amid the distinguished names publicly attesting this miraculous cure, are those of M. Gendron, the eminent oculist, who also, in a long letter, gives all the particulars to the Bishop of Montpellier; M. Pirrault, governor and preceptor of the two children of Dom Joseph Palacios; M. Linguet, of the College of Navarre, and M. Linguet, a physician attending Dom Alphonse in Paris; the two celebrated surgeons, Demanteville and Souchay; Sir Edward Aston, the son of Lord Aston, who made a deposition in public of his knowledge of the case both before and after the cure; M. Rollin, Rector of the University of Paris; M. Roulié des Filtières, who took him to M. Gendron at Auteuil, and many others; as may be seen by reference to Montgeron.

Let us now take the sixth case, because it is another case of blindness. Pierre Gaultier was apprenticed to a saddler at Pezenas, a village of Languedoc. As a child, the small-pox had left two opaque scars on the pupil of the left eye, which partially obstructed his sight. In 1732, in endeavouring to loosen a knot in some harness, the knot gave way unexpectedly, and his awl plunged into his eye. It pierced to the very retina, and left him wholly blind of that eye, and with very defective vision in the other. Every medical man to whom it was shown pronounced the case perfectly hopeless. He was advised to go to Paris, and visit the St. Mèdard tomb, by his confessor. He did so, and returned perfectly cured of the eye which had been pierced by the awl, but with the two scars still remaining on the left eye.

The Jesuits, having much influence in that quarter, were all up in arms; and their adherents declared that it was no miracle, or the scars would have been removed from the left eye. The Archbishop of Sens had poured much ridicule on the cure of Dom Alphonse's eye, because the one which had been totally destroyed for years had not been recreated. Dom Alphonse felt it a great miracle to have one restored. In this case the doctors were consulted; and they declared that, had the scars been removed from the left eye, it would have been an incontestible miracle. By the advice of his confessor, Gaultier once more went to Paris, visited and prayed at the tomb, and returned perfectly free from the scars, and with only a slight mark where the awl had entered the right eye.

Gaultier's father, who was a baker to the army, now demanded his services in Italy. No sooner was he gone, than the Jesuits and the professedly incredulous propagated the report that the cure was not real, and that the Bishop of Montpellier had secreted him in some solitude, that it should not be known. Now the bishop had, like a sensible man, investigated the case by summoning Gaultier, his parents and neighbours, as well as the doctors who had attended him during his blindness from the accident; and finding the whole true as stated, had written to the Archbishop of Sens to assure him of it. The archbishop now replied, reproaching the bishop with making a false statement. The bishop, a man of the most noble character, and warmly esteemed in his diocese, made enquiry after Gaultier, and soon had satisfactory attestations that the solitude in which he was hidden was the midst of the army in Italy—a solitude of forty thousand men, whom, with his father, he was helping to supply with bread!

On Gaultier's return from the army with a pair of excellent eyes, the indignant Jesuits procured an order for his arrest—for the crime, in reality, of being cured by miracle. He escaped, but was caught; and as the soldiers marched him along to the office of the intendant, his grandmother cried out in the streets, 'What is all this about? They do not like that my grandson has been cured by miracle; but they shall not gain their end. As long as God preserves my life, I will proclaim it everywhere, that his eye was put out by an awl, and that it was cured by the Abbé Paris.'

The Jesuits, however, having him once in their clutches, plied him with promises and threats; the least of which latter was, that he should be shut up for life in a dungeon; and the poor fellow consented to sign a paper that he was not really cured; that he could see but very indifferently; and that M. Carisol, his confessor, and M. Milhau, the priest of the oratory, had engaged him to assert that he had been cured by the Abbé de Paris. This is the ground on which the impartal Bishop of Salisbury states that Gaultier, after all, was not cured! But what was the fact? His father appeared before the intendant in great indignation, declaring that his son saw as well as any of them, and that he had been threatened into his denial of the miracle by the Jesuits. He gave the intendant the most convincing proofs of all this; and the intendant at once delivered him to his father. The enraged Jesuits then wrote to Cardinal Fleury, the minister, and obtained the dismissal of M. Carisol and

M. Milhau from their churches, on the representation that they had committed a sacrilegious imposture. The people, in great grief for the loss of their clergymen, to whom they were exceedingly attached, and the Bishop of Agde, who knew their worth, wrote to Fleury, stating their innocence, and the unquestionable cure of Gaultier; and they were restored; the bishop giving to M. Carisol a commission to preach the Advent in all the parishes of his diocese. The expelled ministers returned amid the jubilant exultation of their people; and the young man, now freed from the terror of the humbled Jesuits, openly declared the terrible menaces they had used, and the flatteries they had applied to him, to bring him to make a false confession.

The case of Philippe Sergent deserves some notice. This man was a wool-carder, who had become so paralysed in all his limbs, that he could no longer work at his trade, but had got admission to the Hotel Dieu, being pronounced incurable by all the medical men who saw him. His legs had lost their use; and when he attempted to move on crutches, they were slung up in lists and straps. His friends, hearing of the miracle at the tomb of Abbé Paris, obtained his discharge from the hospital. He got to the tomb by the help of a carter, and was instantly cured, and sprang up and sang Te Deum on the tomb. To the astonishment of everyone, he went about showing himself at the Hotel Dieu, and wherever he was known, and then took a damp cellar, where he recommenced his trade. His wife entreated him to quit the place, the walls of which frequently ran with wet; but he persisted in remaining there nine months, taking no harm. During this time a person called on him, pointed out to him his miserable circumstances, and offered him a hundred pistoles to sign a paper declaring that he had never been cured. He rejected the offer with indignation; but from that time he was hunted down by the most inveterate persecutions. He was compelled to quit Paris; but everywhere the Jesuits had their emissaries at his heels. They chased him successively from Rheims, Dinant, Namur, Mons, and

Liège. He returned to Paris; and, to put an end to the lies of the Jesuits, he wrote down the full account of his paralytic condition and his cure, and deposited it in a public office. The evidence, with the depositions of the doctors, are all given by Montgeron.

The cases of Mademoiselles Thibault and Courronneau are of the most extraordinary kind: the most fearful complications of paralysis and dropsy, cases most publicly known, declared by the most celebrated doctors utterly incurable, yet perfectly and rapidly cured by visits to the tomb. As the whole narrative of these cases, with all the official evidences, are to be found in Montgeron, I shall only extend my notice by a few sentences on the cases of Marie Carteri and Louise Coirin. That of Mademoiselle Carteri was a disease of the lachrymal glands, in which the bones of the nose were partly eaten away by caries, and pronounced utterly incurable. She was not only cured, but the destroyed bone replaced; and one half of her body—dead, as it were, in paralysis for more than twelve years—perfectly restored to vigour. The attestations to these facts by medical men and public officers at Nanterre, her place of abode, and in Paris, are perfect. This is precisely a similar case to that of Mademoiselle Perryer, the niece of the celebrated Pascal, as already related; and, what is most extraordinary, that cure was effected simply by her wiping her eyes with a napkin which had been laid on the tomb, as she was too ill to be carried there. Those who laugh at this may as well at the same time laugh at St. Paul, who sent napkins and handkerchiefs from his own body for the same purpose.

Mademoiselle Coirin was afflicted, amongst other ailments, with a cancer in the left breast for twelve years. The breast was destroyed by it, and came away in a mass; the effluvia from the cancer was horrible, and the whole blood of the system was pronounced infected by it. Every physician pronounced the case utterly incurable, yet by a visit to the tomb she was perfectly cured, and what was more astonishing, the breast and nipple were wholly restored, with the skin pure and fresh, and free from any trace of scar. This case was known to the highest people in the realm. When the miracle was denied, Mademoiselle Coirin went to Paris, was examined by the royal physician, and made a formal deposition of her cure before the public notary. Mademoiselle Coirin was daughter of an officer of the royal household, and had two brothers in attendance on the person of the king. Amongst the clergymen asserting the truth of the cure was Le Pere de Lespin, a supporter of the Pope's bull, the person appointed by the Archbishop of Paris to supersede the curé of St. Etienne du Mont in Paris, who was expelled for resisting the bull. The testimonies of the doctors are of the most decisive kind. M. Gaulard, physician to the king, deposed officially that 'to restore a nipple absolutely destroyed, and separated from the breast, was an actual *creation*, because a nipple is not merely a continuity of the vessels of the breast, but a particular body, which is of a distinct and peculiar organisation.' M. Souchay, surgeon to the Prince of Conti, not only pronounced the cancer incurable, but, having examined the breast after the cure, went of himself to the public notary, and made a formal deposition 'that the cure was perfect: that each breast had its nipple in its natural form and condition, with the colours and facilities proper to those parts.' Such also are the testimonies of Seguier, the surgeon of the hospital at Nanterre; of M. Deshieres, surgeon to the Duchess of Berry; of M. Hequet, one of the most celebrated surgeons in France; and numbers of others, as well as of public officers and parties of the greatest reputation, universally known; all of whose depositions are officially and fully given in Montgeron.

Let us suppose that any or all of these cases *had* been curable by ordinary means, notwithstanding this insurmountable evidence that they were all otherwise—what then? As I have already said, after having been attempted in vain by the most celebrated medical men, and then cured instantly through prayer, they would have been miracles still.

Nobody supposes that the mother of Peter's wife, who was ill of fever, was incurable, and yet no one would venture to deny that the instant cure by Christ was miraculous. It is the fault of all these cavillers, that their arguments are continually making deep incisions into the substance of the Gospels.

Such are these cases which the Bishop of Salisbury, in 'The Criterion,' has ventured to cavil at and deny. On the spot, only five years afterwards, he went only amongst the Jesuit enemies; closed his eyes carefully to these public documents, and decided accordingly. On such rotten and fraudulent foundations has been built the book which has been accepted by our universities as complete authority on these reputed miracles; on such authority has Paley proceeded, and thus our national clergy have been regularly educated to maintain a congeries of the most dishonest and disgraceful statements on the question of miracle. Who shall deny to what enormous extent the conduct of Bishop Douglas has damaged the national faith? We may safely assert, that if the evidence publicly produced on this subject and occasion is not complete, then evidence is utterly unavailing in any case, and need never be referred to. We can well see why the Jesuits, men who hesitate at no fraud to gain their ends, seeing their craft in danger, should violently, and in defiance of all evidence, persist in decrying these miracles; but why an English bishop, born and educated in a religion which has no foundation but that of miracle, should in the face of this irresistible mass of evidence, join the Jesuits, accept their unfounded stories, and retail them as truth, can only be accounted for by the fact that the Church of England has committed itself to an anti-miracle and, therefore, anti-gospel theory, and is determined to maintain it at all costs.

The cases of the Convulsionaires, as they are called—people who, in the progress of these miracles, fell into convulsions—resemble in some points many cases amongst the recent revivals, but they exceed them in the marvellous.

Montgeron, however, gives the fullest proofs of their reality; and even Bishop Douglas admits that many of these patients were *invulnerable* to fire! Many of them were weak women, who received blows on their chests, as they lay on the ground, which in any normal state would have pounded them to a jelly; yet they only expressed pleasure in it. One person, as attested by numbers, lay upon a stout peg fixed in the ground, and eight or ten inches high, sharply pointed, and had half a dozen persons standing on his chest, but without the peg piercing or hurting him. Montgeron says that Jane Moulu, a girl twenty-two or twenty-three, standing erect, with her back against a wall, received upon her stomach and belly one hundred blows of a hammer, weighing from twenty-nine to thirty pounds, which were administered by a very strong man. The girl declared that she could only be relieved by very violent blows. And Carré de Montgeron himself having given her sixty with all his force, the woman found them so inefficient, that she caused the hammer to be placed in the hands of a still stronger man, who gave her a hundred blows more. In order to test the force of the blows, Montgeron tried them against a stone wall. 'At the twenty-fifth blow,' he says, 'the stone upon which I struck, which had been shaken by the preceding efforts, became loose; everything that retained it fell on the other side of the wall, and made an aperture more than half a foot in size.'

Upon other Convulsionaires a plank was laid, and as many men got upon it as could stand, until the convulsions were relieved. Montgeron says he saw a girl thus pressed under a weight enough to crush an ox. The author of the *Vaens Efforts*, an enemy of the convulsionists, corroborates this statement. Dr. Bertrand declares them strange and inconceivable, but too well attested to be disputed. M. de Montegre declares the evidence so complete, and so authentic, as to preclude all rational doubt; but the public acts preserved in the archives are the best proofs. Boyer, a contemporary author, says these Convulsionaires could see perfectly with their eyes bandaged. (*Coup d' Œil sur les Con-*

vulsions: Paris, 1733.) The author of *Lettres sur l' Œuvres des Convulsions*, and many other witnesses, say the same. La Taste, a declared enemy of the Jansenists, declares that he had seen Convulsionaires who divined the thoughts of others, and displayed a knowledge of things impenetrable to all human subtlety. Dr. Bertrand, though opposed to them, admits the same. La Taste, Boyer, and the author of the *Lettres sur l' Œuvres des Convulsions*, all attest that the Convulsionaires spoke in languages that they had never learned, sang songs in languages unknown to the bystanders, and that one woman understood things addressed to her in Hebrew, Greek, and Latin. They, in fact, received those spiritual communications so frequent amongst mediums. It must be understood, however, that these convulsed people were thus affected by evil or disorderly spirits, and came to the tomb of the Abbé to obtain relief, which they did not obtain except with great difficulty. The attempt to designate the convulsions as natural effects is futile, for no natural causes could enable flesh and blood to resist the poundings which demolished a stone wall, and the monstrous pressure described.

CHAPTER IX.

THE SUPERNATURAL AND THE CHURCH OF ENGLAND CONTINUED.

> Truth is a suppliant, who, standing before the threshold, is for ever pressing towards the hearth, from which sin has banished it. As we pass and repass before that door, which it never quits, that majestic and mournful figure fixes for a moment our distracted attention. . . . We have not been able entirely to repudiate the truth; we still retain some unconnected fragments of it; what of its light our enfeebled eye can bear; what of it is proportioned to our condition. The rest we reject or disfigure—we retain but the name of things which we no longer possess.—*Vinet's Vital Christianity.*

BISHOP DOUGLAS, having treated the practical and official statements of Montgeron with such unexampled untruth, proceeds to the wonderful cures of Mr. Valentine Greatrakes, of Affane, in the county of Waterford, Ireland. Mr. Greatrakes was a Protestant gentleman, who had been a lieutenant in the Earl of Orrery's regiment of horse, but had retired to his ancestral estate at Affane, and was clerk of the peace for the county of Cork, registrar for plantations, and justice of the peace. In a letter to the Hon. Robert Boyle he states that, in the year 1662, he had an impulse, or strong persuasion in his mind, for which he could not account, that the gift of healing the king's evil was conferred upon him. He mentioned it to his wife, but she thought it a strange imagination. Mrs. Greatrakes, however, had acted, as many ladies then did, as country doctress to her humble neighbours, and a tenant of Robert Boyle's brother, the

Earl of Burlington and Cork, brought his son to her. Mrs. Greatrakes found him very much afflicted with king's evil about the neck and face, and told her husband, who said she should now see whether it was a mere fancy which possessed him. He laid his hands on the affected parts, prayed to God to heal him, in a few days found him wonderfully amended, and on a second application he was perfectly cured. He continued this practice for three years, not meddling with any other distempers; but the ague becoming frequent in the neighbourhood, he felt impressed to cure it, and succeeded, to his astonishment. He now extended his practice to all kinds of complaints, and cured great numbers, but not all. He says various persons were brought to him who had all the appearance of being possessed with dumb, deaf, and talking devils, and he expelled them, notwithstanding their violent resistance. He names the Mayor of Worcester, Colonel Birch, Major Wilde, and, at York House, London, Sir John Hinton, Colonel Talbot, and many others, as witnesses of such exorcisms.

His fame spread all over Ireland, and in 1666 the Earl of Orrery persuaded him to come to England, to cure Lady Conway of an obstinate head-ache. His plan was purely apostolic; he put his hands on the diseased parts, and prayed to God to heal the sufferer, and when it took place, he gave God thanks for it. He never accepted any remuneration for his cases. It was remarkable that in Lady Conway's case he could do nothing, but during his abode at Ragley, the seat of Lord Conway, where he remained a month, he laid his hands upon more than a thousand persons from the country round, and performed many wonderful cures. The Bishop of Dromore was there most of the time, and bears testimony to his marvellous cures. 'I have seen,' says the bishop, ' pains strangely fly before his hands, till he had chased them out of the body; dimness cleared, and deafness cured by his touch. Twenty persons, at several times, in fits of the falling sickness, were, in two or three minutes, brought to themselves, so as to tell where their pain was, and then he hath pursued it till he hath driven it out at some extreme point. Running sores of the king's evil were dried up, and kernels were brought to a suppuration by his hand; grievous sores, of many months' date, in a few days healed, obstructions and stoppings removed, cancerous knots dissolved in the breast,' &c. All this the bishop thought 'extraordinary, but not miraculous.' What, indeed, could a Church of England bishop allow himself to confess miraculous? The bishop, had he witnessed Christ's miracles, would assuredly have remembered that he was 'a high priest,' and taken good care not to admit that anything was a miracle.

At Worcester, Greatrakes' success was equally remarkable, and by command of Lord Arlington, secretary of state, he came up to court. He then took a house in Lincoln's-Inn-Fields, and for many months continued there, performing the most extraordinary cures. As he was assailed, as a matter of course, by all sorts of calumnies, especially from the medical men, he published an account, before leaving London, of all whom he had cured, with the names and abodes of the individuals. Besides this, the most distinguished men, physicians and others, attested, from personal knowledge, the reality of his cures. Amongst these were the celebrated philosopher Robert Boyle, Sir Nathaniel Holbatch, Sir John Godolphin, Sir Abraham Cullen, Sir Charles Doe, Colonel Weldon, Alderman Knight, Flamstead the astronomer, Dr. Cudworth, who attested the cure of his own son; Nathaniel Hobart, Master in Chancery, &c. Amongst physicians bearing unequivocal testimony to these cures were Sir William Smith, Dr. Denton, Dr. Fairclough, Dr. Jeremiah Astel, &c. Amongst divines, besides the Bishop of Dromore, Dr. Whichcote, attesting his own case; Dr. Wilkins, afterwards Bishop of Chester, Dr. Patrick, afterwards bishop; Dr. George Eames, &c.

John Doe, the son of Sir Charles Doe, relates that he had for three or four years been afflicted by an obstinate and violent headache, which had resisted all the means prescribed by the physicians; that this was attended by bleedings at the nose; that, hearing that Mr. Greatrakes was at the Lord Mayor's, he went to him and begged him to endeavour to relieve him; that Greatrakes asked him where the pain was, and, being told, laid his hand on the place, on which it immediately fled to another place, and Greatrakes laying his hand there, at two sittings completely chased it out of his body; and that he continued ever after quite free from it.

Now how did Douglas deal with these cases? Of course, precisely as with those of the Abbé Paris. When he had stoutly asserted what all the great medical authorities of France, including the royal physicians, had distinctly denied, that those cases were curable; when he had impudently—no other word will express the fact—affirmed that cancerous sores which had destroyed the very bones of palate and nose —that paralysis of limbs, which had defied all the power and science of medicine—were curable; and that an eye put out by an awl could be, by ordinary means, restored, there was no difficulty at all with Greatrakes' cases. It is true Dean Rust said he had seen him immediately cure, by his spittle and a touch of his hand, cases of scrofula which had for years set at defiance all the doctors; cancerous swellings in women's breasts; disperse lumps and hard tumours at once; heal ulcerous sores of long standing; cure deafness, lameness, dimness of sight; banish epilepsy, and cause scabs which covered the whole body, and which for many years had been counted incurable, to peel off and disappear, leaving the skin sound and healthy. Such things in our Saviour's time, or in the primitive Church, or in the Roman Church at any time, would have been recognised as the manifestations of the hand of God in answer to faith and prayer. Whether they were miracles or not, it were not worth while to dispute about till we have settled the precise definition and meaning of a miracle: but it is certain that some of the acts of our Saviour, which the same divines claim as miracles, were not more so than some of Greatrakes' may be affirmed without profanity to be, for both were the gracious works of God. The case of Peter's wife's mother, already noticed, those of various lame and leprous persons cured by Christ, would, if cured by Greatrakes, have been pronounced by those Church of England divines 'something extraordinary, but no miracle.'

The Mesmerists and Magnetists of to-day think their favourite agency the all-sufficient cause. It was, say they, a mesmeric power. True, but who gave Greatrakes that power? He says it came with a strange impression on his mind, all at once, that 'such a power was conferred on him.' This power was manifested precisely as the power of Christ and the Apostles, and was exercised in the same way, with faith and prayer. Prayer was the cardinal part of Greatrakes' system. 'The form of words which he used,' says Dean Rust, 'is " God Almighty heal thee for His mercy's sake; " and if the patients profess any benefit, he bids them give God the praise, and that, so far as I can judge, with a sincere devotion.' In fact, Greatrakes was led by spiritual impression, exactly as the Friends have always professed to be led.

And now, must not everyone admit that these great opponents of all miracles except those of Christ and his immediate disciples, in all their arguments against such miracles as those of the Emperor Vespasian, of the Abbé Paris, and of Greatrakes, were using the two-edged sword of sophistry? That what destroyed the authority of one must destroy that of the other? In fact, these are the very arguments used, according to Origen, by Celsus and others against Christianity. They are precisely the same arguments that Paulus, Strauss, and the Rationalists generally employ against all the miracles of the Old and New Testament. Nothing can be plainer than that Valentine Greatrakes was a most powerful spirit medium, the power being announced to him by a spiritual inspiration, and exercised by him in the real apostolic method, in prayer and faith and thanksgiving to God for his merciful aid; and there can be little doubt but that all his patients, had they had the requisite faith, would have been healed.

I have selected Bishop Douglas, the author of 'The Criterion,' as the most complete specimen of this class of sceptics; but the same features run through a numerous array of his contemporaries, Drs. Dodwell, Chuch, Berrington, &c., Farmer, Paley, and others. As for Douglas, Farmer, and Middleton, my conviction is that they did not really believe in miracle at all, either those of the Old or the New Testament, but they had not the courage to own as much. If they *did* believe in them, they must have been blind indeed not to have seen that their arguments went really to destroy all faith in them, and that they were furnishing weapons to the most thorough-going infidelity. Such blindness is not probable in such shrewd men: and Deism had not then discovered the new cloak of Rationalism under which to undermine the miraculous of the Bible. Had they lived now they would all have been 'Essayists and Reviewers.'

As for Paley, he was of the same cut-and-dried school as Douglas; freely admitting miracle under the covers of the Bible, but sheering all complacently away outside of it. He goes exactly over the same ground. 'Once believe that there is a God,' he says, 'and miracles are not incredible.' He does not go along with Bishop Butler, and say that miracles are but a higher order of nature, but contents himself with saying 'we ascribe miracles to the volition of the Deity.' He sings the old cuckoo-song of the English Church, that 'it having pleased the Deity to vouchsafe a miraculous attestation of Christianity, he left it to work its way patiently on the basis of that evidence. That this was a sort of leaven to leaven universal faith, &c. ('Evidences,' p. 392.) He treats the Abbé Paris' cases just as Douglas does; nay, worse, for with a most despicable ignorance in a writer on 'Christian Evidences,' he makes the monstrous assertion that 'of all the thousands of sick, infirm, and diseased persons who visited the tomb, there were only nine professed cures by the miracles; and that in the face of Montgeron's statement, that above a hundred cases were carefully recorded and attested, and many hundreds well known, though not written down. The reader is now in possession of the real facts, and can properly estimate Paley's veracity; but if there were nine only real cures, they want accounting for. He admits that 'there was something really extraordinary, though mixed with much fraud.' The reader can now judge on which side the fraud was, and that on the publicly recorded testimony of better authority than Paley, namely, the eminent surgeons and physicians who had attended the cases, and pronounced them utterly incurable, and on that of the depositions of numerous witnesses of the highest rank and character, made before the public notaries. If there was really something extraordinary, that also wants accounting for.

But poor Paley ran his head also against ' the pretenders to animal magnetism, working upon the imaginations of their patients,' &c. Here his recent annotator, Archbishop Whateley, has had to correct him : ' At the time,' he says, ' when Paley wrote, he had no means of knowing that the reports of the French physicians, to which he alludes, are other than carefully and candidly made. Time has since brought much truth to light on the subject, and the most diligent and fair-minded enquirers have, for several years, been convinced that though, as was to be expected, many instances of imposition and delusion have occurred, a real, and powerful, and serviceable agent has been discovered.'

And so Time will be continually ' bringing much to light.' It has now brought the conclusions of the committee of twenty Viennese doctors on Odyle Force to the light; and thus writers, in their hasty judgements on new discoveries, will find work for their commentators at a later day. What books will have to be revised on Spiritualism! What notes of correction of learned blunders to be appended to the precipitately dogmatic philosophers! Yet this will never teach learned men better. They will always sneer at the new and wonderful, and after-times will have to sneer at them.

Bishop Douglas made as ludicrous a mistake, in his observations on Methodism, as Paley did on Mesmerism. It was the practice of the Church, in his time, to put down all enthusiasm, and to reduce the spiritual temperature of that community to the freezing point, as the only respectable point. 'Such phenomena,' says Douglas, speaking of spiritual ones, 'are, I believe, extremely common amongst the fanatic Methodists, as they were amongst their predecessors, the French prophets.' And this was the enthusiasm, the fanaticism, which was at the very time arousing hundreds of thousands of souls out of the gelid death-trance into which the anti-miracle theology had thrown the English church. 'By their fruits shall ye know them.' Douglas, when a chaplain in the army, was scandalised by a soldier's wife being affected like those in the modern revivals, though she herself insisted that it was under divine impulse. He says, 'The journals and other works of Wesley and Whitfield furnish an inconceivable number of supernatural phenomena most common amongst their *misled* followers.' 'But as the writings of these gentlemen,' he oddly enough adds, 'are already almost as much forgotten as if they had never been published, and may be difficult to be met with, the reader will have full satisfaction by consulting that excellent treatise, " The Enthusiasm of Methodists and Papists Compared," in which the folly and absurdity are so clearly pointed out,' &c.

Methodism was the *bête noir* of the public at that day, as Spiritualism is at this. It would be rather mortifying to the Bishop of Salisbury, should he take a peep amongst us now, to find himself far more forgotten than Wesley or Whitfield are, or ever were likely to be. It is this despised enthusiasm, these contemned phenomena, which have proved the preserving salt of Methodism, and which have infused through it some returning life and spirit into the Church itself. It was Methodism which, on this side of the channel, rose up to counteract the infidelity of France on the other. The devil on the one side, and God on the other, were producing scenes of wondrous but very different excitement. And it is not the less curious, that whilst Methodism was awaking the mass

of the people from the deadly apathy of a mere nominal
Christianity, the Church and the Dissenters of England were
every day narrowing the grounds of the little faith that was
left, by denying all supernatural life, and thus paving the
way for that callous, soulless, and rootless philosophy styled
Rationalism, which has now avowed itself amongst the State
clergy, and reduced Christ from an historical entity to a mere
'ideal,' or metaphysic abstraction.

We might pursue our notices of the modern opinion of
Churchmen on miracle with the lectures of Bishop Marsh of
Peterborough, of Milman's 'History of the Jews,' and of
Hook, the present Dean of Chichester, in his 'Lives of the
Archbishops of Canterbury.' After reading Dean Milman's
explanations of the phenomena exhibited by Moses in the
wilderness to the children of Israel, one really ceases to
wonder at the declaration of the Scotch divine, Dr. Geddes,
who said Moses made a bonfire on the top of Mount Sinai,
and blew a trumpet in the smoke, and that was the sole
mystery attending the delivery of the law. As for Dr. Hook,
he is nearly as explicit. He says, 'It seems to me inconsistent with the principles of our holy religion to expect the
performances of miracles under the Christian dispensation.
According to the economy of means which we see in all the
works of the Creator, miracles would not be permitted to take
place if not absolutely necessary; and miracles cannot be
necessary to a church which possesses a completed Bible.
They had only been employed as the credentials of the messengers of God, and this employment is no longer required,
when, so far from expecting any fresh message, we are bound
to reject it if proffered.'

One would think, from Dr. Hook's assertion, that there were
no longer needed any 'messengers of God.' What, then, do
the doctor and all his fellow clergymen call themselves?
Are no messengers of God still sent to the heathen? Are
not the preponderating millions of the earth still ignorant of
Christ, or rejecting him when preached to them? Are not
miracles as necessary to missionaries now as they were in the

apostolic age? Dr. Arnold seemed to think they were. Do the preachers of to-day convince and convert all the heathen abroad, and the gainsayers at home, without them? Will they ever be able to do it? On the contrary, are not thousands and hundreds of thousands gone back, and continuing to go back, to rationalism, deism, and atheism? Have they not ceased to believe this 'completed Bible,' because of this very thing, namely, that the miracles—said in its day to be frequent, and to have belonged to every prior age—no longer appear? And is not this a reasonable plea for disbelieving? And can these lost thousands and hundreds of thousands ever be recovered by mere words—by anything short of miracle? Does not evidence, like everything else, wear out, and require renewing? Are not miracles quite as necessary now, to restore faith in the Bible, as they were once to give it? Is not the doctor's own church, spite of the boasted eloquence of himself and his compeers, rapidly crumbling and coming to the ground through this want of miraculous life, which he and they so stoutly resist and disavow? Is not the fall of his own beautiful cathedral tower, in consequence of the removal of its ancient interior supports, typical of that which must happen in the human church itself from equivalent spiritual causes?

But here we are arrived at the spiritual condition of Protestantism, and especially of British Protestantism, and must take our final view of it. What is that view? It is one—whether in the Church or amongst Dissenters, for the spirit of the Church has filtrated into all the surrounding foundations of Dissent—of utter abnegation of the great gifts of Christ to his Church, of spiritual, supernatural power; and of a consequent deadness, outward profession, and incapacity for restraining infidelity, much less for annihilating it. And is it wonderful that it should be so? Could it possibly have been otherwise, when all the present generation —our clergy, our lawgivers, our statesmen, our public writers and teachers, all who combine to originate public opinion— have been educated on the works of Douglas and Paley as university stock-books—when they have been all nurtured and built up into this hard, outward, unbelieving, unspiritual, and earthly condition of mind? What a result is this for poor Protestantism to boast of! To stand up as an isolated fragment in solitary opposition to the whole universe, past and present, in limiting the operations of God in his Church. To stand amid the ages as a thing out of joint, as an excrescence on the goodly growth of the world—as an anomaly, not in harmony with any age that has gone before it, and, therefore, an abortion. A condition of humanity which has thrown itself wholly on its intellect and its genius in physics, and has done marvels in material science and invention, but at the expense of the interior divinity.

It is something to know that this state of things is the direct result of the one-sided excess of Protestantism; the excess of reaction against Popish miracle-mongery, in the first instance, and in the second, as the equally direct vaccination of unbelief from the virus of the infidel writers of our own country, of France and Germany. It is patent to all observation that the progress of infidelity in literature, and the progress of the anti-miracle feeling in the church, have gone on *pari passu*; that the English Church and English Dissent now stand rent from the ancient Anglican and the Primitive Church, in the faith in the supernatural; and that it is not the spiritualists who are the heretics, but the clerical, the scientific, the materialistic, and semi-materialistic classes of to-day. We stand, and will stand, by the all-ancient faith in the divine presence and in the ever active ministry of God's angels. And this great and striking fact of the spiritual apostacy of Protestantism shall be known and insisted upon. For, unless this condition of mind be destroyed by a better tone of education, by the revival of the apostolic life amongst us, the mischief cannot stop here, but will produce yet more psychical damage, more soul-destroying effects.

Let us, then, no longer blink the great fact that the clerical and scientific mind of the present day is in a debauched, degraded, materialised, and crippled condition, derived from educational bias, and from a recent age of sceptical philosophy, in harmony with no age from the foundation of the world. It is not in harmony with the minds of the great men who stand along the whole course of time, on the great plain of history, on the topmost heights of intellect and genius. It is not in harmony with a single page of divine revelation in Old or New Testament. It is not in harmony with the mind of Christ, of the Apostles, of the Fathers, of the other existing churches, of any of the great teachers of the Gentile nations; of Confucius, Zoroaster, Pythagoras, Plato, Cicero, Seneca, or Tacitus; of Dante, or Tasso, or Petrarch; of Luther or Melancthon, of Newton or Bacon, of Pascal or Fenelon, of Hooker or Sherlock or Tillotson; of Baxter or Doddridge; of nearly all the departed heroes of dissent; of Fox or Wesley. It is out of joint, sick and palsied. It is overthrown by the same pride which overthrew Lucifer and the angels, and if ever it is to recover this sublime harmony with all spiritual essences and all historical greatness, and become capable of taking the van in the march of true discovery, it must prostrate its pride in the dust. It must lay its haughty and blinding presumption at the foot of the Cross, and come to Christ in a wise humility; desiring that its spiritual, as well as its physical, eyes may be opened, and that all the revelations of mental philosophy may be made for ever to the babes and sucklings.

But how shall this come to pass in State churches? For this is the manner in which State religions are made. A creed is adopted, articles of faith are prepared and sworn to, and from that moment the subscriber has surrendered the freedom of the Gospel, and become the slave of a system. He can no longer go to the Bible with unfettered hands and faculties. He is bound by a creed; he is wrapped from head to foot in the infrangible meshes of articles. 'Hitherto shalt thou go and no further,' says the fiat of the Church.

> Creeds are the leaden weights dead corpse-men wear
> When they are buried from lone ships at sea,
> Freighted wherewith they never rise again!

One of the most appalling reflections which the human mind can make is the mode of the manufacture of national religions. See, in England, the Church, with nearly all its livings, in the hands of the Government and the aristocracy. The candidates for its offices go up, mixed with those who are to become the distributers of its honours and its substantialities, to the national schools, Westminster, Eton, Harrow, Rugby, &c. There they are prepared with a pagan foundation for a Christian ministry. For sixteen or seventeen years they are steeped in pagan languages, pagan history, poetry, and philosophy to the chin. They are taught to look forward to the universities of the Church, and to prepare themselves for them. In due course they march up there; imbibe implicitly their spirit, their dogmas, their canons, and their articles. They are fashioned and built up into the Church and State mould, and woe to him who ventures to assume any other mould or tone! It matters little, indeed, what is the material of which national religions are erected: they may be wood, or stone, or iron; they may be Mahomedan, Parsee, Copt, or Hindoo; the education is the mortar, and the moment that is set and become hard, the building is unchangeable. It may be destroyed, it can never be remodelled without entire pulling to pieces. Salvation may come to individuals through a Christian independence— with God all things are possible—but whence shall it come for churches? Whence and how shall the Church of England, thus built up with the mortar of such an education, become enfranchised? With such objects, such incentives, such a system, how shall its clergy ever become a miracle themselves, and break through their buildings-up into freedom of faith, into the only gospel of miracle and truth? There is a struggle now going on in its interior, but it is a struggle of interests, and dogmas, and creeds, which are rending its vitals, and shaking its very foundations.

Yet let us not despair. Amid this chaos, this hurricane of worldly passions, we listen, not in vain, for the still small voice of Divine power and resuscitation. The lecture of Bishop Marsh drew from Mr. Penrose a 'Treatise on the Evidence of Scripture Miracles.' In this essay Mr. Penrose ably contends for the continuance of miracles, and that even by evil spirits: a view, he says, fully supported both by our Saviour and St. Paul. Stories of the marvellous, he argues, are to be received with a proper suspicion; but this is not to lead us to reject all such accounts on the ground of improbability. Nothing appeared so strange to the Jews as the acts of Christ; and vast numbers of them never could believe in them. To indulge this scepticism too far, he says, is to fall into the pernicious sophistry of Hume, who, he asserts, certainly was guilty of an egregious contempt of logic in affirming that, because many accounts of miraculous events have been false, none can be true. He treats the rejection of all the accounts of such things by the Fathers, by the Catholics, and others, as an insolent assumption of universal falsehood against them, and maintains that a prudent caution against receiving too readily the narratives of such things can never shut us out from the benefit of whatever evidence can be producible on their behalf.

The essay of Mr. Penrose called forth a noble champion in the Rev. C. W. Le Bas, rector of St. Paul's, Shadwell, a prebendary of Lincoln, and late principal of Haileybury College. Mr. Le Bas wrote an elaborate article on Mr. Penrose's work, in the 'British Critic,' of January 1827, which he afterwards enlarged, and published in a separate volume (Murray, 1828). In this ably reasoned little book, Mr. Le Bas carries out Mr. Penrose's idea of the probability of the continuance of miracles, with many fine trains of thought. He ridicules most happily the love of the marvellous in the antagonists of it. No class, he contends, are so credulous as the opponents of credulity, and none are so averse to any real toil of examination of evidence. They had rather, he says, endure a month on the tread-wheel at

Brixton, than half an hour of the real toil of thinking. He treats the overstrained incredulity of the day as a disease. 'There is a certain class of diseases—tetanus, &c.—incident to the human frame, by which the muscles are brought into such a state of inflexible stiffness and contraction as to resist any violence that can be employed to overcome it.' This state of strength and tone, he says, strange as it may appear, medical men attribute to some debility in the general constitution of the patient ; and he attributes the disease of obstinate incredulity to some similar unhealthy rigidity of mind, quite inconsistent with sound vigour. ' But however this may be,' he continues, ' the existence of such instances is but too notorious. There are persons, unhappily, who have the power of setting their faces like a flint against the proof of any proposition which offends their prejudices, or that stimulates into active resistance certain peculiar elements in their mental composition. With individuals of this class, mathematical demonstration would probably be unavailing. As Cudworth has said, it is credible that were there any interest of life, any concernment of appetite or passion, against the truth even of geometrical theorems—as of a triangle having its three angles equal to two right angles—whereby men's judgements might be clouded and bribed, notwithstanding all demonstration of them, many would remain sceptical about them.' (Cudworth's Preface.)

And adds Le Bas, 'If the Pythagorean proposition, for instance (Euclid I. 47), were to impose on mathematicians the Pythagorean maxim of a strict vegetable diet, what carnivorous student of geometry would ever get to the end of the first book of Euclid ? Or if we could conceive the doctrine of Fluxions had, somehow or other, been combined with an obligation to abstain from the use of wine, does anyone believe that it could have gained its present undisputed establishment throughout the scientific world? Should we not, at this very day, have many a thirsty analyst protesting that he was under an absolute inability to comprehend or credit the system ? ' He thinks, with Mr. Penrose too, that 'there may be many minds too much imbruted in sense, many too much vitiated by pleasure, and others too conceited and overweening to be able to perceive or adopt any proposition contrary to the common opinion.'

Mr. Le Bas quotes, with much approbation, views in full accordance with his own, from Dr. Goddard's Bampton Lecture: 'The Mental Conditions necessary to a due Inquiry into the Religious Evidence Stated and Exemplified' (1824); and he then adds: 'If we are asked why we have a tendency to implicit acquiescence in supernatural attestations, the answer is that we are so constituted—that such is our nature —that our disposition to rest in such testimony is just as much one of the phenomena of the creation as any of the physical properties of matter, that it is an ultimate quality from which there can be no appeal.' He adds that '*no* circumstances can be conceived sufficient to annihilate in us the tendency to such reliance;' that 'excessive scepticism is an unnatural state of mind, brought on by a course of perverse and injurious discipline, and proved to be so by the uneasiness it is sure to inflict; and that the truth is, that of all aberrations of the understanding, sceptism is itself, perhaps, the worst.'

The reappearance of such men, and such sentiments as these, are the lights gleaming over the long dark wintry waste of Protestantism, which assures us that there will yet be a spring, and that it is not far off. It was with much pleasure that, in the Bishop of London's sermon before the Young Men's Christian Association, at St. Andrew's Church, Holborn, in 1859, I read these words: 'As on all other occasions when the Spirit of God has sought to manifest itself, there were some who mocked, and said these men are full of new wine . . . In the new dispensation, after Christ had come upon earth, there was to be a general and universal outpouring of the Spirit. In all the prophetic writings are allusions to this general outpouring of the Spirit. In the outpouring of gifts there are two classes of gifts, the ordinary and extraordinary. . . . No doubt there are great changes yet to come . . . Whatever may result from the present and future state of things, whatever may be the result of the recent religious revival in America, still all cannot fail to be reminded of the necessity of a further outpouring of the Spirit of God.'

The principles thus proclaimed by Penrose, Le Bas, Goddard, and the Bishop of London, carried legitimately out, embrace the whole faith of the Spiritualist. That superhuman revelations are a part of nature, as much as matter is a part of creation : that both good and evil spirits can make such: and that we must use our faculties, or, rather, our spiritual sense, in deciding to what class they belong. Since the date of most of these publications the Cambridge Spiritual Association, called in jest the Cambridge Ghost Club, and including many of the most distinguished members of that university, clergymen and professors of high note, and one or more bishops, has been established to enquire into the existence of spiritual phenomena, and has already decided on the reality of apparitions. The distinguished men who constitute this society give weight to their decisions, and form a pleasant contrast to the more recent outbreak of German Rationalism in the Church. They are signs of life remaining in the old iron-bound stump in the grass.

Still more encouraging is the fact that various clergymen have earnestly examined the claims of Spiritualism, and embraced it as a great truth. Amongst these we may place the Rev. Dr. Maitland, F.R.S., F.S.A. In an essay entitled 'Science and Superstition,' Dr. Maitland, in a keen and scarifying style, ridicules the moral cowardice of such men as Faraday and Sir David Brewster. These are the men, he says, who tell us that scientific men only are capable of observing facts, yet when Sir David Brewster was present when a table rose into the air, he said 'It *seemed* to rise;' that is, he did not know whether it rose or not. And Faraday, when informed that his test for table-*turning* had failed, for tables were daily rising into the air, dared not venture to go and see for himself. Are these, asks the doctor, the men on whose observations we are to depend? He tells them that Spiritualism cannot so be got rid of. 'A man cannot step out and put his foot upon it, as if it were a spider.'

In fact, the present state of Protestantism, opposed, as it is, to the whole history of man, and to the plainest and most precious promises of the Gospel, being out of nature, must of necessity have an end, for

> What though the written word be born no more,
> The spirit revelation still proceeds,
> Evolving all perfection.

It is high time, therefore, to protest against Protestantism, and to come back to the Gospel in its unclipped fulness and life. Let us, therefore, pray daily in this sense—

Panem nostrum quotidianum da nobis hodiè.

CHAPTER X.

SPIRITUALISM IN NORTH AMERICA.

Οὐ γάρ τι νῦν γε κἄχθες, ἀλλ' αἰεί ποτε
Ζῇ τοῦτο, κοὐδεὶς οἶδεν ἐξ ὅπου φάνη.—*Sophocles.*

For this is not a matter of to-day
Or yesterday, but hath been from all time,
And none hath told us whence it comes, or how.

WHEN Spiritualism had, for nearly a hundred years, been exhibiting itself in Germany under a variety of phases, and had enlisted in its cause some of its most distinguished philosophers and *savans*, as I have narrated in my second chapter, it made a new and still more general appearance in the Western hemisphere. It originated in the ordinary visit of what the Germans had denominated a Polter-Geist, or knocking-ghost; but either the temperament of the North-American public was more favourable to its rapid developement, or the time had come in the general scheme of Providence for a more full and decided prevalence of spiritual action; for it spread with almost lightning rapidity, assumed new and startling forms, and speedily established itself a great and significant fact in the convictions of more than three millions of people of all classes, professions, and persuasions. My sketch of the history of this developement in the United States must, necessarily, be slight; its details fill several large volumes, and may be sought for in Capron's history of these events, in 'Footfalls on the Boundary of Another World,' by the Hon. Robert

Dale Owen; in the works of Professor Hare, Judge Edmonds, Governor Talmadge, the Rev. Adin Ballou ; of J. P. Davis, the recent report on American Spiritualism by Mr. Benjamin Coleman, the English 'Spiritual Magazine,' and many other sources.

The spot in which the eventful origin of the American movement took place is thus described by Mr. Dale Owen, who had visited it: 'There stands, not far from the town of Newark, in the county of Mayne, and state of New York, a wooden dwelling—one of a cluster of small houses like itself, scarcely meriting the title of a village, but known under the name of Hydesville; being so called after Dr. Hyde, an old settler, whose son is the proprietor of the house in question. It is a storey and a half high, fronting south; the lower floor consisting, in 1848, of two moderate-sized rooms opening into each other; east of these a bed-room and a buttery, opening into the same room: together with a staircase between the bed-room and buttery, leading from the sitting-room up to the half-storey above, and from the buttery down to the cellar.'

Such was the humble abode where the great American spiritual movement commenced. A Mr. Michael Weekman, it appears, had occupied the house about the year 1847, and had been troubled by certain knockings, for which he could find no explanation. On the 11th of December of that year, Mr. John D. Fox, of Rochester, a respectable farmer, moved into this house, whilst another in the country was building. His family consisted of himself, his wife, and six children; but only the two youngest were staying with them at that time—Margaret, twelve years old, and Kate, nine years. It appears that the family of Mrs. Fox had long previously evinced medium power. She was of French descent, and her husband of German, the original name being Anglicised from Voss to Fox. Mrs. Fox's grandmother had been possessed of second-sight, and saw frequently funerals, whilst living in Long Island, before they really took place. Her sister, Mrs. Elizabeth Higgins, had similar power. When the two sisters were residing in New York, and were about to make a trip by water, Elizabeth Higgins said one morning that they should not go by water, but by land, for she had seen the whole journey in a dream, in which they had not been able to obtain lodging in a certain tavern in the woods, the landlady lying dead in the house. Mrs. Fox replied that this could scarcely be so, for Mr. Mott, the landlord, lost his wife the year before. But all fell out as she had dreamed. The landlord had married again, and his second wife lay then dead, preventing their entertainment. All the circumstances of the journey were exactly as dreamed.

Thus open to spiritual impressions the Foxes entered the house at Hydesville, and from the very commencement they were disturbed by noises, but at first attributed them to rats and mice. In the month of January 1848, however, the noises assumed the character of distinct knockings at night in the bedrooms, sounding sometimes as from the cellar below, and resembling the hammering of a shoemaker. These knocks produced a tremulous motion, since familiar enough to spiritualists, in the furniture, and even in the floor. The noises increased nightly, and occasionally they heard footsteps in the rooms. The children felt something heavy, as of a dog, lie on their feet when in bed, and Kate felt, as it were, a cold hand passed over her face. Sometimes the bedclothes were pulled off. Throughout February, and to the middle of March, the disturbances increased. Chairs and the dining-table were moved from their places. Mr. and Mrs. Fox, night after night, lit a candle and explored the whole house in vain. Raps were made on doors as they stood close to them, but on suddenly opening them no one was visible. It was afterwards found that Mr. and Mrs. Weekman, during eighteen months that they occupied the house, had just the same experience as to the knockings, the sound of footsteps, and the impossibility to catch anyone at a door, which was suddenly opened by them in the very instant of the knockings upon it. The Foxes were far from superstitious; and still hoped for some natural explanation, especially as the annoyances always took place at night. But on March 13, 1848, matters assumed a new aspect. That day, which was cold, stormy, and snowy, they were visited by their son David from his farm, about three miles distant. His mother related to him their annoyances, on which he smiled, and said, 'Say not a word to any of the neighbours about it. When you find it out, it will be one of the simplest things in the world.' And in this belief he returned home.

But the knockings were unusually loud. The bed of the children had been moved into the room of the parents to give them confidence, and they were told to lie still, even if they heard noises. But scarcely had Mrs. Fox lain down, when the noises became violent, and the children shouted out, ' Here they are again!' They sat up in bed, and Mrs. Fox arose and called her husband. He tried the sashes to see if they were shaken by the wind, and as he did so the little lively Kate observed that the knockings in the room exactly answered the rattle made by her father with the sash. Hereupon she snapped her fingers and exclaimed, ' Here, old Splitfoot, do as I do!'

The child had evidently heard it suggested that it was the devil who made the noises, and if so, he was an obliging devil, for he immediately responded to the challenge. This at once attracted attention. Kate Fox made the mere motion with the thumb and finger, and the raps regularly followed the pantomime, just as much as when she made the sound. She found that, whatever the thing was, it could *see* as well as hear. ' Only look, mother!' she said, bringing together her thumb and finger as before. The rap followed.

' This at once,' says Mr. Owen, ' arrested the mother's attention. " Count ten," she said, addressing the noise. Ten strokes were distinctly given. " How old is my daughter Margaret ? " Twelve strokes ! " And Kate ? " Nine ! " And what can all this mean ? " was Mrs. Fox's thought. But the next question which she put seemed to refute that idea " How many children have I ? " she asked aloud. Seven strokes. " Ah!" she thought, "it can blunder sometimes." And then aloud, " Try again !" Still the number of raps was seven. Of a sudden, a thought crossed Mrs. Fox's mind. " Are they all alive ? " she asked. No answer. " How many are living ? " Six strokes. " How many are dead ? " A single stroke ; she had lost one child.

'She then asked if it was a man ? No answer. Was it a spirit ? It rapped. She next asked if the neighbours might hear it, and a Mrs. Redfield was called in, who only laughed at the idea of a ghost; but was soon made serious by its correcting her, too, about the number of her children, insisting on her having one more than she herself counted. She, too, had lost one; and when she recollected this, she burst into tears. The spirits always reckon all the children, whether so-called dead or alive, as still living. They admit of no such thing as death.'

Mr. Owen, in relating these facts, whilst he gives just credit to Kate Fox for observing the *intelligence* of the rapping cause, does not forget that such a fact has frequently been observed before, but had never been followed out. It is to Mrs. Fox, rather than to her daughter, that we are indebted for following it out. Mr. Owen refers to the answers by knocks elicited by Mr. Mompesson in 1661, and by Glanvil and the Wesley family. But there had been such evidence of spiritual intelligence much earlier than that. At Rushton-hall, near Kettering, in Northamptonshire (as noticed in ' Notes and Queries,' vol. viii. p. 512), this occurred to Sir Thomas Tresham, as appears by one of his letters. Whilst his servant Fulcis was reading to him in the ' Christian Resolution' after supper in the year 1584, on beginning to read the treatise of ' Proof that there is a God,' there were *three loud knocks* as if it had been with an iron hammer, to the great amazement of Sir Thomas and of his two servants present. In the famous case of Mr. Mompesson's haunted house at Tedworth in 1661, as fully detailed by Glanvil, it was soon observed that, on beating or calling for any tune, it would be exactly answered by drumming.

When asked by a gentleman present to give three knocks, if the drummer had set it on, it gave the three knocks and no more. Other questions were put, and answered by knocks exactly; and that in the presence of Sir Thomas Chamberlain, of Oxford, and many others. Glanvil himself says that, being told it would imitate noises, he scratched on the sheet of the bed, five, then seven, then ten times, and it returned exactly the same number of scratches each time. Melancthon relates, that at Oppenheim, in Germany, in 1620, the same experiment of rapping and having the raps exactly answered by the spirit which haunted a house, was successfully tried. Dr. Henry More relates, that at the house of Sir William York, at Leasingham, in Lincolnshire, in 1769, a spirit imitated all the sounds made by the servants and workmen. In the famous Wesley case, the haunting of the house of John Wesley's father, the Parsonage at Epworth, Lincolnshire, in 1716, and for two months afterwards, the spirit used to imitate Mr. Wesley's knock at the gate. It responded to the Amen at prayers. Emily, one of the daughters, knocked, and it answered her. Mr. Wesley knocked a stick on the joists of the kitchen, and it knocked again, in number of strokes and in loudness exactly replying. When Mrs. Wesley stamped, it knocked in reply.

Now it is wonderful, after these and many other such instances, that the knockings were not improved into dialogue by question and answer. The gentleman at Tedworth, who put a direct question regarding the drummer, and was directly answered by affirmative knocks, was on the very threshold of discovery, had he pursued his enquiries. But the following out was left to American acuteness. What is still more wonderful is that the discovery of discoursing with spirits by means of the alphabet should also have been left to this time. By asking questions of the ghost, it was successively ascertained by responsive knocks that it affirmed itself a spirit, and that of a man murdered in that house four or five years ago. Then a neighbour of the name of Duesler asked it to rap out its name on the repeating of the alphabet, and this was accomplished. Here the way to full dialogue was staring the people in the face, yet we are told that it was only on the suggestion of Isaac Port, a member of the Society of Friends, four months afterwards, and at Rochester, that the alphabet was tried for full and regular communication. And yet, as we have seen, the use of the alphabet had been well known for this purpose 1484 years before, namely, in the reign of the Emperor Valens, A.D. 364. Nay, it would seem to have been known far earlier; for the spirit-pendulum, consisting of a ring at the end of a thread, according to Professor Kieser, was used in the ancient service of Hydromantia. Peucer says Numa Pompilius thus used it in augury. The ring in this use is suspended over a bowl of water so as not to touch it, and on the pronunciation of a certain charm the string dashes about and strikes at a circle of letters on the rim of the bowl, thus spelling out the answer. Casaubon says the pendulum is of no use without the charm, that is, the invocation of the spirits. There have been many instances of the successful use of the spirit-pendulum in modern times. See the 'Spiritual Magazine,' vol. ii. p. 249, for the experience of Dr. Eymard, of Lanchatre, in France, who pronounces it 'moved by an unseen and intelligent agent.' See also a similar experience by Mr. Welton, in a communication from Mrs. Welton, in the 'Spiritual Magazine,' i. 142. Thus, however, at Rochester, in North America, was rediscovered the employment of the alphabet in conversing with spirits, upwards of 2,500 after its familiar use by Numa Pompilius, and nearly 1,500 years after its notorious use in the reign of the Roman Emperor Valens. And such is the profound ignorance of history in our days that our *literary* men call this ancient knowledge a *new trick*!

The neighbours being called in by the Foxes on this memorable night of the 31st of March 1848, grew to a crowd of seventy or eighty persons. Numbers of questions were put to the spirit, which replied, by knocks, that it was that of a travelling tradesman who had been murdered by the then tenant, John C. Bell, a blacksmith, for his property. That his name was Charles B. Rosmer, and that his body had been buried in the cellar by Bell. The servant girl living with the Bells at that time, Lucretia Pulver, gave evidence that she had been suddenly sent away at the time the pedlar was there, and sent for back afterwards; had found the cellar floor had been dug up, and that Bell afterwards repaired the floor in the night-time. The pedlar had never been seen afterwards; and on the floor being dug up, to the depth of more than five feet, the remains of a human body were found.

The sensation produced by the publication of these events was immense. The Fox family became the centre of endless enquiries. Margaret, the elder of the two young girls, going on a visit to her married sister, Mrs. Fish, at Rochester, the sounds went with her, as if they 'had been packed amongst her clothes.' Public meetings were called, and committees were appointed to examine into the phenomena. There were soon plenty of assertions that the little girls, the Foxes, were impostors, and produced the sounds by their knees and toe joints; even one of their relations, a Mrs. Culver, declared that Kate Fox had taught her how it was done. But Mrs. Culver's statements would not stand the test of close enquiry. The little girls were submitted to a committee of ladies, who had them stripped, laid on pillows, and watched in such a manner that they could not possibly make any sounds with knees or toes without discovery; still the sounds went on, on walls, doors, tables, ceilings, and not only where the Misses Fox were, but in scores of other places. The spirits, having found a mode of making themselves heard and understood, seemed determined to be heard to some purpose. They made their knockings in the house of a Mr. Grainger, a wealthy citizen of Rochester, where no Misses Fox were. They appeared in that of a Doctor Phelps, at Stratford, Connecticut, a man of the highest character for intelligence and worth; they frequently cut to pieces the clothes of one of his boys; they threw down glasses, porcelain, snuffers, candlesticks, or dashed them against the windows. He threw open his house to the observation and enquiry of all visitors, but no one could account for what was thus destructively going on. He says 'I have seen things in motion above a thousand times, and in most cases where no visible power existed by which the motion could be produced. There have been broken from my windows seventy-one panes of glass, more than thirty of which I have seen broke before my own eyes.'

But everywhere the manifestations were not so mischievous. They assumed the forms of rapping, but of rapping under great variety of phases. On the outside and inside of a door at the same time, or simultaneously at opposite doors, on the floor, on the walls, ceilings, on tables, chairs, in the inside of cupboards and drawers, on the back of the red-hot fire-grate, on the pages of books that people were reading, on the persons of the people themselves. Individuals were speedily discovered to be mediums, or persons through whose atmosphere the spirits were enabled to show their power. Where these persons were present, tables and chairs and other furniture would be moved about, raised from the ground; and in some cases, so powerfully, that six full-grown men have been known to be carried about a room on a table, the feet of which did not touch the floor, and which no other person touched. Handbells rose up, flew about rooms, and rung, as it appeared, of themselves. People became media of all kinds: musical, writing, drawing, healing media. That is, persons who knew no music had an involuntary power of playing excellent music on a pianoforte; other pianos played of themselves. People unacquainted with drawing drew striking sketches by merely laying their hands on paper. Others wrote messages from the spirits, communicating intelligence of deceased friends, which filled their friends with astonishment. Circles were everywhere found to receive their manifestations; and, so early as 1852, Philadelphia alone reckoned 300 circles, and in 1853, there were 30,000 media in the United States.

It is not to be supposed that all this went on without opposition. On the contrary, all the old Protestant leaven was dreadfully violated by this extraordinary demonstration. The press, the pulpit, the scientific chair, were all in agitation against it. It was denounced as imposture, humbug, blind imbecility, vilest superstition; and by the religious, on the other hand, as downright demonry and sorcery. No matter, its wonderful facts were open to everyone who chose to see them, and people believed their own senses rather than the wild satires of learned folly. The Rev. W. R. Hayden, writing in 1855, said, 'Eight short years ago, not a single individual in the United States was known as a spiritualist: at this date 2,500,000, at a moderate estimate, profess to have arrived at their convictions of spiritual communication, from personal experience. The average rate of increase has been 300,000 per annum.' In two more years we find it stated in the 'Spirit Journals' of America, that the number of convert spiritualists were upwards of three millions, a number equal to the united members of all the thirty thousand American churches; far outstripping the conquests of Lutheranism or Methodism in their Augustan periods. Amongst these were statesmen, members of congress, foreign ambassadors, judges of the higher courts, clergymen in great numbers, lawyers, doctors, and professors. Amongst them were Judge Edmonds; Dr. Hare, the great electrician; a Protestant bishop; Professors Bush and Mapes, of New York; and Channing, of Boston.

A new class of teachers had sprung up amongst them, namely, trance-speakers, who professed to speak from direct inspiration; and eminent amongst these were Mrs. Cora Hatch, Mrs. Henderson, and Miss Emma Hardinge, an Englishwoman. Their discourses were represented as in the highest style of eloquence; that they had not less than 500,000 hearers on Sundays, and that hundreds went away without being able to get entrance, though the largest halls in the largest cities were engaged for this new class of preachers. The literature was already become voluminous,

Mr. Partridge, of New York, having alone published nearly a hundred volumes. There were twenty papers and periodicals devoted to the cause.

In proportion to the spread and success of spiritualism were the endeavours of the stereotyped class of minds to explain it away. With the stereotyped religionist it was simply profane delusion, or diabolic agency, for some got so far; with the general run of people it was 'all folly and nonsense,' infatuation, and an epidemic. With the stereotyped literary man it was imagination, for it is wonderful what can be ascribed to imagination when needful. With the scientific it was either sheer imposture or merely subjective impression. A Dr. Rogers lit upon a theory which, for a time, was deemed utterly crushing. Baron Reichenbach had brought to the aid of physiologists his odyle force, a mere modification of magnetism or electricity, or both, according to his own assertion, but exhibiting peculiar powers. As he attributed to it a great deal of the action of the brain, Dr. Rogers at once invested it with the power of originating a spurious sort of thinking, independent of the mind of the individual. This he termed reflex cerebral action. Now, he supposed that the odyle had the power of laying the mind to rest, of placing it in a sort of dormant state, and then of throwing certain 'mundane influences' on the brain, which were reflected, as from a mirror, back again, and came out through the organs of speech, though the hand in writing or drawing as a kind of imagery or ghosts of thought—mere reflections, however, of these 'mundane influences.' By a stretch of imagination, he conceived the brain of one man in this condition to come into *rapport* with the brain of another, and the two to receive jointly and reflect back through the organs of the two, these 'mundane influences,' as a stereoscope unites two separate pictures into one. The explanatory theory was far more complex and unaccountable than the simple conception of a spirit impressing and speaking through a mind in full consciousness. There also wanted philosophic truth at the bottom of the theory; though it is true that the mind can and does carry on a sort of second inferior, or habitual consciousness, so that exterior observation, talking, acting, do, at the same time, go on in walking, or even speaking, while thinking intensely on some topic. This consciousness is an act of the mind, and not merely of the brain. The brain as simply matter can have no action except what it receives from *mind*, either that of the individual himself or of another mind, embodied or disembodied, acting upon it. That 'mundane influences,' or strange, wandering, floating ideas, should come into contact with a person's brain, willy-nilly, and there shape themselves into order and intelligible ideas, and processes of ratiocination, and state facts known to no one present, sometimes occurring at the moment on the other side of the globe, sometimes not to take place for years, was a theory more wonderful and incredible, besides being contrary to all our consciousness and experience, than a hundred such theories as that of simple spirit impression. It wanted, moreover, to account for this great and persistent fact, that none of these reflected 'mundane influences,' these co-operating actions of mutually biologized brains, these wandering manes, or hobgoblins of unappropriated thought-matter in the air, ever shaped themselves into the declaration that they were odyle, od, or any other oddity, but in all cases and places, at all times and under all circumstances, in thousands and tens of thousands, and millions of instances, that they were spirits, and nothing else. The uniformity, ever recurring, ever existing, of these impressions and facts, was, by all the rules of logic and philosophy, a triumphant, incontestable proof of their own truth.

A Professor Mahan followed Dr. Rogers in this endeavour to turn the human brain into a monster Frankenstein, self-acting, ruthless, a shadow dealing only in shadows; ghostly, yet without any ghost. Amongst the learned and scientific men who rose preeminently above the prejudices of their caste, and dared to look the phenomena in the face, and applied to them the true tests of evidence, were Professor Hare and Judge Edmonds.

Dr. Hare was the most famous practical chemist and electrician of the United States. He was born in Philadelphia in 1781, and died there May 18, 1858, of course aged 77. At the early age of twenty he was a member of the Philadelphia Chemical Society, and there made his first and most important discovery, the oxy-hydrogen blow-pipe, which led to the discovery of the celebrated Drummond Light. By means of this apparatus, he was the first able to render lime, magnesia, iridium, and platinum fusible in any considerable quantity, and perhaps the first to procure calcium in a pure metallic state, and strontium without alloy of mercury. He first announced that steam is not condensible when combined with equal parts of the vapour of carbon. He invented the valve-cock or gallows screw, by means of which perfectly air-tight communication is made between cavities in separate pieces of apparatus. He made improvements in the voltaic pile, which enabled the American chemists to apply with success the intense powers of extended voltaic couples long in advance of the general use of similar combinations in Europe. In 1816 he invented the calorometer, a form of battery by which a large amount of heat is produced with little intensity. The perfection of these forms of apparatus was acknowledged by Faraday in 1838, who adopted them in preference to any he could devise (Experimental Researches, 1124, 1132). It was with these batteries that the first application of voltaic electricity to blasting under water was made. This was in 1831, under the personal direction of Dr. Hare. In 1818 Dr. Hare had been appointed Professor of Chemistry in the Medical School of the University of Pennsylvania, and he occupied this post till 1847 with distinguished ability, that is, for twenty-nine years, when he resigned. The 'American Cyclopædia' describes him as 'a frequent speaker at public meetings; and in conversation, especially when it assumed an argumentative character, he discoursed with great ability. His external features were in harmony with the strength and massiveness of his intellect. His frame was powerful and remarkable for its muscular developement, and his breast was large and finely formed.' Judge Edmonds, who knew him, says:—' He was an excellent man, and all who knew him loved him for his purity, simplicity, and candour.' He adds that his courage arose from the fact that he did not know what it was to conceal or disguise the truth.

Such was the man who, when spiritualism forced itself on his attention, received it, as other scientific men, as a mere delusion of the senses. He read Faraday's explanation, and thought it was convincing. A Mr. Holcomb, of Southwick, Massachusetts, had repeated the experiments of Faraday, and wrote to him to say that they evidently failed; that he had himself seen musical instruments played upon without any hands touching them, and heavy articles moved without any visible cause. Dr. Hare replied that he still concurred with Faraday; but, unlike Faraday, when he was informed of such facts, he determined to test these too. He therefore introduced himself to a lady, a celebrated medium, and watched carefully the phenomena. When he saw tables and other articles moved, and intelligible communications given through raps, he set to work and invented machinery, to cut off all direct communication between the medium and the results. He continued the experiments for two years with indefatigable industry, ingenuity, and care. The details of them may be seen in his work on spiritualism: 'Experimental Investigation of Spiritual Manifestations.' The result was an overwhelming mass of facts, utterly demolishing the Faraday theory. The demonstrations were mathematically correct and precise; first, of a power beyond that of human, or of any known mundane agency; second, of intelligence not derived from minds in the body. Here, then, was one great step gained: the phenomena were real, and not reconcileable to any physical theory. The next question to satisfy himself upon was, whether they proceeded from distinct disembodied spirits. To decide this point, Dr. Hare adopted this plan.

He had gradually become himself developed as a medium;

and, sitting down at his own table, he frequently received communications professedly from his father and a deceased sister. One day, on the spirit calling herself his sister presenting herself at his table, as manifested through raps, he told her he wished her to do him a little service. She replied that she would if it were in her power. He was then on a visit at Cape May, about a hundred miles from Philadelphia; and he requested her to go to Philadelphia, and desire Mrs. Gourlay, the medium, to get Dr. Gourlay, her husband, to call at a certain bank and ask the note-clerk a question as to the passing through of a bill, and bring him the answer by half-past three. The spirit promised, and was absent for half-an-hour; but had then returned with the answer. Dr. Hare made no other communication to Mrs. Gourlay on the subject; but on his return to Philadelphia, in about a fortnight, he enquired of Mrs. Gourlay if she had received any message from him during his absence. She said yes, and under very extraordinary circumstances. She was receiving a communication from her spirit-mother, when the communication suddenly stopped, and his spirit-messenger gave her commission. It was attended to by Dr. Gourlay, and the answer returned to him by the spirit. Dr. Hare then went to the bank, and ascertained from the note-clerk that Dr. Gourlay called on the day named, asked a question, and received the answer, which had been returned to Dr. Hare by the spirit-messenger. Dr. Hare was thus assured that he had had an actual spirit-messenger, and was perfectly satisfied.

But other doubts had to be destroyed in him by spiritualism. He had all his life been a determined infidel, disbelieving in God, the immortality of the soul, and in revelation. He had told Judge Edmonds that he had collated and published offensive passages from the Bible to impeach the validity of the so-called revelation; that he would put down spiritualism also, which claimed to be a revelation. Having convinced himself, however, of his first error as to spirit, his further enquiries convinced him of the truth of the Christian revelation, and a little time before his death he called on the Judge, and said his sister, who had been dead many years, had come to him, and so thoroughly identified herself to him, as to convince him it was herself, and that she still lived. He had reasoned thus: 'If she lives, I shall live also, and there is an immortality; if an immortality, there must be—there is a God. But,' said he, 'Judge, I do not stop there, I believe in revelation, and in a revelation through Jesus of Nazareth. I am a Christian.' A grand answer to the *cui bono*.

In speaking of the conversion of Professor Hare to Christianity, Judge Edmonds says, ' In the introduction to my second volume of " Spiritualism " I published some twenty letters from different persons, showing that the writers of these letters were but a few of the long list of such conversions.' Professor Hare himself, in his work, says that five-and-twenty thousand persons had been converted from atheism and deism to Christianity, in the United States alone, in his time. Dr. Gardner, of Boston, goes further in the ' Banner of Light,' and says, ' Millions in our country have, like myself, become convinced of the immortality of the soul, who were sceptical before the interposition of spirit-communion.' What so-called Christian Church of to-day can produce such testimony to its spiritual life?

As Professor Hare determined to explode the impositions of spiritualism by scientific enquiry, so did Judge Edmonds by the acumen of legal sagacity. We have this on his own evidence: ' I went into the investigation, originally thinking it a deception, and intending to make public my exposure of it. Having, from my researches, come to a different conclusion, I feel that the obligation to make known the result is just as strong; therefore it is, mainly, that I give the result to the world. I say mainly, because there is another consideration which influences me, and that is the desire to extend to others a knowledge which I am conscious cannot but make them happier and better.' The Judge was born in Hudson, U.S., in 1790. He received a classical education, and entered on the study of the law in his eighteenth year. He entered the office of Martin Van Buren, the Ex-President, in 1819, and in 1820 commenced practice in his native town. He edited a newspaper some time, and became an officer in the militia. By successive degrees he became a senator of Columbia, a member of the State Senate, President of the Senate, a commissioner to the Indian tribes, inspector of the prison at Sing-Sing, Circuit Judge, Judge of the Supreme Court, Judge of the Court of Appeals, &c. On avowing his conviction of the truth of spiritualism, he was assailed by such vituperation and slander that he resigned his judgeship, and before returning to his practice at the bar, which the custom of his country allowed, he made a tour of two months, boldly to lecture on and spread his new faith. He went from Boston in the east to the Mississippi in the west, as far south as the Ohio River, and as far north as the Milwaukie, on Lake Michigan. He says that in this tour he found spiritualism so generally diffused, and every spiritualist, whatever his previous opinion on the subject, so invariably an anti-slavery man, that he declared on his return that spiritualism would prove the death-blow of slavery; that it nearly decided the Presidential election in 1856, and decided it altogether in 1860. If this be correct, spiritualism originated the present terrible conflict in the United States, to end in God's purposes, no doubt; but what, who shall yet say?

At the bar Judge Edmonds, notwithstanding his spiritualism, speedily rose to a first-rate practice, and some time ago was elected by men of all parties to the office of Recorder of New York, one of the most important and responsible positions in the gift of the people. This office he respectfully declined. We may complete the sketch of the worthy judge by the testimony of a very competent witness, the Hon. N. P. Tallmadge, late U.S. Senator, and Governor of Wisconsin:—' I knew him as a man of finished classical education, a profound lawyer, astute in his investigations and in analysing testimony, unsurpassed in legal opinions, and in the discharge of his high judicial duties; and, above all, I knew him to be a man of unimpeachable integrity, and the last to be duped by an imposture, or carried away by an illusion.' The judge tells us that he first turned his attention to the raps, but soon found them appearing so far from the mediums, sometimes on the tops of doors, and in all parts of rooms where the mediums had never been before, and where they could not reach; appearing at all times, travelling in carriages, on railroads, or at times when the hands and feet of the medium were all held. 'After depending on my senses,' he says, 'as to the various phases of the phenomena, I invoked the aid of science, and with the assistance of an excellent electrician and his machinery, and of eight or ten intelligent, educated, shrewd persons, I examined the matter. We pursued our enquiries many days, and established to our satisfaction two things: first, that the sounds were not produced by the agency of any person present, or near us; and, secondly, that they were not forthcoming at our will.'

This was acting in a rational common-sense manner, very different to the cowardly conduct of scientific and learned men in England, who, after taking a glance at spiritualism, and finding it very shattering to their philosophy, contented themselves with observing it at a distance. In the course of these investigations the judge saw a great variety of physical phenomena. Amongst others, a mahogany table, having only one central leg, and with a lamp burning upon it, lifted from the floor at least a foot, in spite of the efforts of those present, and shaken backwards and forwards as one would shake a goblet in his hand, and the lamp retain its place, though its glass pendants rang again. The same table tipped up with the lamp upon it so far, that the lamp must have fallen off unless detained there by something else than its own gravity; and a dinner bell, taken from a high shelf in a closet, rang over the heads of four or five persons in that closet, then rang around the room over the heads of twelve or fifteen persons in the back parlour, was then borne through the folding doors to the farther end of the front parlour, and then dropped on the floor. Of such things, he says, that he saw hundreds of cases, and such things are now so familiar that they need no citing. He proceeded to the examination of the higher phenomena—communications from deceased friends, questions often put only mentally, and answered openly by the alphabet. He himself became a writing and drawing medium. He found his inmost thoughts read and stated by the spirits. He heard the mediums use Greek, Latin, Spanish, and French words, when he knew that they were wholly ignorant of any language but their own. He heard conversations in foreign and unknown tongues by those unacquainted with either. He addressed a request through a public journal, 'The Banner of Light,' for well attested cases of persons who spoke or wrote languages which they had never learned, to be given with names of persons and places, so that they might be scrutinised and proved; and in his 'Letters on Spiritualism' he gives, besides other cases under his own observation, twenty-four letters from different reliable persons, with names and dates detailing very extraordinary instances of such cases. In his 'Spiritual Tracts,' Tract No. 6, he gives many other examples of such cases in well-known persons, occurring in the presence of himself and others, whose names are given, and amongst those thus speaking, his own daughter, and a daughter of Governor Tallmadge. These 'Tracts' and 'Letters' may be procured of Mr. Pitman, No. 20 Paternoster Row, for a few shillings, and anyone can thus examine these statements for himself.

In a word, Judge Edmonds became fully convinced, as any person must who pursues a like honest and commonsense course, when the matter of enquiry is a fact. His daughter, who for a long time was greatly averse to spiritualism, became by force of over-ruling evidence also convinced; became a striking medium, frequently speaking languages that she had never learned; and both father and daughter have remained firm and active promoters of the truth. The judge lost his wife some years ago, but soon received messages from her, and he records of spiritualism that 'there is in it that which comforts the mourner and binds up the broken heart; that which smooths the passage to the grave, and robs death of its terrors; that which enlightens the atheist, and cannot but reform the vicious; that which cheers and encourages the virtuous amidst all trials and vicissitudes of life; and that which demonstrates to man his duty and his destiny, leaving the latter no longer vague and uncertain.'

Professor Hare and Judge Edmonds may be taken as the examples of a large class of the learned and scientific in America, amongst them Governor Tallmadge, Professors Mapes and Gray, men of great eminence and universal recognition. The Rev. Adin Ballou has left his opinions in an admirable little work on the subject, and many others have written voluminously in its defence. Theodore Parker, the celebrated Unitarian minister, though not a professed spiritualist, bore this testimony to the spiritualists : 'This party has an idea wider and deeper than Catholic or Protestant, namely, that God still inspires men as much as ever; that He is imminent in spirit and in space.'

But this was not the case with all the learned and scientific. Many of them attacked spiritualism with an increasing acrimony, equal to any such melancholy exhibitions in England. At Buffalo, Drs. Schiff, Richmond, and others, professed to have examined and exposed the frauds of mediums; but they were answered and exposed themselves. At Boston, Dr. Gardner challenged Professors Felton, Gordon, and Dwight of Harvard College, Cambridge, and others of that university who had made violent attacks on spiritualism in the newspapers, to appoint a committee of twelve disinterested men in June 1857, to test the medium, Mrs. R. M. Henderson. This committee sat at times during three weeks, the professors attempting various tricks, showing anything but a fair spirit, and drawing up a report that the facts were not real, and yet that they were hurtful to morals! The same Professors expelled a Mr. Willis from the college for being an avowed medium. The undaunted Dr. Gardner invited a committee of gentlemen of the press to make a similar examination, Mrs. Brown and Miss Kate

Fox being mediums, and many of these gentlemen reported that the results were genuine and satisfactory. Again, Dr. Gardner invited the governor, council, and legislature of Massachusetts to a public examination of the claims of spiritualism, Mrs. Ada Coan being the medium. A committee of members of the legislature was appointed, and upwards of thirty intelligent tests of spiritual presence were given. At the close the committee declared their belief that the demonstrations were conducted in the fairest possible manner, there being neither collusion nor fraud.

The religious world did not omit to examine into the claims of spiritualism.

The Rev. Charles Beecher, at a regular meeting of the Congregational Association of New York and Brooklyn, was appointed to investigate the 'Spiritual Manifestations.' It should be borne in mind that he is the pastor of a regular orthodox church. In his elaborate report, made after a most careful and laborious examination of these phenomena, he assumes the hypothesis that 'spirits can only obtain access through prepared odylic conditions;' that this was the mode of communication by the ancient prophets, and to substitute any other theory 'cuts up by the roots large portions of the Scriptures.' And he adds, 'Whenever odylic conditions are right, spirits can no more be repressed from communicating than water from jetting through the crevices of a dyke.' Mr. Beecher concludes by saying:

'Whatever physiological law accounts for odylic phenomena in all ages, will in the end inevitably carry itself through the Bible, where it deals with the phenomena of soul and body as mutually related, acting and reacting. A large portion of the Bible, its prophecies, ecstasies, trances, theophanies, and angelophanies, are more or less tinged with odylic characteristics. The physiology, the anthropology of the Bible is highly odylic, and must be studied as such. As such it will be found to harmonise with the general principles of human experience in all such matters, in all ages. If a theory be adopted everywhere else but in the Bible, excluding spiritual intervention by odylic channels *in toto*, and accounting for everything physically, then will the covers of the Bible prove *but pasteboard barriers*. Such a theory will sweep its way through the Bible, and its authority, its plenary inspiration, will be annihilated. On the other hand, if the theory of spiritual intervention through odylic channels be accepted in the Bible, it cannot be shut up there, but must sweep its way through the wide domain of popular " superstitions," as they are called, separating the element of truth on which those superstitions are based, and asserting its own authoritative supremacy.'

Similar views have been avowed by the Rev. Henry Ward Beecher, one of the most vigorous and eloquent preachers of America. In a sermon on Ephesians i. 13, 14, he declared that he had often been in that state which links us with another and a higher life. 'One of these occasional openings into the other world; a state in which the invisible world is more potent and real than the visible world; and in which we see through the body and discern the substance of eternal truths.'

The discussions betwixt the spiritualists and anti-spiritualists of America have been infinite; and many of the most violent opponents have, of late years, owned their entire conversion to the truth they had so energetically spurned at.

Amongst the various forms of spiritual manifestation in the United States, besides the physical ones already spoken of, the more intellectual ones of spirit-writing, spirit-drawing, and performance of music are very remarkable. In some of these cases writing and drawing were done through the hands of mediums, in others without any human hand at all, directly by spiritual agency, and in presence of numerous witnesses of high character. Specimens of these may be seen by the English reader in the English 'Spiritual Magazine' (vol. ii., from p. 432), and at various intervals since. These are professed to have been done in the presence of Mr. Benjamin Coleman of London, Judge Edmonds, Mr. Gurney, and others. The account of

'Spiritualism in America,' by Mr. Coleman, published in the 'Spiritual Magazine,' and up to a certain date republished by Mr. Pitman, 20 Paternoster Row, contains some of the most amazing statements on the subject ever yet made public. In the 'Spiritual Magazine,' from time to time, are still published letters from a distinguished gentleman of New York, in which the frequent appearance of the gentleman's deceased wife and of Dr. Franklin to him, and other well-known friends, are unquestionably unequalled in the annals of the marvellous. Fac-similes of letters written by the deceased lady are given, and it is solemnly stated that the witnesses have not only seen, but touched these spirits, and handled the clothes and hair of Franklin. I have seen some of the letters themselves, and compared them with the lady's letters whilst in the body, and the identity of the cheirography is perfect.

Some of the musical demonstrations have been of an extraordinary character, but are attested by too many and capable witnesses to be disbelieved. Amongst these are those of what are called 'The Davenport Boys,' and of Koons' Rooms in Ohio. The 'Davenport Boys,' children of a family of that name at Buffalo, were declared to be the mediums of a band of musical spirits, of whom 'King,' the spirit of an Indian, was the leader. We have accounts of the visits to these boys by Mr. Partridge, publisher, New York, Dr. Halleck, Professor Mapes, Mr. Miltenberger, and Mr. Taylor. They state that on being introduced into the room they found, on a table in the centre, a guitar, tambourine, speaking-trumpet, bell, and ropes. At the far end of the room sat the two medium boys. The hands of these boys were securely tied, as well as their feet, and they were tied to the wall. The room was made dark, and instantly the instruments flew about the room, playing over the hearers' heads, and often touching them; King frequently speaking through the trumpet. On restoring the light the boys were found fast tied as at first. In one instance, the 'Cleveland Plaindealer' says, the sceptics not only tied the boys down to the benches with their hands behind them, but put iron handcuffs on them and locked them. The music proceeded all the same. Again, the keys which locked the handcuffs were placed aloft in a box, and the spirits were desired to reach them and unlock the handcuffs. It was done instantly. Mr. Partridge asked the spirits why they did not perform in full light; they replied because it would injure the mediums, by drawing too much force from them. Mr. Partridge, whilst listening to the music, found himself suddenly tied hand and foot, and with the rope round his neck, in a most intricate manner; and as rapidly untied. Mr. Coleman, at p. 443 of the 'Spiritual Magazine' (vol. ii.), gives us an account of the visit of Professor Mapes to the 'Davenport Boys' which accords with all the others. Professor Mapes, Mr. Coleman tells us, is one of the most powerful intellects of America, a profound chemical philosopher, who, like Dr. Hare and Judge Edmonds, grappled with spiritualism in the hope of exposing an imposition; but was driven, step by step, from his original position into complete belief. Like Hare, till forty-five years of age, he was a materialist. Mr. Coleman gives us Professor Mapes's visit to Koons' Rooms, which entirely accords with those of Mr. Partridge and others.

This Mr. Koons was a farmer, living in a log hut amongst the mountains of Ohio, in Milford district, Athens County, twenty-five miles north of M'Connelsville, forty-two miles from Lancaster, and sixty-seven from Columbus. 'No man,' says Mr. Partridge, 'ever travelled so hilly a country anywhere else; and, when you got into Koons' vicinity, you found the essence of hills personified; there was no such thing as a level spot to put a house upon.' Yet for hundreds of miles round did people flock thither to witness the extraordinary scene, and listen to the strange spirit-bound play performing daily. Koons had built a wooden hut for this purpose, in the centre of which stood a table with a frame or rack upon it, on which hung various musical instruments;' two fiddles, a guitar, a banjo, an accordion, a French horn, a tin-horn, a small drum, a tea-bell, a triangle, and tambourine. Koons and his son Nahum took their fiddles and tuned them. The shutters were closed; and, in the account of a Mr. John Gage, Koons then said, " Well, King, you are here!" for the spirit of King, the Indian, was also band-master here. The moment Koons and his son began, the whole of the instruments struck up, and played with such power and energy as to be actually alarming. The whole house was on a jar and vibrating in perfect time with the music; and I knew no mortal hands held the instruments. The tambourine made rapid circles in the room, and was beaten with such violence that it seemed it must be dashed to pieces; and darted from place to place, so that I thought it must strike me. Drum, harp, accordion, French-horn, all played together, and a strange, unearthly voice would sing in concert with the music. Between the tunes there was a talking through the horns, and these circled through the room over and around us at the same time.'

Koons handed to the spirits some phosphorus in a bit of paper, with which the tambourine-player rubbed his hands, so that they became visible, and could be seen whirling the tambourine over their heads with a rapdity, here and there, like flashes of lightning, or more like the flickering of a light thrown from water on a mirror than anything else. The shining hand made blows causing a sensible rap where it touched, and also wrote them a long letter. The visitors all shook hands with the spirits. The accounts of Mr. Partridge and Professor Mapes are precisely similar. The professor says that at the exhibition of the Davenport Boys he conversed half an hour with John King, who spoke through a trumpet. He shook hands with him, and received a most powerful grasp. His friends Dr. Warren and Dr. Wilson, and others, were with him, and all experienced the same things.

Another of the American phenomena were the Kentucky Jerks. These are described by the Rev. Jacob Young in his Autobiography. He saw them so early as 1804. These appear to have been of a very disorderly kind. A Mr. Doke, a

Presbyterian clergyman, was first seized by the jerks, which twitched him about in a most extraordinary manner, often when in the pulpit, and caused him to shout aloud, and run out of the pulpit into the woods, screaming like a madman. When the fit was over, he returned calmly to his pulpit and finished the service. People were often seized at hotels, and at table would, on lifting a glass to drink, jerk the liquor to the ceiling; ladies would at the breakfast table suddenly be compelled to throw aloft their coffee, and frequently break the cup and saucer. The long plaits of hair then worn down the ladies' backs would crack like whips. Some attributed the cause to the devil, some to an opposite source. A certain clergyman vowed that he would preach it down; but he was seized in the midst of his attempt, and made so ridiculous that he withdrew himself from further notice. Camp meetings were seized with it, and hundreds would be affected with the jerking simultaneously. It was looked upon by many as a judgement for the immorality of the age.

Those singular people the Shakers or Shaking Quakers, who have eighteen communities in the United States, who maintain the primitive order of things, and have all things in common, are spiritualists to a man. They claim their origin from John and Jane Wardley, formerly Friends, of Bolton in Lancashire, who joined those of the Camisards or Prophets of the Cevennes who came to England. In 1758, they were joined by Ann Lee, the daughter of a blacksmith of Manchester, and being persecuted by the mob, and Ann, who had become the head of the society, and was called Mother Ann, being treated as a madwoman, and put into an asylum for several weeks, they went to America, where it was revealed to Ann that they should increase and become a people in peace and freedom. \ They arrived in the States in 1774, but were at first very poor and compelled to separate to obtain a livelihood. But in 1776, they founded an establishment near Albany. They afterwards founded others at New Lebanon, near Hudson, and at Hancock. They claim to have greatly enjoyed the apostolic gifts of healing, of prophecy, speaking in unknown tongues, and singing new and spiritual songs. They have been led by the Spirit, they aver, into a deep and holy experience, and they have been inspired, not only by the Holy Spirit, but by other spiritual intelligences, with whom they have daily and hourly communion. In 1856, one of them, named F. W. Evans, wrote to Robert Owen, informing him 'that seven years previous to the advent of spiritualism, the Shakers had predicted its rise and progress, precisely as they have occurred, and adding that the Shaker order is the great medium betwixt this world and the world of spirits.' He continued,—

'Friend Robert, it appears that you are now a spiritualist. Spiritualism originated amongst the Shakers of America. It was also to and amongst them a few years ago, that the *avenues* to the spirit-world were first opened; when for seven years in succession a revival continued in operation among that people, during which period hundreds of spiritual mediums were developed throughout the eighteen societies. In truth, all the members, in a greater or less degree, were mediums. So that physical manifestations, visions, revelations, prophecies, and gifts of various kinds, of which voluminous records are kept, and, indeed, "divers operations, but all of the same spirit," were as common as gold in California.'

He says that these spiritual manifestations were of three distinct degrees. The first being for the complete convincement of the junior members; the second for the work of judgement, the judging and purifying of the whole people by spiritual agency; and the third, for the ministration of millennial truths, to various nations, kindreds, tribes and people, in the *spirit-world*, who were hungering and thirsting after righteousness. And that spiritualism in its outward progress will go through the same three degrees in the world at large, being only yet in its first degree in the United States. Spiritual manifestations, he maintained, were God's answer to the hearts' cry of earnest men and women, seeking facts, not words, in attestation of the ' Word of Life.'

Mormonism must be set down as one of the disorderly phases of American spiritualism. To those who have read both sides on the subject and history of Mormonism, there can be little doubt that the thing has originated in real spiritual agency, but not of the purest kind. The Mormons, one and all, claim a miraculous origin for it. They declare that the gifts of prophecy, of healing, of seeing visions, are amongst them; and they record abundant instances of curing the most violent complaints, by the prayers o the church and the laying on of hands. Orson Pratt, one of their great oracles, says, ' We believe that wherever the people enjoy the religion of the New Testament, there they enjoy visions, revelations, the ministry of angels, etc. And that wherever these blessings cease to be enjoyed, there they also cease to enjoy the religion of the New Testament.' He says, ' New revelation is the very life and soul of the religion of heaven; it is indispensably necessary for the calling of all officers in the church. Without it, the officers of the church can never be instructed in the various duties of their calling. Where the Spirit of Revelation does not exist, the church cannot be comforted and taught in all wisdom and knowledge, cannot be properly reproved and chastened according to the mind of God, cannot obtain promises for themselves, but are dependant upon the promises made through the ancients. Without new revelation, the people are like a blind man groping his way in total darkness, not knowing the dangers that beset his path. Without prophets and revelators darkness hangs over the future; no city, people, or nation understand what awaits them. Without new revelation, no people know of the approaching earthquake, of the deadly plague, of the terrible war, of the withering famine, and the fearful judgements of the Almighty, which hang over their devoted heads. When the voices of living prophets and apostles are no longer heard in the land, there is an end of perfecting and edifying the saints; there is a speedy end to the work of the ministry: there is an end to the obtaining of that knowledge so necessary to eternal life: there is an end to all that is great, and grand, and glorious, pertaining to the religion of heaven : there is an end to the very existence of the Church of Christ on earth, there is an end to salvation in the celestial kingdom.'

Whatever of error and folly there may be in Mormonism, this at least is genuine and gospel truth. It is only what John Wesley had said before in fewer words,—' The real cause why the gifts of the Holy Ghost are no longer to be found in the Christian Church is because the Christians are turned heathen again, and have only a dead form left.' Their organ, the 'Millennial Star,' says, 'The Latter-Day Saints *know* that the angels do here converse with men. They *know* that the gifts of the Holy Ghost are manifested in these days by dreams, visions, revelating tongues, prophecies, miracles, healings.' Orson Pratt says, and a tract, published by the Latter-Day Church, called 'The Book of Mormon confirmed by Miracles,' gives numerous proofs of the truth of his assertions, that 'nearly every branch of the church has been blessed by miraculous signs and gifts of the Holy Ghost, by which they have been confirmed, and know of a surety that this is the Church of Christ. They know that the blind see, the lame walk, the deaf hear, the dumb speak, that lepers are cleansed, that bones are set, that the cholera is rebuked, and that the most virulent diseases give way through faith in the name of Christ, and the power of His Gospel.' He adds, 'that these things are not done in a corner; they are taking place every day, and before tens of thousands of witnesses.'

Well, there is nothing to be said against this, unless we could prove it to be utterly false. The doctrine is a true doctrine. Every church, except the Protestant Church, not only asserts the same, but claims to have ample evidence of it. The ancient church, the Roman, the Greek, the Waldenses, the Camisards, the early Friends, Luther himself, and many individuals even amongst Protestants. Greatrakes was a great healer in the apostolic fashion. Madame Saint-Amour, who had been educated in Romanism, but who became a Swedenborgian, discovered in 1826 that she possessed the same power of healing diseases as Gassner, and Greatrakes, by the power of the Spirit of Christ. She was the wife of Major Saint-Amour, and herself of high Dutch connection; her uncle, General Drury, being commander at the Hague, under the Stadtholdership, and under Louis Buonaparte, and her cousin M. Van Mann, minister of justice in the Netherlands. Madame Saint-Amour, however, made no hesitation as to whether she should injure her worldly position. She went to Nantes in September 1828, and began her benevolent mission. It was soon rumoured that a lady had arrived from Paris, who cured sickness and chronic ailments by prayer. The whole place was thrown into a state of excitement. Some declared that the apostolic times were come again; others that these miracles originated in some occult art, rather than in religion. The sick who were cured kindled the enthusiasm of those who yet awaited their turn. A cripple, who had left his crutches with Madame Saint-Amour, hastened to prostrate himself at the shrine of St. Semilian, exclaiming, 'She cures everything!' A child carried to her in his sister's arms, returned home on foot, followed by a crowd, uttering their astonishment at the miracle. Passengers were stopped by the wondering crowd before Madame Saint-Amour's house; there was much questioning, and replies were given that struck the hearers with amazement. Throngs increased; the street was completely blocked, so that carriages could not pass. The very steps up to her door were crowded with sick and maimed, seeking help. From six in the morning till night, the invalids remained waiting their turn. Numbers waited all night, to be among the earliest admitted next morning. Wherever she went, they stood in her way as if nailed to the ground; they were confident that if they could but touch her dress they should be cured. Many even went so far as to declare that she was the Virgin Mary herself in disguise.

M. Richer, the celebrated editor and commentator on Swedenborg, went to judge for himself. It is well known that the Swedenborgians are violently hostile to any one possessing supernatural gifts but Swedenborg himself. They seem to think that he had a patent for miracle, and that no one must invade it to the end of the world; but M. Richer was astonished at what he saw, and honestly confessed it. He heard Madame Saint-Amour saying to the crowd of afflicted applicants, 'Do you believe in God? Do you believe that God, who created heaven and earth, has power to heal you?' And when they confessed their belief, she prayed that they might be healed, and laid her hand on them. He saw with amaze the wonders which ensued: saw her melted into tears of joy and gratitude to God in the midst of the miracles that He wrought by her hands; saw her witness with rapture the change from pain and suffering in her patients, to ease and strength; saw her cast herself on her knees in speechless gratitude to the Giver of all good, amid the restored invalids around her.

For three days the excitement continued to increase. From all sides arrived the sick, full of astonishment at the relations which they heard. They came from Tours, Saumur, Rochefort, Angers, Rennes, from the Maine and Loire, from Vendée, Morbihan, and other distant places. It may safely be asserted that not a place in the Lower Department of the Loire but sent some patient to the capital of the district. The wealthy were struggling to get Madame Saint-Amour to lionise her in their saloons; and to escape for awhile from the incessant crush of eager people around her, she accepted invitations to distant quarters. But everywhere augmenting crowds poured after her, and everywhere in her way you saw sick and curious people who prayed the favour of addressing her. It was in vain that at night she endeavoured to persuade the throngs to disperse; they would remain in order to secure her services in the morning, and you might see her hands stretched from the windows to call down blessings on the immoveable crowd. As she endeavoured to drive along, she administered cures from the windows of her carriage. The streets and gateways of the houses she visited were speedily besieged, and four sentinels at every door were not sufficient to keep back the people. Every vehicle in the city on hire was taken to carry applicants to her; crowds of workmen abandoned their employments to get a sight of her. In every circle she and her cures were the subject of conversation; at the exchange, in the college, in the saloons, in the inns and in private houses; and it was declared that no such things had ever before been heard of, except in books.

But all at once it was discovered by the Church that Madame Saint-Amour was a heretic Swedenborgian! The priests were instantly in arms: a meeting of the clergy was called by the Archbishop, and as the monks of St. Stephen had declared to Columbus that there was no such continent as America, the clergy of Nantes declared that these miracles were not the work of Christ but of witchcraft. The crowds were told that if God sent such miracles it would be through a priest, and not through a woman. The cry of heresy and devilry was raised against her, and Madame Saint-Amour was speedily compelled to escape from the city and district.

Madame Ehrenborg, a Swedish lady, who has published three very interesting volumes of her travels on the continent, when at Nantes since these events took place, was shown the portrait of Madame Saint-Amour, and was assured by various persons of highest character in Nantes that the narrative of these extraordinary cures was perfectly correct. Madame Saint-Amour is said to have gone to join her son in Algiers.

To return to the Mormons; they claim only a general Christian claim as to miracles, and if they had not introduced polygamy into their system, the world would have little to lay to their charge. This they do, however, under patriarchal precedent, and on the ground that the authority of the Old Testament is not to be impeached any more than that of the New. They ask where, indeed, the practice is forbidden in the Gospels? and to this it is not easy to find an answer in express terms. All zealots have a wonderful propensity to fall back on the Old Testament. The Scotch Covenanters and the English Puritans appealed to it for their martial warrant. So did the German peasants in the Bauern Krieg. And we may ask whether even polygamy is worse than, or as bad as, that immoral system of murder called war, now defended by so-called Christians all the world over, and who, with banners blessed by the churches, strew all the fields of earth with the bodies of their fellow-men? For my part, I am no defender of Mormon polygamy, but I am still less an admirer of the bloody spirit of the so-called followers of the Prince of Peace. I believe that both systems originate in a spiritualism that is not from above. Without such 'a biologising from below' it is as impossible that the pretended Christian world of to-day could perpetuate the Satanic spirit of war—that bloody burlesque on 'the gospel of peace'—as that the Mormons could have grown in a few years from a solitary country lad, with his miraculous tablets of gold, and Urim and Thummim, into hundreds of thousands still rapidly streaming from the British Isles to the Salt Lake, and constituting a fast-growing state, which bids defiance to all the power of North America. In what are called enthusiasm and fanaticism, there is a spiritual orgasm which inspires, inflames, and attracts men, and gives them life and potency, whether for good or for ill, without which zeal would soon die out, and the energy of progression cease. Effects can only equal their causes, and mere enthusiasm and fanaticism are not causes adequate to the vast results of Mormonism. They are temporary and evanescent impulses; the career of Mormonism is something strong and permanent. That which acts widely and lastingly on men's spirits must be spirit, and nothing short of it. That it is not altogether a pure spirit, may render it the more efficacious with impure human nature; and, probably, no small part of the success of this Mormon manifestation is, that it has much of the Christian truth mixed with an enticing spice of demonry.

Amongst the innumerable mediums who have arisen in

America, besides those trance and lecture mediums already referred to, the three most remarkable, or most familiar on this side of the Atlantic, are Daniel Dunglas Home, Andrew Davis Jackson, and Thomas L. Harris. All these are perfectly distinct in the character of their mediumship, and in the field of their spiritual missions. Mr. Home is an exhibitor of what are called physical phenomena, but which are spiritual agencies acting on matter. Through him raps have been given and communications made from deceased friends; tables have been raised into the air, or have moved themselves, as it were, from one place to another in the apartment; his hand has been seized by spirit influence, and rapid communications written out of a surprising character to those to whom they were addressed. Spirit hands have appeared, which have been seen, felt, and recognised frequently by persons present or those of deceased friends; bells have been lifted up and rung about a room; persons in their chairs have been suddenly transported from one end of a room to another; he himself has been frequently lifted up and carried, floating, as it were, through a room near the ceiling. Numbers of such facts are recorded in the 'British Spiritual Telegraph,' and the 'Spiritual Magazine,' as well as in the 'Cornhill Magazine,' with the names and testimonies of well-known witnesses. Such manifestations have been made in very many of the houses of our leading nobility, cabinet ministers, and gentry, in the palaces of nearly half the principal monarchs in Europe. I myself have been witness to many of these phenomena through Mr. Home. The fact that the English press has made a great outcry against the truth of these statements is no proof that they did not take place, but only of the astounding ignorance of the press that all history abounds with such facts; that in all times they have been familiar phenomena, attested by the most celebrated men; and that for the last fifteen years they have been so common in America, that they have convinced 3,000,000 of people. In America, all these phenomena have displayed themselves in far greater force than here.

Mr. Home's mission seems to have been to go forth and do the preliminary work of restoring faith by the performance of these outward marvels. Till that foundation was laid there could be no faith in higher and more psychical efforts. He was the herald of more interior truths. By a remarkable dispensation, like the apostles of old, he was taken from the class which had no power in itself, that all the power might be seen to come from on high. He was, though of old and aristocratic descent, from the Homes of Scotland, a poor Scotch adopted boy in America. Whilst quite a child, the spiritual power manifested itself in him to his own terror and annoyance. Raps came around him on the table or desk where he sat, on the chairs, or walls of the room. The furniture moved about and was attracted towards him. His aunt, with whom he lived, in consternation at the phenomena, and deeming him possessed, sent for three clergymen to exorcise the spirit; but as they could not do it, she threw his Sunday suit and linen in a bundle out of the chamber window, and pushed him out of doors. Thus was Daniel Dunglas Home, at the age, I believe, of eighteen, or thereabout, thrust a homeless youth into a world without friends. But the power that was upon him raised him friends, and sent him forth to be the planter of Spiritualism all over Europe. By circumstances that no man could have devised, he became the guest of the Emperor of the French, of the King of Holland, of the Czar of Russia, and of many lesser princes. The narrative of these events is to be found in numerous articles in newspapers, and in the Spiritual Journals of America, France, and England. Mr. Home returned from this unpremeditated missionary tour amongst principalities and powers, endowed with competence, and loaded with testimonies of the thanks and approbation of emperors, kings, and queens. At the Tuileries on one occasion, when the emperor, empress, a distinguished lady, and himself only were sitting at a table, a hand appeared, took up a pen and wrote, in a strong and well-known character, the word NAPOLEON. The hand was then successively presented to the several personages of the party to kiss.

It is not my business here to detail the long and well-substantiated series of the supernatural circumstances attending Mr. Home's career. They would form a volume of themselves, and, I hear, that it is Mr. Home's intention himself to record them. My concern only is to note his place in the history of spiritualism, as the herald of a coming restoration of faith in the indissoluble union of the natural and supernatural, of disembodied and embodied spirits, which Protestantism, in what the Rev. John Henry Newman calls its 'dreary development,' has for a time destroyed. Mr. Home has not assumed any other character than the foundation layer. He has not pretended to enunciation of merely spiritual views. He has not come forth as the prophet, but only as the seer. And his work has not been the less important or less valuable. Without the foundation stone, there can be no building. Without faith, promulgation of sublime and spiritual truths would fall dead, upon dead souls. They would be like the rays of the sun not falling on the solid and respondent earth, but on the barren vacuity. In vain would Jacob's ladder have invited the angels, who issue from temporary bodies to climb it to heaven, had not its foot been set upon the earth. Men sunk in their spiritual condition to the earth, must have manifestations of the earth first to awake them. For this reason the much-despised and ridiculed physical manifestations have come first, as the *only* ones adapted to the degraded physical status of men, many of them at the same time imagining themselves peculiarly enlightened and refined. It was truly said by Abraham to Dives that it was useless sending *him to his brothers*, because, they, doubtless, were in a condition in which one rising from the dead would have been to them no fitting or effective message. A wooden chair dancing, or a money-table lifting itself up before their sordid eyes, would have spoken much more intelligible things.

The office of Mr. Home has been the first great and necessary office of awakenment; as the watchman crying the approaching hour of the morning of recompleted man, he has done much, and there remains much yet to do.

But perhaps nothing connected with Mr. Home has given more profound evidence of the truth and tendencies of the consoling and divine effects of spiritualism, than the circumstances attending the decease of his most interesting wife. Mrs. Home, who was a Russian lady of high family, died at the age of only twenty-two. From the moment that it was announced to her that her complaint, consumption, was past cure, she exhibited no alarm or regret at the prospect of death. She had learned, by conviction of the truth of the views of her husband, that death was only apparent. She had long been in daily communication with the spirits of her departed friends; and the life about to open before her was certain, and beautiful beyond conception. Moreover, the Greek Church, in which she had been educated, has always recognised the Saviour less as the Crucified than as the Arisen, the triumphant over suffering and death; and her faith and feeling were in glad accordance with it. The Bishop of Perigeux, in France, near which place she died, and who administered to her the last sacrament, remarked that 'though he had been present at many a death-bed for heaven, he had never seen one equal to hers.' Can the end of any genuine Christian spiritualist be otherwise?

The office of Andrew Jackson Davis, the next typal man, has been different. It has been that of the seer and the scribe. Mr. Home's province was not to write but to act: Mr. Davis's has been to enter more spiritually into the spirit-world, and to write and publish what has been revealed to him. Mr. Davis has not only made known his interior revelations, but has written his own life under the name of 'The Magic Staff.' Like Mr. Home, Davis has been taken from the class of naked humanity; from that of human beings standing isolated in their bare human nature, unsupported, unrecommended by the adventitious circumstances of education, wealth, or connection. The work he had to do was to be conspicuously the work of his Maker, and developing itself from the faculties and inspirations of invisible spirit. His toils and endowments were from the great storehouse of the soul-world, and not from the manufactories, schools, or coffers of men.

Andrew Jackson Davis was born in 1826, in Blooming Grove, Orange County, New York State. He was one of six children of a very poor village weaver and cobbler. Both his parents were illiterate, but from his mother he seems to have inherited the clairvoyant faculty. He received only five months' schooling at the village school, and it was found impossible to teach him anything there.

Afterwards he was, as a boy, employed successively in a flour-mill, a shop, and on a farm. During his solitary hours in the fields he saw visions and heard voices. His parents removed to Poughkeepsie, and he was apprenticed to a shoemaker. He then became the clairvoyant of a mesmeric lecturer, and in this situation excited wonder by the revelations he made, and acquired the name of the Poughkeepsie Seer. This was in 1843, five years before the Rochester knockings were announced. In his clairvoyant state Davis not only declared that the power of seeing into and healing diseases was given; but he prescribed for scores who came most successfully, stating their symptoms in a manner that surprised the patients and equally so several accomplished physicians who attended the *séances*. In his 'Harmonia' he has described the wonderful scenes opened up to him in this condition. His clairvoyance was advanced into clairscience. He beheld all the essential natures of things; saw the interior of men and animals as perfectly as their exterior; and described them in language so correct that the most able technologists could not surpass him. He pointed out the proper remedies for all the complaints, and the shops where they were to be obtained. The life of all nature appeared laid before him; and he saw the metals in the earth like living flames, and lights and flames emanating from every portion of the living structure of men and animals. The most distant regions and their various productions were present before him. Everything appeared to him, as to all clairvoyants, clothed with its peculiar atmosphere; not only living forms, but every grain of salt or sand, the minutest bones and tendrils, mineral and earthy subtances, had this coloured atmosphere. As George Fox and Swedenborg before him, he declared that the whole of creation was opened to him; that he saw the names of all things in their natures, as Adam saw them. He saw how every animal represented some one or more qualities of men and their vices or virtues, just as Fox and Swedenborg had asserted, and he gave even Greek and Latin names to things, whilst in his ordinary state he could not even write or speak decent English. These facts are attested by eminent physicians whose names have been published by themselves.

In this state he had his vision of 'The Magic Staff,' as it were, a rod of gold which he was told to take, to try and walk with, leaning on it, and believing on it; and on the staff was written his life's motto, ' *Under all circumstances keep an even mind.*' On this staff, he tells us, he has continued to lean.

In 1845 he delivered 157 lectures in New York whilst in the clairvoyant state. These went to give a new Philosophy of the Universe, and were published in a volume called 'Nature's Divine Revelations,' amounting to 800 pages. Edgar A. Poe and Professor Bush were amongst his wondering hearers, and the latter has attested that those parts of the lectures which he heard were faithfully transferred to the book. Since then Mr. Davis has been a very voluminous writer, as his 'Great Harmonia' in 5 volumes, ' The Philosophy of Special Providence,' ' The Philosophy of Spiritual Intercourse,' ' The Penetralia,' ' The Present Age and Inner Life,' and ' The Magic Staff' testify. Besides this he edits the 'Herald of Progress.' Mr. Coleman's account of him represents him as a man of substantial outward as well as inward developement. ' I was,' he says, ' agreeably surprised to find him bright, active, and solidly intelligent, with nothing of the dreamy mystic about him. His personal appearance is extremely prepossessing, with a massive and most intellectually formed forehead, prominent nose, long black hair, and profusely flowing beard.' He told Mr. Coleman that he spends one half of his time in his garden, the other half in his study, and visits his office in the city only one day in the week, when he sees all sorts of enquirers, and still prescribes spiritually and gratuitously.

One of the characteristics of Mr. Davis's spiritualism is, that it is not Christian, but simply theistic. This, no doubt, belongs to his place in the progressive order of developement. He is in the hands of pagan or rather pantheistic spirits, and represents the ancient philosophic paganism. Mr. Home represents the earlier, primitive, and patriarchal cycle where outward miracles appeared as a natural portion of life. This may have for its object to attract and reintroduce to spiritual relations those great masses of society which the negation of Protestantism, and the intense selfishness of nominal Christians, have driven far away from Christianity, and made it but another name for priestcraft and masked ambition. Though to us it may be an unsatisfactory, to others, drawn by negative religion into the Cimmeria of scepticism, it may be a reconciling gradation. And accordingly out of the sphere of Davis was developed Harris, who step by step has ascended into the highest region of Christian spiritualism.

We find that Mr. Harris, wonderfully attracted by the 'Divine Revelations of Nature' of Davis, became one of his most enthusiastic disciples. But that was not the place where he was to stay. The Christian must develope out of the pagan cycle. In his earlier spiritual inspirations Harris became a poetic medium, and dictated whole epics, under the supposed influence of Byron, Shelley, Keats, Pollok, &c. Whoever were the poetic spirits who infused those poems, they are specimens of poetry of the highest order. Speaking of the 'Lyric of the Golden Age,' Mr. Brittan, the publisher, says, and not more eulogistically than justly, 'This lyric has scarcely less than Miltonic grandeur. The descriptive parts are wonderful as illustrations of the compass of our language. It would severely tax the capabilities of the most gifted mind to coin its phraseology alone, which, however, is neither strained nor far-fetched, but natural, flowing, and melodious as a valley brook.'

But the instantaneous manner in which these poems—a whole volume of 300 or 400 pages at a time — were thrown off is still more amazing than their high merit itself. Mr. Brittan tells us that the 'Lyric of the Golden Age' (381 pages) was dictated by Harris, and written down by Mr. Brittan in *ninety-four* hours. In a similar manner was produced the 'Lyric of the Morning Land,' and other volumes. In the production of poetry we know no similar achievements. But the progress of Harris into an inspirational oratory is still more surprising. He claims, by opening up his interior being, to receive influx of divine intuition in such abundance and power as to throw off under its influence the most astonishing strains of eloquence. This receptive and communicative power he attributes to an internal spiritual breathing corresponding to the outer natural breathing. As the bodily lungs imbibe and respire air, so, he contends, the spiritual lungs inspire and respire the divine aura, refluent with the highest thought, and purest sentiment, and that without any labour or trial of brain. Swedenborg teaches the same mystery, and Catholics also of devotional temperament.

Görres, in his 'Christliche Mystik,' asserts that this 'vital breathing,' however, descends into the human being through the crown of the head, and reissues by that, and is in intimate connection with the rays and circlets of light seen on the heads of saints (vol. ii. p. 330, 'Innere Begründung der Lichterscheinungen'). Whatever be the process, those who heard Mr. Harris during his visit to this country in 1860 had abundant proofs of the magnificent results. His extempore sermons were the only perfect realisation of my conceptions of eloquence; at once full, unforced, outgushing, unstinted, and absorbing. They were triumphant embodiments of sublime poetry, and a stern, unsparing, yet loving and burning theology. Never since the days of Fox were the disguises of modern society so unflinchingly rent away, and the awful distance betwixt real Christianity and its present counterfeit made so startlingly apparent. That the preacher was also the prophet was most clearly proclaimed by his suddenly hastening home, declaring that it was revealed to him that 'the nethermost hells were let loose in America.' This was before the public breach betwixt North and South had taken place; but it soon followed, only too deeply to demonstrate the truth of the spiritual intimation.

In these three typal mediums have been designated the three stages of Spiritualism:—the patriarchal or preparatory, the Pagan, and the Christian. In the general character of American Spiritualism has been displayed, in equally unmistakable features, the previous social and spiritual condition of that country. Those who thought that a dispensation from the invisible world should be all of a divine nature have been horrified to perceive that it partook largely of an opposite nature, the demoniac. That was an expectation out of nature itself, contrary to the world's history, in which the evil has ever come in hot haste on the heels of the good. Never, in any age of the world, did demon activity abound so much as at the Christian advent. It is a trite truism, that where God pours out His Spirit most abundantly, it is next abundantly met by the blasts of hell. American Spiritualism, therefore, though it has shown divine features, and produced deep and serious Christian effects, bringing back large numbers from atheism and deism to Christianity, has also largely shown features of a lower and more repulsive kind. And this must inevitably have resulted from the condition of the churches there previous to this avatara, as described by both American and European travellers. The curse of slavery had entered into the deepest vitals of the moral life of the country, North as well as South.

An English traveller, Mr. W. Robson, of Warrington, four or five years ago, writing to the Boston 'Liberator,' said—'In England, there is a kind of somnambulic life in the churches, mistaken by long habits of thought for health and vigour; but, with you, in America, it is the foul life of the charnel-house, the loathing rottenness of corruption, that is mistaken for the same thing. With us, there is a general formalistic acknowledgement of the truth, and in the low vegetating kind of life found in the churches there is not so much visible Satanic and diabolical that you can take up and shake in their faces, to arouse and alarm them: but here the very brotherhood of man is denied and scouted, the divine truth lying at the basis of a God-derived humanity, and of the necessity of Christian salvation rejected with scorn.' As the Church of England is responsible for the war-spirit which prevails, having hallowed it by its Te Deums, fasts, and thanksgivings, so the churches in America are responsible for the enslavement of four millions of the African race. Dr. Channing says, 'Slavery could not exist an hour, were it not supported by the American churches!' Another writer says, 'Eight hundred ministers in the South are slaveholders. The number of slaves held by church members is incredible, and it is a fact, that out of 20,000 clergymen, North and South, there are not a score consistent advocates of freedom. It is literally a church of dumb dogs that dare not bark. This terrible conspiracy against humanity will appear more plainly by a reference to the leading organisations of orthodox theology. The American Tract Society is the wealthiest society in America, with an annual income of 400,000 dollars, an army of 500 men, 300 of whom labour in the Southern and South-Western States, holding 14,000 prayer-meetings annually, distributing millions of tracts and periodicals, denouncing zealously the sins of dancing, Sabbath breaking, sleeping in church, novel reading; but it has never, during the thirty-three years of its existence, uttered a word, or published a line, against the oppression, injustice, robbery, and villany practised on the negro. They have made it heresy to deny the doctrine of the Trinity; total depravity, endless misery, for all who do not recognise their theology; but no heresy to sell little children for gain, to nullify the marriage relation, to make merchandise of the image of Christ.

'The American Sunday School Union, an organisation for supplying Sunday Schools with religious books, with large resources, never give the slightest testimony against this sum of all villanies. On one occasion, having reprinted an English tract, "The Life of Joseph," a little girl asked a school teacher what was the difference between selling Joseph and selling Cato or Pompey. The alarm was given, and the book was suppressed, and afterwards reprinted without the selling scene!

'Within a stone's throw of where I am writing,' says this author, 'there is a Congregational Southern State Library, containing 2,000 volumes, but not a volume against oppression. The American Bible Society has lent its influence to build up the slave power by twice refusing a donation of 5,000 dollars, presented to them by the American Anti-Slavery Society, on condition that, in the distribution of the Bible, slaves should be included. The Board of Foreign Missions, the Methodist Book and Sunday School Unions, the Presbyterian and Episcopalian publishing houses, all are steeped in the same blinking sin of crouching before slavery, and permit their church members to hold slaves.'

In such a state of society, of moral cowardice and glaring hypocrisy, the spirits of evil were certain to seize on these rotten parts, and revel in them. Hence, on the outburst of Spiritualism, such members, sunk in this lowest depth of spiritual corruption, were instantly possessed by spirits of like tone. Hence, in the ranks of spiritualism and spirit mediums, there appeared such persons, who stood forth mere atheists, deists, pagans, of no creed but infidelity. Like attracts like; and spirits of their stamp claimed kindred with those, enveloped them, and taught them the doctrines of the hells, or of the dubious and intermediate regions. As the Shaker W. F. Evans said —' These are brought to judgement, for their inner life was made manifest by the spirits who claimed them and indoctrinated them.' This was inevitable, for they who hoped that all teaching from the invisible world would be true, were as ignorant of the real condition of the spirit world, as they who, seeing evil, denounced *all* as evil. As the whole of this history has shown, the good and the evil issue equally from the spirit world, and all must make their election. As in Christianity, so in Spiritualism, the battle of heaven and hell is for ever going on. Woe to those who ally themselves to the one!—well for those who, by prayer and faith, seek the support and teaching of the other, that is, of the Holy Spirit and its ministering angels.

In America, the curse of slavery—which thus fearfully corrupted the churches, and sent its taint into the innermost vitals of society—has brought its terrible retribution in this present fratricidal war, fraught with its gigantic horrors. As Harris was warned, the nethermost hells are there broken loose in truth, and there can be little question that the spirits who infested many of the regions of American Spiritualism, promulgating contempt of Christianity, and emitting the fœtid steams of a low and poisonous vulgarity, which have filled many of the American spiritual journals, are the same who are now rioting in the blood of brothers, and festering the woods of the South with the mutilated relics of their victims.

On the other hand, a large portion of the American spiritualists, like Hare and Edmonds, Harris, Owen, Newton, and others, have made a noble stand for Christianity, truth, and purity, and the purifying effects of the better Spiritualism are becoming more visible. Judge Edmonds tells us that to a man the American spiritualists have declared against the monster crime of slavery; Hare long ago said that Spiritualism there had converted 25,000 infidels; and the writer whom I have been quoting says: ' Spiritualism has banished scepticism and infidelity from the minds of thousands, comforted the mourner with angelic consolations, lifted up the unfortunate, the outcast, the inebriate, taking away the sting of death, which has kept mankind under perpetual bondage through fear—so that death is now, to its million believers,

> The kind and gentle servant who unlocks,
> With noiseless hand, life's flower-encircled door,
> To show us those we loved.'

And there can be no doubt that this purifying and Christianising operation is the great mission of Spiritualism under Providence, though to the secularised and the paganised mind, hardened into mere conventional churchism, bowing only to the god of this world, it may come with searching, withering fires, with a horror of great darkness, and with shakings of the earth and its heaven-defiant institutions.

CHAPTER XI.

SPIRITUALISM IN ENGLAND.

Then they cried with a loud voice, and stopped their ears.
Acts vii. 57.

It is amusing to see how the arguments and positions on both sides, which were all gone over by us ten or twelve years ago, are now reproduced with you, and with so strong a resemblance, that one might almost talk of plagiarism.—JUDGE EDMONDS *of New York, in a letter, October* 12, 1861, *on the Spiritualistic Discussions in England.*

SPIRITUALISM in England, in its more physical phase, is but a reflection and a weaker reproduction of Spiritualism in America. This is so very much the case, that had it not further developements of its own, it would be sufficient simply to note the fact, and pass on. All that has occurred in regard to rapping and gaining intelligence by the alphabet, to the lifting and moving of tables, chairs, and other articles of furniture, to the floating of persons, the appearance of spirit-hands, and even spirit forms, to the ringing of bells and playing on instruments, and the like phenomena, have, on the whole, been more powerfully exhibited in America than here. We have seen tables often enough lifted by invisible power from the floor; seen them give answers to questions by rising and sinking in the air; we have seen them in the air keep time by their movements to a tune playing on a piano; seen them slide about the floor of a room, laying themselves down when touched, and refusing to do anything for a fortnight together, but thus to creep about the floor whenever touched. We have heard bells ring in the air, and seen them thus ringing move about a room; seen flowers broken from plants, and carried to different persons, without any visible hand; seen musical instruments play correct airs apparently of themselves, and even rise up, place themselves on a person's head, and there, just over it, but not touching it, play out a well-known air in fine style. We have heard remarkable predictions given through mediums, and which have come literally to pass; heard wonderful descriptions of scenes in the invisible world made by persons in clairvoyant trance, which would require the highest imaginative genius to invent or embody in words; have seen writing done by pencils laid on paper in the middle of the floor, not within reach of any person present, and innumerable such things; but all these have been done more powerfully and perfectly, in hundreds and thousands of cases, through a course of fifteen or sixteen years previously in America. I believe no person has seen in England a large table, with six full-grown persons upon it, float through a room without touching the floor; yet such things have been done repeatedly in America. With the exception of the smashing to pieces of the table of Dr. —— at a lunatic asylum in Kent, a table made to resist the efforts of maniacs, and which had resisted them all successfully, I know of no physical achievement of the spirits in England equal to those common in America, and even there it was through the mediumship of Mr. Squire, an American. See the 'Spiritual Magazine,' vol. i. p. 161, for Dr. ——'s account of this interesting case, the doctor to that time having been a violent opponent of and disbeliever in these phenomena.

All the great physical mediums have been Americans, or from America. Mrs. Hayden in 1852 was, I believe, the first who introduced the phenomena in England, then Mr. Home in 1855, and Mr. Squire in 1859. Besides these there have been visits made by Dr. Randolph, a trance-medium; Dr. Redman; Mr. Harris, poetic, preaching, and trance-medium, and some others, one or two of whom have been real mediums, but from the wrong side of Spiritualism.

Spiritualism, therefore, in its latest developement in England, came clearly from America, but has not here, even in its American missionaries, produced physical effects by any means equal to those which, by all attestations, have been common in the United States. Perhaps the destruction of Dr. R——'s table, through Mr. Squire, in February 1860, is the nearest approach to the vigour of American theurgy. In the English atmosphere, and the English mind, the spiritual agency has met with a more resistant principle than in the New World. Probably our denser atmosphere, less electrical and magnetic in its character, and our different telluric conditions, are less favourable to the transmission of spiritual impressions, but more probably the chief obstruction lies in the indurated and materialised tone of the English mind. The Americans are conspicuously a more nervous and excitable people than we are. They have grown up rapidly under new climactic influences, new blending of blood and international indiosyncracies. They have shown a singular genius for mechanical inventions, and an audacity approaching to rashness in inaugurating new social schemes, new religious organisations, and vast plans of political dominion. Their minds, like their institutions, have shot up with a rapidity of growth resembling that of tropical jungles, and have, in consequence, greater openness and receptivity.

As for us, for the last two centuries, we have been undergoing a double process of induration. Trade, and Protestant abjuration of spiritual relations, have been mutually doing the work of internal petrifaction and ossification upon us. State Churchism—sapping the vitality of our consciousness, dulling our religious sensibility, and substituting secular ambition and hierarchic pride for the pure love of Christ and of souls—has handed us over, the only too willing victims of commercial cupidity. These, insensibly but rapidly actuated by the wonderful progress of physical science, colonial expansion, manufacturing immensity and their confluent streams of wealth, luxury, and social aspiration, and our literature and theology saturated with foreign importations of infidel and semi-infidel philosophy, have produced a condition of general mind and opinion more destructive to a healthy faith than any period of the world, the most pagan or most corrupt, ever saw. It is notorious that foreign churches see and feel in Anglicism a hard, unspiritual, domineering, and worldly tone, which strikes them with astonishment.

For these causes the English press and pulpit have merely repeated the opposition to Spiritualism which America had already shown, but with additional pugnacity, and with an utter absence of originality. They recommenced the attack, just terminated in America after a ten years' combat, as if it had sprung up under their eyes a totally new phenomenon. That it had been familiar to all ages and nations; that in those ages and nations just the greatest men and greatest minds had demonstrated its reality; that the greatest historians and philosophers had described all its forms and settled all its diagnoses; that the Bible, the New Testament, the Church, at every period and in every country, had overflowed with it; and that in Germany, for the last hundred years, it had forced itself on the attention and the conviction of many of its chief philosophers, had passed almost unnoticed in America. But still more extraordinary was it to see, that when, besides all this, in America every argument against it had been exhausted in ten years of conflict, and when three millions of converts had been the imposing result, the whole was lost on the English educated public as though it had never been. Our literary men and clergy appeared to have been profoundly asleep during this long and fiery battle, and when the turn came to them, only started up, and gathering the abandoned weapons of American journals, turned over again all the old arguments, without adding a single new one. Judge Edmonds, in the motto to this chapter, has recorded the astonishment of America at the threadbare English imitation of the attack in the United States.

Professor Hare said, long ago, whilst looking on the

unequal strife in America itself—'The wisest man who speaks in ignorance speaks foolishly to the ears of those who perceive his ignorance.' In this ridiculous light must our newspaper and periodical writers have appeared to the people of America, who had for ten years fought the same battle, and exhausted the whole quiver of objections. What figures must our Faradays and Brewsters have cut in the eyes of a whole population familiar with the facts they were denying as with their daily food. The particulars of the opposition of these eminent men I pass over, as they will shortly be given by Mr. Home in a memoir of himself.

Another remarkable feature of this English onslaught on Spiritualism has been, that where the opponents did not borrow American worn-out arguments, they pillaged those which the old Pagan Romans had hurled at Christianity. When they called spiritualists impostors and tricksters, all well-read people saw that they were stealing the weapons of Julian the Apostate, who called St. Paul τὸν πάντας πανταχοῦ τοὺς πώποτε γόητας καὶ ἀπατεῶνας ὑπερβαλλόμενον Παῦλον (a fellow who outwent every other, as a deceiver, by tricks which he performed through magic, Apud Cyril l. 3). When they taunted spiritualists with the stupidity of their belief, they only imitated Julian again, who used to taunt the Christians with having stupidly elevated the son of a carpenter into a God. When they wanted terms of ridicule, they went to Tertullian for raillery used by the Pagans against the Christian faith. 'And here they will say, "And who is this Christ of yours, with his tale of wonders? Is he a man of common condition? Is he a magician? Was he stolen away from his crucifixion? From the sepulchre by his disciples? Is he now in hell? Is he not in heaven? And to come quickly from thence also with a quaking of the whole universe, with a shuddering of the world, and the wailing of all men, save the Christians, as the Power of God, and the Spirit of God, and the Word, and the Wisdom, and the Reason, and the Son of God?"'

The 'Evangelical Quarterly Review' could not accept Spirit-

ualism because it was 'too *undignified* for a spiritual revelation of God.' The remark was simply stolen from Lactantius, who quotes it as used against Christianity. In the 4th b., 22nd c. of that father's 'Divine Institutions,' on 'True Wisdom and Religion,' we have the very words:—
'Negant fieri potuisse, ut natura immortali quidquid decederet. Negant denique *Deo dignum*, ut homo fieri vellet, seque infirmitate carnis oneraret, ut passionibus, ut dolori, ut morti scipsum subjiceret, quasi non facile illi esset, ut citra corporis imbecillitatem se hominibus ostenderet, eosque justitiam doceret (si quidem id volebat) majore auctoritate, ut professi Dei,' &c. 'They deny it to be possible for an immortal to put off his immortal nature. They deny it *to be worthy of God* to become man, and to load Himself with the infirmity of the flesh, and subject Himself to its passions, its misery, and its death. As though it had not been easy to Him, without the frailty of the body, to show Himself to men, and to teach them righteousness, if He wished it, with greater authority as God avowed.' The Pagans go on to argue, that God would have given thus a higher prestige to celestial precepts, and could have' enforced them by divine power. Why, then, did He not come, as God, to teach them? Why should He come in so humble and imbecile a form that He should be despised by men, and subjected to punishment? Why should He expose Himself to violence from miserable mortals? Why not repel the hands of men by His power, or escape them by His divinity?

How frequently have we had to listen to this class of borrowed arguments. Why, said the learned heathen, did not God come as God? Why, say the anti-spiritualists now, do not His angels come openly as angels? Why do they confine themselves to modes of communication as strange to the wise now, as Christ's mode of coming was to the wise then?

And all this time, in England, thousands and tens of thousands were daily sitting down in their families and circles of intimate friends, and were quietly, and as people of common sense, successfully testing those angels under their own mode of advent, and finding them real. And both in America and here, as well as in most of the continental nations, this private mode has been the great mode of enquiry and convincement. Not one man in a hundred has ever seen a *public* medium. Public mediums have, in reality, only inaugurated the movement : it has been, of necessity, carried on by private and family practice. In this domestic prosecution of Spiritualism, equally inaccessible to the vulgar sorcerer and the interested impostor—where every person was desirous only of truth, and many of them of deep religious truth—the second stage of spiritual developement, the more interior and intellectual, has been reached by a very large community. For there is, indeed, a very large section of society who are sick of mere empty profession, or still more disgusted with the dreary cheat of scepticism, and who have been long yearning for some revelation of the immorta hopes of earlier years in some substantial and unmistakable form. They have found this in the daily visits of their departed friends, coming to them with all their old identities of soul, of taste, or common memory of glad or trusting incidents, of announcements of Christian truth, and of God's promised felicity. They have listened again and again to the words of their beloved ones, bidding them take courage, for there was no death, no place for darkness or death ; but that around them walked their so-called departed, ready to aid them and comfort them in their earth's pilgrimage, and to receive them to immediate and far more glorious existence.

That great cry which has, at one time or other, ascended from the universal human heart, for positive and personal assurance of the reality of the Christian promises, and the reunion of beloved friends, had been going up from theirs; and they had felt how comparatively small is the value of all the evidences given to others, and especially to the ancient world, weighed against one such evidence *to themselves.* All human souls have felt this ; all have cried, ' How long, O Lord, wilt Thou continue to me a God who hidest Thyself?'

Mrs. Crawford, in the 'Metropolitan Magazine,' in 1836, tells us that the then Lord Chedworth was a man who suffered deeply from doubts of the existence of the soul in another world; and that he had a friend, very dear to him, as sceptical as himself. Whilst one morning relating to his niece, Miss Wright, at breakfast, that his friend appeared to him the night before, exactly as he appeared in life, and told him he died that night at eight o'clock, and that there *was* another world, and a righteous God who judgeth all—and whilst Miss Wright was ridiculing the idea of the apparition—a groom rode up the avenue bringing a letter announcing the fact of his friend's sudden death at the time stated by the spirit. Mrs. Crawford adds, 'The effect it had upon the mind of Lord Chedworth was as happy as it was permanent; all his doubts were at once removed, and for ever.'

To such a certainty, and comfort to a single mind tortured with doubts, what is the value of the finest sceptical writing that ever was written?

We are told that the Rev. J. H. Tuttle, pastor of a leading universal church in America, on receiving convincing messages from deceased relations, exclaimed, 'What a glorious thing it is to *know* that we are to live on through eternity.' He had long preached this doctrine to his people, backing it by many splendid arguments from Scripture and reason, but now he *knew* it, and felt it a very different thing. Zschokke, on his father's death, implored him on his knees, and in an agony of tears, to reappear to him. Shelley, the poet, in his 'Hymn to Intellectual Beauty,' one of his very earliest compositions, tells us that he wandered through churches and ruins to implore a ghost to appear to him, but in vain:—

> While yet a boy I sought for ghosts, and sped
> Through many a listening chamber, cave and ruin,
> And starlight wood, with fearful steps pursuing
> Hopes of high talk with the departed dead.
> I called on poisonous names with which our youth is fed:
> I was not heard: I saw them not.

But though Shelley could meet with no ghost then, he did

in after life, and the first that we hear of seemed sent to answer his youthful enquiries: —

'One night,' says Lady Shelley, in her 'Memorials of Shelley,' 'loud cries were heard issuing from the saloon. The Williamses rushed out of their room in alarm. Mrs. Shelley also endeavoured to reach the spot, but fainted at the door. Entering the room, the Williamses found Shelley staring horribly in the air, and evidently in a trance. They waked him, and he related that a figure wrapped in a mantle came to his bedside and beckoned him; he followed it into the saloon, when it lifted the hood of its mantle, ejaculated " *Siete sodisfatto ?* "—are you satisfied? and vanished.'

Again: — 'After tea,' says Mr. Williams in his Diary, 'while walking with Shelley on the terrace, and observing the effect of moonlight on the waters, he complained of being unusually nervous, and stopping short, he grasped me violently by the hand, and stared steadfastly on the white surf that broke upon the beach under our feet. Observing him sensibly affected, I demanded if he were in pain; but he only answered, " There it is again! there! " He recovered after some time, and declared that he saw, as plainly as he then saw me, a naked child—Allegra, who had recently died —rise from the sea, and clasp its hands, as if in joy smiling at him.'

Lord Byron also, in his letters to John Murray, says that, a few days before Shelley's tragic end, he and others distinctly saw him walk into a wood, though they knew that he was at the time several miles away.

We find the same yearning breaking forth from the hearts of pious bishops like Heber, men set to comfort others with the assurances of the future. 'I know not,' he says, 'indeed, who can know? whether the spirits of the just are ever permitted to hover over those whom they loved most tenderly; but if such permission be given—and who can say it is impossible?—then it must greatly diminish the painful sense of separation which even the souls of the righteous may be supposed to feel.' But with what more impetuous agony this cry for spiritual evidence burst from the vehement soul of Burns:—' Can it be possible that, when I resign this frail feverish being, I shall find myself in conscious existence? When the last gasp of agony has announced that I am no more to those that knew me, and the few who loved me; when the cold, stiffened, unconscious, ghastly corse is resigned unto the earth, to be the prey of unsightly reptiles, and to become in time a trodden clod, shall I yet be warm in life, seeing and seen, enjoying and enjoyed? Ye venerable sages and holy flamens, is there probability in your conjectures, truth in your stories of another world beyond death, or are they all alike baseless visions, and fabricated fables? What a flattering idea is a world to come. Would to God I as firmly believed it, as I ardently wish it!'

And what should have prevented this divine and positive evidence visiting the soul of Burns, as it visited bards and prophets of old—in the still small voice of the Holy Spirit, soft as the whisper of a zephyr, but distinct and certain as a note of thunder, or in the voice or shape of some dear departed one—but the death-frost of a creed which had exiled all such visitations? While men were crying in despair for this natural aliment of the soul, for this higher communion necessary to the life of spirit as air is to the life of matter, the demon of infidelity was complacently harvesting them into his dreary garner.

The clever author of ' The Apocatastasis, or Progress Backwards,' an American book, says:—' To say nothing of older pantheistic theories and pantheistic men, as Spinoza, Hobbes, &c., or of the atheistic spawn of Germany, not without their influence, direct or indirect, now and here: have we not, in our own time and language, popular writers of highest talents, who with wide, deep, and insidious power, subvert the foundations of all proper human responsibility? For pantheism, and the " Eternal Laws," know or teach only the responsibility appropriate to animals. Widespread, and fearful to humanity in men, is this influence. Witness, as a single specimen of it, in " The Life" of poor

Sterling, a soul capable of the truest and fullest spiritual life and developement, perishing in the serpent folds of atheistic sophistry, like an unhappy beast in the embrace of the anaconda.'

It is in trampling underfoot this horrible vampire of the soul, Infidelity, in restoring the ruins of a godlike faith, by direct and daily repeated evidence, that Spiritualism in England has achieved hitherto its greatest triumph. Who shall express the consolation, the profound and assured peace and joy that it has spread around it, where the cold forms of churches, and the sounding brass and tinkling cymbals of materialised preachers, had failed? Quietly stealing on from fireside to fireside, without pretence, without parade, it has gone up from the middle ranks of life to the highest aristocratic regions, and down to the humblest abodes of working men. It has sat down with the sad and bewildered members of every insensate fraction of an orthodoxy, which rejected miracle in a blind obstinacy, and has sent them away rejoicing in the fall of Materialism, that reign, as Baron Guldenstubbe styles it, of Satan *par excellence*. Whilst men, wise in their own conceit, and too conceited to examine, were writing violent philippics against it, they saw and were satisfied. And in the train of this reaccepted power followed gifts full of interest, grace, and fresh assurance. In England, Spiritualism has been more generally received in a religious spirit than in America. It is rare to find any of its disciples pagans, as so many Americans have boasted themselves, so that at one time the American spiritualists separated themselves in Christian spiritualists and Not-Christian spiritualists. There have been a considerable number here who have pursued it more as an amusement than, as it is, a great and solemn agent for the overthrow of Infidelity; but the majority have fully perceived its more elevated and sacred nature. In the works and periodicals which have appeared in its advocacy, this nobler spirit has been almost universally conspicuous. With the best part of American spiritualism it has kept pace in its legitimate operations. Here, as there, it has brought back numbers of men from atheism, or from a condition little better or more comfortable. I speak this from actual knowledge of such cases.

Great numbers of English spiritualists have developed into writing and drawing mediums, and some of these have already reached an excellence far beyond anything in this department, as far as I can learn, yet witnessed in America. I may refer, in proof of this statement, to the water-colour drawings of Lady Ellis; to those of Mrs. William Wilkinson, which have been seen by many hundreds of persons connected with art and literature; and to the pencil drawings of my daughter, Mrs. Watts. Of my own little experience in this branch of spiritual art, I have already spoken. In musical mediumship, I have, in an earlier page, noted a very remarkable example.

We read in the spiritual journals of America of ladies who have been in the habit of seeing spirits as they see people, from childhood. This is fully confirmed by similar cases familiarly known to myself in this country. Two in particular, Mrs. N―― and Miss A――, are well known to a very wide circle, in which they have for years given such daily proofs of this faculty, that no fact is more thoroughly established. It was Mrs. N―― to whom the spirit of Captain Wheatcroft appeared in London the same evening that he appeared to his own wife at Cambridge, and informed her that he was killed that day before Lucknow, and that his body was not then buried. 'The thing that I wore,' he said, 'is not buried yet.' The whole case is related by Mr. Owen in his 'Footfalls.' The circumstance had been related by Mrs. N―― to myself, before Mr. Owen took up the matter. It will be seen, in Mr. Owen's narrative, that the return of the killed at the storming of Lucknow did not agree, in the date of the death of the captain, with that of the apparition. To both the ladies the apparition was on November 14, 1857; the return stated the death on the 15th. Had the return been correct, the spirit must have appeared the day before its departure. The solicitor to the captain's family communicated this discrepancy to the War Office, and requested that reference should be made to Lord Clyde as to the correctness of the date in this instance. This was done, and Lord Clyde returned answer that the date was correct — the death took place on the *fifteenth*. Here the ghost and the War Office were at variance, but a letter subsequently received from a brother officer proved the ghost to be right, and the War Office, in consequence, corrected its date. These ghosts, however visionary and unreal some people think them, can on occasion show themselves more exactly accurate than people in the body.

I could relate many equally curious proofs of the validity of Mrs. N——'s statements on this point. One may suffice. The first time that she was in my house, she said that she saw the spirit of a young man standing near one of the party. She described him so exactly, that we immediately recognised him. It was a person whom Mrs. N—— never had seen or heard of. No remark was made further, but on a subsequent visit, in order to test the matter, we produced a number of miniature portraits of our friends of past days, without at all referring to Mrs. N——'s former sight of the spirit. The moment she cast her eyes on one of the portraits, she put her finger on it, saying, 'That is the young man I saw here.' It was in truth the person she had described.

Miss A—— is also one of the ladies who saw the apparitions of Squire and Dame Children, at Ramhurst, in Kent, the particulars of which are also given by Mr. Owen in his 'Footfalls.' These particulars were also well known to me before Mr. Owen took up the subject, and discovered, by a visit to Ramhurst and to the British Museum, in consequence, facts regarding Squire Children and his family known only at Ramhurst through the apparitions, the memory of the family there having almost wholly died out. Amongst the particulars communicated to Miss A—— by Squire Children was the date of his death, which Mr. Owen, after much search in the MS. department of the British Museum, found to be perfectly correct.

Amongst the most remarkable spirit mediums of modern times is Elizabeth Squirrell, whose revelations took place before Spiritualism, in its present avatara in England, had taken place. Elizabeth Squirrell may be said to be the Seeress of Shottisham, as Mrs. Hauffe was the Seeress of Prevorst. There is a striking similarity in their cases. Both had their bodily frames so weakened by disease, and their nervous system so excited, that the spiritual life within predominated over the bodily life without; the communion with the spiritual world was opened up, and they became not only clairvoyant of what was around them, but prophetic of what was approaching. Both were maligned and charged with imposture, and both found some candid people who were ready to examine thoroughly into their cases, and thus became witnesses to the honesty of the accused, and to the extraordinary nature of their visitations. The main difference was that Madame Hauffe sank under her complaints; Elizabeth Squirrell has, I understand, in a great measure, recovered from hers.

Elizabeth Squirrell was born at Shottisham, in Suffolk, five miles from Woodbridge and thirteen from Ipswich, in 1838. Her father appears to have been in trade there, and was the son of the late Baptist minister of Sutton, a neighbouring village. At three years of age she fell into a severe illness, which probably laid the foundation of her future malady, though she recovered her health, and for several years used to walk three miles daily to school and back, six miles altogether. It appears to have been in her twelfth year that she was suddenly attacked with illness at school, and this attack grew more and more complicated for years. At first she experienced a weakness in the back, a severe pain and pressure on the head, then violent epileptic fits, spasmodic contractions, paralysis of the limbs, and eventually loss of power to swallow, lock-jaw, which continued twenty-one weeks, and finally she lost sight and hearing. Her sense of smell disappeared in the nose, but she could inhale odours through the mouth. All her senses, except feeling, were shut up, and she lay in a most enfeebled and suffering condition. Doctor after doctor was called in, who attributed her complaint to as many causes as there were doctors; ossification of the heart, water on the brain, a tumour, and so on. She was sent to the hospital at Ipswich, and returned worse; her case was declared hopeless.

It was soon noised abroad that this poor girl, when about fourteen or fifteen, had lost all power to swallow, and had lived without taking any nourishment whatever for twenty-five weeks. The thing was denied, though there are numerous cases of the kind on record, the celebrated Englebrecht's amongst them; there was a great rush of people to see the case, and a loud outcry of imposture succeeded. Both she and her parents were accused of being in complicity to deceive, for the purpose of obtaining money. Three separate committees were appointed of watchers. The second, on which there were several clergymen, imagined that they had discovered fraud, and broke up quarrelling amongst themselves, and setting abroad the most damaging reports. A third and still more rigorous watch of twelve persons was appointed, who reported, everyone signing his or her own statement, all most unequivocally asserting that no food could possibly have been taken during fourteen days' watch, night and day, the parents being excluded from the room. All declared their conviction that both parents and child were honest, conscientious people, and that Elizabeth herself was not only innocent of all deceit, but was a very sincerely religious and highly gifted girl. Various medical men of more liberal character visited her, and, after careful examination and enquiry, confirmed this opinion. Amongst these Dr. Johnson, of Umberslade, published a very interesting visit to her. Dr. Garth Wilkinson and Dr. Spencer T. Hall, both gentlemen well acquainted with such cases, gave decided opinions on the truth of her extraordinary condition. Some clergymen were equally fair, and amongst them the Rev. W. A. Norton of Alderton. But this did not prevent the Baptist Society at Stoke-Green, Ipswich, expelling both parents and daughter, because they asserted that Elizabeth had for more than a quarter of a year lived without taking sustenance; and still worse, because she asserted that she had seen angels and departed spirits.

In fact, the poor girl had become a thoroughly clairvoyant subject. She saw spirits about her, amongst them her guardian angel; and in her mesmeric sleep she saw her own internal condition, the seat and nature of her complaints, and could distinctly, in these sleeps, foretell the approach of greater illness, or of alleviation—when she should be able to swallow again, and when a return of her inability to swallow would occur. In her waking condition, she knew nothing whatever of what she had seen or said in her mesmeric sleep; and her attendants wisely did not communicate this to her, so that they could judge of her truthfulness and consistency. In her mesmeric sleeping, she spoke of her waking condition as of another person, as if two spirits occupied one body, one sleeping as the other awoke, and vice versâ. She always called her waking condition ' My waking,' and said, ' My waking is very ill—very ill indeed;' or ' My waking' will suffer so and so; but always added, ' It does not know of this, and don't you tell it, for it would distress it.' The attendants always found her prognostics occur to the letter, and exactly as to time.

My notice of this extraordinary case must necessarily be brief, but the whole account of it has been published by one of the watchers, and may be had of Simpkin and Marshall.

Mesmeric and homœopathic treatment eventually restored her. One of the most remarkable occurrences which took place during her illness was the ringing of a glass tumbler, which had been set on the table near her with flowers. This ringing first called her mother into the room, who supposed her daughter had struck it with something soft, but she denied it, and the mother watching it, soon heard it ring out again in the same musical manner. Many other persons then, from time to time, witnessed it, and they found that it always rung when they were conversing on spiritual and elevating subjects, as in confirmation of what was said. One person who went to pray by her heard it above fifty times, and generally when he was thus engaged, and declared that his emotions on hearing it were indescribable. On several occasions it rang in sharp notes when assistance was wanted, for Elizabeth was subject to faintings, and her mother running in on one occasion, found her in so insensible a condition, that she was convinced that without instant aid she would have died.

It was soon said that the sound came from a harmonica that she concealed in the bed, but it was amply proved that the ringing commenced many weeks before she obtained the harmonica, and above forty people hearing the glass ringing when this could not be the case. She herself well observes that no earthly advantage was to be gained by pretending that the glass thus supernaturally rung, as it was sure to be laughed at; but she adds, 'It has decided many an uncertain surmise, dispelled many a fear, and unmistakably announced the presence of some spiritual envoy.' And what in all this is so barbarously obscene and impious? Is it not written in the Old Testament, 'The angel of the Lord encampeth round about them that fear him?' And is it not written again in the New Testament, 'Are they not all ministering spirits, sent forth to minister?' &c.

One of the most satisfactory features of this case is the brightness and intelligence of this young sufferer of fifteen. With only a simple village education, she writes with a spirit, a vigour, a sound sense, that few persons possess at any time of life. Like the Seeress of Prevorst, she wrote a good deal of poetry, and in a very sweet and genuinely poetic vein. An eminent London surgeon, who went down to see her, says with much truth :—' I am quite of opinion that Elizabeth Squirrell possesses extraordinary genius for her years, and that all she says teems with so much good sense, good taste, and genuine piety, that all she utters deserves to be preserved. Her powers of sight and hearing being obliterated, of course she is desirous to hold communion with herself, and this constitutes a new state of existence.' He adds, ' It is most shameful that people should prejudice this case. I confess that I went down with one impression, and returned with another.'

But all were not so self-reliant or so charitable as this liberal medical man. The parents of Elizabeth were ruined in their trade, and compelled, from the persecuting spirit of those about them, to remove to Ipswich to endeavour to get a livelihood. It seems that Elizabeth has since been in London, seeking to support herself as a needlewoman: on enquiring after her, I understood that she was again gone down into the country. Similar cases of extreme clairvoyance abound, where the parties, when in the sleep, and with eyes blindfolded, could see everything around them, even to distant dwellings, and could read anything written at a considerable distance; but few cases have been so complete as that of Elizabeth Squirrell, who, in actual blindness, possessed this wonderful faculty of sight.

The literature of English Spiritualism already numbers several works of solid merit, and which may be studied by enquirers to great advantage. It is not necessary to do more than mention the titles of these works, which may be procured through any bookseller from the publishers in London. Mrs. Crowe's ' Night-side of Nature;' her translation of the ' Seeress of Prevorst,' and her subsequent work on Spiritualism itself, have been repeatedly referred to in this work, and strongly recommended to the reader. Her ' Night-side of Nature' is one of the best-reasoned works in the language on the subject. There is a little volume of Mr. Rymer's on Spiritualism, containing some of the earliest occurrences regarding it in England, as he was one of the first convinced. Mr. Andrew Leighton has edited a shilling edition of Adin Ballou's work on ' Spirit Manifestations,' and prefaced it with a very excellent introduction. Mr. Newton Crosland's ' New Theory of Apparitions,' and Mrs. Crosland's ' Light in the Valley,' should have a careful perusal. They are very important, and only came out too early, the subject then being almost wholly unknown, except by mere and absurd report. Mr. William Wilkinson's little volumes on 'Spirit Drawings,' and on the 'Revivals,' cannot be left unread by anyone who would thoroughly inform himself on these subjects. They are ably and philosophically written, and I would particularly recommend to the reader's attention the chapter in the latter on 'the Dynamics of Prayer.'

For some of the most extraordinary, in fact, the most extraordinary phenomena of recent spiritualism, the reader must go to Mr. Benjamin Coleman's 'Spiritualism in America,' being the report of what Mr. Coleman saw in a visit to the United States in 1861, made for the express purpose of examining into the facts and condition of spiritualism there. A little work called 'Angel Visits,' by Miss Helen Faucit, presents the reader with an individual's experience on the subject.

'The Confessions of a Truth Seeker' are full of knowledge of spiritual history, and the arguments of opponents are dealt with in a very felicitous manner. Mr. John Jones's 'Natural and Supernatural' is a storehouse of very curious knowledge on the subject. Mr. Dale Owen's 'Footfalls on the Boundary of Another World,' are too well known to need mention. Mr. Barkas, of Newcastle-on-Tyne, has lately added another work on the subject, of much interest. To those who would acquaint themselves with the facts and arguments of English spiritualism, I need only say that these are to be found in the 'Yorkshire and British Spiritual Telegraphs,' for several years, now discontinued, and the 'Spiritual Magazine,' in current publication. Most or all of these may be procured at Mr. Pitman's, 20 Paternoster Row.

And this is all that now seems necessary to say on English spiritualism. Making its way quietly but steadily—already more widely pervading the ranks of literature and science than many of its professors find it prudent to avow—already numbering many clergymen of one creed or another, who find it necessary to avoid martyrdom by approaching it as Nicodemus did Christ; the time is not far off when it will assume a more broad and open aspect. The ravages of infidelity with its many faces or rather masks, are becoming so fearful, and are showing themselves so rampantly in the very penetralia of the Established Church, that there must be a remedy, or the day of Christ's second advent may be declared at hand; for very soon there will be no faith left on earth, except in the Roman Catholic fold which yet needs vigorous purging, and in this the growing church of spiritualism, which opens its arms to the gospel in all its original investments of power, natural and supernatural.

Distinguished Churchmen seem more and more becoming sensible of this. I have already recorded remarkable words of the Bishop of London, uttered at a Young Men's Association Anniversary, and we find him again, in a sermon delivered in Westminster Abbey, as reported in the *Times,* saying, ' The especial lesson taught by Jacob's dream was, that God constantly controlled our thoughts, and that *we were constantly in connection with the world of spirits,* whilst we thought we were far away amid worldly things. He entreated those whose thoughts turned heavenwards, not to check them; for they might be certain that they were enlightened by the same glorious presence which cheered Jacob in the wilderness.' And we find the Rev. E. Bickersteth declaring that ' No part of divine truth can be neglected without spiritual loss; and it is too evident that the deep and mysterious doctrines of revelation respecting evil spirits and good spirits *has been far too much disregarded in our age.'* We find Hallam in his ' Literature of Europe' (vol. i. 275-6), asserting the same thing, and that ' an indifference to this knowledge of invisible things, or a premature despair of attaining it, may be accounted an indication of some moral or intellectual deficiency, some scantiness of due proportion of mind.' We have the present Dean Trench, in his ' Notes on the Miracles,' stoutly declaring the doctrine of the miraculous. ' The true miracle is a higher and purer nature coming down out of the world of untroubled harmonies into this world of ours which so many discords have jarred and disturbed, and bringing this back again, though it be but for one prophetic moment, into harmony with that higher.' Stating this to be a nature is stating it to be perpetual, and, therefore, as much belonging to now as then. We find the Rev. Professor Kingsley as strenuously defending miracle, and affirming that 'the only difficulty lies in the rationalist's shallow and sensuous views of nature;' with much more of the kind in his 'Westward Ho!' and other works. We find the Rev. F. D. Maurice in one of his recent 'Tracts for Priests and People,' asking why things true in the Gospels should not be true in the days of Queen Victoria? These are all symptoms of a need strongly felt in the ecclesiasticism of the day.

NOTE.—Whilst this is going through the press, a phenomenon of a most extraordinary kind has shown itself in America. Mr. Mumler, a photographer of Boston and a medium, was astonished, on taking a photograph of himself, to find also by his side the figure of a young girl, which he immediately recognised as that of a deceased relative. The circumstance made a great excitement. Numbers of persons rushed to his rooms, and many have found deceased friends photographed with themselves.

The matter has been tested in all possible ways, but without detection of any imposture. An account of the particulars will be found in the 'Spiritual Magazine' of December 1862, and of January of the present year, and specimens of these spirit-photographs are now published by Mr. Pitman, Paternoster Row.

CHAPTER XII.

OPPOSITON TO NEW FACTS.

> Vertentem sese frustra sectabere canthum,
> Cum rota posterior curras, et in axe secundo.
> PERSIUS.
> Thus rendered by Dryden —
> Thou, like the hindmost chariot-wheels, art curst,
> Still to be near but never to be first.

IT will be as well here to devote a chapter to some of those numerous facts which should act as a warning to opponents not to gibbet themselves as obstructors of truth to future times. It will be well employed if it save but one reasonable creature from adding his name to the long catalogue of those who, whilst they think they are doing God service, are merely persecuting His truth.

The Creator of man, He who knows all the springs and motions of the human heart, when He was in Christ on the earth, said to His messengers of His great new truths, 'Behold, I send you forth as lambs amongst wolves' (Luke x. 3). This is His announcement of the inevitable consequences of the mission of truth to the end of the world. Persecution is the eternal heritage of truth. There is a deadly enmity to truth in the spirit of the world, which no knowledge, no experience, no infinitely repeated folly will ever cure. The world hates new truths, as the owl and the thief hate the sun. Mere intellectual enlightenment cannot recognise the spiritual. As the sun puts out a fire, so spirit puts out the eyes of mere intellect.

The history of this hatred of truth is the same in the Pagan and the Christian world. Socrates, Pythagoras, and many others, fell under it. But it is most strikingly demonstrated in the history of Christ and His church. The Jews, the educated classes of that time, who had studied the prophets, and carried the institutions of Moses to the utmost perfection, still wanting the spiritual vision, when Christ came covered with all the signs of prophetic history, could not see Him. But what it did to Christ and His apostles, it had done long before. It ridiculed Noah's building the ark for a hundred years, till the flood came, and swept all the sneerers away. It made the life of Moses for forty years a torment, and after a thousand miracles in the wilderness. It caused the pagans to roast, boil, and hew in pieces the early Christians.

Nor was it less operative amongst the early Christians themselves. They ridiculed the discoveries of science, as the scientific ridiculed their Christianity. In his twenty-fourth chapter, 'De Antipodibus, de Cœlo ac Sideribus,' Lactantius laughs at the notion of there being such things as antipodes, thereby showing that the theory of the rotundity of the earth and of antipodes was held, as we know it was, by Macrobius, Pliny the Younger, Cleomenes, and others. Lactantius is quite merry at the idea of 'homines quorum vestigia sint superiora quam capita;' whose heels are higher than their heads. Is it possible, he asks, for 'fruges et arbores deorsum versùs crescere? pluvias et nives et grandinem sursùm versùs cadere in terram?' that is, for fruits and trees to grow downwards! rains, and snow, and hail to fall upwards to the earth! for fields, and seas, and cities, and mountains to hang upside down? The reason, he says, by which they came to such absurd ideas was, that they saw the sun and moon always setting in one place, and always rising in another, and not knowing the machinery by which they were conveyed when out of sight, they thought the heavens must be round, and, therefore, the earth must be round too. Nay, according to him, they had actually made an orrery. 'Itaque et aëreos orbes fabricati sunt, quasi ad figuram mundi eosque cælarunt portentosis quibusdam simulacris, quæ astra esse dicerunt.'

Thus the earth was, according to these philosophers (some of them of the first century of the Christian era, probably earlier still), round, and the planets were represented the same, and as circulating round it. Then followed what Lactantius regarded as a very monstrous notion. Si autem rotunda etiam terra esset, necesse esse, ut in omnes cœli partes eamdem faciem gerat; id est, montes erigat, campos tendat, maria consternat. Quod si esset, etiam sequebatur illud extremum, ut nulla sit pars terræ quæ non ab hominibus, cæterisque animalibus incolatur. Sic pendulos istos Antipodes cœli rotunditas adinvenit. 'That is, if the earth were round, it would follow of necessity, that it would everywhere present the same face to the heavens; it would elevate its mountains, extend its plains, diffuse its seas. And if this should be, then this extreme condition would follow too, that there would be no part of the earth which might not be inhabited by men and other animals. And thus the rotundity of the earth is actually made to introduce pendulous antipodes!'

But if you ask, says our learned Christian Father—and he was a very learned man of his age, and did able battle with the heathen and their mythologies—how all these things are prevented flying off from the round earth, and dropping into the lower regions of space, they tell you that it is a law of nature that the most ponderable substances tend to the centre, and are united to the centre as you see the spokes in a flying wheel; whilst the lighter substances, as clouds, smoke, and fire, are carried from the centre, and mount towards the heavens.

Assuredly, if we have not specific gravity here, soon after the Christian era, we are on the skirts of it. 'Quod si quæras ab iis, qui hæc portenta defendunt, quomodò non cadunt omnia in inferiorem illam cœli partem; respondent, hanc rerum esse naturam, ut pondera in medium ferantur, et ad medium connexa sint omnia, sicut radios videmus in rotâ; quæ autem levia sunt, ut nebula, fumus, ignis, à medio deferantur ut cœlum petant.'

Lactantius cannot, he says, account for the people continuing to defend such absurdities, except that, once taking up wrong premises, they are sure to go on maintaining them; though he thinks the philosophers are sometimes knowingly quizzing, and only do it to show their ingenuity and astonish people. When the learned laugh at Lactantius, let them reflect for a moment, that spiritualism may be just as true now as that the world was round, and that there were antipodes in his time.

The same spirit pursued through all the middle ages the children of the light, by its grand institution, the Inquisition, furnished with every species of machinery for crushing, burning, racking, and tearing out the truth. It fought desperately against the Reformation, and poured all its fury on Huss, Jerome of Prague, the Lollards, Waldenses, Huguenots, on Fox, on Wesley, and on every religious reformer.

It stood in the path of even physical progress, and laughed. It is the Fool and the Alguazil of every age, even to physical progress. We all know the stories of Galileo, of Harvey, and Jenner; they are worn threadbare in holding them up as warnings. It put Solomon de Caus in the Bicêtre as a madman for asserting the power of steam. The 'Edinburgh Review' called on the public to put Thomas Gray into a strait jacket, because he affirmed that there ought to be railroads. Gall says that such was his treatment for introducing phrenology, that he could not have lived through it, had he not been supported by one man who knew the value of science, and that the learned even did not restrain their premature jokes and squibs till they had made some research.

A writer in the 'Homœopathic Review' says, 'In the sixteenth century, the French parliament solemnly interdicted the use of antimony as a medicine, and the Faculty of Paris not only forbade the employment of *all chemical remedies*, but would not allow them even to be mentioned in theses and examinations. In the same century, the discovery of the valves in veins by Amatus Lusitanus was denied and ridiculed by the chief anatomists of the day : whilst Harvey's farther discoveries were treated as madness. In the seventeenth century the medical profession was roused to fury by the introduction of *Peruvian Bark*. This remedy was not brought in through the portals of the college ; and the new discovery, to use the words of Boniland, had to be " baptised in tribulation." The physicians of Oliver Cromwell allowed him to die of ague rather than administer the hated specific. In the same century, the President of the College of Physicians committed Dr. Groenvelt for daring to prescribe *cantharides* internally.

'In the eighteenth century Jenner was ridiculed, lampooned, and excluded from the honours and privileges of the College of Physicians because he advocated vaccination. In the nineteenth, the discovery of Laennec was, for a time, scouted by the medical authorities. " I have not," one professor sneeringly remarked, " a sufficiently fine ear to hear the grass grow : " and at a medical banquet, a sort of dinner of the Medical Association of the day, it was proposed to test the qualities of the wines by percussing the bottles. If we pass from medicine to general science, how the volume teems with stories of blind opposition to everything involving a change of opinion.'

The writer then cites the case of Galileo, so well known, and of Columbus, ridiculed and rebuffed by the learned men of Genoa, Portugal, and Spain, and then, having proved the truth of his theory of another continent, dying brokenhearted amid the hatred and envy of those who feared conviction. Of Franklin, bravely erecting his lightning conductor amid the jeers of his fellow-citizens, and not only so, but amid those of the Royal Society of London. Dr. Ashburner, in the ' Spiritual Magazine,' has called attention to the following fact in ' Lardner's Manual of Electricity,' in the ' Cabinet Library,' i. 47. ' When these and other papers, proposing that an iron rod should be raised to a great height in the air, to convey electricity from the clouds to the earth, by Franklin, illustrating similar views, were sent to London and read before the Royal Society, they are said to have been considered so wild and absurd that they were received with laughter, and were not considered worthy of so much notice as to be admitted into the " Philosophical Transactions." Dr. Fothergill, who appreciated their value, would not permit them to be thus stifled and burked. He wrote a preface to them and published them in London. *They subsequently went through five editions!*'

The writer then cites the case of Perdonnet, the engineer, earning the character of a madman by predicting in a lecture at the *École Centrale*, the success of railways. He adds, ' Then have we not some pleasant stories of the French academicians, —the Sir Benjamin Brodies of the day—the *crême de la crême* of philosophers ? In 1805 Napoleon the First applied to the Academy to know if concentrated steam, according to Fulham's process, could propel a vessel. The question was answered by a burst of laughter, and the emperor was extremely mortified for having showed his ignorance. The same body of philosophers rejected the proposition to light by gas as an impossibility ; and years afterwards, Arago was received with bursts of contemptuous laughter when he wanted to speak of an electric telegraph, his learned compeers declaring the idea to be perfectly Utopian. To these instances he might have added the ridicule and persecution of Hahnemann, for the introduction of homœopathy, and of Reichenbach, for the discovery of the odyle force.

It is a curiosity of science that Benjamin Franklin, who had himself experienced the ridicule of his countrymen for his attempts to identify lightning and electricity, should have been one of the committee of *savans* in Paris in 1778, who examined the claims of mesmerism, and condemned it as absolute quackery ! This opinion was seconded by another commission, which commenced its sittings in February 1826, and continued its labours for five years. The report of the commission, however, recommended that *physicians* only should be allowed to practise mesmerism, forgetting that it was unmedical men who had forced the science on the medical men. Mr. Rich shrewdly observes, that as soon as the Church recognises mesmerism, and we believe spiritualism too, it will then consider it very proper that only clergymen should practise them.

The 'Scottish Review,' in an able article, some years ago, reminded its readers that the establishment of the Royal Society was opposed because it was asserted that 'experimental philosophy was subversive of the Christian faith.' The elder Disraeli shows that telescopes and microscopes were at first denounced as 'atheistic innovations, which perverted our organ of sight, and made everything appear in a false light.' In the outcry against Jenner, the Anti-Vaccination Society, in 1806, execrated vaccination, as a horrible tyranny 'for forcing disease on the innocent babes of the poor—a gross violation of religion, law, morality, and humanity.' It was declared by learned men that it would make children 'ox-faced,' that there were already symptoms of sprouting horns on children, and that they would have the visages of cows and the bellowings of bulls ! It was declared a diabolical invention of Satan, a tempting of Providence, and was practical sorcery and atheism.

When machines were invented for winnowing corn, a dreadful outcry was raised in Scotland, that it was an impious attempt to supersede God's winds, and raise a devil's wind. One Scotch clergyman refused the holy communion to all who used this 'devil's' machine. The readers of 'Old Mortality' will remember the indignation of honest Mause Headrigg, at her son Cuddie having 'to work in a barn wi' a new-fangled machine for dighting the corn frae the chaff, thus impiously,' said the alarmed Mause, 'thwarting the will of Divine Providence, by raising wind for your leddyship's ain particular use by human art, instead of soliciting it by prayer, or waiting patiently whatever dispensation of wind Providence was pleased to send upon the sheiling hills.'

When a route was discovered across the Isthmus of Panama, a priest named Acosta, in 1588, declared that, too, a resistance of Divine Providence and His finite barriers, which could only be followed by plagues and curses. When forks were introduced into England, they were denounced by the preachers, who declared it 'an insult on Providence not to touch our meat with our fingers.' The abolition of slavery was treated in the same manner by many religious people, as an impious attempt to put aside the curse on Ham and his posterity; and like arguments are still used against the attempts to convert the Jews, a people, it is said, rejected for their rebellion and crucifixion of Christ.

There is a large class of persons at the present day who may, with much profit, digest this list of facts. After reading it, no one will feel himself obliged to add his name to the catalogue of bigoted obstructives.

CHAPTER XIII.

THE PHILADELPHIAN BRETHREN.

> There are sown the seeds of Divine things in mortal bodies. . . .
> It may be a question whether such a man goes to heaven, or heaven comes to him; for a good man is influenced by God himself, and has a kind of Divinity within him.
> SENECA's *Morals, Le Strange's Translation*, p. 159.

WE have brought down the 'History of the Supernatural' to our own time. But there are many incidental emanations of it lying, as it were, outside of our track, and yet essential to a complete panoramic view of it. These I shall now, in a few concise chapters, endeavour to bring up; confining them to occurrences since the Reformation. One of the earliest objects which courts our attention is a sort of Protestant association of the 'Friends of God,' under the name of

THE PHILADELPHIAN BRETHREN.

This society was founded by Pordage, a clergyman who was deprived of his living under the commonwealth, and studied medicine, and practised it as a physician till his death, in 1698. He might be styled the English Böhme, whom he had studied and admired. He wrote clearly and with great strength. His chief work, 'The Divine and True Metaphysic,' is in three volumes. The chief members of his society were Thomas Bromley, Edward Hooker, Jane Leade, Sabberton, and others. They used to meet for worship to the number of twenty persons or so, and, according to their accounts, had wonderful, or actual apparitions of good and evil spirits. Some of those of Pordage will be thought very extravagant by many; but if we admit of apparitions at all, it will be difficult to prescribe to them the precise shapes and circumstances in which they shall come, especially if they are evil ones. Much discussion has taken place of late years on the circumstance of ghosts appearing in the very dress which they used to wear on earth, and retaining the fashion of ages ago; and many have thought it a very good reason to deny apparitions at all on this account, saying that they might believe in a spirit, but not in the spirit of a coat. But this is only saying that we are ignorant of the habits and endowments of the spiritual world. When spirits appear, it is necessary that they should be able to identify themselves; and, by whatever means, they evidently have the power. Professor Hare says they possess a will-power far transcending our highest conception, and that it is a portion of *creative* power, conferred by God on spirits, to render them capable of executing His commissions. The faculty, which we ourselves possess, of creating or receiving from the creation of spirits, in our dreams, the most lifelike pictures of places, things and persons, is a part of this wonderful faculty.

When, therefore, we read the strange relations of Pordage, it is only necessary to remember this spiritual potence; and, in the history of the saints, we have abundant examples of presentations of evil beings equally extraordinary. The first of these occurred to Pordage in 1651. As he was asleep in his bed, he was awakened by the violent flinging back of his curtains; and he saw, standing before him, the figure of a person named Eberhard, whom he had well known. The figure was very distinctly seen by the light of the fire in his room; and, after standing some time, it withdrew through a side door. Pordage, it seems, had been accustomed to apparitions; so he turned over, and fell asleep again. But a second time he was awoke, and saw a gigantic figure standing with an up-torn tree on his shoulder, and a huge sword in his hand. As he felt that this was an evil thing, he determined to fight it; and, getting out of bed, he attacked the figure with a walking-stick. He calls it a magical conflict; by which he means the divine magic, or power, which Christianity gives good spirits over bad ones. His fight, he says, lasted for half an hour, when the giant vanished. Scarcely was he gone, however, when he, or another spirit, returned in the shape of a winged dragon, which filled half his chamber, and, as he fought with him, breathed flames upon him, by which he fell into a swoon; but an invisible hand raised him up, and he continued the fight till morning.

Pordage declares that his wife was a witness of the whole of these battles, and the shapes, as plainly as himself; and such was the opinion of the veracity of Pordage, that even his opponents did not doubt that he believed that he had seen and done this. Pordage related all the next day to the members of his society; soon after which time they had very lively visions of hell and heaven, which appeared daily to nearly all the members for a month. Pordage relates, that in these visions, which, he says, they saw both inwardly with the eyes of the spirit, and outwardly with the eyes of the body, they beheld the Prince of Darkness, and damned souls in the shape of men, pass by in grand procession in chariots of clouds, and surrounded by lesser spirits in swarms. The spirits which drew these chariots were in shape of dragons, tigers, bears, and other beasts. They saw countless hosts of them, like an army, which stood outside, whilst others came through the glass into the room. When they closed their eyes they saw these visions just the same. The true cause of seeing, he says, was in the opening of their inner eyes and of the divine union of the inner and outer vision into a perfect oneness. They saw that glass, walls, locked doors, formed no obstacle to their ingress or egress, and that they could change their forms at will, whether into those of men or beasts. This continued for weeks; and some of the members received much injury to their health from the infernal stenches and effluvia. During the whole of this time, whether together or alone—whether by day or by night—they were sickened and disgusted by a detestable taste of mixed sulphur, soot, and salt, and felt continual wounds and stabs, and burning, as from poisoned arrows and the stings of scorpions.

But what was most remarkable, the devils painted on the glass of the windows and on the tiles of the house all kinds of extraordinary figures of men and animals, which appeared continually to move, as if alive. On the tiles of the fireplace they had drawn the two hemispheres of the earth full of men and beasts, which also appeared to move. When the visitation was over, they attempted to wash these out, but they found them indelible, and could only get rid of them by breaking them up with a hammer. The matter had made a great public sensation, and numbers of people, magistrates and others, made a particular examination of the circumstances, and proved the truth of them.

These statements, extraordinary as they are, have been, in many particulars, corroborated by events of to-day. In the case of Mary Jobson, of Sunderland, published by Dr. Reid Clanny, physician to the Duke of Sussex, the sun and moon, and other things, were painted on the ceiling in colours, which her father whitewashed over once or twice, but they still came through, and were seen by hundreds of people, several medical men amongst them, and could only be destroyed at last by destroying the plaster. The wonderful powers of representation and presentation in varied forms is one of the most remarkable and best-attested facts of modern spiritualism. Spirit-writing and spirit-drawings now exist in abundance. Of the former, Baron Guldenstubbe, of Paris, possesses upwards of a thousand specimens, and has published fac-similes of some of them, in his work 'Pneumatologie Positive.' These will be noticed hereafter.

Jane Leade.

Amongst the most distinguished members of the Philadelphian Brotherhood was Jane Leade, a lady of a titled family of Norfolk, married to her cousin, William Leade. She was a woman of accomplished education, and intellectual character. After her husband's death, she said that she had a visit from his spirit, and from that time she retired from the fashionable world, and devoted herself to religious life, and joined the society of Pordage, in whose family she had lived some time. She speaks, like him, of the magical power possessed by believing Christians, but this so-called magic is plainly no other than the theurgic power possessed by the Church in a state of living faith. She says, in her numerous writings, that the time comes when there shall be on earth a community of the enlightened and sanctified, who shall live as really new-born into the world of God and the angels. That the highest attainment of the divine Sophia, of which she continually speaks, is the possession of the magical power which issues from God, and is communicated by Him to those who are willing to receive it.

'Am I asked,' she says in her 'Revelation of Revelations,' 'what this magic power is? I answer, it is a marvellous truth penetrating into the soul of those who receive it, transpiercing the inner life and changing the blood, into a together-flowing and life-giving light resembling flame. It is the power of God in the person of Christ and of the Virgin, and, in a pure virginal spirit, is the pervading and overshadowing power of God, and which by degrees, as a spiritual root, continues to spread itself, and to pass over into others.' 'This power,' she says again, 'places him who possesses it in the condition to exert power over the various departments of creation, over plants, animals, minerals, so that when many work together in this power, nature will be reshapen into a paradisiacal state, and the so-called miracles of the ancient times will again be wrought as nothing extraordinary.'

'How are we to arrive at this power? Through the new birth and through faith, that is to say, through the accordance of our will to the Divine will, which, as St. Paul says, makes everything obedient to us.' This is precisely what our Tennyson says, that 'our will is never so much ours as when it is God's.' Jane Leade lived to the age of eighty-one, by which time the Society had reached a hundred members, including learned and professional men, lawyers, clergymen, physicians, merchants, &c. Her writings were published in twelve volumes, and translated into German by one of her admirers, Loth Vischer, of Amsterdam. The chief of these are 'The Revelation of Revelations,' 'The Laws of Paradise,' 'The Wonders of God's Creation revealed to the Authoress;' and 'The Theologia Mystica.'

ANTOINETTE BOURIGNON.

This lady may be classed with the Philadelphian Society, for her views were precisely the same, though she was a Catholic. She was born at Ryssel, in Flanders, in 1616. From her earliest childhood she showed an unconquerable aversion to the ordinary society of the world, and as unconquerable a drawing to religious retirement and feeling. As she grew up her parents determined to marry her to some man of standing, in whose house she would be obliged to mix in the society of the world. But she steadfastly resisted all such offers, and desired to enter a convent, to which her parents would not consent. She fitted up her private closet as a little chapel, where she had her altar and her religious books. There she declared that she had a spiritual manifestation which determined her future course of life. After the death of her parents, which was during her early years, she opened the ladies' school of which I have spoken, and where the witch fit broke out amongst her scholars, when the school was in the full tide of popularity; for Antoinette Bourignon was a woman of much talent and accomplishment. The secret of this may be found in the enmity of

St. Saulieu, a Capuchin priest, who had professed to desire to open a boys' school on her plan, and through her means obtained the necessary money. Having got this, he thought fit to keep it for his own purposes, and offered to abandon his order and marry Antoinette. Horrified at his villany, she broke off all friendship with him. The Jesuits then endeavouring to obtain the spiritual direction of her school, and being also rejected, the Capuchin and the Jesuits combined to drive her away by the stratagem related. Her school being taken possession of by the authorities, to avoid further persecutions she fled. She afterwards lived in Holland, at Hamburg, and in other places in Germany. There she continued to diffuse her religious ideas both by her conversation and by her pen. Her works are numerous: 'The Light Risen in Darkness,' 'The Light of the World,' 'An Admirable Treatise of Solid Virtue,' &c.

The misfortune of Antoinette Bourignon was her attractions as a woman of education, talent, and deep feeling, so that her admirers, instead of assisting in her views, were continually falling in love with her, and wanting to marry her. All such overtures she rejected, having but one great object, the devotion to and promotion of vital religion. The celebrated Poiret went so far as to separate from his own wife, and then offered his hand to her, which she, as usual, rejected. The great naturalist, Swammerdam, was one of her most zealous disciples. She died in 1680, in the same year as Swammerdam, at the age of seventy-four.

Her writings had excited a great sensation, especially in Germany, and her proselytes and enemies were equally zealous. She was denounced as a Sabellian, an Origenist, and a Gnostic; but she seems to have been simply a woman who had so clear a perception and love of spiritual, that is, vital Christianity, that nothing else had any charms for her. Her writings are excellent, and show that she had obtained the true view of Christianity and of the world. When a child, she used to implore her parents to take her to where the Christians lived, not being able to reconcile the doings of those about her to Christian precepts. She says that she derived all her knowledge from the Spirit of God speaking to her spirit. She expresses no astonishment at the darkness of the so-called Christian world, but says it will yet grow darker, for Christ said that He should not come till it was midnight.

She had seen and known that Christianity was a spiritual reality; that the spiritual world was as objective as the outer world to the unsealed eye and the fully developed soul; and she was in the same condition and category as the long line of so-called mystics, which stretches through every age of the world—a class of people supposed to live amid mere imaginations, but who have found a substantial verity; for no empty imaginations can satisfy strongly-feeling, deeply-seeing souls, for years, and through whole lives.

CHRISTINA PONIATOWSKI AND ANNA MARIA FLEISCHER.

During the thirty-years'-war, as in all times of trouble and excitement, many mediums appeared, who might be classed with the Philadelphian Brethren. Amongst them were Kotter, Plaustrar, Felgenhausen, Warner, Reichard, Drabicides, and others. The most remarkable were three ladies, Eve Margaret Frölich, the wife of a Swedish colonel, Anna Maria Fleischer, and Christina Poniatowski. Christina Poniatowski, the daughter of a Polish nobleman, announced the defeat of Austria and of Wallenstein, through Gustavus Adolphus, and carried her prophecy to Wallenstein, but was kept from his presence, and only delivered it to his wife. 'Commenius,' says Wallenstein, 'though a great believer in astrology, was much amused by Christina's letter, saying the Emperor received letters from Rome and Constantinople, but he from heaven.' However, on December 11, 1628, she saw, in a vision, Wallenstein walking in a bloody cloak, and attempting to scale the clouds by a ladder which broke, and he fell to the earth vomiting blood, smoke, and poison, and an angel proclaimed his certain destruction. This took place in 1634, when he was assassinated in Egra.

Christina Poniatowski was afterwards attacked by a fever, died to all appearance, and lay as dead for many hours, when she revived again and lived, was married, and enjoyed sound health for many years.

Anna Maria Fleischer was a lady of Freyberg, who, when she was in her prophetic, or clairvoyant ecstasy, was lifted into the air, and floated sometimes from one to nearly nine yards high. This is related by Andreas Möller, the superintendent of Freyberg, and by Corrodi, a man never accused of superstition. Anna Fleischer used to say that a boy in bright habiliments often appeared to her, but in the costume of the time, for which reason the wise ones said he could be no angel. He announced that the licentiousness and usuriousness of the time, the drunkenness, and destruction of so much corn in making brandy, would bring after them the wrath of God, war, pestilence, dearness, and change of religious conditions. Those who heard these things laughed, but the things came, and that in unspeakable horror.

CHAPTER XIV.

SPIRITUALISM AMONGST THE DISSENTERS.

An indifference to this knowledge of invisible things, or a premature despair of attaining to it, may be accounted an indication of some moral or intellectual deficiency, some scantiness of due proportions of mind.—HENRY HALLAM's *Literature of Europe*, vol. i. pp. 275, 6.

Nous sommes intimement convaincus que le triomphe final du Spiritualisme entraînera avec lui le rétablissement complet de l'autorité de la Sainte Écriture, cette parole de Dieu qui renferme la plus haute sagesse révélée aux hommes par la disposition des anges de l'Eternel.— BARON GULDENSTUBBE, *Pneumatologie Positive*.

THOUGH Dissenters have but too much imbibed the want of faith in the invisible, which has so terribly laid waste Protestantism, yet there have not been wanting many of their greatest men who, from time to time, have borne unreserved and eminent testimony to the reality of spirit and spirit influences. These honest and clear-sighted men have taken the same ground that Professor Hare has more recently taken—that even the despised department of apparitions furnished more substantial evidence of the immortality of the soul than all the reasonings of the philosophers. Even the highest arguments of Plato were but mere suppositions of an hereafter, but the merest ghost was a positive proof of it. 'How,' asks Hare, 'is it that the theologians, at least, cannot see, if scientific and natural philosophers do not, the immense, the all-important value of spiritualism as a weapon against the atheist and the deist?

Once let it be proved that the *phenomena* of spiritualism are real, and the sceptic and the atheist lose every argument on which they build. If it be admitted that spirits really do visit us, and prove it both by moving matter and showing a spiritual intelligence, there is an end of all argument. These are facts, and take their place immovably in the very centre of the arena of positivism. They may deny what is related only on the evidence of men nearly 2,000 years ago, but they cannot deny the evidence of men now living in thousands and in tens of thousands. They cannot deny the evidence of all their senses, and of their understanding. The great triumph of Christianity then comes, as it must come, from the positivism of spiritualism. It proves Christianity by analogy; it adds a new and invincible force to all historic and moral proofs of it.'

'Comte's positive philosophy,' Hare says, 'after all, is merely negative. It is admitted by Comte that we know nothing of the *sources* or *causes* of Nature's laws: that their origination is so perfectly inscrutable as to make it idle to take up time in any scrutiny for that purpose. He treats the resort to the Deity as the cause, as a mere abstraction, tending to comfort the human mind before it has become acquainted with the science, and doomed to be laid aside with the advance of positive science.'

'Of course, his doctrine makes him avowedly a thorough *ignoramus* as to the *causes* of laws, or the means by which they are established, and can have no basis but the *negative* argument above stated, in objecting to the facts ascertained in relation to the spiritual creation. Thus, whilst allowing the atheist his material dominion, spiritualism will erect within and above the same space a dominion of an importance, as much greater as eternity is to the average duration of human life, and as the boundless regions of the fixed stars are to the habitable area of this globe.' (p. 26.)

This was the strong point which the most able minds of dissent saw from the first, and which caused them to accept proofs of apparitions, and proofs derived from dreams fulfilled, even where they did not care to encounter the Sadduceeism of the age by reasoning much upon the subject. Amongst the earliest and most outspoken of the Nonconformists who derived a great argument for the immortality of the soul from this source, was the venerable Richard Baxter. In his 'Saint's Everlasting Rest' he has introduced a regular treatise on apparitions, and he also wrote an express work on the subject, only a few months before his death, called 'The Certainty of the World of Spirits fully evinced by Unquestionable Histories of Apparitions and Witchcrafts, Operations, Voices, &c.; proving the Immortality of Souls, the Malice and Misery of Devils and the Damned, and the Blessedness of the Justified. Written for the Conviction of Sadducees and Infidels.'

As his observations on this head in the 'Saint's Everlasting Rest' were written nearly forty years before, it shows how settled a principle was supernatural agency in his mind. He assigns as a reason for the work, that notwithstanding his strong religious convictions of the truth of the Gospel, the immortality of the soul, &c., yet the devil every now and then infused very uncomfortable doubts into his mind, and that he found all confirming helps useful; and amongst those of the lower sort, apparitions and other sensible manifestations of the certain existence of spirits themselves invisible, and especially that such evidences were good for them who were prone to judge by sense. What strengthened him must strengthen others, and therefore he collected such accounts, and not to please men with the strangeness and novelty of such stories.

Baxter's spiritualism in his 'Saint's Everlasting Rest' will be found in the second part, and they who may be inclined to treat him as a dreamer had better first see what the greatest writers of his time and since have said of him. Dr. Kippis, in the 'Biographia Britannica,' takes a very high estimate of him. Job Orton, in 'Doddridge's Memoirs,' places him above Rowe, Henry, Doddridge, and Watts; and Orme says, Baxter would have set the world on fire while Orton was lighting a match. Addison and Dr. Johnson pronounce the highest encomiums on him. Johnson says his works are *all* good. Grainger, in his 'Biographical History,' says: 'Men of his size are not to be drawn in miniature;' and Wilberforce, though the Church of England had expelled Baxter, insisted on still claiming him as 'one of its highest ornaments.' Archbishop Usher and Bishop Wilkins, Drs. Barrow, Manton, Bates, and other great Churchmen, vie in praising him, and the Hon. Robert Boyle not the less.

He assures us that he did not accept stories of apparitions without proper investigation. 'I am,' he says, 'as suspicious as most in such reports, and I do believe that most of them are conceits and delusions; yet, having been very diligently inquisitive in all such cases, I have received undoubted testimony of the truth of such apparitions; some from the mouths of men of undoubted honesty and godliness, and some from the reports of multitudes of persons, who heard or saw. Were it fit here to name the persons, I could send you to those yet living, by whom you would be as fully satisfied as I; and to houses that have been so frequently haunted with such terrors, that the inhabitants successively have been witnesses of it.'

He shows us that knockings were known in his days, that is, previous to 1691. 'There is now,' he says, 'in London, an understanding, sober, pious man, oft one of my hearers, who has an elder brother, a gentleman of considerable rank, who having formerly seemed pious, of late years does often fall into the sin of drunkenness. He often lodges long together here in his brother's house, and whenever he is drunk, and has slept himself sober, something knocks at his bed's-head, as if one knocked on a wainscot. When they remove his bed, it follows him. Besides other loud noises on other parts where he is, that all the house hears, they have often watched him, and kept his hands lest he should do it himself. His brother has often told it me, and brought his wife, a discreet woman, to attest it; who avers, moreover, that as she watched him, she has seen his shoes, under the bed, taken up, and nothing visible to touch them. They brought the man himself to me, and when we asked him how he dare sin again after such a warning, he had no excuse. But being persons of quality, for some special reasons of worldly interest, I must not name him.'

Here we have all the characteristics of a medium in the seventeenth century. The noises appeared *where he was*. They suspected him of making them, as they suspect mediums now, and held his hands that he should not do it, yet it was done all the same, and his very shoes when standing under the bed were lifted up.

Baxter quotes 'Learned, godly Zanchius, De Potentia Dæmonum,' and shows from him that even demons are valuable proofs of spirit life. He draws no argument against spiritualism, as the illogical religious of to-day, but sees that they confirm religion. 'Zanchius,' he says, 'wonders that any should deny that there are such spirits, as from the effects are called hags or fairies; that is, such as exercise familiarity with men, and do, without hurting men's bodies, come to them and trouble them, and, as it were, play with them. I could,' he says, ' bring many examples of persons still alive that have experience of these in themselves; but it is not necessary to name them, nor, indeed, convenient. But hence, it appears that there are such spirits in the air, and that when God permits them, they exercise their power on our bodies, either to sport or hurt.'

But neither Zanchius nor Baxter find any argument in these lower grade of spirits for denouncing spiritualism altogether. On the contrary, they found grand arguments upon the fact. ' Having,' they observe, ' not only the certainty of God's word, but man's daily experience, for their existence, they find their use in it.' These devils do confirm our faith of God, of the good angels of the kingdom of heaven, of the blessed souls, and of many things more which the Scripture delivereth. *Many deny that the soul of man remaineth and liveth after death*, because they see nothing go out of him but his breath; and they come to that impiety that they laugh at all that is said of another life. But we see not the devils; and yet it is clearer than the sun that this air is full of devils; because, besides God's word, experience itself doth teach it.

Baxter knew as well as we that this faith was the faith of all ages and nations. ' Gregory, Ambrose, Austin, Chrysostom, Nicephorus, &c., make frequent mention of apparitions, and relate the several stories at large. You may read in Lavater de Spectris, several other relations of apparitions, out of Alexander ab Alexandro, Baptister Fulgatius, and others. Ludovicus Vives " De Veritate Fidei" saith, that among the savages in America, nothing is more common than to hear and see spirits in such shapes both night and day. The like do other writers testify of those Indians; so saith Olaus Magnus of the Icelanders. Cardanus de Subtilit. hath many such stories. So Johan. Manlius in Loc. Common. Collectan. de Malis Spiritibus et de Satisfactione. Yea, godly, sober Melancthon affirms that he had seen some such sights or apparitions himself; and many credible persons of his acquaintance have told him that they have not only seen them, but had much talk with spirits.'

From Lavater de Spectris, he gives, on the testimony of many different persons, recitals bearing all the fixed characteristics of such things. Of persons who had the bed-clothes pulled off them; others who felt something lying on the bed; others who heard it walking in the chamber by them, speaking, or groaning, and passing in and out through locked doors. Other persons under spirit-influence spoke Greek and Latin; and saw what was doing at incredible distances, Thus honest Baxter confirms prior and subsequent ages by a testimony wholly according with theirs; neither because he feels evil does he pronounce all evil, but rationally infers that because there is evil, there must be good too, for such is the evidence of all nature, all history, and all revelation.

A curious discovery is made in reading him. He incurred, he says, in 1655, the troublesome acquaintance of one Clement Writer, of Worcester, an infidel; and, in order to refute his arguments, wrote his 'Unreasonableness of Infidelity.' In this we find that the grand argument of David Hume, which has given him so much notoriety, and the character for so much logical acuteness—namely, that a miracle is incapable of such proof from human testimony as to entitle it to belief—was, in reality, Clement Writer's more than a hundred years before. Writer's words are—'Whatever reality might have belonged to the miracles of Christ, they cannot be proved so as to oblige us.' The idea is identical, and deprives Hume of all originality on this subject; whilst it affords an essential argument for the perpetual recurrence of miracles. The idea is become the stock dogma of every infidel, to which spiritual phenomena are the only valid answers.

To Baxter we must add his celebrated contemporary, Bunyan. It is a striking fact, and creditable to spiritualism, that the authors of two of the most universally popular works in this or any language—'The Pilgrim's Progress' and 'Robinson Crusoe'—were both deeply rooted in this faith. In those charming narratives, which have been the wonderlands of all children since they were written—which have been read with the same enthusiasm in all languages, and by the holders of all creeds, and of which the beauty never fades, and the love never declines, even with declining years— we have the conceptions of two of the most decided spiritualists that ever lived. They were too boldly honest to deny the solemn assurances of the leading intellects of past times; they were too intimately acquainted with the soul and the surroundings of humanity, not to see and feel the perpetual action of the invisible world on the invisible within us. De Foe wrote a work expressly on the subject; John Bunyan wrote one which is altogether a spiritual composition. His pilgrim is one who sets out from this world to the world to come entirely on the faith of Christ and His miracles. He is led and defended by angels; and whether he treads the Valley of the Shadow of Death, amid the pitfalls of

Satan, and stung by the arrows of Apollyon, or climbs the Delectable Mountains, and takes entrancing views into the land of Immanuel, he knows that all these things are realities, and not mere dreams and allegories. The very mode in which the 'Pilgrim's Progress' is communicated, stamps it as spiritual intromission. Like Raphael, Coleridge, with his 'Christabel,' Schiller, according to his own confession, and many others, ideas not his own fell on him. Whilst he was, in fact, actively engaged in writing something else, the idolon of the 'Pilgrim' presented itself—shooting across his normal train of thought—and bore him away into a new and more marvellous track:

>Now when at first I took my pen in hand,
>Thus for to write, I did not understand
>That I at all should make a little book
>In such a mode ; nay, I had undertook
>To make *another*, which, when almost done,
>Before I was aware, I this begun.

Precisely in the manner of spiritual suggestion; the whole plan of his work was not revealed to him at once ; the matter was given him by degrees:

>And thus it was : I writing of the way
>And race of saints in this, our gospel day,
>Fell *suddenly* into an allegory
>About their journey, and the way to glory,
>In more than twenty things which I set down.
>This done, I *twenty more* had in my crown ;
>And they again began to multiply
>Like sparks that from the coals of fire do fly.

The biographers of Bunyan have been extremely jealous of any imputation of a borrowing of the idea of the 'Pilgrim' from any prior author. That there had been a number of such works, and almost under the exact title, is notorious. So early as the fourteenth century, Guillaume de Déguilleville, a priest of the Abbaye Royale of St. Bernard, at Chagles, wrote his 'Romaunt des Trois Pélérinages,' in which a pilgrim sets out on the same heavenward journey, is conducted by a beautiful female called God's Grace, and encounters the like enemies, perils, and triumphs. The second part of this 'Pilgrim's Progress' was translated into English, and printed by Caxton, as the Pilgrimage of the Soul, in 1483, of which we have lately had a beautifully illustrated version. Then there was the 'Pilgrim of Perfection,' written by William Bond, a monk of Sion Monastery, and printed in 1526, by Wynkyn de Worde. In 1627 Boetius Adam Bolswaert published at Antwerp a Pilgrim's Progress, in a set of engravings, in which the Slough of Despond, the Valley of the Shadow of Death, and Vanity Fair are clearly discernible. This 'Pilgrim's Progress' was speedily republished in French, Spanish, Dutch, and other languages, long before Bunyan was born. There was, moreover, in English, ten years before Bunyan's, 'The Parable of the Pilgrim,' by Simon Patrick, Bishop of Ely. Still earlier (namely, in 1591), 'The Pilgrimage to Paradise,' by Leonard Wright; in 1613, 'The Pilgrim's Journey towards Heaven,' by William Webster; 'The Pilgrim's Passe to Jerusalem,' 1659, and others.

Thus the idea, and even the main features, of a 'Pilgrim's Progress' were familiar enough to have passed amongst the people of a religious turn, and were such as were very likely to have done so, and to have taken deep hold on their minds. If Bunyan had not actually read any of them, they might have come, like the 'Babes of the Wood' and kindred things, orally to the cottage fireside, and seized on his youthful imagination in their most insinuating form. It is, therefore, just as probable that Bunyan had thus sucked in, by the domestic hearth, or in some of the tinkering rounds of his father, in which he accompanied him, the idea of the Pilgrim, which his after spiritual experiences and Scripture reading the more endeared to him; as it is certain that he threw into *his* Pilgrim a far higher tone and a more brilliant originality than distinguished any of his predecessors. But this tone and fascinating originality, we are assured by him, came suddenly, he knew not how, into his mind, when occupied by another topic. Whence? What if the disembodied author of the

'Trois Pélérinages,' or of the 'Pilgrimage of the Soul,' had, with a higher and wider range of vision, a more perfect knowledge, gathered in the spirit-world itself, thus poured this ennobled and consummated version of his work into the brain of Bunyan, giving it a new and eternal career on earth, making it a new missionary of God in the world of probation?

This, it will be said, is a theory which robs men of originality, and makes them but the mediums, not the authors of their writings. But what are the brightest men but such mediums? Whence come originality and new intellectual emotions? from men, or from above? Is there anything that we possess, spiritually or intellectually, that comes not from God, descending through the chain of His angels? We might as well say that every fruit or product of earth does not come first from the sun in its vivifying light and heat. No man could be so prompt as Bunyan to empty himself of the origination of anything great and glorious, and to ascribe it to the Power who has made the pattern of all things seen here below, primarily in the heavens.

Not only in his writings—none of which bear any resemblance in originality and fresh beauty to the 'Pilgrim's Progress'—but in his preaching, Bunyan distinctly attributes the life and motive power to spiritual agency. He says, ' I have with soberness considered that the Lord, even in my childhood, did scare and affrighten me with dreams.' Thus he dreamed dreams expressly sent from God. But not only so, but all the steps by which he was drawn from his wickedness, as a poor, ill-taught, and demoralized tinker, accustomed to the utmost degree of profanity and crime, he felt to be from the direct hand of God. All the horrible temptations, and terrifying assaults and persuasions to despair and to self-destruction, he knew too well to be the work of actual devils, and not mere imaginations or abstract ideas of 'personified evil.' They were to him as actual and substantial as he has made them to his Pilgrim. The experience of Christian was wholly and absolutely his own. He knew that the voice which at last struck home to his conscience, and arrested his

career of crime, was a real voice from heaven, and no fancy.
'But the same day, as I was in the midst of a game of cat,
and having struck it one blow from the hole, just as I was
about to strike it a second time, a voice did suddenly dart
from heaven into my soul, and said, "Wilt thou leave thy
sins and go to heaven, or have thy sins and go to hell?" At
this I was put into an exceeding maze. Therefore, leaving
my cat on the ground, I looked up to heaven, and was as if
I had, with the eyes of my understanding, seen the Lord
Jesus looking down upon me, as being very hotly displeased
with me, and as if He did severely threaten me with some
grievous punishment for these and other ungodly practices.'
He was playing at cat on a Sunday.

Everyone is familiar with the long and agonizing spiritual
struggle of Bunyan before he emerged into a full sense of
the Divine forgiveness and acceptance; and those who regard
these as the mere effects of an excited imagination, have yet
to learn a sound and practical psychology. It was a schooling
necessary to produce a great and effectual teacher of the
process of Christian regeneration. He heard, occasionally,
such unmistakeable voices from God's spiritual guardians
and trainers in the heavenly life, 'that once,' he says, 'above
all the rest, I turned my head over my shoulder, thinking
surely, that some man behind me half a mile, had called me.'
He adds, 'I did see and feel that it was sent from heaven to
awaken me.' The voice, no doubt, was as real as that which
came to the child Samuel in the Temple; and the suggestion
of the devil was as real and more apparently compulsory.
'I was bound in the wings of a wind,' he says, 'that *would*
carry me away to *bolt* out some horrible blasphemous thought
or other against God or Christ His Son, and the Scriptures.'
So mighty was the evil power that endeavoured to sweep
him away on the wings of the wind to evil, that he says,
'I did sometimes kick; I did shriek and cry; and these
things did not make me slack my crying.' He felt the
spiritual presence of the devil at his side. 'I have thought,'
he says, 'that I felt him behind me, pulling my clothes.'

There are plenty, now-a-days, who have felt the actual pullings of spirits, both good and evil. I, myself, a few years ago, might have deemed this impression of Bunyan's a strange fancy; I have now seen too much to think its being a simple matter of fact anything extraordinary. In these respects the experiences of Bunyan greatly resemble those of Luther; and neither of these strong and honest-souled men were what is called *rational* enough to restrict such phenomena first to the Bible, and then to explode them altogether. Like Luther, Bunyan ascribed to demoniac influences storms, wrecks, blights, and the like. He had, at times, most splendid and life-like visions, and inward revelations of Divine grace. His ministerial work was shown him by impression. 'I have observed that, where I had a work to do for God, I have had, first, as it were, the going of God upon my spirit, to desire I might preach there. I have also observed that such and such souls in particular have been strongly set upon my heart, and I stirred up to wish for their salvation; and that these very souls have, after this, been given in as fruits of my ministry.' Though Bunyan and the Friends could not understand each other, in this respect they are of one testimony. When on his trial, he had direct words from God put into his mouth, as Christ had promised to His followers. 'I say God brought the words, for I had not thought of them before; they were set evidently before my mind.' The judges, like our worldly-wise men now-a-days, attributed his faith to 'Beelzebub, to the spirit of delusion, and the devil.'

Bunyan had a firm belief in divine judgements, and direct interpositions for the defence of God's people, and open punishment for their persecutors; and he records many curious instances of these. Such was the philosophy of John Bunyan, who learnt it from his Bible as he trudged with his tinker's budget through fields and lanes round Elstow, or lay a prisoner in Bedford jail, twelve long years for conscience-sake. They were not fancies that steeled him to all this endurance, when a few words of meek compliance would have set him at large. They were not fancies which enabled him to sacrifice every earthly enjoyment, to do stout battle with Pope and Pagan, and to show us the way to batter down Doubting Castle.

In an 'Account of the Parish of Aberystwyth,' by Edward Jones, printed in 1779, we find Baxter's arguments of the proofs of the immortality of the soul also used by the author, who was an Independent minister. 'I reasonably apprehended,' he says, ' that a well-attested relation of apparitions and agencies of spirits in the world is a great means to prevent the capital infidelities of Atheism and Sadduceeism, which get much ground in some countries; for in Wales, where such things have often happened, and still do in some places, though but seldom now, we scarce meet with any who question the being and apparition of spirits.'

Mr. Jones, like most Welsh people, had had experiences of this kind of his own. He says, that when a very young boy, going with his aunt, Elizabeth Rogers, early in the morning, but after sunrise, he saw, near his father's house at Pen-yr-Keven, the likeness of a sheepfold, with a door towards the south, and over the door, instead of a lintel, the dried branch of a tree. People were coming out, all dressed in an old costume, the men in white cravats, and one fair woman in a high-crowned hat and red jacket, whom they seemed to honour. He thought the bough over the door was of hazel, and everyone in passing under it made an obeisance. The fair and well-formed countenance of the woman, he says, still remained very clear in his memory. He says, such apparitions were common about Havodavel and Kevenbach, and that the people of Monmouthshire called the Fairies, 'Mother's Blessings and Fair Folks of the Wood,' though they were not blessed spirits.

Dr. Doddridge had a strong faith in a revelation by dreams, and the Rev. Samuel Clarke relates one which made a wonderful impression upon the Doctor. In this dream he imagined he saw Death and the passage of his spirit into the invisible world. He was met by an old man and conducted to a palace, more beautiful than anything he had ever seen on earth, and was told that was his present residence. When he looked round him in a noble saloon, he saw a golden cup standing on a table, with the embossed figures of a vine and clustering grapes upon it. This, he was told, was the cup in which the Saviour drank new wine with His disciples in His kingdom. He then heard a *rap* at the door, and was told that this was *the signal of his Lord's approach,* and *intended to prepare him for the interview.* The Saviour then entered, and he threw himself at His feet and was raised up by Him, and was presented with the cup, of which he drank. When the Lord left him, he again looked round the apartment, and, to his astonishment, saw that it was hung round with the pictures of his whole life, in which nothing of importance was omitted. He then saw how he had been led and protected by divine and angelic agencies, and the joy thus diffused through him was inconceivable. On awaking, the impressions continued so vivid, that tears of joy flowed down his cheeks, and he said that he never, on any occasion, remembered to have felt sentiments of devotion, love, and gratitude equally strong.

Dr. Isaac Watts, a great man amongst the Dissenters, author of a system of logic, but better known to everyone by his religious hymns, not only strongly advocated the fact of apparitions, but wrote an essay to prove a separate state of the soul betwixt death and the general resurrection. In this he says, 'The multitude of narrations which we have heard of in all ages of the apparitions of the spirits or ghosts of persons departed from this life, can hardly be all delusion and falsehood. Some of them have been affirmed to appear upon such great and important occasions as may be equal to such an unusual event; and several of these accounts have been attested by such witnesses of wisdom, prudence, and sagacity, under no distempers of imagination, that they may justly demand belief.' He quotes, in confirmation of such a theory, the appearance of Christ walking upon the water, when His disciples took Him for a spirit, the appearances of Christ after His resurrection, and other scriptural passages. He thinks the appearance of apparitions a strong proof of an intermediate state, whence they can return for special divine purposes.

The celebrated Countess of Huntingdon, a daughter of the Earl of Ferrers, who became a great disciple and patroness of Whitefield, who was her chaplain, was a firm believer in spiritual agencies. She was one of the most energetic and remarkable persons of her time. After the death of Whitefield, she took the management of his converts, founded schools and colleges, and built chapels; so that the society acquired the name of Lady Huntingdon's Society. In her 'Life,' in 2 vols. 8vo. by the Rev. Alfred New, we find abundant evidences of spiritualism.

Her husband, the Earl of Huntingdon, who was remarkable for scarcely ever having a consciousness of dreaming, dreamed one night that Death, in the semblance of a skeleton, appeared at his bed's foot; and, after standing awhile, untucked the bed-clothes at the bottom, crept up the bed, and lay between himself and his lady. His lordship told his dream in the morning to the countess, who affected to make light of it; but the earl died of apoplexy in about a fortnight after, in the fiftieth year of his age (vol. i. 74).

In the same work, a very extraordinary circumstance is recorded as occurring to Whitefield. On taking his text, at an open-air meeting in Yorkshire—' It is appointed unto men once to die,' &c.—a shriek took place in the audience; and Mr. Grimshaw hastened up to him to say that a person had fallen down dead. After pausing a moment, he again repeated the text; and another shriek followed from the spot where Lady Huntingdon and Lady Margaret Ingham were standing; and it was announced that the destroying angel had taken away another soul.

About three years before, the Countess of Huntingdon went to establish a congregation in Brighton, a gentlewoman, who lived in the vicinity of the town, dreamed that a tall lady, whose dress she particularly noticed, would come to Brighton, and be the means of doing much good there. One day she happened to meet her ladyship in the street; and, fixing her eyes upon her, exclaimed, 'O madam, you are come!' Lady Huntingdon, surprised at the singularity of such an address from an entire stranger, thought at first that the woman was deranged. 'What do you know of me?' asked the countess. 'Madam,' replied the person, 'I saw you in a dream three years ago, just as you appear now:' and she then related the whole dream to her. An acquaintance sprang up between them; and Lady Huntingdon was made instrumental in her conversion. The lady died about a year afterwards, in full assurance of hope, through Jesus Christ (vol. i. 313).

In 1763 the countess lost her daughter, Lady Selina Hastings. 'During her illness, Lady Huntingdon had every day many promises given her of God's kindness to her daughter, all which she interpreted in the carnal sense, like the Jews, and thought her daughter would recover, and do well again. By this means she was wonderfully supported, and her spirits were kept up to the last. And when the Lord let her see things were otherwise intended than she thought, then He had prepared for her a fresh fount of comfort' (vol. i. 333). Mr. Romaine, who relates this, does not tell us how Lady Huntingdon received these assurances; but it is probable that it was by the *Sortes Biblicæ*, which we find, from a great humourist of her faith, Mr. Berridge, vicar of Everton, Cambridgeshire, was in use amongst them. He informs us that he had sought direction as to his taking a wife, by kneeling down, praying, and then opening the Bible, and had been thus repeatedly determined against it. He says, 'This method of procuring Divine intelligence is much flouted by flimsy professors, who walk at large, and desire not that sweet and secret access to the mercy-seat, which babes of the kingdom do find. During the last twelve years I have had occasion to consult the oracle three or four times on matters that seemed important and dubious, and have received answers full and plain. Was not this the practice of the Jewish church? and can we think that God will deny that direction to the Christian church which He freely granted to the Jewish? Is not access to the mercy-seat more free and open than before? I believe perplexed cases are often sent on purpose to teach us to enquire of the Lord. By leaving the oracles of God, we make an oracle of man; and we are properly chastised for our folly. . . . . Where is faith? Buried under mountains, and not removing them. However, this oracular enquiry is not to be made on light and trifling occasions, and, much less, with a light and trifling spirit. Whoever consults the oracle aright, will enter on the enquiry with the same solemnity as the high priest entered into the Holy of holies; neither must this be done but on a high day: not on trifling occasions, but on very important concerns. And whoever thus consults the Word of God as his oracle, with a hearty desire to know and do God's will, I believe will receive the information' (vol. i. 389). He says, people have received answers to their first enquiries, and never afterwards, because they have asked of mere trivial matters; and that, though God is willing to be consulted, He is not willing to be trifled with.

Towards the end of Lady Huntingdon's life, Lord Douglas, a Papist living at Brussels, invited her to visit him there, promising her much success amongst the Catholics. Lady Huntingdon, always ready to spread the gospel, accepted the invitation, and had a new equipage prepared for the journey, but being obliged to stop at different places in England on her way to Dover, on the concerns of her chapels, it gave time for letters to arrive from Brussels, apprising her that Lord Douglas's invitation was a plot to get her assassinated there, as well as any of her preachers who might accompany her. She properly attributed this timely delay as a direct interposition of Providence. Like Stilling, and Müller of Bristol, she had frequent instances of such interpositions. A gentleman who assisted her in the management of Spafields Chapel called one day at her house to expostulate with her for the impropriety of entering into engagements for another chapel in the metropolis, without having the means of honourably fulfilling them. Before he left the house her letters arrived. As she opened one her countenance brightened, and her tears began to flow. The letter was to this effect:—'An individual who has heard of Lady Huntingdon's exertions to spread the gospel, requests the acceptance of the enclosed draft, to assist her in the laudable undertaking.' The draft was for five hundred pounds, the exact sum for which she stood engaged. 'Here,' she said, 'take it, and pay for the chapel, and be no longer faithless, but believing!' (vol. ii. 508).

The late Mr. Priestly, visiting her a few days before her death, she said, 'I cannot tell you in what light I now see those words, "If a man love me, He will keep my words, and my Father will love him, and we will come unto him, and make our abode with him." To have in this room such company, and to have such eternal prospect, I see this subject now in a light impossible to describe' (vol. ii. 510).

After her death, Lady Anne Erskine took her place in the management of the society, and declared her experience of the same timely supplies as Lady Huntingdon had received—on one occasion, at a moment of utmost need, and when the necessary funds could not be looked for from any particular quarter, a lady calling and presenting her with £500. This Lady Anne predicted her own death. On going to bed she said, 'The Lord will reveal Himself to me to-morrow,' and the next morning she was found apparently in a calm sleep, but actually dead in her bed.

Lady Huntingdon expended upwards of £100,000 in her religious labours, and not only established the colleges of Trevecca in Wales, and of Cheshunt, near London, but built with her own funds numerous chapels in different parts of the kingdom. She was the means not only of introducing religion amongst the poor, but also amongst the rich and titled. Her drawing-room was crowded by aristocracy, where Whitefield and sometimes Wesley preached to them. Amongst the hearers were Lord Chesterfield, Lord and Lady Dartmouth, Bolingbroke, the Duchess of Bedford, Lord and Lady Dacre, Lords Townshend, Northampton, Tavistock, Lyttelton, Trafford, Edgecombe, and many others; the Duchesses of Hamilton, Richmond, &c.—in fact, whole crowds of nobility. Amongst those who came within her circle, were Pope, Akenside, Drs. Watts and Doddridge; Blair, author of ' The Grave '; Col. Gardiner; the father of Godwin was one of her preachers, and thus the grandfather of Mrs. Shelley; Romaine, Toplady, Fletcher of Madeley, Venn, John Newton, Dr. Haweis, and many other clergymen of the Establishment, Rowland Hill, &c., were of her society ; and almost every town and village of Wales bears testimony to the extensive effect of her labours in the chapels of Calvinistic-Methodists. She was the first to originate the enquiry into the abused school charities of England by her successful restoration of the school and hospital of Repton, in Derbyshire, to reformed activity ; and Lord Chesterfield, a judge of human character, has left his statement, that she possessed one of the most balanced, sagacious, and masculine minds that he ever met with.

But the story of a person of similar name, but of humblest plebeian origin, is not much less remarkable than that of the countess. William Huntington was the son of a poor farm labourer in Kent, and was born in 1744. His parents were the poorest of the poor, and his childhood was passed in hunger and hardship ; but from his earliest years he had the strongest convictions of the ever-present providence of God, and he learned to throw himself entirely on His care, and grew to have a firm faith that he would always be provided for. He called God his banker, and he has written his autobiography, calling it ' The Bank of Faith.' In this he relates the most extraordinary occurrences, by which he was promised relief from his difficulties, and which promises were always fulfilled, though often at the last moment, and after the most severe trials of his faith. From a poor serving boy, however, at 'Squire Cook's, he gradually grew into a coal-heaver, and relapsed into deism. He married, returned to his religious life, went to live at Sunbury, joined the Calvinistic Methodists, and became a preacher. At first, his preachings were only in obscure places, but his ministry so much widened that he came to keep a horse, extended his labours to London, grew very popular, and finally he married the widow of Sir James Sanderson, Alderman of London, and passed the latter part of his life as a man of wealth. For a full idea of the spiritualism of Huntington, the reader must refer to his 'Bank of Faith,' or to a condensed account of him in the 'Spiritual Magazine,' vol. i. 77. His life is a series of dreams, prophecies, and prevision, but, above all, remarkable for the prevailing intimations of help that was to come from time to time, and which did come unfailingly, proving not only a general but a particular and directly interfering Providence.

Amongst recent instances of spiritual belief, we may select the avowal of it by the Rev. Isaac Taylor, the celebrated author of 'The Natural History of Enthusiasm,' 'The Physical Theory of another Life,' &c., one of the ablest reasoners of our time. Speaking of communications from the deceased to the living, he says, 'The supposition of there being a universal persuasion totally groundless, not only in its form and adjuncts, but in its substance, does violence to the principles of human reasoning, and clearly is of dangerous consequence.' In another place he asserts his literal belief of the demoniac possessions of the New Testament, refusing to reduce them to mere diseases. We cannot deny their reality without destroying altogether the authority of the Scriptures. 'The gospel narrations in these instances are of a kind not to be disposed of by the hypothesis of accommodation; but are of a plain, historical complexion, such as that, if they are rejected as untrue, we are bound to withdraw our confidence altogether from the reporters, as competent and trustworthy witnesses of facts.'

Another great authority amongst the Independents is

Dr. John Campbell, the minister of the Tabernacle Chapel, Finsbury, and editor of the 'British Banner,' &c. With that massive vigour which distinguishes his style, during the controversies regarding spiritualism in 1852, he delivered in the 'Banner' this verdict in November of that year:—' A proud philosophy of impious scepticism, of course, pours contempt upon all such alleged facts and circumstances. That much credulity, some superstition and delusion, and, it may be, some cunning craftiness and selfish imposture, may have mixed up with such things, we feel it impossible to deny; but that the whole shall prove delusion is more than we are prepared to grant. Along with the sad mass of base coin, we are strongly inclined to believe that there was a portion of that which was genuine. We see no reason for starting with it as a first principle, that such things are impossible, unnecessary, and, therefore, non-existing. We are sometimes met with the question of *cui bono*? We deny our obligation, as a condition of rational faith, to prove the *cui bono*. It may exist where we see it not, and have important ends to accomplish with which we are unacquainted. We conceive, that what was in the ages preceding those of the apostles, and what occurred in their days, may occur again.'

A great mass of corroborative statements might be drawn from Methodist writers and preachers, but, as I shall deal separately with Wesley and his followers, I shall reserve these cases for that chapter. Perhaps I ought to place the testimony of Mrs. Schimmelpenninck here; for, as she was educated a Friend, it would be difficult in her after life to appropriate her strictly to any particular church. In her 'Autobiography' she gives many proofs of her faith in spiritual intercourse. In her first volume (p. 225), she says, 'The connection between the visible and invisible world is one of the greatest of all questions, and it must ever remain a subject of deepest concern, especially to *regenerate* man.' She adds, that nothing but a lapse into a grosser and more material state, can annihilate that interest. As for all those who had pooh-poohed this belief amongst her contemporaries, she says, 'At the end of sixty-five years, all those from whose lips I heard the sentiment have learned that it is the invisible world which constitutes the *only reality*, and that those pressing interests which they once conceived of as vivid realities, have proved to be the passing shadows.'

She records a striking providence occurring to her aunt, Lady Watson, by which she saved the life of her husband by sending out a boat in a storm to save a person in jeopardy on an insulated rock, without knowing who it was, but which proved to be Sir William Watson himself. She defends miracles zealously. She declares the creation the greatest of standing miracles. She says, 'It has pleased God to create man with moral sentiments,' and asks 'whether it would not be the greatest of improbabilities, that, having bestowed on him this gift, He should afford him no means for its exercise on a true object. But how can this object be known but by a revelation of the mind of God from God Himself? And how can that revelation be given from Himself to a creature formed in the image of the Divine Trinity, without a revelation which speaks with a triple voice to his threefold being? To the spirit of man by the Divine Spirit; to the senses of man by the outward signs of power, and to his understanding by deductions from both? This being the case, the reality of a communication by miracles to the senses of man involves no greater improbability than the fact that God should have given man a revelation at all' ('Life,' p. 219).

Mrs. Schimmelpenninck, in her autobiography, also gives us the remarkable dream and apparition of Mr. Petty, the son of Lord Shelbourne, on the authority of Dr. Priestley, who was librarian to Lord Shelbourne at the time. Mr. Petty dreamed that he rode in a strange dark, old carriage to High Wickham, which was the burial place of the Shelbournes, and, on being carried out (for he was weakly), he saw that the carriage looked like a hearse, and there was a long train of mourning carriages after it. He was but a youth, under twenty, and imagined that it prognosticated his death. Dr. Priestley endeavoured to persuade him out of the fancy; as Lord Shelbourne, however, was from home, he thought it best to send for the medical man, who ordered Mr. Petty not to go out of doors on any account, as the weather was cold, being January, and his chest weak. The medical man, calling a day or two after, was surprised to see Mr. Petty come running down the drive from the house to meet him, regardless of his prohibition. Before he reached him, however, he disappeared behind some shrubs, and the doctor, thinking he eluded him to avoid being scolded, drove on to the house, where he learned, to his astonishment, that Mr. Petty had just expired, not having been out of the house at all. Dr. Priestley, who thought the noises at Mr. Wesley's, at Epworth, had been the result of some trick, appears to have been differently impressed by these events. Mrs. Schimmelpenninck says this account was not only given her by Dr. Priestley, but was confirmed to her many years after by Dr. Allsop of Calne, the medical man who attended Mr. Petty on the occasion.

I will close this chapter with the remarks of another distinguished Unitarian—a class of religionists, perhaps, farther removed than even the Church of England from spiritual impression. Mr. Theodore Parker says of spiritualism: 'Let others judge the merits and defects of this scheme—it has never organized a Church—yet, in all ages, from the earliest, men have more or less freely set forth its doctrines. We find these men amongst the despised and forsaken; the world was not ready to receive them. They have been stoned and spit upon in all the streets of the world. The "pious" have burned them as haters of God and man; the wicked called them bad names and let them go. They have served to flesh the swords of the Catholic Church, and feed the fires of the Protestants, but flames and steel will not consume them; the seed they have sown is quick in many a heart—their memory blessed by such as live divine. These are the men at whom the world opens wide the mouth, and draws out the tongue, and utters its impertinent laugh; but they received the fire of God on their altars, and kept living its sacred flame. They go on, the forlorn hope of the race; but Truth puts a wall of fire about them, and holds the shield over their heads in the day of trouble. The battle of truth seems often lost, but is always won. Her enemies but erect the blood scaffolding where the workmen of God go up and down, and, with divine hands, build wiser than they know. When the scaffolding falls the temple will appear.'

Thus the leading minds of all classes of Dissenters have admitted the truth of spiritualism; the greater the mind the more prompt its conviction, the more candid its testimony.

CHAPTER XV.

GEORGE FOX AND THE FRIENDS.

> They called themselves by the pleasant name of Friends; the pious called them, the Children of the Light; the baser sort, quaking at the Light, called them Quakers.— GERARD GROESE.

> There exist folios on the human understanding and the nature of man, which would have a far juster claim to their high rank and celebrity, if, in the whole huge volume, there could be found as much fullness of heart and intellect as bursts forth in many a simple page of George Fox.—COLERIDGE's *Biographia Literaria.*

> This man, the first of the Quakers, and by trade a shoemaker, was one of those to whom, under ruder form, the Divine idea of the universe is pleased to manifest itself; and across all the hulls of ignorance and earthly degradation, shine forth in unspeakable awfulness, unspeakable beauty on their souls; who, therefore, are rightly accounted prophets, God-possessed.—THOMAS CARLYLE.

HENRY VIII., who established the Reformation in England, died in 1546; George Fox, the first of the Society of Friends, was born in 1624, and in 1646, exactly a hundred years after the death of the royal reformer, as he was walking towards Coventry, was struck with a sudden wonder how all were said to be Christians, both Protestants and Papists, and that it was said that all true Christians must have been born again, and thus passed from death to life, a fact which he found it hard to believe of very many of his contemporaries. In fact, the more honest George pondered on this subject the more was his amazement; for surely, from all the accounts that we have of the condition of genuine Christianity, there was very little of it at that time.

Protestantism, patronised, if not introduced, by royalty into England, had, under state pressure, assumed a very odd shape. Checked, and driven, and thwarted by kingly and queenly caprices, it had become a very hybrid and stunted thing. It had abjured voluntarily many of the gifts of the church of Christ, as those of curing by laying on of hands, prophesying and working miracles, thus having lopped off a number of its own limbs; and this circumstance, cooperating with the royal tinkering of the faith, had done wonders in introducing a strange death-in-life sort of religion. Having abandoned all faith in the supernatural, very few people believed in the action of the Holy Spirit on the spirit of man. Nothing brought so much ridicule on the Friends as their assertion that they were moved by the Spirit. It became a common mode of scoffing at them to say that 'the Spirit moves them.' Nay, it is still thought rather witty to say that 'the Spirit moves them.' As for being born again, in George Fox's day it was ridiculed by bishops and clergy as the height of absurdity. To be a Christian was to go to church, to adjourn thence to the ale-house, and drink and swear lustily; and to be a heretic was to go to a Dissenting chapel, dubbed by law a 'conventicle,' and to be fined twenty pounds for it. Such was the condition to which legal and regal Protestantism had reduced this country in a hundred years.

We need not take the evidence of George Fox and the Friends solely on this point. Richard Baxter was Fox's contemporary, and a clergyman of the legal church too. In Orme's life of the venerable Richard, it is stated that 'before or about the time that Richard was born — 1615 — an important change took place in his father. This was effected chiefly by the reading of the Scriptures; for *he had not the benefit of Christian association, or the public preaching of the gospel.* Indeed the latter privilege could scarcely be enjoyed in that county—Shropshire. There was little preaching of any kind, and that little was calculated to injure rather than to benefit. In High Ercall, his place of residence, there

were four readers in the course of six years, all of them
ignorant, and two of them immoral men. At Eaton-Constantine, also a place of his abode and hereditary property,
there was a reader of eighty years of age, Sir William
Rogers, who never preached, yet had two livings twenty
miles apart from each other. His sight failing, he repeated
the prayers without book, but to read the lessons he employed
a common labourer one year, a tailor another; and at last
his own son, the best stage-player and gamester in all the
country, got orders and supplied one of his places. Within
a few miles round were nearly a dozen more ministers of the
same description; poor, ignorant readers, and most of them
of dissolute lives. Three or four who were of a different
character, though all conformists, were the objects of popular
derision and hatred, as Puritans. Where such was the character of the priests, we need not wonder that the people
were profligate, and despisers of those who were good. The
greater part of the Lord's Day was spent by the inhabitants
of the village in dancing round a maypole, near Mr. Baxter's
door, to the no small distress and disturbance of the family '
(p. 2 'Baxter's Life,' by the Rev. William Orme).

'From six to ten years of age, Baxter was under four
successive curates of the parish, two of whom never preached,
and the two who had the most learning of the four drank
themselves to beggary, and then left the place. At the age
of ten he was removed to his father's house, where the old
blind man, Sir William Rogers, of whom we have already
spoken, was parson. One of his curates, who succeeded a
person who was driven away on being discovered to have
officiated under forged orders, was Baxter's principal schoolmaster. This man had been a lawyer's clerk, but hard
drinking drove him from that profession, and he turned
curate for a piece of bread. He only preached once in
Baxter's time, and then was drunk! From such a man,
what instruction could be expected? How dismal must the
state of the country have been when they could be tolerated
either as ministers or teachers! His next instructor, who

loved him much, he tells us, was a grave and eminent man, and expected to be made a bishop. He also, however, disappointed him, for, during no less than two years, he never instructed him one hour, but spent his time, for the most part, in talking against the factious Puritans. In his study, he remembered to have seen no Greek book but the New Testament; the only Father was Augustine De Civitate Dei; there were a few common English works, and, for the most part of the year, the parson studied " Bishop Andrew's Sermons "' (p. 3).

'When Baxter went to renew his labours at Kidderminster, 1646—the same year that George Fox opened his eyes to the state of things around him—he found an ignorant vicar, and, at a chapel in the parish, an old curate as ignorant as he, that had long lived upon ten pounds a year and the fees for celebrating unlawful marriages. He was also a drunkard and a railer, and the scorn of the country. " I knew not," says Baxter, " how to keep him from reading, though I judged it a sin to tolerate him in any sacred office. I got an augmentation for the place, and an honest preacher to instruct them, and let this scandalous fellow keep his former stipend of ten pounds for nothing; yet could never keep him from forcing himself upon the people to read, nor from celebrating unlawful marriages, till a little before death did call him to his account. I have examined him about the familiar points of religion, and he could not say half so much to me as I have heard a child say. These two in this parish were not all: in one of the next parishes, called the Rock, there were two chapels, where the poor ignorant curate of one got his living by cutting fagots, and the other by making ropes. Their abilities being answerable to their studies and employments "' (p. 101).

Whilst a hundred years of legal Christianity had brought the Established Church to such a pass as this, we may suppose that there were people existing who were looking out for something more satisfactory, for the Bible was let loose amongst them, by translation, to do its eternally revolutionising work—'turning the world upside down;' and Baxter tells us that there were five sects in his day, the Vanists, or followers of Sir Harry Vane, the Seekers, the Ranters, the Behmenists and the Quakers. We will not trouble ourselves with honest Richard's account of these sects, for if it be not more correct than that which he gives of the Quakers it is not very valuable. We may turn to George Fox, however, and shall find him confirming the general state of religion in the country as given by Baxter.

George Fox was born at Drayton, in Leicestershire, in July 1624. His parents were of the Church of England; his father a weaver, and George himself was put apprentice to a shoemaker who dealt in wool and cattle. George does not seem to have had much to do with the shoemaking: he took most delight in attending to the sheep and to farming operations. He was early visited by religious convictions, and sought enlightenment from the clergy around him. It was not likely, however, that such ministers as Baxter has described could do him much good. He fell into great distress of mind, and walked many nights by himself in great spiritual troubles and sorrow. The clergyman of his parish, one Nathaniel Stevens, so far from communicating spiritual light, drew from George, and used to make his sermons out of what he heard from him in conversation. George, therefore, went to an ancient priest at Mansetter, in Warwickshire, and endeavoured to learn from him the causes of his despair and temptations, but this 'ancient priest' had no better counsel for him than 'to take tobacco and sing psalms.' But George signified that he was no lover of tobacco, and as for psalms, he was not in a state to sing. Then the priest bade him come again, and then he would tell him many things. But when George came the priest was angry and pettish, for George's former words had displeased him; and he was so indiscreet, that what George had told him of his sorrows and griefs he told again to his servants, so that it got amongst the milk-lasses, and grieved him to have opened his mind to such a one; and he saw they were all miserable comforters. Then he heard of a priest living about Tamworth, who was accounted an experienced man, and therefore he went to him, but found him like an empty hollow cask. 'Hearing, afterwards, of one Dr. Cradock, of Coventry, he went to him also, and asked him whence temptations and despair did arise, and how troubles came to be wrought in man? Now as they were walking together in Dr. Cradock's garden, it happened that George, in turning, set his foot on the side of a bed, which so disturbed that teacher, as if his house had been on fire, and thus all their discourse was lost, and George went away in sorrow, worse than he was when he came, seeing that he found none who could reach his condition. After this he went to one Macham, a priest of high account, and he, no more skilful than the others, was for giving George some physic, and for bleeding him. But they could not get one drop of blood from him, either in the arms or the head, his body being, as it were, dried up with sorrows, grief, and trouble, which were so great upon him, that he could have wished never to have been born, to behold the vanity and wickedness of men; or that he had been born blind, and so he might never have seen it, and deaf, that he might never have heard vain and wicked words, or the Lord's name blasphemed' (Sewel's History of the Christian People in derision called Quakers, vol. i., pp. 8-12).

Fortunately for George Fox, he was driven from seeking spiritual aid from all such 'empty casks,' to the true means, his Bible, and earnest solitary prayer for Divine illumination. He retired into the fields and spent whole days and nights reading and praying in a hollow tree. Here he found what is divinely promised, that to those who knock it shall be opened; that those who seek spiritual teaching from the Divine Spirit itself shall find it. His darkness, his doubts, his despair, gradually cleared away, and he came to see the 'truth' developed to his understanding, pure and free from all school glosses. Never since the original proclamation of the gospel to the simple fishermen of Galilee, had its noble reality been so completely manifested. It came to him unclouded, unimpeded by any preconceived or preinculcated notions or conventionalisms. There were, in his hollow oak, no 'royal reasons' to warp God's truth, no college logic to cramp it; pure and unadulterated it issued from the Divine mind as the waters of Siloa's fount, which

> Flowed fast by the oracle of God.

It came forth in all its august but simple greatness, and Fox, a soul of the most honest and intrepid mould, embraced it with that love and faith which are ready not only to die for it, but to suffer all contempt and wrong for it whilst living. Lord Macaulay, in his 'History of England,' has treated Fox as a fanatic ignoramus, and little better than an idiot. It was the only judgement to which such a man as Macaulay could come. Fox must be an idiot to a man like Macaulay, and Macaulay must have been an idiot to him. Macaulay was essentially an outward, worldly-minded man, a man given up to Whiggism and standing well with the world; and verily he had his reward. Fox was the exact antipode of such a man. Fox was no fool; on the contrary, he was a man, though destitute of much human education, possessed of a masculine understanding, of a power of reason against which the florid rhetoric of Macaulay would have stood no more chance than did the ablest sophisms of the ablest men of the times; judges, officers, clergy, statesmen, of Cromwell himself, as may be seen by his history. Macaulay with his mere worldism could no more understand a man of the intellectual calibre of Fox than a monkey's subtlety can comprehend the massive sagacity of an elephant. The one was all superficial expedience, the other all internal truth; the one having no root in the eternal soil of principle, the other all heart and principle; the one worshipping at the shrine of popularity and personal advantage, the other worshipping only the eternally true, the eternally holy, and despising every temporary profit or glory which could interpose itself in his life and death struggle towards it. Such men must remain longer than suns and systems remain; while truths are truths, and selfisms are selfisms, idiots, inconvertible idiots to each other; with this difference, that Fox could have seen through and through Macaulay at a glance, whilst Macaulay could never fathom the profound greatness of Fox. The religion of Fox became, like that of the first apostles, a religion in which spiritual truth went for everything, mundane considerations, mundane reservations, mundane balancing of advantage, for nothing. With him all was for God and the insurmountable truth; all for man and his eternity, without any temptation from man as a favour-bestowing or praise-bestowing creature of a day. The mountain standing in the vastness and the solidities of nature knows nothing of the sheep which grazes it, or the butterfly which sports over its herbage, and they cannot comprehend the solid and age-enduring mountain. When they can understand each other, then Foxs and Macaulays will understand each other, and not till then.

Fox was developed into the highest phase of spiritualism, that of direct communion with the Divine mind, by the same means as the apostles and saints in all ages have been developed and baptised into it, by opening their souls in solitude and prayer to the Eternal Soul in a sublime unflinching integrity. In this silent and perfect dedication to its infiltrations, in a heroic submission to its meltings and mouldings, he found all the outward husks of human theories, the outward shadow of self-indulgence, self-weakness, self-cravings, and self-wisdom, drop away, and a pure, calm, resplendent wisdom and strength rise up in clear vision, and make him a free man of the universe, triumphant over pride, passion, and temporal desire in the power and unity of God.

He had now rapidly to unlearn what he had learned in established teachings of the age. 'As he was walking in a field, on a First-Day morning, it was discovered unto his understanding, that to be bred at Oxford or Cambridge was not enough to make a man a minister of Christ. At this he wondered, because it was the common belief of the people; but for all that, he took this to be a Divine revelation, and he admired the goodness of the Lord, believing now the ordinary ministers not to be such as they pretended to be. This made him unwilling to go any more to church, as it was called, to hear the priest Stevens, believing that he could not profit thereby; and therefore, instead of going thither, he would get into the orchard or the fields, by himself, with his Bible, which he esteemed above all books, seeking thus to be edified in solitariness. At this, his relations were much troubled; but he asked them whether John, the Apostle, did not say to the believers, that "they needed no man to teach them, but as the anointing teacheth them." And though they knew this to be Scripture, and that it was true, yet it grieved them, because he would not go to hear the priest with them, but separated himself from their way of worship; for he now saw that a true believer was another thing than they looked upon it to be; and that being bred at the universities did not qualify a man to be a minister of Christ. Thus he lived by himself, not joining with any, nay, not of the dissenting people, but became a stranger to all, relying wholly upon the Lord Jesus Christ.'

Fox, in fact, found himself like Abraham, called to go forth from his father's house and his kindred, from all old teachings, associations, and notions, for he was appointed one of those who have to revitalise the Church, and bring it back to its original faith and power. He had to go forth, with the Bible in his hand and the fire of God in his soul, to bring men back from set forms and dead rituals, to the simple religion of the Bible: and it is the Bible, in such hands, which has continually to fight with mere human formalities and dead shells of profession. It is this which has produced all the changes and reforms that have appeared in the Christian Church yet. It overthrew paganism—it split asunder popery—it ruined monkery in this country—it destroyed it in Spain. The Catholics were deeper in worldly wisdom than the Church of England: they knew it to be an enemy, and they treated it as an enemy: they kept it down and out of sight as long as they could. Henry VIII. and Elizabeth were wiser in this respect than their successors. Henry passed an Act, in 1539, called 'The Bloody Statute,' in which he decreed that 'no women, artificers, apprentices, journeymen, husbandmen, or labourers, should read the New Testament, on pain of death:' and Elizabeth was equally averse to it. She did not wish the people to read at all, lest it should make them less submissive. She disliked even preachings, lest the mischievous principles of Christianity should steal abroad through it; three or four preachers in a county she declared quite sufficient. Such was the policy of the Catholic Church, and of the cunning founders of the English Church; but now the Bible had been allowed to walk abroad over the whole land, the peasant had learned to feel himself a man, and the man an immortal creature—the child of God — the heir of precious rights and deathless hopes; a being too good to be trodden on by priestly pride, or robbed by priestly pretences. It was because the peasants of Scotland had, in every mountain glen and-lowland hut, listened to the animating topics and precious promises of the 'big ha' Bible,' that they had risen and resisted the bloody emissaries of the church. And now, throughout England, in city and hamlet, in field and forest, the great charter of man was studied, and was ready in the hands of 'the man in leather,' to cast down everything that was opposed to freedom of spirit and independence of purpose.

Amongst these inquiring spirits, or Seekers, as they were called, George Fox went forth, in 1647, directing his first course into Nottinghamshire and Derbyshire. 'During all this time, he never joined in profession of religion with any, but gave himself up to the disposal of the Lord; having forsaken not only all evil company, but also taken leave of father and mother, and all other relations; and so he travelled up and down as a stranger on the earth, which way he felt his heart inclined, and when he came into a town, he took a chamber to himself there, and tarried sometimes a month, sometimes more, sometimes less, in a place, lest, being a tender young man, he should be hurt by too familiar a conversation with men' (Sewel, vol. i. p. 15).

As he had forsaken the priests of the establishment, so he left the separate teachers, too, because he saw there was none amongst them all that could speak to his condition. And when all his hopes in them and in all men were gone, then he heard, according to what he relates himself, a voice, which said, 'There is one, even Christ Jesus, that can speak to thy condition.' Having heard this, his heart leapt for joy, and it was showed him why there was none upon the earth that could speak to his condition, namely, that he might give the Lord alone all the glory.

He was now in a continual progress of spiritual teaching by inward revelation. He learned experimentally that Christ is the light that truly enlighteneth any man who cometh into the world, and this became so fundamental a doctrine of his, that the people who gathered about him were at first called 'The Children of the Light.' Yet he was a diligent reader of the Scriptures, that speak at large of God and Christ, though he knew him not but by revelation, as he who had the key did open. George was in the highest state of mediumship and of spiritualism, namely, in direct communication with the Spirit of God, and his followers cultivated this highest condition, and laid down their whole system upon it, paying little attention to the secondary condition of ministrations through angels, which has been the more particular dispensation of this more material age. Yet we shall see, that he and his Friends showed themselves distinguishers of dreams, casters out of evil spirits, healers in the name of Christ, and predicters of events, etc. They possessed many of the gifts of the true Church, though they desired above all to walk in the immediate power of the Divine Spirit, and to call all men to this communion as the source of all Christian teaching and edification. So much was this the case, that they were accused of not believing

Λ.3798-3800.3801.3805.

MISREPRESENTATIONS OF THE FRIEND

in the outward Christ, who died at Jerusalem, b
taught that the outward death of Christ ther
would avail little, without the inward life and
quickening and reforming power of His Spirit.
calumny has even been reiterated in our time, a
honest but misinformed Richard Baxter. The I
Philip, in his lives of Whitefield and of Bunya
Wardlaw, of Glasgow, have repeated the calumɪ
allowing Friends to be Christians on that account
truth of the matter being, that whilst they ful
and proclaimed their belief in the outward Chris:
the first to draw attention to the great doctrin
dwelling and regenerating life in the soul, then ɫ
myth, but now from the Quakers re-admitted
credence. In the Articles and Homilies of the
England, indeed, this doctrine existed, but at ɪ
had ceased to exist in the credence of the clerg
continually ridiculed by them when asserted by]

Amongst the people whom Fox came amongst,
who believed much in dreams; but he taught theɪ
very necessary distinction betwixt one kind of ɩ
another. He told them there were three sorts
Multiplication of business produced dreams:
whisperings of Satan in the night seasons, and
also speakings of God to man in dreams—facts
firmed by modern spiritualism. Amongst his
spiritual openings he had several precisely of the
since to Swedenborg. 'In Nottinghamshire it
Lord to show him that the natures of those thing
hurtful without were also within, in the minds
men; and that the natures of dogs, swine, viperɛ
of Cain, Ishmael, Esau, Pharaoh, etc., were in tl
many people. But since this did grieve him, he
Lord, saying, "Why should I be thus, seeing]
addicted to commit these evils?" And inwaɪ
answered him, "That it was needful he should h
of all conditions; how else should he speak to all cɩ

He also saw that there was an ocean of darkness and death, but withal an infinite ocean of light and love, which flowed over the ocean of darkness, in all which he perceived the infinite love of God' (Sewel, vol. 1. p. 18).

Again he says, 'I saw into that which was without end, and things which cannot be uttered; and of the greatness and infiniteness of the love of God, which cannot be expressed by words; and I have been brought through the very ocean of darkness and death; and the same eternal power of God which brought me through those things was that which afterwards shook the nation, priests, professors, and people. . . . And I saw the harvest white, and the seed of God lying thick on the ground, as ever did wheat, which was sown outwardly, and none to gather it, and for this I mourned with tears.' ✶

The shaking which came through Fox, of priests, people, officers, magistrates and learned men, was a great revolution, little understood at the present day. Of late there has been much talk of Quakerism dying out, and sundry books have been written to show the causes of it; but those who supposed such a thing, little knew what Quakerism was or is. It is not a religion of caps and coats, but of the great principles of the New Testament, which at that day lay trodden under foot. Fox went on under a process of revelation till he saw the whole mighty scheme of the gospel in its grandeur and fullness. He came to despise all mere outer forms, and to grasp the inward and eternal principles of Christian truth— THE TRUTH, as he emphatically termed it. This consisted in the doctrine that Christ is the Word, the Light, and the Comforter, which enlightens every man which cometh into the world, and leadeth into all truth. That by opening our hearts to this Divine and ever-present teacher, we have all truth in ' the two great books of God, the Bible and Nature,' opened up to us. That in Christ we are born again new creatures, and trained up into perfect men in Christ Jesus. Like Wesley, religion,—that Christ's religion is free and self-sustaining. That it is utterly opposed to all despotism in creed, or in politics; to usurpation of the personal liberties of men; to all giving and receiving of titles of worldly honour and flattery. He refused, on this account, to pay what he called hat homage, by taking off his hat to people, and to use ' you ' to a single person. All these things, he asserted, sprang from pride and an inordinate self-love and vanity, and how truly this was the case was seen by the resentment and the persecution which the refusal of them occasioned. He rejected baptism by water, and the Sacrament of the Lord's Supper, as non-essential forms, the baptism of the Spirit being the true and essential baptism; and that, if we commemorated the Last Supper, though only recommended to Christ's own immediate disciples, we ought also to wash one another's feet, as a ceremony more strictly enjoined. He taught that tithes were anti-Christian, both tithes and those to whom they were given, being terminated with the tribe of Levi. He showed the impropriety of calling that a church which was only the meeting place of the church, and generally styled those steeple-houses. Never was there such a stripping away of the old rotten bark of ecclesiasticism, so thorough a return to the naked truth of the gospel. Such a system was sure to bring down a tremendous tempest of persecution, and the whole history of the Society of Friends down to the Act of Toleration by William III., is a history of as frightful and ruthless persecutions as ever fell on any Christian body from any church calling itself Christian. The history of these awful ' sufferings' fill a huge folio volume. The Five Mile Act, the Conventicle Act, and the Oath of Allegiance and Supremacy, were made the means of fleecing the Friends by wholesale. Fox and his disciples could not take any oath at all, seeing that Christ had most explicitly said, ' Swear not at all,' and, therefore, this oath was made a continual snare to them. Fox had soon vast numbers of serious enquirers of all ranks flocking to him, and as they declared that the gospel ought to be preached freely—' freely ye have received, freely give'—the clergy saw that, if this succeeded, their craft was gone for ever. Therefore, clergy, and magistracy, and soldiery, came down on these modern apostles, 'who turned the world upside down,' and they were plundered and thrown into prison by thousands. Fox, and nearly all his eminent followers, passed many years in prisons,—such dens of filth, inclemency, and wickedness, as now strike us in the description with amazement—2,500 Friends were in prison at one time, and 369 died there! In Bristol, at one time, every adult Quaker was in prison for his faith, and the children still met, in spite of the beatings and insults of their persecutors, who struck them in the face, as they were accustomed to do the women, whom it was a favourite plan to drag by the hair, pinch their arms till black and blue, and prick them with bodkins and packing-needles. When this would not do, they banished them to the colonies and sugar plantations, and sold them for slaves, where their doctrines soon spread, and persecution became as hot as at home, especially in New England, where the famous PILGRIM FATHERS exceeded all others in monstrous fines, flogging of women from town to town, cutting off ears, and hanging! These people, who had fled from England on the plea of escaping persecution for religion there, turned the most savage of persecutors, showing that their boasted love of religious freedom was but inspissated selfishness.

All this time at home (that is, for thirty years), the Friends were stripped of their property by means of the before-named enactments, the informers receiving one-third of the spoil. They were charged ten pounds a piece for attending a Friends' meeting, and twenty pounds a-piece if they opened their mouths to defend themselves, on the pretence that they preached! Their meeting-houses were pulled down—those in London, by Sir Christopher Wren! Their very beds were dragged from under them, and one woman's body was torn from the grave. From 1655 to the end of this persecution, half-a-million of money or money's worth was wrenched from them. One clergyman said he would rather see all the

Quakers hanged than lose a sixpence by them. The informers lived jovially on them. They entered freely into their houses, kept the keys of their doors in their pockets, and declared that they would eat of the best and drink of the sweetest, and these rogues of Quakers should pay for all. When they complained to Archbishop Sancroft of these villanies, he coolly replied, 'There requires crooked timber to build a ship!'

How the students of Oxford behaved themselves at this period deserves recording: — 'The students of Oxford fell on two women Friends, who presumed to preach in the town, and to advise these same youngsters to amendment of life. They dragged these females to the pump of St. John's College, pumped on their necks and into their mouths till they were almost dead; after which they tied them arm to arm, and inhumanly dragged them up and down the college, and through a pool of water; and finally flung one of them, Elizabeth Fletcher, a young woman, over a grave-stone into a grave, with such violence, that she died in consequence. Then these religious students — this was in 1658 — these embryo prophets of a nation, came into a meeting-house there, and drew a Friend out by the hair of the head. The proctor himself pulled John Shackerly by the hair, and out of doors, from Richard Bettin's house, and violently thrust out others. And several times the scholars threw stones and dirt at Friends, and broke the doors to pieces; and broke the windows several times; and took away the key of the door; and knocked tenterhooks into the keyhole; and pulled up part of the porch; and came into the meeting, and turned up the seats that Friends sate on; and rid upon the backs of men and women like wild horses; and brought gunpowder and squibs, and fired them, and set the room on a smoke, and among people under their clothes, like to set the house on fire, and to undo people; and have shot bullets amongst Friends to knock out their eyes; stamping wildly and unruly, like tavern fellows, crying, " *Give us beer and tobacco!* " And the scholars have come into the meeting, among the people of God, and called for wenches, or harlots, like fellows that haunt ill houses; and brought strong beer into the meeting, and drank to Friends, and because they have refused to drink, have thrown it on their necks, and clothes, and bands, and have sung vile songs, and cursed and swore. And several times came into the meetings blowing and puffing with tobacco-pipes in their mouths, cursing, swearing, and stamping, making the house shake again, and insulted the women too shamefully for description. And the scholars have come into the meeting to act Tobit and his dog; and one of them divided his filthy stuff into uses and points, after the manner of priests; and another raised doctrines of a tinker and cobbler, and many more wicked actions, by mockings and scoffings, and filthy language; and these scholars have been so shameless that, after meeting, they have pressed in by violence, and taken meat from off the table; taken the bread and pottage out of the pot, like greedy dogs lapping them up; and stole and carried away the Friends' books. One Friend they dragged into *John's* College; threw beer upon him, struck, and beat, and pinched him, till he lost his consciousness; and then thrust pins into his flesh, and kept him there scoffing at him, and asking him, "*If the Spirit did not move him now?*"

'But I am weary,' says Besse, 'of transcribing their abominations, and shall cease with this remark, which, however severe, is just and natural—namely, had those scholars been expressly educated for ministers of the devil, they could not have given more certain proofs of their proficiency' (Besse's 'Sufferings of the People called Quakers,' i. 565).

These are singular features of the state of the national church and its universities in George Fox's times, and of what people suffered for spirituality then. We spiritualists of to-day walk in silken slippers, and are let off with a harmless sneer or two. Having shown what Fox and the Friends endured for spiritualism, we may again revert to a few more traits of its peculiar character.

The power evinced during some meetings was such that

the house seemed to be shaken, and, on one occasion, a clergyman ran out of the church lest it should fall on his head. This was at Ulverstone, but the thing was of frequent occurrence. In 1648 George Fox had 'an opening,' such as Swedenborg records of himself. ' The creation was opened to me; and it was showed to me how all things had their names given them, according to their nature and virtue. And I was at a stand in my mind whether I should practise physic for the good of mankind, seeing the nature and virtue of the creatures were so opened to me by the Lord.' He says that the Lord showed him that such as were faithful to Him would be brought into the state in which Adam was before the fall, when the natures of all things were, by the divine unity, known to man, and that so they would come to know the hidden unity in the Eternal Being. He was shown that the professions of physic, divinity, and law were all destitute of the true knowledge and wisdom necessary for these professions, and that nothing but this divine illumination could bring them into it. It was shown him, however, that his labour was not to be physical but spiritual. It was at this time that he felt a certain assurance of his acceptance with God.

At Mansfield Woodhouse he found the gospel gift of command over disordered spirits manifested in him. There was a distracted woman under a doctor's hands, being bound and with her hair loose. The doctor was trying to bleed her, but could get no blood from her. Fox desired that she might be unbound, and he then commanded her in the name of the Lord to be still; and this had such effect that she became still; her mind settled, she grew well, and became a convert to his doctrine, and remained perfectly sane till her death. Soon after at Twycross he restored a person who was ill by prayer. 'There being in that town a great man, who had long lain sick, and was given over by the physicians, he went to visit him in his chamber; and having spoken some words to him, he was moved to pray by his bedside, and the Lord was entreated, so that the sick man was restored.' A still more remarkable case is recorded by him in his 'Journal.' 'After some time I went to a meeting at Arnside, where Richard Myer was, who had been long lame of one of his arms. I was moved of the Lord to say unto him, amongst all the people, ' Stand upon thy legs;' and he stood up, and stretched out his arm that had been lame a long time, and said, " Be it known unto you, all people, that this day I am healed." Yet his parents would hardly believe it; but, after the meeting was done, they had him aside, took off his doublet, and then saw it was true. He came soon after to Swarthmore meeting, and there declared how the Lord had healed him.'

These cures by spirit-power Fox regarded but as incidental objects of his mission; but we should have been glad to have had the particular record of others; for such there were, and numerous ones, according to his account. 'Many great and wonderful things were wrought by the heavenly power in those days; for the Lord laid bare His omnipotent arm, and manifested His power to the astonishment of many, by the healing virtue whereof many have been delivered from great infirmities, *and the devils are made subject to His name*, of which particular instances might be given beyond what this unbelieving age is able to receive or bear.' Still we have a considerable number of instances of the healing power of God exerted in the early history of the Friends. At Ulverstone, Sawtrey the justice of peace, set the people upon George Fox, who beat him so terribly with cudgels that he fell senseless on the common to which they had dragged him ; ' but, recovering again, and being strengthened by *immediate* power, he stood up, and, stretching out his arms, said with a loud voice, " Strike again, here are my arms, my head, and my cheeks." Then a mason gave him such a heavy blow over the back of his hand with his rule that it was much bruised, and his arm so benumbed that he could not draw it to him again, so that some of the people cried out, " He has spoiled his hand for ever." But he, being preserved through the love of God, stood still, and after a while felt such extraordinary strengthening power that he instantly recovered the vigour of his hand and arm' (Sewel, i. 77).

In the ferocious treatment which the early Friends received, they were often wounded so desperately that, to all ordinary ideas, they never could recover; but they bear continual testimony to a supernatural healing. Miles Halhead, one of their preachers, 'was so beaten and abused at Skipton, that he was laid for dead; nevertheless, by the Lord's power he was healed of all his bruises; and within three hours he was healthy and sound again, to the astonishment of those that had so abused him, and to the convincing of many (*Ibid.* p. 91). Soon after the same undaunted soldier of Christ was attacked by a mob at Doncaster, which was again urged on by the priest; was once more knocked down, and beaten, as was supposed, to death. In the evening, however, he entered a chapel, and, sorely bruised as he was, he preached, and at the conclusion of his discourse 'the Lord made him sound of all his bruises' (p. 93). William Dewsbury, another eminent Quaker minister, was set upon at Coldbeck, and was nearly killed by the mob; but was healed in the same astonishing manner' (p. 96). Barbara Blaugdone, a most courageous female minister, was so cruelly flogged at Exeter for preaching that the blood flowed all down her back; but she only sang during the operation, so that the enraged beadle laid on with all his might to make her cry out, but in vain; for, says the historian, 'she was strengthened by an uncommon and more than human power.' She afterwards declared that her feeling was above all suffering.

Another evidence of the existence of Christian spiritualism amongst the early Friends was their power of seeing into the internal state of people, and often of foreseeing, through this, calamities about to befall them. Barbara Blaugdone, already mentioned, having 'a concern'— that is, an impression — in her mind, to speak to the Lord-deputy of Ireland regarding the persecution of the Friends, an attempt was made to impose upon her. As she knew neither the person of the deputy, nor those of the chief people about him, when she was brought into the drawing-room a person presented himself as the deputy. She stood silently, and the room being full of people, they asked her why she did not do her message to their lord. She answered, 'When I see your lord, then I shall do my message to him.' Her internal monitor assured her that this was not the deputy. Soon after he came in, and sate down, and she immediately addressed him on the subject of her concern.

George Fox meeting with James Nayler, one of the ministers of the society, was 'struck with a fear concerning him—a sense of some great calamity that was like to befall him.' The next time that he saw him was in Exeter gaol, in consequence of some fanatic proceedings which became of national notoriety, and to be mentioned anon.

George Fox, going to Hampton Court to speak with the Protector Cromwell, regarding the persecutions of the Friends, met him riding in Hampton Court Park, and before he came at him, he said he perceived a waft of death to go forth from him, and coming to him, he looked like a dead man. Having spoken to Cromwell of the persecutions of Friends, he desired him to come to Hampton Court the next day; but, on going there, he found him too ill to be seen, and in a day or two he died — September 3, 1658.

Innumerable instances of this clairvoyance might be given, but I shall only add that the celebrated Robert Barclay, author of the 'Apology,' in a letter to Heer Adrian Paets, the Dutch ambassador to Spain, in 1676, amongst other features of Quakerism, gives some striking explanations of this internal sense. 'This divine and supernatural operation in the mind of man is a true and most glorious miracle, which, when it is perceived by the inward and supernatural sense, divinely raised up in the mind of man, doth so evidently and clearly persuade the understanding to assent to the thing revealed that there is no need of an outward miracle.' He adds that the voice of God in the soul is as convincing as the truth of God's being, from whom it proceeds (Sewell, ii. 252). 'It is no less absurd to require of God, who is a most pure Spirit, to manifest His will to men by the outward senses, than to require us to see sounds and hear light and colours; for as the objects of the outward senses are not to be confounded, but every object is to have its proper sense, so must one judge of inward and spiritual objects, which have their proper sense, whereby they are perceived. And tell me, how doth God manifest His will concerning matters of fact, when He sends His angels to men, since angels have not outward senses, or, at least, not so gross ones as ours are? Yea, when men die, and appear before the tribunal of God, whether unto eternal life or death, how can they know this, having laid down their bodies, and therewith their outward senses? Nevertheless, this truth of God is a truth of fact, as is the historical truth of Christ's birth in the flesh' (*Ibid.* p. 253). From all this Barclay contended that the soul had its own senses, as distinct from the outward senses as the natural senses are distinguished from each other by their specific difference, and that it is through these senses that God, a spirit, directly addresses the human soul.

Robert Barclay had a prognostic of the murder of Archbishop Sharpe. It is thus recorded by his son, Robert Barclay, of Urie:—'On the third day of May, as he was travelling home from Edinburgh in his coach, Archbishop Sharpe was murdered; it being very remarkable that, some days before the murder, Robert Barclay, being upon a journey to the yearly meetings at Edinburgh, in company with his wife's sister, and they being on horseback, at the East Ferry, as they passed by the kirk which belonged to the archbishop, close to the end of the town, they heard a most terrifying howling noise, which was astonishing. Upon which, they sent the servant to look into the church through the windows, who could then perceive nothing, but no sooner returned to them than the noise began again, and continued till they rode out of hearing. This account both he and his sister gave immediately after, and she in my hearing repeated the same, but a few years ago, to a company visiting her at her own house in Newcastle, consisting of Quakers and others. This I mention as a fact, without any other reflection.'

The early Friends declare in many places that they heard internal voices as clear and distinct as outward voices. The wife of Miles Halhead, who had been greatly opposed to his leaving his home so much to travel in the ministry, at length wrote to him, ' Truly, husband, I have something to tell thee. One night, being in bed, mourning and lamenting with tears in my eyes, I heard a voice saying, " Why art thou so discontented concerning thy husband? I have called and chosen him to my work, and my right hand shall uphold him." It went on to say, that, if she became content, it would bless her and her children for her husband's sake ; if not, it would bring a great cross upon her. This alarmed her, but did not cure her, and her only son was soon after taken from her by death. Then she saw the cross menaced, and submitted to God's will' (*Ibid.* i. 92.) Marmaduke Stevenson, one of the Friends hanged by the Pilgrim Fathers, says he heard a distinct voice saying, 'I have ordained thee a prophet to the nations.' Catherine Evans, who, with her companion, Sarah Cheevers, was thrown into the Inquisition at Malta, heard a voice saying, ' Ye shall not die!' and on that voice they calmly relied, and, after many sufferings and threatenings, came out safe. When some English ships arrived, and endeavours were made for their liberation, the voice distinctly said they could not go yet; and then, spite of all efforts at that time, it proved so.

Visions were as frequent amongst them as voices. George Fox says, that, going up to the top of Pendle Hill in Yorkshire, ' the Lord opened to him, and let him see a great people to be gathered in those parts, and especially about Wensleydale and Sedberg. He saw them in white raiment coming along a river side to serve the Lord.'

Catherine Evans, already mentioned, whilst in the Inquisition at Malta, and threatened with being burnt alive with her companion, and being kept in suspense for several days on this subject, saw 'in a dream a large room, and a great wood fire in the chimney; and she beheld one sitting in the chair by the fire in the form of a servant, whom she took to be the Eternal Son of God. Likewise she saw a very amiable well-favoured man-child, sitting in a hollow chair over the fire, not appearing to be above three-quarters of a year old, and having no clothes on but a little fine linen about the upper parts, and the fire flamed about it, yet the child played and was merry. She would then have taken it up for fear it should have been burnt, but he that sat in the chair bade her let it alone. Then turning about, she saw an angel, and he that sat in the chair bade her take up the child, which she did, and found it had no harm; and then awakening, she told her dream to Sarah, and desired her not to fear, since the heavenly host thus followed them, (Sewel, i. 406). Daniel Baker, a minister who went to Malta to obtain the release of these ladies, had a mountain shown to him in a dream where he had to deliver a testimony; on coming to Gibraltar, he saw that this was the very mountain, and, though the captain of the vessel would not consent to his going on shore, the ships were detained there wind-bound till he was allowed to go and deliver his message, and on the next day a fair wind sprang up, and the fleet set sail.

When the Turks were making great progress against Austria, George Fox saw a vision of the Turk turned back, and told his friends that this would be the case; and in a few months, contrary to general expectation, it took place. James Nayler, warned by what befell him, cautioned Friends to try their visions, etc. by the inward test of the Divine Spirit. 'If there appear to thee voices, visions, and revelations, feed not thereon, but abide in the light and feel the body of Christ, and therewith thou shalt receive faith and power to judge of every appearance and spirits, the good to hold fast and obey, and the false to resist.' Sound advice, and that of St. John.

Another gift of the church, the spirit of prophecy, was liberally conferred on Fox and the Friends. At Gainsborough, a man having uttered a very false accusation against Fox, he called him a Judas, and announced that Judas's end would be his. The fellow soon after hanged himself, and a stake was driven into his grave. At Swarthmore, he announced to Sawtrey, the persecuting magistrate, that God had shortened his days, and that he could not escape his doom. The man drowned himself. A similar doom he announced to another persecutor, Colonel Needham, whose son desired him to cut him off, and who sent him prisoner to Cromwell. Needham was hanged as one of the judges of Charles I. Barbara Blaugdone, being confined in a most abominable prison in Dublin, wrote to Judge Pepes, who unjustly condemned many of the Friends, that the day of his death was at hand—God was calling him to his account. The night after she got out of prison, the judge, according to her prediction, died of apoplexy in his bed. 'A certain woman came once into the parliament with a pitcher in her hand, which she, breaking before them, told them so should they be broken to pieces, which came to pass not long afterwards.' Thomas Aldam, a minister amongst Friends, who had in vain protested against the persecutions under Cromwell, took off his cap, tore it to pieces in his presence, and told him so should the government be rent from him and his house. George Bishop, a minister, in a letter dated the 25th September, 1664, to the king and two houses of parliament, distinctly predicted the plague of London, which broke out in December of the same year, and swept away 100,000 people. This letter he had delivered to both the king and members of parliament. As it is short and decided, we may as well quote it entire. ' To the King and both Houses of Parliament, thus saith the Lord:—" Meddle not with my people because of their conscience to me, and banish them not out of the nation because of their conscience; for if ye do, I will send my plagues upon you, and ye shall know that I am the Lord!" Written in obedience to the Lord by his servant, George Bishop; Bristol, the 25th of the Ninth Month, 1664.'

George Fox predicted the desolation of London some years before the fire took place; but two of his disciples again predicted it more distinctly still. Thomas Briggs went through Cheapside and other streets preaching repentance to the inhabitants, and declaring, like Jonah at Nineveh, that, unless they repented, London should be destroyed. 'Thomas Ibbit of Huntingdonshire, came to London a few days before the burning of that city, and, as hath been related by an eye-witness, did, upon his coming thither, alight from his horse, and unbutton his clothes in so loose a manner, as if they had been put on in haste, just out of bed. In this manner he went about the city on the sixth day, being the day he came thither, and also on the seventh day of the week, pronouncing judgment by fire which should lay waste the city. On the evenings of these days some of his friends had meetings with him to enquire concerning his message and call, to pronounce that impending judgment, in his account whereof he was not more particular and clear, than that he said he, for some time, had a vision thereof, but had delayed to come and declare it as commanded, until he felt, as he expressed it, the fire in his own bosom; which message or vision was very soon proved to be sadly true, the fire lasting nearly four days, and destroying thirteen thousand two hundred houses.' It broke out September 2, 1666, the very day following the second day's announcement by Ibbit. So amazed was the prophet at the prompt and terrible fulfilment of the prediction, that he nearly lost his own life in it, standing in Cheapside before the flames with his arms stretched out, till one Thomas Matthews with others forced him away.

More striking, complete, and terrible predictions than these scarcely occur in the Scriptures themselves. It is equally remarkable that nearly all the leading persecutors of the Friends perished by sudden and awful judgments. One Barlow, a preacher at Exeter, turned lawyer, grew rich by the spoils in Oliver's days, but afterwards became as suddenly poor. Many of the New England persecutors, one of whom when a Friend quoted St. Paul, 'For in God we live and move, and have our being,' was irreverent enough to reply, 'And so doth every cat and dog,' were visibly punished for their former cruelty. Endicot the governor, died of a hideous disease, and his stench was so loathsome before his death that scarcely anyone could go near him. Major-general Adderton, who scoffed at Mary Dyer when she was going to be hanged, and who, warned of God's judgments by another Friend, replied, 'But the judgments are not come yet,' was killed by a fall from his horse, and lay a horrible spectacle. Norton the clergyman, one of the fiercest of the persecutors, died suddenly, and with a groan saying, 'The judgment of the Lord is upon me.' Bellingham, governor after Endicot, went mad, and died a raving maniac. Sewel says that it was reported that a curse long rested on the vicinity of Boston, and that, on enquiry into the truth of it from persons well knowing the neighbourhood, the report was confirmed. That for twenty miles round Boston no wheat would grow to perfection. Sometimes insects destroyed it, sometimes other things, till the owners despairing let the ground go to waste; yet beyond that circuit, dyed with the blood of the Quakers, the soil was most fruitful. Colonel Robinson of Cornwall, one of the worst persecutors, and who used to call on the other justices to go with him fanatic-hunting, was killed by his own bull whilst George Fox was in that neighbourhood. A Quaker lady, having her maid with her, preached in Dieppe, but was cruelly used by the mob. A Mr. Dundas conducted them to their lodgings at a Scotchman's, but he shut the door in their faces; he then led them to his own lodgings, but his landlady refused them entrance. At length he got them away by ship. Two things he afterwards noticed: that the Scotchman who shut his door upon them died within the year, and the house of his landlady who refused them entrance was burnt down. A ship freighted with Quakers, banished to the British plantations in America, never could reach there, but after being driven from place to place, put them ashore in Holland, whence they returned to their own country. Henry Marshall, priest of Crosthwaite in Westmorcland, a bitter persecutor of Friends, fell downstairs and was killed by fracture of his skull. Christopher Glin, priest at Butford, another persecutor, was struck blind in his pulpit, and remained so for life. To these specific instances Sewell adds, 'Many others of the persecutors, both justices, informers, and others, came to a miserable end; some being by sudden or unnatural death, and others by lingering sicknesses, taken out of this life; while some who, by spoil, had scraped much together, fell to great poverty and beggary, whose names I could set down and mention, also time and place, and among these some rapacious ecclesiastics, who came to a sad end; but I studiously avoid particularising such instances, to avoid the appearance of grudging and envy. Some of them signified themselves the terrible remorse of conscience they felt, because of their having persecuted the Quakers, insomuch that they roared out their gnawing grief, mixed with despair, under the grievous pains they suffered in their body' (vol. ii. 237).

As is usual, in all times of great spiritual development, the devil managed to put in for a share of it. On the dark side of spiritualism rose up Lodovick Muggleton and his coadjutor John Reeves, who declared themselves the two witnesses spoken of in Revelations xi. 3. Reeves soon died, but Muggleton lived a good while, and put forth a number of publications of the most wild and blasphemous character, and had followers named Muggletonians. He professed to be sent by the Holy Ghost, and pronounced eternal damnation on the Quakers, and declared that 'no infinite Spirit of Christ, nor any god could detain them from his sentence and curse.' That to him were given the keys of heaven and hell, and that he 'was set over all other gods and infinite spirits whatever,' &c. &c.

The Friends did stand battle against this effusion from the inferno; but what grieved them much more deeply was

the breaking out of a disorderly spiritualism within their own
pale. We have seen that George Fox had been struck with
a feeling of something unsettled and unsound in the spiritual
condition of James Nayler, one of the most gifted and intellectual of the ministers of the society. This James Nayler
was a native of Ardesley, near Wakefield, in Yorkshire, who,
at the time of his offence was scarcely forty years of age.
He was the son of a man of some landed property; had
received a good English education; had been an Independent in religion, and a quarter-master in the troop of
General Lambert, but discharged on account of failing health.
He seems to have been of a sensitive and highly poetical
temperament, and thus liable to be carried off his feet by the
excitements of the times. He was convinced of Quakerism
by George Fox at Wakefield in 1651, when he was about
thirty-five years of age. As he was at plough in the field,
he said he heard a voice bidding him go forth from his father's
house, and had a promise given with it that the Lord would
be with him: whereupon he did exceedingly rejoice that he
had heard the voice of God whom he had professed from a
child, and endeavoured to serve. He endeavoured to set
out on his mission, but his courage failed, and he said the
wrath of God was so upon him, that he became a wonder,
and it was thought he would have died. Afterwards he
went, and found himself, he said, provided for in a wonderful
manner from day to day. He then went to London, and by
the brilliancy of his preaching immediately made a great
sensation. He particularly excited the admiration of certain
enthusiastic women, Martha Simmons, Hannah Stranger,
and Dorcas Erbury, who fell into extravagant flatteries of
him, calling him the Everlasting Son of Righteousness, the
Prince of Peace, &c. It was the fault of Nayler that he
allowed these expressions, attributing them as applied not to
himself, but to Christ within him. This appears to have been,
through the darkest hours of his aberration, his real idea;
never for a moment did he conceive himself to be Christ, but
to be acting in the power of the indwelling Saviour, and the

homage as described to that Saviour. The words and conduct of the women, however, admitted of a worse meaning, and Nayler was reproved by the Friends for permitting them. In this state Nayler went down into the West of England, and made an entrance into Bristol with one Thomas Woodcock going bare-headed before him, and these wild women spreading scarfs and handkerchiefs in his way, and crying, ' Holy, holy, to the Lord God of Hosts!' They were all taken up and cast into prison. From Bristol they were carried to London, and the case made one of parliamentary enquiry. It is a remarkable circumstance, that the chief business of one whole session was the discussion of Nayler's case. A committee of the whole house sate twelve times, morning and afternoon, on it; for whilst a simple imprisonment of a few months would have been enough to have brought both Nayler and his foolish followers to their senses, there was a predominating party of the same hard, persecuting Independents, which had supplied America with its Pilgrim Father persecutors, and these would not be satisfied without some ferocious exhibition of cruelty. There was no proof that Nayler had ever uttered a single blasphemous word. On the contrary, when questioned whether he were the Christ, he emphatically and constantly denied it, saying only that he held, according to the New Testament, that Christ was in him, and that according to St. Paul, he was a reprobate if this were not the case. These are the words of his examination before the magistrate:—

Justice Pearson.—' Is Christ in thee?'

Nayler.—' I witness Him in me; and if I should deny Him before men, He would deny me before my Father which is in heaven.'

Justice Pearson.—' Spiritually, you mean.'

Nayler.—' Yea, spiritually.'

Justice Pearson.—' Is Christ in thee as a man?'

Nayler.—' Christ filleth all places, and is not divided: separate God and man, and he is no more Christ.'

This was the uniform language of Nayler; he never

departed from it: he was perfectly clear and orthodox in his faith on this point; his fault was that he was led into a personal exaltation by the flatteries of his followers, and that he did not reprove and reject their blasphemous language. There were charges also of criminal conversation with some of these women; but this was never proved, and was indignantly denied by him. In fact, Nayler was a simple-minded but imaginative man, and led by the wily tempter into the acceptance of the wild flatteries of the women by the blinding of his judgement. But he was no blasphemer himself. There was a general persuasion of this, and numerous petitions were made to parliament, and earnest applications to Cromwell by people of other persuasions for his treatment rather as one under a temporary delusion than as a blasphemer. But Cromwell was in the hands of the Independent ministers, especially of Reynolds, Griffith, Nye, Caryl, and Manton. He would not effectively interfere, and parliament, after violent debates, sentenced him to be whipped through London and through Bristol, to be set in the pillory, branded with 'B' for blasphemer, in the forehead, and his tongue bored through with a hot iron. The whole of this diabolic sentence was carried out with the most horrible rigour, notwithstanding the most vehement remonstrances from the public. Nayler underwent the punishment with stoical patience, and in the subsequent solitude of his prison came to the most sincere penitence for his folly, and wrote to the Friends, acknowledging this, and soliciting their forgiveness. The conduct of the Friends, on the occasion, was generous and just; for though the affair was calculated to injure their cause deeply, they never charged James Nayler with more than a temporary subjection to the delusions of Satan, and received him again to their full sympathy and affection.

But the grief of his fall had sunk deep into his own soul; he lived only about four years, in a mood of most affecting penitence, humility, and tenderness of spirit. The circumstances of his end are singularly pathetic. He was on his way northward towards his native place, when near Huntingdon he was robbed on the highway, and left bound. Probably he received at the time fatal injuries; for, being carried to a Friend's house near King's Rippon, he died in a few hours, at the latter end of the year 1660, aged forty-four.

About two hours before his decease he spoke in presence of several witnesses the following words—words which express more vividly and tenderly the suffering and divine nature of Christian truth, according to my idea, than any to be found in the whole compass of religious literature:—

'There is a spirit which I feel, that delights to do no evil, nor to revenge any wrong; but delights to endure all things, in hope to enjoy its own in the end. Its hope is to outlive all wrath and contention, and to weary out all exaltation and cruelty, or whatever is of a nature contrary to itself. It sees to the end of all temptations. As it bears no evil in itself, so it conceives none in thoughts to any other. If it be betrayed, it bears it; for its ground and spring is the mercies and forgiveness of God. Its crown is meekness, its life is everlasting love unfeigned, and it takes its kingdom with entreaty, and not with contention, and keeps it by lowliness of mind. In God alone it can rejoice, though none else regard it, or can own its life. It is conceived in sorrow, and brought forth without any to pity it; nor doth it murmur at grief and oppression. It never rejoiceth but through sufferings, for with the world's joy it is murdered. I found it alone, being forsaken. I have fellowship therein with them who lived in dens and desolate places of the earth, who through death obtained this resurrection and eternal holy life.'—JAMES NAYLER.

Peace to the gentle manes of James Nayler! happier and more enviable in his fall than his barbarous enemies in their day of triumph; for he found in that what their savage souls never knew, the immortal patience and immortal forgiveness of a tender soul baptised in suffering, and raised with Christ into the spirit of a perfect and infinite love.

This article, from the abundance and greatness of its material, has run to such extent, that I must end it abruptly. The system of the Friends was entirely so spiritual a system, that they could not make a single religious movement without spiritual guidance. It compelled them to refrain from all outward manufacture of ministers; God alone could make and qualify such. They were compelled to refrain from all forms, formulas, rituals, and ceremonies. They could only sit down together, and seek and receive the ministrations of the Divine Spirit. As that Spirit is promised to all who sincerely seek it, there could be no exceptions from its operations and endowments. As God is no respecter of persons, so there could be no difference of ranks and titles in the church, except such as He individually put on His members. The Friends could neither pray nor preach without immediate influence from the Spirit of Christ. However much the Society has since changed, however much it has since lost, however much it has cooled in its zeal and conformed to the spirit of the world; however much the growth of wealth has corrupted it, it has never abandoned its faith in the purely spiritual nature of its jurisdiction. Those who of late have seen it relaxing certain strictnesses, abandoning certain forms of costume, opening itself up to more liberal views of art and science, and social life, and have imagined that the day of Quakerism was drawing to a close, were never more mistaken. Quakerism being simply and solely primitive Christianity, can never die out. As it never could be circumscribed within the bounds of a sect—George Fox never wished it to be so—so the sect of Quakers may perish, but its principles must eternally remain. Those proclaimed by Fox and his Friends have now gone out from them into all bodies of the Christian world. The doctrine of the immediate influence of the Spirit of God, of the anti-Christianity of war, of slavery, of the pride of life, of the emptiness and deadness of all mere ecclesiastical forms; the doctrines of the true baptism being the baptism of the Spirit, the true Lord's Supper the daily feeding on the bread of life, which, like the manna in the wilderness, is spread every day before every soul. These doctrines have gone forth, or are going forth from the Society of Fox, never to return till they reach the ends of all the earth.

Never did a Christian body hold so firmly to their standard of truth against the scorn and the scornings of the world. Firm in their faith, no terrors, not those of death, could daunt them for a moment. When all other sects complied, they stood immovable, even to the smallest iota of conscientious conviction, and they were the first to wring from the government the rights of marrying and burying, and exemptions from oaths, with other privileges. They gave to Christian testimony a more manly stamp. The very name of Quaker became the highest of burlesques; for they never *quaked* at whatever man or tyrant could inflict upon them. They who nicknamed them so, were, in fact, the Quakers.

This high and entirely spiritual nature of Quakerism has exhibited itself in every period of its existence down to this hour. I could bring a whole volume of instances of the acting of the Friends under immediate spiritual guidance. William Penn, in founding Pennsylvania, showed his practical reliance on the doctrines of the New Testament. When all other settlers declared the American Indians not to be trusted, when Cotton Mather, a minister of the Pilgrim Fathers, declared them to be the children of the devil, and that, if he had a pen made of a porcupine's quill and dipped in aquafortis, he could not describe all their devilishness; when they were hunted down by so-called Christians with blood-hounds, and exterminated with fire and sword, Penn went to them unarmed, in Christian kindness, and made that just treaty with them which Voltaire says was the only treaty ever made without an oath, and the only one never broken. I must, however, refer the reader to the lives and works of Friends of all periods for plenty of spiritual manifestations. Instances of the ministers in their preaching having particular states suddenly communicated to them, and their preventing suicides and other crimes, are frequent. Extraordinary providences, and rescues from imminent perils, are of common record amongst Friends. John Roberts of Cirencester used to be consulted by his neighbours on the loss of cattle, etc., and after a short silence he would invariably tell them where to find them. See also the lives of John Woolman, David Sands, of Stephen Grellet, a minister whom I knew, and whose memoirs have been recently published; of Elizabeth Fry, or, indeed, the life of almost anyone of the ministers and eminent men amongst them at all times. As no denomination of Christians has ever recurred so fully and firmly to the primitive practice and condition of the Christian church, so none has received more brilliant and convincing proofs that the gospel in which they trusted is no cunningly devised fable. The promises by Christ of supernatural powers to His church have been firmly believed and fully demonstrated amongst the Friends.

CHAPTER XVI.

MADAME GUYON AND FENELON.

Whenever can there be A CHURCH that is not a church of gifts ? No man can make himself; still less can a church. THE SPIRIT in all its universality is the professed gift of the New Jerusalem; the Spirit hymning all praises, lifting all hands in prayer, that cast forth all demons; blessing all labours; healing all sorrows ; speeding all arts, piercing all veils, and catching the reflex of its Lord in all sciences; opening heaven and hallowing earth; the Spirit to do more than can be written, is the offer of the Lord to His everlasting Church.
DR. GARTH WILKINSON.

Open thy soul to God, O man, and talk
Through thine unfolded faculties with Him
Who never, save through faculties of mind
Spake to the Fathers.
HARRIS'S *Golden Age.*

THE history and opinions of Madame Guyon and of the Archbishop of Cambray are so well known that we need not go at great length into them. All the world knows that the spirituality of their religion was the cause of all their persecutions and misfortunes. Madame Guyon had adopted the opinions and sentiments of the early Christians rather than of the Roman Church. That religion was not a mere thing of human hierarchies or political institutions, but an act and habit of the soul, in which it entered into communion with the King and Saviour of souls, and was and could be subject to Him alone. It is true that the Fathers and the early ascetics so much lauded by the church had held precisely the same views; but that was before the church had established its despotism, and afterwards it was too late to cry down the Fathers and the recluses. It is true that numbers of the holy men and holy women of the church, as St. Bernard, St. Francis de Sales, St. Francis d'Assissi, and numbers of others; and that still more numerous female saints, as Sts. Theresa, Catherine of Sienna, and many more, had held the same opinions, and had in reality been canonised for them; but these saints and saintesses had held them submissively to the papal hierarchy in monasteries and convents, and in full deference to confessors and superiors. Madame Guyon, on the other hand, did not scruple to set the monitions and demands of the Holy Spirit above the monitions and demands of any human authority. She claimed a certain independence of opinion which cannot be admitted in the Roman Church, where the right of private opinion has been so absolutely extinguished. This was the grand secret of her persecutions, and of those of Fenelon, who accorded with her entirely in his faith.

Jeane-Marie Bouvèries de la Mothe was born at Montargis, in 1648. Her family was of considerable distinction, and she was married at the early age of sixteen to the celebrated M. Guyon, who owed his rank and fortune to the successful undertaking of the canal of Briare. At eight-and-twenty she was left a widow, with three very young children. She was remarkable already for her deep and ardent piety, and for her works of benevolence. Meeting with the Bishop of Geneva in Paris, in 1680, he persuaded her to settle at Gex, and assume the management of an institution for the education of Protestant young ladies. At Gex she found Father Lacombe, whom she had known in Paris, who held her own religious views, and who was now appointed the superior of the institution. They greatly strengthened each other in their religious faith and zeal.

The relatives of Madame Guyon, alarmed at a tone of mind certain to bring her into trouble with the orthodox dignitaries and priests, and professing serious fears of injury to the fortunes of her children on that account, Madame Guyon, influenced by a more real regard for her children than was probably felt by their zealous relatives, agreed to surrender the care of these to them, and, to show her disinterestedness, at the same time surrendered what is called *la garde noble* of these children, the right to enjoy their income till they were of age. This income amounted to 40,000 livres, or about 1,600*l.* a-year, a handsome revenue at that period in France. She had left herself but a very modest provision; but she soon found, as is but too common with Catholic institutions, that this at Gex wanted her to resign this modicum in its favour. She declined the proposal. This, of course, was resented, and Madame Guyon found it necessary to withdraw. Father Lacombe had left the institution before, and had become the director of a convent of Ursuline nuns at Thonon, in the Chablais; and thither she betook herself. She afterwards removed to Verceil and Turin. In all these places she zealously, as a duty of conscience, propagated her religious views : and that with the warm approval of various bishops and distinguished persons. In 1687 she returned to Paris, and published two works, 'Moyen court et facile pour faire Oraison,' and 'L'Explication mystique du Cantique des Cantiques.' In the meantime Father Lacombe had published his ' Analyse de l'Oraison mentale,' and Harlay, Archbishop of Paris, quickly denounced them as heretical; and Lacombe was arrested and sent a prisoner to the castle of Lourdes, in the Pyrenées, where he remained ten years. Madame Guyon was also arrested and confined in a convent in the Rue St. Antoine. But her great friends Madame Maisonfort, the Duchess de Bethune, and the Duchess de Beauvilliers, appealed to the all-potent mistress of Louis XIV., Madame Maintenon, and managed so much to interest her in Madame Guyon that she was quickly released, had various interviews with the royal mistress, and won so much on her favour that she was introduced by her to her aristocratic nunnery at St. Cyr to inspire the nuns with her devotion. This, which appeared at the moment a great triumph, proved, as it was certain to do, the source of all Madame Guyon's wrongs and troubles, and, at the same time, of all those of Fenelon.

The Archbishop of Paris, and Desmarais, the Bishop of Chartres, were quickly at the Maintenon to point out Madame Guyon's heresies, and that cold and politic soul immediately took the alarm, and pointed out no end of heresies in the works she had previously admired intensely. To bring down the Maintenon on her was the same thing as to bring down on her Louis, the devoted tool of the Jesuits, and the whole batch of courtier bishops. The Bishop of Chartres expressed his astonishment at finding a woman mixing herself up with matters of the church, and sitting, as it were, ex-cathedra, to teach a system of spirituality which, he said, though falsely, she had the audacity to originate. Madame Guyon was not only promptly ejected from St. Cyr, but the nuns were ordered to cease to read anything of hers, and it was recommended that her doctrines should not be spoken of, even to their spiritual fathers. Cardinal Noüilles, subsequently Archbishop of Paris, and, far more fatally, the celebrated Bossuet, Bishop of Meaux, declared against her. Madame Guyon demanded that commissioners, half ecclesiastical, half lay, should be appointed to enquire into the orthodoxy of her writings and the purity of her conduct, which was also arraigned. The commission was appointed, but only of ecclesiastics, consisting of Bossuet, Noäilles, and M. Tronson. In vain Madame Guyon protested, these ecclesiastics sate for six months at Issy on her writings and conduct. They were compelled finally to admit Fenelon; but, as they could not agree, Bossuet and Noäilles themselves issued a condemnation not only of Madame Guyon's writings, but of 'the Spiritual Guide' of Molinos, the 'Easy Practice' of Malaval, and the 'Analysis of Mental Prayer' by Lacombe. Fenelon, however, prevailed on Bossuet to give Madame Guyon a most decided and honourable testimony to the perfect purity and propriety of her conduct. During this investigation Madame Guyon had, by the advice of Bossuet, retired to the monastery of the Visitation at Meaux. It was the plan of Bossuet to keep her there under his authority, and thus suppress her religious activity; but, on receiving so complete a

clearance of her moral character, she immediately quitted
Meaux, as resolved as ever to propagate what she believed
to be the eternal truth confided to her of God. This step
greatly astonished and confounded Bossuet, and he lost no
time in getting her arrested, through the influence of the
royal mistress, and thrown into the prison of Vincennes.
Meantime, Harlay was dead, and Noüilles, the weak coadjutor and facile tool of Bossuet, became Archbishop of Paris.
The Maintenon, therefore, wished him to ask what he would
like to be done with Madame Guyon, her *friends*, and
papers. Foremost among these friends there hinted at was
Fenelon, now become the Archbishop of Cambray, much to
the chagrin, on second thoughts, of both Louis and his
mistress. Bossuet now became the mortal enemy of both
Madame Guyon and Fenelon, expressed his ecstasy at the
imprisonment of Madame Guyon, and prophesied this
mystery would now be chased from the pale of the church.
From this moment Bossuet appears as the ferocious and
implacable persecutor, and stands in a frightful contrast to
the piety of Madame Guyon and the noble meekness of
Fenelon.

Madame Guyon was subjected to a close examination by
her enemies within the walls of the prison of Vincennes;
but she stoutly maintained the truth and gospel character of
her opinions, and defended Father Lacombe as a most holy
and unoffending man. Fenelon had the boldness to write to
the Maintenon, declaring that the doctrines held by Madame
Guyon were precisely those held by Angely de Foligny, St.
Francis of Sales, St. Francis of Assissi, St. Theresa, St.
Catherine of Sienna, and St. Catherine of Gênes. He
showed that neither Bossuet nor Noüilles were at all
acquainted with the subject which they had undertaken to
condemn. This was especially true of Bossuet, who was at
this very time busily reading, for the first time, the writers
whose opinions were in accordance with those of Madame
Guyon. The consequence of Bossuet's new studies appeared
in a work called a 'Relation du Quietisme.' Fenelon

condemned it as Jesuitical, and drew up his admirable
'Explication des Maximes des Saints sur la Vie intérieure.'
This celebrated work, amply showing that the doctrines so
firmly condemned by Bossuet and his clique were the
doctrines of all the most celebrated Fathers of the church,
roused the burning hatred of Bossuet, and he resolved not
only on the destruction of Fenelon, but of his *protégé*
Madame Guyon. The latter was consigned to the Bastile,
and Bossuet instigated Louis XIV., through his mistress, to
ruin Fenelon. That gentle and humble Christian was,
accordingly, banished to his diocese in French Flanders, and
every endeavour was made to induce the Pope to condemn
his maxims of the saints. The Pope was thrown into the
utmost perplexity. The book was notoriously based on the
doctrines of the greatest Fathers and founders of the church;
to condemn it was to condemn them. He hung back as long
as he could; but, compelled to move by the power of the
French king, who was continually spurred on by his mistress
and her ferocious flatterers, the priests, headed by Bossuet, he
at length appointed a numerous commission of cardinals to
examine the book; but half decided one way, half another.
Bossuet had his nephew constantly at the Papal Court to
watch and urge on the proceedings; and, when all their
malice appeared hopeless, they got Louis XIV. to write a
most menacing letter to the Pope. Not satisfied with this,
Bossuet procured, through the king, a condemnation of the
book, by the Sorbonne whilst before the Pope. Alarmed at
the threats of Louis of France, the Pope consented to condemn
the book; but he did it in the gentlest terms, avoiding to pronounce it *heretical*, and at the same time writing to Fenelon
to assure him of his profound affection and veneration for his
character.

Fenelon, a true son of the church, submitted his private
judgement to the judgement of the Holy See, so far as to bow
to the censure; but he still declared that he regarded this
sentence as directed against his imperfect demonstration of the
doctrines, not against the doctrines themselves, which he

maintained to be the sound and unchangeable truth. No one sympathised more sincerely with Fenelon and mourned more deeply the disgraceful persecutions of Fenelon, than the Duke of Burgundy, his royal pupil, whom he had trained up from a most insolent and ungovernable lad into a noble and accomplished prince. Heir to the throne, he disregarded the anger of his grandfather, and visited the archbishop in his distant diocese.

Nothing could exceed the disappointment of Bossuet at the mildness of the papal censure, and at the noble resignation of Fenelon. So far from crushing him, the proceeding raised him to an unexampled popularity. In the midst of these attacks upon him appeared his famous work 'Telemachus,' and flew all over Europe, awaking in every country of the world the most rapturous admiration of its author. At the same time, Fenelon was living in the midst of his people, like a common parent to his diocese, exhibiting one of the most lively examples of genuine Christian wisdom and benevolence that the world ever saw. The triumphant enemies, the Dutch and Germans, whom Louis had so long invaded and pillaged, now under the able command of Marlborough, with an English army, and Prince Eugene, were daily approaching the frontiers of France, and humiliating the proud French king. But amid the retribution poured on his head, they took care to exempt the territory of Cambray from the smallest violence. The universally beloved and venerated character of Fenelon was its palladium, and every wish of his was law to the victors. Amid the ravages of hostile armies all around, Cambray, for the sake of Fenelon, remained not only untouched, but a carefully guarded region. Such honours, the direct consequence of Fenelon's Christian greatness, were gall and poison to the malicious mind of Bossuet; and, to complete his mortification, Fenelon came out with an answer to his 'Narrative of Quietism' of such irresistible eloquence and splendour, as drew the most rapturous applause, not only from all France, but all Europe. Bossuet did not live long under the ever-growing popularity of the man whom he had laboured so fiercely and long to crush, and whom he had dared, in spite of his sublime gentleness, to style a ferocious beast, and to accuse him of being another Montanus with his Priscilla. Both Fenelon and Madame Guyon saw him expire some years before them; the one issuing from the Bastile to spend the remainder of her days in peace and pious happiness at Blois, near her daughter; the other falling asleep gently amid his sorrowing people, one of the most eminent examples of a true disciple of a gentle, suffering, and benevolent Saviour, that the world has yet seen.

And what were the doctrines which drew on these distinguished Christian friends this tempest of persecution from the political priests and powers of that day? They were nearly the same which the primitive church held; which Christ taught, and which the Friends hold now: that the essence of religion consists not in ceremonies and dogmas, but in walking in close communion and in humble teachableness with Him who said, ' If any man love me, he will keep my words; and my Father will love him, and we will come unto him, and make our abode with him.' It was a belief that this visitation of the Son and of the Father is open to every seeking soul; and that in this divine abode with it, they will teach it all heavenly wisdom; and build it up into all truth, and unto everlasting life. That through this communion of God offered to every son of Adam, that state of things shall come to pass when men shall no more seek to men, shall no more say every man to his brother, ' Know the Lord; for all shall know Him from the least unto the greatest.'

It was this knowledge and communion which Madame Guyon taught and experienced, and which the priests and bishops saw, if allowed to go on, would speedily put an end to their craft, and, therefore, made them begin to cry lustily, ' Great is Diana of the Ephesians!' Madame Guyon was one of the most distinguished writing mediums that ever lived. She declared that whatever she wrote did not proceed from herself, but was given through her hand by the Holy

Spirit. She was equally open to the divine influx in all her thoughts. That influx was the life and substance of her religion. In the language of Wordsworth:—

> In such access of mind, in such high hour
> Of visitation from the living God,
> Thought was not; in enjoyment it expired.

The following passages from her autobiography are essential Quakerism, as essentially the doctrine of Swedenborg, of Harris, of Wordsworth, of a thousand God-visited souls of holy men and women, as they are essentially the highest form of spiritualism. 'During my extraordinary sickness the Lord gradually taught me that there was another manner of conversing among souls wholly His, than by speech. I learnt then a language which before had been unknown to me. I gradually perceived, when Father Lacombe entered, that I could speak no more, and that there was formed in my soul the same kind of silence towards him as was formed in it with regard to God. I comprehended that God was willing to show me that men in this life might learn the language of angels. I was gradually reduced to speak to him only in silence. It was then that we understood each other in God, after a manner unutterable and all divine. At first this was done in a manner so perceptible—that is to say, God penetrated, us with Himself—in a manner so pure and sweet, that we passed hours in this profound silence, always communicative, without being able to utter one word. It was in this that we learned, by our own experience, the operations of the heavenly word to reduce souls into unity with itself, and what purity one may arrive at in this life. It was given me to communicate this way to other good souls, but with this difference, that I did nothing but communicate to them the grace with which they were filled, while near me, in this sacred silence, which infused into them an extraordinary strength and grace, but I received nothing from them; whereas, with Father Lacombe, there was a flow and return of communication of grace, which he received from me, and I from him in the greatest purity.'

Here we see the same laws of mediumship operating in the divine element, as in the mesmeric. Madame Guyon, as the fuller vessel of divine life, which she calls grace, communicated this to the less-developed souls around her. She perceived virtue go out of her as Christ did when touched on earth; but with Father Lacombe, a spirit as richly developed and life-charged, she felt no mere outflowing, but flux and reflux, as of a divine sea.

'All those,' she continues, 'who are my true children, are drawn in their minds at once to continue in silence when with me; and I have the like tendency to impart to them in silence what God gives me for them. In this silence I discover their wants and failings, and communicate to them in an abundant plenitude, according to their necessities. When once they have tasted of this manner of communication, every other becomes burthensome to them. As for me, when I make use of speech, or the pen, with souls, I do it only on account of their weakness, and because either they are not pure enough for the interior communication, or because it is yet needful to use condescension, or for the regulation of outward affairs. It was in this ineffable silence that I comprehended the manner in which Jesus Christ communicated Himself to His most familiar friends, and the communication of St. John, when leaning on his Lord's bosom at the supper of the Passover. It was not the first time that he had seated himself that way, and it was because he was most proper to receive those communications, being the disciple of love. I began to discover, especially with Father Lacombe, that the interior communication was carried on, even when he was afar off, as well as when he was near. Sometimes our Lord made me stop short when in the midst of my occupations, and I was favoured with such a flow of grace, as that which I felt when with him — which I have also experienced with many others, though not in a like degree; but more or less feeling their infidelities, and knowing their faults by inconceivable impressions, without ever having been mistaken therein.'

It was for the experience and the teaching of this great doctrine of Christ and the early Church that Madame Guyon, Fenelon, Father Lacombe, Michael Molinos in Spain, and the Friends in England, were so furiously persecuted by people who bore the outer name of Christians without a knowledge of its inner life. And how little do religious professors of to-day understand this spiritual developement, by which souls are opened to the impulse of the spirit-life around them, by which God and his ministering spirits can operate upon and communicate with them, and by which the wealth of the invisible world becomes accessible to incarnated spirits. By which, as George Fox said, ' States can be discerned,' and 'the infallible guide' be followed as confidently as a child follows the guiding hand of a father; a state in which Wordsworth says of his Wanderer:—

> No thanks he breathed, he proffered no request,
> Rapt into still communion that transcends
> The imperfect offices of prayer and praise,
> His mind was a thanksgiving to the Power
> That made him; it was blessedness and love!

CHAPTER XVII.

THE PROPHETS OF THE CEVENNES.

> They, the Cevennois, had many among them who seemed qualified in a very singular manner to be the teachers of the rest. They had a great measure of zeal without any learning; they scarce had any education at all. I spoke with the person who, by the queen's order, sent me among them to know the state of their affairs. I read some of the letters which he brought from them, full of a sublime zeal and piety: expressing a courage and confidence that could not be daunted.
> —*Testimony of Bishop Burnet to the* '*Prophets of the Cevennes.*'—'*His Own Times*,' vol. iv. p. 159.

IN most of our English histories we come upon slight and passing notions of certain insurrections in the the Cevennes, a mountain region of the south of France, against the oppression of Louis XIV., to which some aids of money, arms, and men, were sent by the government of Queen Anne, but which never reached the insurgents in question. These insurgents were Protestants, and, therefore, deemed worthy of the sympathies of Protestants; but we learn little from such histories of the results of this sympathy. We find, however, that a number of those insurgents made their way to this country. That they professed to be prophets; to be divinely inspired by the Holy Ghost, and to be enabled by the Divine Spirit to perform miraculous acts, like the members of the primitive church. This pretension, we learn, immediately startled and disgusted the English Church of that day, both Established and Dissenting; a loud cry was raised against these French Protestants as fanatics. The Bishop of London called the attention of the French Church in the Savoy to them; the French Church summoned them before its consistory, and the prophets rejected their authority, declaring that they had no masters but God. This made the outcry against them wild. Dr. Edmund Calamy, a great nonconformist divine, whose name would be more correctly spelt Calumny, in the indignation of a fossil divinity, which denies the possession of the spiritual life which Christ promised to his Church, and which the Church once had, but has relinquished for itself, and refuses to its neighbours, preached mightily and bitterly against these poor refugee foreigners, for presuming to have the spirit and living works of the Saviour. He presented his book, called a 'Caviat,' to the queen, calling angrily for the punishment and expulsion of these blasphemers. Accordingly, the unfortunate Cevennois were denounced, put in the pillory and made very glad to escape from this land of boasted toleration.

There were, however, certain gentlemen who took the trouble to enquire for themselves into the real history, lives, and opinions of these unhappy men, these who sought bread and protection from Englishmen, and received not merely a stone, but many stones and rotten eggs. These gentlemen, amongst whom were Sir Richard Bulkeley and Mr. Lacy, gentlemen of fortune and station, came to the conclusion that the objects of this terrible outcry were simple, honest, pious men, and in the possession of all the spiritual gifts to which they laid claim. Thereupon it was immediately sounded abroad that Sir Richard Bulkeley was a little crooked man, whom the prophets had promised to make, through the spirit, as tall and straight as a poplar, and still more strange things were predicated of Mr. Lacy, the other great defender of the Cevennois. Agnes Strickland, in her 'History of the Queens of England,' retails all these *on dits* gravely, and accuses these gentlemen of countenancing some 'rubbish like modern mesmerism!' Poor Agnes!

Unfortunately for these aspersions on the champions of the unfortunate Prophets of the Cevennois, we have the testimony of Bishop Burnet, quoted above; and we find Dr. Josiah Woodward, a clergyman of high standing in the Established Church, at the very time that he was writing against the Cevennois, declaring the gentlemen who stood by them to be men of such high character that they cannot for a moment be suspected of countenancing imposture; adding his belief in the sincerity of the unhappy Cevennois themselves, though not crediting their assumed inspiration, but treating them as sincere enthusiasts, whom English Christians ought to pity and send home to their mountains, instead of persecuting them. Still more unfortunately for the calumnies heaped by the hard doctrinal divinity of the time on these poor French Protestants and their defenders, we have looked into the accounts given of them by Sir Richard Bulkeley and Mr. Lacy, and find these the relations of men calm, rational, and religious, having every mark of proceeding from sound logical heads and honourable hearts. In 'The Impartial Account of the Prophets,' by Sir Richard, he gives us the mode by which he went to work to know all about them. He enquired whether the phenomena which they presented proceeded from contrivance, disease, satanical delusion, or the Holy Spirit of God? Whether these people had any motives of ambition, gain, or a desire to serve themselves by embroiling us with our enemies? Again, he tried if he could reconcile these phenomena to frenzy or madness; to enthusiastic melancholy, or epileptic convulsions? But he was driven from all such explanations by the sober sense, sound health, genuine piety, and simple truthfulness of these people. 'I found them,' he says, 'not men of impiously hardened consciences, as they must have been, to profess to be actuated by the Holy Spirit, as the Prophets did, when they knew the contrary; but men of sober lives and conversation; men of good character; pious and devout Christians, and having the fear of God before their eyes.' He found them possessing 'an extraordinary spirit of prayer and praise to God; the gifts of prophecy, of exhortation, of discerning spirits, of languages, of the ministration of the same spirit to others; and some earnest of the gift of healing; all which were proofs that the Holy Spirit gave in the Apostles' times; and these being shining evidences of its being from God, I durst not,' he says, 'from some little clouds that now and then seem to our understanding to darken its lustre, conclude that God was not in it, or to take upon me, in my faint light, to determine what the All-wise and All-unaccountable will or will not do to us, that are worse than the dust before him.'

Such were the cross-lights that gleamed upon me from the opposite statements of the time, as to these 'Prophets,' which, from the natural and honest tone of the brave Sir Richard, little and crooked man as he was, but with a soul evidently 'as tall and as straight as a poplar,' led me strongly to suspect that the stories of Dr. Edmund Calumny and Co. were just such as beset Christianity, and every new developement of Christianity, in the persons of Luther, Fox, Swedenborg, Whitefield, Wesley, and others. I turned to enquire what our English writers, historians, or travellers have had to say about them since, but I could find little light amongst them. The Rev. Mr. Smedley, in his 'History of the Reformed Religion of France,' indeed, treats them in the true unbelieving spirit of orthodoxy, as fanatics; 'ignorant people, deranged by enthusiasm,' &c.

The tone of this hard-shell orthodoxy not seeming to me capable of accounting for the marvels which not only Bulkeley and Lacy, but the numerous witnesses who deposed to the truth of their relations, before the magistrates in England, boldly asserted, as given in 'The Cry from the Desert,' and the 'Theatre Sacré des Cevennes,' both published in London at the time, I turned to the French authorities. To Coquerel's 'Histoire des Eglises du Désert,' Peyrat's 'Histoire des Pasteurs du Désert,' Bruey's 'Histoire de Fanatisme,' 'Memoirs de Jean Cavallier,' 'Histoire de Camisards,' 'Les Lettres de Flèchier,' to Louvreleuil, Lebaume, Court; 'Lettres de Racine,' and to others, friends and enemies, and what a scene burst upon me! What a scene of tyranny and persecution, sublime in its very horrors! What a scene of heroism, of devotion, of biblical faith and biblical spiritualism, in a simple race of mountaineers! What a scene of glories and sufferings wrought by the demonry of kings and priests, and the bared arm of the Almighty, stretched forth in all the majesty of ancient times amongst a simple and trodden-down people! What a spectacle of poor men lifted by the power of the devil, and the mightier power of God, amid their magnificent mountains and their rushing rivers, poor, obscure shepherds, pastors, and wool-combers, into heroes and martyrs equal to the most renowned of the most soul-inspiring times. Earth has few such stories; let us give a brief account of it.

The history of the endeavours of the Popish Church to tread out all real Christianity, a Church calling itself the Church of the Lord, yet doing the most decided work of the devil, never was equalled by the barbarities of any pagan nation. If we had a history of hell, what could it be but a history in which those who still retained any traces of heaven, would be tormented by every imaginable invention of cruelty, in which every demoniac fury would be exercised to crush out the last spark of faith and virtue? Such is the history of the great Roman heresy; the anti-Christ of Paul, if ever there was one, in which dragonades, inquisitions, burning of people alive, and breaking them on racks and wheels, crushing them with iron boots, and the most exquisite tortures of every kind, figure from age to age. We, in this country, had our share of this devilry, from which Tophet itself might have learned fresh lessons of torment, during the days of bloody Mary and of the popish Stuarts; but what has been the fate of England, in this respect, to that of the continental nations, where the great delusion still reigns in darkness and strength? The Albigenses and Waldenses have left a fearful story of Rome's exterminating cruelty against the gospel of Christ. Protestantism was literally and utterly extirpated in Bohemia and Moravia by the extirpation of the population. I have traversed the melancholy plains of those countries, and the curse of Rome's annihilating fury seems yet to brood over them. What horrors were perpetrated in Styria, in the Palatinate, in Flanders, in Spain and Italy! In some of these countries popery utterly burnt out and hewed to pieces Protestantism with its myrmidons called inquisitors, alguazils, jesuits, priests, and soldiers. But in no country was the reign of intellectual tyranny, of a fearful and remorseless war on Protestantism, endured so long, and which presented so many horrors, as in France; and for this simple reason, that the government has never been able to destroy totally the remnant of God's martyrs. We need not tell the long story of the Huguenots, nor recall the night of St. Bartholomew. Henry IV. signed the blessed edict of Nantes, and Louis XIV. revoked it. Then burst forth, with renewed fury, all the murderous soul of Rome. Then again were the poor Protestants hunted down, ruined, imprisoned, murdered by priests, bishops, mayors, intendants, and soldiery, at the command of a man whom historians have delighted to laud as Le Grand Monarche, the great Louis Quartorze, one of the most debauched, unprincipled, tiger-souled, and terrible monsters who ever sat on a throne, and made war on all the rights of Europe;—the exterminator of Protestantism, the desolator of all neighbouring nations. Let the burnt and reburnt Palatinate; let desolated Flanders, and the butcheries committed on his pious and simple Protestant subjects of the south of France, for ever stamp him as the monster he was, and heap shame on the heads of his flatterers and fools!

In few countries is there a region more beautiful than that of Provence and Languedoc in the south of France. The Vivcrais, the Cevennes, Rouergue, Gevaudan, and the lovely regions in which stand Montpellier, Nismes, Uzes, St. Hippolite, and Somiere. A country of old volcanic mountains, old forests, rapid torrents, and elysian valleys; a country watered by the superb Rhone, the Gardon, and the Ardêche. This paradise of a country, inhabited by a brave and simple race, descended from Roman blood, from the ancient colonies of Nismes and Narbonne, was the one on which Louis XIV. and his brutal minister, Louvois, especially let loose the tempest of their persecuting rage. The only crime of the people was, that they would not worship God according to the domineering and superstitious rites of Rome. For this, this much lauded monarch, politically blind as he was bigotedly remorseless, destroyed or scattered into all the nations round, FIVE HUNDRED THOUSAND of the best and most devoted subjects that ever king had, with all their trades, their ingenuity, and their industry. Amongst these, too, were some who rose to high eminence in the English and other armies, and fought against the tyrants. Such were Schomberg and Ruvigny, generals of our William III., who became severally Duke of Leinster and Earl of Galway. But it was chiefly on the people of the Viverais, and above all on those of the Cevennes, that he hurled his desolating vengeance.

He haughtily commanded them to attend mass, and conform to popery. They steadfastly refused. He then marched down armies to compel them, or to root them out. In 1685 took place the revocation of the Edict of Nantes. Finding that neither soldiers nor prisons, nor the savage violence of priests and magistrates, had any effect in putting down the Protestant churches, Louis determined to banish every Protestant pastor from the country. 'If they are already imbecile,' he said, 'let them stay and rot; if they are of vigorous mind, chase them out!' Accordingly, there was seen the mournful sight of every minister compelled to quit his native hills and his flock. But the weeping people would not be left behind. One thousand five hundred and eighty pastors quitted for ever the soil of France, followed to the frontiers by the vigilant eyes of soldiers and police. These good men scattered themselves all over Europe; and, on their people coming after them, established new churches. Among them were some very eminent men: Claude, Dubosc,

Dumoulin, Juricu, Abadie, Beausobre, Lenfant, Pajon, Bayle, brother of the lexicographer; the world-renowned Saurin, Basnage, Tronchin, Ancillon, Constant, Candolle, &c. Of these, Claude and Saurin settled at the Hague, Dubosc at Rotterdam, Ancillon at Berlin. Their flocks abandoned their homes and country, and hastened after them into voluntary exile. Amongst these were 15,000 gentlemen and 2,300 elders.

'They arose in silence,' says Peyrat, 'and departed in crowds; men, women, children—a desolate throng. They stole away privately from their paternal roofs, from their native villages; and in small knots sought to escape from their country. Muleteers, though forbidden under severe penalties, dared the enterprise for good pay, and led them, by unfrequented ways, to the nearest frontiers. The fugitives disguised themselves as muleteers, or colporteurs, or beggars; ladies, whose satin slippers had never before touched the grass, walked forty or fifty leagues in wooden shoes, as peasant-women; and gentlemen carried packages or trundled wheel-barrows, to escape the cognisance of the guards on the frontiers. Soon, the evacuation of the country became so alarming—for the revocation of the edict had deprived two millions of people of the protection of the laws—that Louis issued the most stringent orders that no single Protestant should be permitted to quit the country. Marshal Montrevel, the military commandant of the Cevennes, published them there. Every person who quitted the country suffered confiscation of his whole property. Every person attempting it, though in vain, suffered the same confiscation, and was condemned, if a man, to the gallies for life; if a woman, to perpetual imprisonment. If they stayed in the country they were forbidden to sell their real property for three years, or their personal at all, under the same penalties; and, being thus nailed down to their native places, they were all liable to the same penalties if they attended Protestant places of worship, or gave any assistance to ruined or starving Protestants.

Thus given up a prey to the priests, informers and soldiers, confiscation and the gallies, or death, were denounced against all captains who dared to take them out by sea. The whole Protestant population of the south was now at the mercy of the sword and the plunderer. Their houses were rifled and burnt, their crops destroyed, and themselves thrust into the gallies by thousands, till they could hold no more; and then the prisons were filled to repletion—and such prisons! They were pits and dungeons swarming with vermin, and reptiles engendered by the filth; abysses unvisited by the sun! The unhappy people could neither stand upright, sit, or lie down. They were let down into these horrible depths with ropes, and came up only to be flogged, mutilated, rent on the rack, or broken alive on the wheel. Many, after some weeks' confinement, issued from these infernos without hair and without teeth! Carrion and the garbage of cattle were flung into these pits for their food. They weltered in sloughs of impurity; their bodies became bloated; their skins peeled off like wet paper; they were, in effect, living corpses. At length, to disencumber these hells of horror and contagion, Louis was compelled to ship them off in rotten transports to America, indifferent whether they reached land or the bottom of the ocean.

But as the most active and pitiless use of fire, sword, plundering, racking, torturing, hanging, and murdering in these slaughter-house prisons, could not bend these poor, but brave Christians, Montrevel, the general, and Baville, the intendant, determined to lay waste the country of the Cevennes, and exterminate every Protestant. They, therefore, divided the whole territory into sections, and distributed to every section its troop of soldiers, who went to work to destroy every house, lay waste with fire every field, and kill every man, woman, and child they could find. They left only a few towns, to which the Catholics might flee till the massacre was complete. Driven by these merciless measures to rebellion, the Cevennois rose and defended themselves. They got up into the mountains, and into the forests, laid up their grain and provisions in huge caverns, and every man, who had any kind of arms, became a soldier. Yet, what a handful against a host! The highest calculation gives only 3,000 Cevennois in arms at once; some authors declare that there never were more than 2,000; whilst the king's troops, disciplined in the great wars of the time, and the militia, amounted to 60,000 men, commanded by the best generals of France.

But the handful of brave mountaineers, trusting in God, determined not to die tamely. They elected leaders, and rushed down on their enemies, scattering them and slaying them to a marvel. One of their first attempts was to rescue a number of their unhappy brethren and sisters and their children out of the hands of the Abbé Chayla, the prior of Laval, archpriest of the Cevennes, and inspector of missions in Gevaudan. This man had a crowd of priests about him, and they persecuted the Protestants mercilessly. The cellars of Chayla's palace were crammed with victims, whom he and his priests daily tortured. Sometimes they ran from one to another beating them with cudgels till they were out of breath. They stretched them on the rack; they invented new modes of torture. They made them close their hands upon burning coals; they wrapped their fingers in oiled cotton, and set fire to it. They tied their victims' hands and feet, and lifting them up, plunged them down on the floor on their faces. They tied them down in the shape of beasts on all fours, and kept them for days in that cramping posture, unable to look upward. Their victims could only escape, the men by money, the women by loss of their honour. At length the indignant people marched down upon him, demanded the release of his victims, and as he and his impious coadjutors only answered by firing on them, they burst in, burnt the house over his head, killed him, and led away the prisoners, singing a hymn of triumph.

Then rose the blood of the long-oppressed, and the war went on for ten years. Terrible were the deeds done by the sixty thousand soldiery with all their massacres, their dragonades, their conflagrations, their racks, gibbets, and hangings. Terrible and wonderful were the retaliations of the little 2,000. The limits of a single chapter forbid me to follow the course of this marvellous story, more wonderful, more desperate, and more triumphant than that of the Scottish Covenanters. It is a story of volumes, not of a chapter. But what concerns us is, that the source of their triumphs and their deeds which rung through Europe, was SPIRIT-UALISM—spiritualism of the most exalted, the most biblical, and the most unprecedented character. Spiritualism which demands for its recorded facts the utmost stretch of faith, but attested by a cloud of witnesses, enemies as well as friends, such as no history, the most universally accepted, can surpass for weight, for numbers, for ascendance, or trust-worthiness.

When the wretched people were driven to desperation, when the blood-hounds of despotism, and the hell-hounds of Antichrist surrounded them with fire and artillery, with overwhelming thousands, and with daily and insatiate carnage, then they cried mightily to God, and God came visibly to their rescue. They were seized with an extraordinary power and passion of inspiration. They were shaken and agitated by it, as clairvoyants are moved, and are, as it were, transfigured. Then they broke forth in prophesyings; in declarations of trust in God; in exhortations to prayer and newness of life. They foretold all that was necessary for their safety and their success. It was immediately revealed to some one of them where the enemy was marching against them and in what numbers, and thus they were always ready to surprise and route them. Every action was regulated by their oracles, which never failed. Whether they should fight or flee, should hide or advance, was clearly told them. If a traitor came among them, he was at once pointed out; if their enemies were planning means for their destruction, they saw them as if present, and heard their discourse. Men, women, and children spoke, under inspiration, not in the ordinary patois, but in the purest French; children of only twelve months and less, who had never before used speech, spoke to the amazement of hundreds present, and the words of such children were received as implicitly as those of the oldest and wisest amongst them. These startling facts stand in the testimony of numbers, and some of them of the highest rank and fame. It is not possible to enter into these details here; they are all fully stated in the works to which I have referred; and they show the real source of the unparalleled triumph of the little band of the Cevennois for years over the mighty armies of France.

From the moment that any man received the influence of the spirit, it was observed that he became a new man, whatever had been his life before, and nothing could seduce him from his purity of life and devotion to the cause. 'The spirit,' say some of these heroes themselves, 'inspired all the military manœuvres, and animated the courage of the chiefs in battle. They had no knowledge of war, nor of any other thing. Everything was given them miraculously.' 'The spirit encouraged the soldiers,' says M. Fage in the 'Theatre Sacré.' 'When about to go into battle, and the spirit said, "Fear nothing, my child, I will guide thee, I will be with thee:" I rushed into the melée as if I had been clad in iron; as if the arms of the enemy were of wool. Happy in the words of God, our little boys of twelve, struck right and left like valiant men. Those who had neither swords nor guns did wonders with blows of a staff, or a cudgel. The bullets whistled about our ears like hail, but as harmlessly. They cut through our caps and coats, but they did no hurt.' Cavallier says that they frequently found them in their shirts, quite flattened, but having made no wound.

Those who were told by the spirit beforehand that they should fall went resignedly to their martyrdom; the rest fought in confident assurance of safety, and declared with Cavallier that they often found the flattened balls betwixt their shirts and skin. This was the grand secret of those wonders of valour which astonished all Europe, and confounded the most experienced of the royal generals. The sufferings of the Cevennois, however, were terrific. Four hundred towns and villages were reduced to ashes, and the whole country for twenty leagues was left a desert. But the hunted Protestants had made terrible reprisals. They destroyed every cross, image, and symbol of popery that they came near, levied heavy contributions, and had slain one-third of the royal army.

And all this was accomplished by poor simple peasants and artizans. The whole movement was purely among the people. They were led and instructed by none of the gentry; these had escaped abroad, or were almost wholly Catholic; Rowland, their commander-in-chief, was a vine-dresser; Cavallier, their great warrior, the David of their army, who was a beardless boy when he stood forth as a prophet and a leader, and was only nineteen when he terminated his career in the Cevennes, was a peasant and a baker. Catinat was a watcher of horses on the hills of Vivens. Seguier, Castanet, Saloman, Ravanel, and La Belle Isabeau, the prophetess, were all carders of wool. Elie Marion was the only one of a family of superior grade. Yet all these conducted their share of the command and of the management of the general affairs, with an ability and success which astonished beyond all measure their high-born and accomplished opponents, and covered them with continual defeat. These, not self-instructed, but God-instructed men, conducted the civil affairs of their community, of a population driven from their homes, reduced to beggary, and to daily peril of the most frightful nature; thrown, in fact, on their hands in one gigantic mass of helplessness and misery, with the same brilliant sagacity as they did the war. They took care to bring in from the enemy abundant provisions and clothing; cattle, sheep, corn, and wine. They constructed vast magazines of ammunition, and of all necessary stores, in caverns in the hills, and in the depths of forests. They quartered themselves and their dependent people in the castles and chateaus of their enemies. They had their hospitals and their retreats for the wounded and invalids, and made up for want of surgical skill, in many cases, by tender care and native ingenuity. Yet they had surgeons among them too.

The great leaders of the Camisards, as they were called— from Camis, the dialectic name for a shirt, because they helped themselves to clean shirts wherever they went, or, more probably, from the black blouse which they wore, that they might not be easily seen at a distance, whence they were called 'The Invisible Phantoms,'—were Rowland and Cavallier. Rowland Laporte was a man of about forty; sedate, thoughtful, and endowed with the capacity for managing the general affairs. By his wisdom and prudence, all was kept in order, and every one fitted into his or her place. His providential watchfulness, under the immediate guidance of a higher Providence, inspired confidence, and diffused order and harmony through the whole Camisard community. He, as well as every commander, was a prophet or medium, and exhorted, and prayed, and prophesied in their assemblies. These assemblies were held in the open air, sometimes in the glades of the forests, sometimes in the courts of the old chateaus. To them the people, men, women, and children, ran, in the midst of danger, from the woods and hiding-places, carrying with them their bibles, rescued from the flames of their burning houses, and listened intently to the words of the inspired, and to their hymns of faith and triumph, till the men, women, and children became capable of the most astonishing deeds.

Cavallier was the great genius, the great hero of the Camisards. Youth as he was, of low stature, of a simple, fair, and ruddy countenance, and with his long hair rolling in waves over his shoulders, he was capable of carrying with him the spirits of all around him, both when he delivered an inspired harangue or led them to the battle. At his right hand always rode the gigantic and intrepid Ravenel, with his bushy beard and wild hair, on his left his younger brother Daniel, a mere boy, on a fine young charger. At the head of their cavalry they rushed down into the plains, and spread terror amongst soldiers, priests, and the Catholic population. They had, through inspiration, knowledge of the movements of their enemies, and laid ambushes for them, and overthrew them with amazing slaughter. Cavallier had a touch of the hero of romance in him. He would dress himself and his followers as royal soldiers, and thus obtain admittance to the castles and forts, dine with the commandants, and then astonish them by seizing them, leading them out of their strongholds, and setting these on fire. He entered the towns in disguise, and made himself master of all the projects of the king's officers. The people conceived for him the most enthusiastic admiration. They looked upon him as, under God, their great deliverer, and this, at length, led to the fall of the Camisards. They began to trust more in the instruments than in the God who made them. The chiefs arrayed themselves in the splendid uniforms of the slain king's officers. They adorned themselves with gold chains, and ruby and diamond rings. Cavallier, Rowland, Ravenel, Abraham Mazel, and the rest, might be seen in their broad hats and feathers, and their scarlet coats, mounted on their proud chargers. Cavallier rode a noble white horse which had belonged to Colonel La Jonquiere, and which he took afterwards with him to the war in Spain. They lived in the castles and chateaus of ancient nobles, and called themselves dukes and counts; but their followers always persisted in simply calling them their brothers. Rowland styled himself Duke of the Cevennes, and declared the country his, won by his sword. They had, though still pious and brave, forgotten partly the rock whence they were hewn, and their glory departed.

Louis finding that his successive generals and successive armies availed nothing, sent against them the subtle Villars, who afterwards coped with Marlborough on the plains of Flanders. Villars soon comprehended that he might, perhaps, extirpate the whole race by a vast struggle and a tremendous massacre, but that he could never subdue them. He tried art and flattery. He invited Cavallier to meet him and gave hostages for his safety. They met at Nismes, and what a scene was that! The people streamed from all surrounding towns, from villages and farms, to gaze on the hero of the Cevennes. They crowded round in dense and eager thousands on thousands, kissing his feet and his garments, as he rode proudly on his white steed, with his little troop of Camisards opening the way for him with their swords, and Ravanel and the young Daniel riding on each side of him. The proud marshal and Cavallier met in the gardens of the old monastery of the Franciscans; and the bland and polite royal general poured the subtle poison of flattery into the ear of the young mountaineer. He spoke of the fame which he had won wide through the world; of the wish of the king to make him the commander of a regiment of his brave Camisards, to fight, not against him, but against his enemies. He offered freedom of conscience, though not liberty to have churches, for the brave Protestants of the Cevennes. Cavallier demanded other guarantees and privileges; but Villars told him the king's goodness and the king's word were the best guarantees to loyal subjects; and the weak youth, weak without his spiritual guide, fell. He signed the contract, and signed it without consulting his chief—Rowland.

When Cavallier returned to the hills to proclaim the achievement of liberty of conscience, and to call away with him his regiment of heroic Camisards to fields of distant glory, what a reception was that! What a wild and fearful scene! 'What liberty? What security?' demanded the indignant Rowland. 'No: unless the Camisards had liberty to worship God, not in holes and corners, not in deserts and caverns only, but in their own churches, with all the rights and guarantees of citizens, they would live and die with their arms in their hands.'

A terrible shout and a howl of fury, mingled as with the rolling of thunder and the hissing of serpents, burst round the astonished youth from the frantic Camisards. 'Traitor! Betrayer!' and not Liberator and Saviour, rushed from the lungs of the thousands of infuriated Camisards—from the men whom he had so long led to battle, and who dreaded no death at his command. In vain he explained and reasoned; they would not hear him, till Rowland said, 'Though we cannot agree with our deluded brother, let us not part in anger,' and embraced him. Then the hearts of all the soldiers melted a little, as they thought on old times; and when the heart-stricken young champion said, ' Let those who love me follow me,' forty strode forth from the ranks and followed him. Forty only who now loved him! Forty only who had followed his banner as the banner of God—of certain victory! Forty only of all those who had seen the wonders of his young arm, and rushed into the hottest battle at his trumpet voice, now followed in silence the melancholy hero and the young Daniel; for the gigantic Ravanel—to this moment faithful to God and Cavallier—now stood firmly faithful to God alone. He waved his sword vehemently, and shouted with the Camisard soldiery, 'Live the sword of the Eternal! Live the sword of the Eternal!'

That was the fall of the Camisards. The glory of the Cevennes, and its wondrous warfare under the banners of the Almighty, and the visible armies of the angels—visible to the prophets in their hours of ecstasy—was over. From the year 1701 to 1705 was the period of the most marvellous revelation, and conflict, and victory. Cavallier and his little troop—melancholy, and ominous of evil done with good intent, and of evil coming—were sent under guard to Versailles. Cavallier had been told, in one of his illuminated hours, that he should speak with the king; and he did speak with him, and boldly and eloquently, for the oppressed people of his mountains, and of the beautiful south; but he found quickly that he was only speaking to an old and bloated bigot, surrounded by the most corrupt and priestly influences—a sensual and priest-ridden slave—though the nominal monarch of France. When he reminded him of the treaty made with Marshal Villars, in a voice of thunder he bade him be silent;

and the Camisard then knew that he was betrayed. Some friendly voice now whispered to him to fly, ere the Bastile shut in him and his party for ever. But it was not to the Bastile, but to the fortress of Brisac, that the treacherous king had destined them; on the way, they rode off in the night, and reached the frontier and safety.

The subsequent history of Cavallier was more fortunate than that of his late brother chieftain. He went to Holland, and, collecting a regiment of French Protestant refugees, he fought gallantly in Savoy, and in Spain, against the persecuting Louis. At the battle of Almanza, his regiment of Camisards finding themselves face to face with one of Montrevel's old regiments, which had helped to lay waste the Cevennes, the embittered enemies—countrymen, but Catholic and Protestant—rushed on each other with fixed bayonets, and, without firing a shot, fought with such fury that only three hundred out of both regiments, according to the Duke of Berwick, were left alive. After that Cavallier came to England. His world-wide fame gave him high distinction, and led to wealth. He married, in Holland, a daughter of the famous Madame Dunoyer, of Nismes, and by that marriage became nephew of Lachaise, the persecuting confessor of Louis XIV., and, nominally, brother-in-law to Voltaire! He wrote his Memoirs, and became the Governor of Jersey, which post he held till his death, which occurred in Chelsea, in 1740. But was he happy as he was prosperous? When he was introduced at Court, Queen Anne asked him whether the Lord still visited him, as he did in his native mountains; and the wealthy and *fortunate* (?) ex-Camisard chief burst into tears, hung his head, and was silent!

The rest of the Camisard leaders refused any compromises—refused the delusive and soon violated treaty. But the charm was broken; the Divine Spirit, which had blazed in unclouded glory upon them, was veiled in a great measure, if not withdrawn. Confidence had received a shock by the defection of Cavallier, and suspicion and weakness crept in. Rowland, the brave, the good, and the wise, had become, in his own imagination, the Duke of the Cevennes, and boasted to have won it by his sword. He was soon suffered to fall into the hands of a traitor, and was killed, gallantly defending himself against an ambushed and overwhelming force. There was no longer any head, any centre of union. Every chief commanded his own independent section of Camisards, who fought bravely, but were overpowered. Some surrendered on condition of being allowed to quit the country; others were taken and put to death with horrible tortures, being kept without sleep, or broken, inch by inch, on the wheel. The leaders all gone, the poor people endured a condition of sad oppression. No regard was paid to the treaty; and there remains a long history of wars and trampling violence till the outbreak of the Revolution.

There is none so sad a story as that of the Protestants of the south of France till 1787, when Louis XVI. was compelled to pass a much boasted, but pitiful edict of toleration. The edict granted the mere right to worship, and legitimated marriages amongst Protestants; but it rigorously excluded them from the exercise of every civil, judicial, or political function, and subjected them to the domination of the established church, which had perpetrated upon them a hundred years of the cruellest martyrdom, and yet scowled on them with the eyes of a wolf still licking its bloody jaws.

It is a singular fact that it was not to the so-called Christianity of the country, but which was, in truth, the devil's counterfeit of it, that the French Protestants owed their liberty, their restoration to human rights—but to Infidelity; to that scepticism and atheism which the tender mercies of the *soi-disant* Christianism had generated; to that disgust, universal and inexpressible in France, which the oppressions and suppressions, the dungeons, the racks, the fires, the insolence and the darkness of Antichrist had created, and which, cooperating with and encouraging political despotism, evoked the tempest of the national indignation, which destroyed both throne and altar. Read the haughty words of Louis XVI.'s emancipatory edict of 1787: 'Pour cette grâce royale, vous serez assujettis au service de l'état et à l'entretien de la religion catholique, seule dominante; mais du reste, vous demeurez à jamais exclus de toutes fonctions d'administration, de judicature, d'enseignement, et privés de tout moyen d'influence dans le royaume. En un mot, vous n'obtiendrez de nous ce que le droit naturel ne nous permet pas de vous refuser.'

But Voltaire gave the signal, and magistrates, philosophers, and literary men became the organs of tolerance, the echoes of the mighty voice of Ferney. Tolerance was the word of universal order: procurators general, Rippert de Montclar, Servan, la Charlotais, demanded it from parliament; Turgot and D'Alembert, in journals and pamphlets; Fenouillot de Falbaire, in the theatre, in his drama of 'The Honest Criminal;' Paris, France, demanded it in thunder. The new philosophy penetrated through all the pores of superannuated society, and decomposed it utterly, as the air decomposes a corpse. It was not monarchy, it was not Christianity, but the National Assembly, which proclaimed the freedom of the mind; and yet it is remarkable that that Assembly elected, as one of its first weekly presidents, a pastor of the Church of the Desert, a son of the martyrs of the Cevennes, Rabaut Saint Etienne! And when the dungeons of Antichrist were thrown open, they found in them crowds of miserable beings the sight of whom could have drawn tears from a Caligula. The victims of the holy and infallible church, chiefly women, overwhelmed at the idea of deliverance, fell at the feet of their liberators, and could express their sensations only by sighs and tears. Many of them were eighty years of age; one, of fifty-three years old, had passed thirty-eight in prison! Marie Durand, sister of the martyr of that name, had been cast into her dungeon at five years of age, and had passed all her life there!

The fiery conflict of the prophets of the Cevennes had at length its triumph. This was the issue of its inspirations and its martyrdoms. The mighty had fallen, but the weak, mighty in God, had remained—Protestantism survived all the dragonades. At the revocation of the Edict of Nantes, the Protestants of France were calculated at two millions;

they are now calculated at three millions, after the enormous numbers who were destroyed, or who emigrated to America, to the Cape of Good Hope, and to most of the countries of Europe. 'Let us conclude our history,' says Peyrat, 'by an observation which is the conclusion natural and consolatory. It is, that the result of this gigantic dragonade—of this political oppression—has been almost null. That the greatest wound given to French Protestantism has been the expatriation of half a million of its children; yet they remain no fewer in number. The Cevennes have given to the world a great and salutary lesson. They have proved that the apostleship of the sword is impotent to convert souls; and that, in order to triumph over a despotism the most colossal, it is only necessary for the weakest people to suffer in silence and to hope. Happy are they who believe, who love, and who hope.'

And the picture which he draws of these Camisard spiritualists, so late as 1840, is beautiful. 'The tourists who to-day traverse these mountains, pondering on the tragic events of which they were the theatre, admire with an involuntary astonishment the profound calm—the serenity of spirit—of these hospitable populations. Their calamities have not left one particle of resentment in their souls, to embitter the pious and the martial traditions which they recount to the stranger. The vestiges of persecution have as completely disappeared from the soil as from their hearts, only the inhabitants of some cantons have not rebuilt their churches—they continue to worship in the desert. How often, in my wanderings, have I suddenly heard arise in the distance a psalmody, simple, grave, and somewhat monotonous, but of a profoundly religious character, which the winds have borne to me across the woods, mingled with the murmur of torrents, and the tinkling of the bells of the flocks and herds. I have hastened towards it, and have soon discovered, on the skirts of the forest, or in some meadow, two or three hundred of the faithful listening, in pious absorption, to the words of their pastor, stationed on a rock at the foot of some ancient oak, which canopied him with its branches.

'Ah! how tame becomes every form of worship after that adoration in the wilderness; amid that living nature which mingles its majestic voice with the hymns of man; under a heaven whose transparent depths permit the mystic spirit to catch glimpses of the invisible. Our emotion is doubled when the desert, like the Champ Domergue, is a spot consecrated by the prayers and combats of their ancestors. The pastor there, the minister of Vialas, is the descendant of the patriarchal Elie Marion. The young catechumens bear the names of warriors and martyrs; for the religious families, the descendants of the inspired Camisards, remain yet almost entire. The Seguiers are remaining in the villages near Magestavols. The posterity of Castanet, under the name of Mallaval, descended by the female line, still inhabit the cottage of that chief at Massavaque. The Mazels are a populous tribe. The Maurels, descended from the sister of Catinat, are small proprietors, farmers, and coopers in Caila. The Cavalliers, prosperous also, have quitted Ribaute; but the stock of the Laportes—the family of Rowland—of which an off-shoot is transplanted to St. Jean-du-Gard, flourishes still in the ancestral house of Massoubeyran; and the youngest of these shoots has received the name of his illustrious great-uncle, the Camisard general, ROWLAND LAPORTE.'

The Camisards who reached this country, and amongst them, the brave Elie Marion, the other Cavallier, and numbers besides, were ready to confirm the truth of the most startling relations to be found in the histories of these Cevennois, with their blood. For abundant testimonies of the most unimpeachable kind, the reader may refer to the 'Pastoral Letters' of the celebrated Jurieu, printed A.D. 1688 and 1689; to the treatises of Messieurs Benoist, Brueys, the Marquis de Guiscard, and M. Boyer; to the letters of M. Calcdon, Madame Verbron, the Marquis de Puysegur; and to the testimonies in form of twenty-six eye and ear-witnesses, during their sojourn in London, on oath before Sir Richard Holford and John Edisbury, Esq., masters in Chancery, in 1707, namely: Messieurs Daudy, Facio, Portales, Vernett, Arnassan, Marion, Fage, Cavallier, Mazel, Dubois, Madame Castanet, Madame Charras, and others; all Camisards distinguished in this great struggle, and whose descendants at the present day recount with pride their share in these amazing events, and maintain their verity. M. Brueys, in his 'History of Fanaticism,' admits that they are facts proved upon trial, and rendered authentic by many decrees of the parliament of Grenoble, by the orders of the intendants, by judgements or sentences judicial, by verbal proceedings, and other justifying proofs. 'Catholics of good sense,' admits M. Brueys, 'know not what to think of these things; and the only way out of their perplexity is to attribute the miracles to the devil, or to the amazing force of enthusiasm.'

The last argument would be equally fatal to the Catholic miracles. But we are assured, by no less authority than that of the London 'Athenæum' of March 26, 1859, in an article on Trollope's 'Decade of Italian Women,' that no amount of enthusiasm will account for such phenomena. 'It needs something more potent than all this. There is a supernatural and spiritual agency which Mr. Trollope does not take into the account. The religious element environs us all; "it is about our path and about our bed;" we all live on the threshold of the invisible world; every time a man kneels down in prayer, in church or chamber, he addresses himself to "the awful presence of an unseen power." St. Catherine dwelt in the heart of that great mystery; ordinary men and women live in the visible present, and do not dwell "in worlds unrealised;" yet the great movements which have stirred the hearts of men like trees of the forests by a strong wind, have had their rise in a fanatical enthusiasm, or some religious idea; we say fanatical, because we would express the vehement, absorbing devotion to *an idea stronger than the man himself, which would be in-*

sanity if it were not INSPIRATION. Men and women carried away, rapt in a religious idea, have all the small hopes, fears, and motives, and self-interests, which make men cowardly and inconstant, burnt out of them; their belief in the wisdom and help which come from above, gives them that entire and perfect will which has no flaw of doubt to mar its unity. *They have united themselves to a strength not their own, and* TRANSCENDING *all human obstacles;* and " it works in them mightily to will and to do," as one of them expresses it. This mysticism is not amenable to any of "the laws of right reason;" it appeals to the deep-seated religious instinct, which is the strongest feeling in man's nature, and underlies all the differences of clime and race, and "makes of one blood all the nations of the earth." Catherine had this religious enthusiasm; she had that *faith which could work miracles* and remove mountains.'

This is a candid confession from a journal which, on so many occasions, has pooh-poohed any idea of the supernatural. What Catherine of Sienna did, the Camisards, by the same sublime and omnipotent power, did in a still higher degree. ' The number of the prophets,' says Brueys, an enemy of theirs, ' was infinite; there were many thousands of them. Some of the things done, and fully recorded and attested, as already said, both in histories and before public authorities, surpass all ordinary belief. Women shed tears of blood, and men were placed in great piles of wood, like the martyrs, and these were set on fire, so that the flames met over their heads; and yet they came out, when all the wood had burnt down to ashes, unharmed. The place, time, and witnesses of these facts are all stated, and a selection of them may be seen in the ' Spiritual Telegraph' for 1859, p. 236. After the trial of this ordeal on Clary, one of their prophets and leaders, in the presence of Colonel Cavallier, and thousands of spectators, at Serignan, in August 1703, the people burst into a simultaneous singing of a French version of the 104th Psalm:—

> Bénis le Seigneur, ô mon âme !
> Seigneur ! maître des dieux, roi de l'éternité,
> Sur ton trône éclatant, ceint d'un manteau de flamme,
> Tu règnes ; couronné de gloire et de beauté !

Even the historians of these scenes, who assume the ground of impartiality, and relate them with the qualifications, 'as they believed,' 'as they assert,' 'as they thought,' we find continually forgetting themselves, and breaking out into the most ample admission of their own faith in these marvels. Thus Peyrat, in his 'History of the Pastors of the Desert,' iv. 179, uses language with which I will conclude this chapter.

'Since Voltaire, it is difficult, in France, to speak of prophecies and prodigies, without being overwhelmed with sarcasm and derision. Nevertheless, ecstasy is an incontestible and real condition of the soul. Phenomenal to-day, it was common in the infancy of the human race: in the early days of the world, when God loved to converse with man in his innocence, on the virgin soil of the earth. It was a kind of sixth sense, a faculty by which Adam contemplated the invisible, conversed face to face with the Eternal Wisdom, and, like a child with its mother, lived with his Creator in the delicious groves of Eden. But after the fall, heaven became closed, God rarely descended among the lost race; man's divine essence was withdrawn from him, and the prophetic gift was only at intervals accorded to extraordinary messengers, charged with words of menace more frequently than those of love. All the primitive nations, Indians, Persians, Phœnicians, Greeks, Latins, Celts, Scandinavians, have had their Yogees, their Magi, their Seers, their Hierophants, their Sibyls, their Druids, their Bards and Scalds, living in solitude, proclaiming the future, and commanding the elements. Scripture, so to say, is but the history of the Hebrew prophets, defenders of the Mosaic law, and teachers of the people of Israel. Their miraculous appearance was irregular till Samuel, who united them into a body, and established the sacred school of the prophets on

Mount Najoth. When the Jews became unfaithful to the Mosaic institution, the democratic judge, reluctantly conceding their desire, gave them, as a counterpoise to royalty, the school of the prophets, which became a kind of theocratic tribunal.

'The prophets, in effect, appear always in the Bible as the divine tribunes of the people, perpetually in conflict with the kings, whom they deposed and put to death, and who persecuted and exterminated them in return. The giant of the Hebrew prophets was Elijah. The Tishbite appears to have had for a soul the lightning of Jehovah itself. In the caves of Carmel, where he lived like an eagle, in the presence of the sea, and above the clouds, the terrible prophet watched at once over Jerusalem and Samaria. To attest his divine mission, the Lord gave him empire over the elements. At his voice the sun consumed the earth, the clouds arose from the sea, fire descended from heaven upon the altar, and devoured the sacrifice. His mission terminated, the prophet ascended to Jehovah in a car of fire drawn by the steeds of the tempest. Elijah comprehends in himself all the gigantic and sombre poetry of the heroic ages of the Jews. The Reformation poured into the modern world, like an inundation, the Hebrew genius and the civilisation of the East. Rome, in sealing up the Bible, had closed its springs. Under the rod of Luther, who smote the rock, the divine stream boiled forth impetuously. The modern nations, fainting from their tempestuous pilgrimage across the middle ages, precipitated themselves into these lakes of life. They plunged into them, they revivified, they purified themselves, like birds which, after torrid heat, drink and wash themselves in the fountains. In this universal regeneration, they were born again demi-Israelites. Heirs of the people of God, who are themselves for the present rejected, they to-day enjoy their laws, their customs, their phrases, their names, their hymns, their symbols, even to their very prophecy, and to those extatic visions in which God appeared to the patriarchs in the deserts of Asia. The revolutions of the Protestants have elevated their faith, which, in the tempestuous fires to which it has been subjected, has sometimes boiled over all bounds, rising like steam towards the clouds, and descended in storms. The German Reformation produced the Anabaptists and the Peasant War; the English Reformation, the Puritans; and the Revocation of the Edict of Nantes, the Camisards.'

CHAPTER XVIII.

THE WESLEYS, WHITEFIELD, AND FLETCHER OF MADELEY.

> All cannot fail to be reminded of the necessity of a further outpouring of the Spirit of God.—THE BISHOP OF LONDON, 1859.

> My serious belief amounts to this—that preternatural impressions are sometimes communicated to us for wise purposes, and that departed spirits are sometimes permitted to manifest themselves.
> SOUTHEY's *Colloquies*.

> And what is strangest upon this strange head
> Is, that, whatever bar the reason rears
> 'Gainst such belief, there's something stranger still
> In its behalf, let those deny who will.
> LORD BYRON.

THE rapidity with which vital religion dies out, under a political machinery for perpetuating it, is most strikingly manifested in our own history since the Reformation. We have seen what was its condition a hundred years after Henry VIII., notwithstanding the hammerings and contrivings of those royal church masons and carpenters, the Tudors and the Stuarts. Fox and his friends, Baxter and Bunyan, revived its life for awhile; but the religious temperature fell fast again till the time of Wesley and Whitefield, and what it was then, Watson, in his admirable criticism on Southey's 'Life of Wesley,' tells us. It had not only fallen prone itself, but had pulled down the dissenting *vis vitæ* with it. 'The body of the clergy,' he says, 'neither knew nor cared about systems of any kind; in a vast number of instances they were immoral—often grossly so. The populace in large towns were ignorant and profligate; the inhabitants of villages added, to ignorance and profligacy, brutish and barbarous manners. A more striking instance of the rapid deterioration of religious light and influence in a country scarcely occurs, than in ours from the Restoration till the rise of Methodism. It affected not only the church, but the dissenting sects in no ordinary degree. The Presbyterians had commenced their course through Arianism down to Socinianism, and those who held the doctrines of Calvin had, in too many instances, by a course of hot-house planting, luxuriated them into the fatal and disgusting errors of Antinomianism. There were exceptions; but this was the general state of religion and morals in the country, when the Wesleys, Whitefield, and a few kindred spirits went forth to sacrifice ease, reputation, and even life itself, if necessary, to produce a reformation' (p. 129).

Every successive attempt to break up this religious torpor, to renew Christian life in the public, has been violently opposed by the established church. We have seen how it treated Fox and his friends, how it treated Baxter and Bunyan; we have now to see how it greeted the spiritual life-breathing of Wesley, Whitefield, and their contemporaries in the eighteenth century. That such men should be met by scorn, misrepresentation, and persecution, is the direct proof of the great need of their appearance. To say that a man is a religious reformer, is to say that he is a Spiritualist. Nothing but a 'new out-pouring of the Divine Spirit' can awake life in the dry bones of defunct profession, in the freezing masses of materialism and worldly debasement. Wesley, Whitefield, and their fellow apostles, produced a wonderful change in the religious character of their age, and have left lasting and beneficent traces of their labours in the public mind. They roused even the stagnant church which abused and rejected them. A new and commendable activity has ever since been visible in the establishment. It has exercised a greater moral control over its clergy, and has entered into a zealous competition with dissenters for the education of the people ; but, again, this very activity has degenerated into a morbid condition, having no claims to a genuine spiritualistic character. It is running wildly into two extremes : the one of forms and rituals, tending to the outward ; the other of infidel rationalism. Between these we look in vain for the ancient spirit of the gospel, which claims boldly the heritage of apostolic powers, and works in that overshadowing of the Holy Ghost which made the mighty preachers of all times, and can alone cause the waters of eternal life to gush from the cold rocks of our daily calculating world. The formalism and the learnedness of the mere letter that killeth, which are the great features of our time, must perish in some new ' outpouring of the spirit,' or Christianity must perish altogether. This hybrid state is, from the very laws of nature, a barren state, and tends to death. But the plan of Providence cannot be impeded by the selfishness and grossness of men and their institutions ; new and unlooked-for outbreaks of the invisible strength of the ages will take place, and amid the clouds and hissing winds that accompany them, herald new spiritual springs. Let us encourage our faith by reviving the circumstances of the despised but triumphant advent of Methodism.

John Wesley was cradled in the very abode of the supernatural ; haunting spirits surrounded his childhood's pillow, and walked beside him in his school-boy rounds. The extraordinary events which took place in the parsonage of his father at Epworth, in Lincolnshire, and which were attested not only by Mr. Wesley and Mrs. Wesley, but by every member of the family which was present at the time, have acquired a world-wide notoriety ; and it were as easy to deny the existence of the Wesley family itself as to deny these manifestations. No case of spiritual disturbance was ever so thoroughly proved, and that by such a number of persons of education and of freedom from superstition. We have the written accounts in narratives and letters of Mr. Wesley himself, the father of John Wesley, and incumbent of

Epworth, who kept a regular diary of the occurrences; of Mrs. Wesley, in four letters to her sons, who were at the time at school at Westminster and the Charterhouse; in letters from six of the Miss Wesleys to their brothers. We have the written account of the Rev. Mr. Hoole, the vicar of Haxey, an adjoining parish, who was called in by Mr. Wesley to hear the noises; and the account of Robin Brown, the man-servant, in a letter to John Wesley. All these evidences will be found at length in the notes to the first volume of Southey's 'Life of Wesley.' I shall, therefore, content myself with copying John Wesley's narrative of these disturbances based on these documents and on personal enquiries on the spot. This narrative was published by him in the ' Arminian Magazine' :—

' When I was very young, I heard several letters read, wrote to my elder brother by my father, giving an account of strange disturbances which were in his house at Epworth, in Lincolnshire.

' When I went down thither, in the year 1720, I carefully enquired into the particulars. I spoke to each of the persons who were then in the house, and I took down what each could testify of his or her own knowledge. The sum of which was this :—

' On December 2, 1716, while Robert Brown, my father's servant, was sitting with one of the maids, a little before ten at night, in the dining-room, which opened into the garden, they both heard a knocking at the door. Robert rose and opened it, but could see nobody. Quickly it knocked again and groaned. " It is Mr. Turpine," said Robert; " he has the stone, and uses to groan so." He opened the door again, twice or thrice repeated. But still seeing nothing, and being a little startled, they rose and went up to bed. When Robert came to the top of the garret stairs, he saw a hand-mill, which was at a little distance, whirled about very swiftly. When he related this, he said, " Nought vexed me but that it was empty. I thought, if it had been full of malt, he might have ground his heart out for me." When he was in bed, he said he heard, as it were, a gobbling of a turkey-cock, close to his bedside; and soon after, the sound of one tumbling over his boots and shoes; but there were none there; he had left them below. The next day, he and the maid related these things to the other maid, who laughed heartily, and said, "What a couple of fools you are! I defy the thing to frighten me." After churning in the evening, she put the butter in the tray, and had no sooner carried it into the dairy, than she heard a knocking on the shelf, where several pancheons of milk stood, first above the shelf, then below. She took the candle, and searched both above and below; but being able to find nothing, threw down butter, tray and all, and ran away for life. The next evening, between five and six o'clock, my sister Molly, then about twenty years of age, sitting in the dining-room, reading, heard as if it were the door that led into the hall open, and a person walking in that seemed to have on a silk night-gown, rustling and trailing along. It seemed to walk round her, then to the door, then round again; but she could see nothing. She thought "It signifies nothing to run away: for whatever it is, it can run faster than me." So she rose, put her book under her arm, and walked slowly away. After supper, she was sitting with my sister Sukey, about a year older than herself, in one of the chambers, and, telling her what had happened, she made quite light of it; telling her, "I wonder you are so easily frightened: I would fain see what would fright me." Presently a knocking began under the table; she took the candle and looked, but could find nothing. Then the iron casement began to clatter, and the lid of a warming-pan. Next the latch of a door moved up and down without ceasing. She started up, leaped into bed without undressing, pulled the bed-clothes over her head, and never ventured to look up till next morning. A night or two after, my sister Kitty, a year younger than my sister Molly, was waiting as usual, between nine and ten, to take away my father's candle, when she heard one coming down the garret stairs, walking slowly by her, then going down the best stairs, then up the back stairs, and up the garret stairs; and at every step it seemed the house shook from top to bottom. Just then my father knocked; she went in, took his candle, and got to bed as fast as possible. In the morning she told this to my eldest sister, who told her, "You know I believe nothing of these things; pray let me take away the candle to-night, and I will find out the trick." She accordingly took my sister Kitty's place, and had no sooner taken away the candle than she heard a noise below. She hastened down stairs to the hall, where the noise was, but it was then in the kitchen, where it was drumming on the inside of the screen. When she went round, it was drumming on the outside, and so always on the side opposite to her. Then she heard a knocking at the back kitchen door; she ran to it, unlocked it softly, and when the knocking was repeated suddenly opened it, but nothing was to be seen. As soon as she had shut it the knocking began again; she opened it again, but could see nothing. When she went to shut the door, it was violently thrust against her; she let it fly open, but nothing appeared. She went again to shut it, and it was thrust against her; but she set her knee and her shoulder to the door, forced it to, and turned the key. Then the knocking began again, but she let it go on, and went up to bed. However, from that time she was thoroughly convinced that there was no imposture in the affair.

'The next morning, my sister telling my mother what had happened, she said, "If I hear anything myself, I shall know how to judge." Soon after, she (Emily) begged her to come into the nursery. She did, and heard in the corner of the room as it were the violent rocking of a cradle; but no cradle had been there for some years. She was convinced it was preternatural, and earnestly prayed it might not disturb her in her own chamber at the hours of retirement, and it never did. She now thought it was proper to tell my father; but he was extremely angry and said, "Sukey, I am ashamed of you; these boys and girls frighten one another, but you are a woman of sense, and should know better. Let me hear of it no more." At six in the evening, he had family prayers as usual. When he began the prayers for the king, a knocking began all round the room, and a thundering knock attended the Amen. The same was heard from this time every morning and evening, while the prayer for the king was repeated. As both my father and mother are now at rest and incapable of being pained thereby, I think it my duty to furnish the serious reader with a key to this circumstance.

'The year before King William died, my father observed my mother did not say Amen to the prayer for the king. She said she could not, for she did not believe the Prince of Orange was king. He vowed he would never cohabit with her till she did. He then took his horse and rode away, nor did she hear anything of him for a twelvemonth. He then came back and lived with her as before, but I fear his vow was not forgotten before God.

'Being informed that Mr. Hoole, the vicar of Haxey, an eminently pious and sensible man, could give me some farther information, I walked over to him. He said, " Robert Brown came over to me, and told me your father desired my company. When I came, he gave me an account of all which had happened, particularly the knocking during family prayers. But that evening, to my great satisfaction, we had no knocking at all. But between nine and ten a servant came in, and said, " Old Jefferies is coming"—that was the name of one that died in the house—" for I hear the signal." This, they informed me, was heard every night about a quarter before ten. It was towards the top of the house on the outside, at the north-east corner, resembling the loud creaking of a saw, or rather that of a windmill, when the body of it is turned about, in order to shift the sails to the wind. We then heard a knocking over our heads, and Mr. Wesley, catching up a candle, said, " Come, sir, now you shall hear for yourself." We went up stairs; he with much hope, and I, to say the truth, with much fear.

When we came into the nursery, it was knocking in the next room; when we were there, it was knocking in the nursery. And there it continued to knock, though we came in, particularly at the head of the bed, which was of wood, in which Miss Hetty and two of her younger sisters lay. Mr. Wesley, observing that they were much affected, though asleep, sweating and trembling exceedingly, was very angry, and, pulling out a pistol, was going to fire at the place from whence the sound came. But I catched him by the arm, and said, " Sir, you are convinced this is something preternatural. If so, you cannot hurt it; but you give it power to hurt you." He then went close to the place, and said, sternly, " Thou deaf and dumb devil, why dost thou fright these children that cannot answer for themselves?—come to me in my study, that am a man." Instantly it knocked his knock, —the particular knock which he always used at the gate— as if it would shiver the board in pieces, and we heard nothing more that night.

' Till this time, my father had never heard the least disturbance in his study; but the next evening, as he attempted to go into his study, of which none had any key but himself, when he opened the door it was thrust back with such violence as had like to have thrown him down. However, he thrust the door open, and went in. Presently there was a knocking first on one side, then on the other; and, after a time, in the next room, wherein my sister Nancy was. He went into that room, and, the noise continuing, adjured it to speak, but in vain. He then said, " These spirits love darkness, put out the candle, and perhaps it will speak." She did so, and he repeated his adjuration; but still there was only knocking, and no articulate sound. Upon this he said, " Nancy, two Christians are an overmatch for the devil. Go all of you down stairs; it may be when I am alone it will have the courage to speak." When she was gone, a thought came in, and he said, " If thou art the spirit of my son Samuel, I pray thee knock three knocks, and no more." Immediately all was silence, and there was no more knocking all that night. I asked my sister Nancy, then about fifteen years old, whether she was not afraid, when my father used that adjuration? She answered she was sadly afraid it would speak when she put out the candle; but she was not at all afraid in the daytime, when it walked after her, as she swept the chambers, as it constantly did, and seemed to sweep after her. Only she thought he might have done it for her, and saved her the trouble. By this time all my family were so accustomed to these noises that they gave them little disturbance. A gentle tapping at their bed-head usually began between nine and ten at night. Then they commonly said to each other, " Jeffery is coming; it is time to go to sleep." And if they heard a noise in the day, and said to my youngest sister, " Hark, Kezzy, Jeffery is knocking above," she would run up stairs, and pursue it from room to room, saying she desired no better diversion.

' A few nights after, my father and mother were just gone to bed, and the candle was not taken away, when they heard three blows, and a second, and a third three, as it were, with a large oaken staff, struck upon a chest which stood by the bed-side. My father immediately rose, put on his night-gown, and hearing great noises below, took the candle, and went down; my mother walked by his side. As they went down the broad stairs, they heard as if a vessel full of silver was poured upon my mother's breast, and ran jingling down to her feet. Quickly after there was a sound, as if a large iron ball was thrown among many bottles under the stairs; but nothing was hurt. Soon after our large mastiff dog came and ran to shelter himself between them. When the disturbances continued he used to bark, and leap, and snap, on one side and the other, and that frequently before any person in the room heard any noise at all. But after two or three days he used to tremble and creep away before the noise began; and by this the family knew it was at hand, nor did the observation ever fail. A little before my father and mother came into the hall, it seemed as if a very large coal was violently thrown upon the floor, and dashed all in pieces; but nothing was seen. My father then cried out, " Sukey, do you not hear that? All the pewter is thrown about the kitchen." But when they looked, all the pewter stood in its place. Then there was a loud knocking at the back door. My father opened it, but saw nothing. It was then at the front door. He opened that, but it was still lost labour. After opening first the one, then the other several times, he turned and went up to bed. But the noises were so violent all over the house that he could not sleep till four in the morning.

'Several gentlemen and clergymen now earnestly advised my father to quit the house; but he constantly answered, "No; let the devil flee from me; I will never flee from the devil." But he wrote to my eldest brother at London to come down. He was preparing to do so, when another letter came, informing him that the disturbances were over after they had continued the better part of the time, day and night, from the 2nd of December to the end of January.'

In this summary by John Wesley, a number of curious incidents are omitted which occur in the statements of the other members of the family. In the elder Wesley's account, the noise of smashing the bottles under the stairs had been heard before by Miss Emily Wesley; and in the same account is mentioned the sound of dancing in a matted chamber which was vacant and locked up. The vicar procured a stout mastiff to watch outside the house, to make sure that the noises were no trick by any living person there. He says that, when one of his daughters knocked, the spirit answered in the same way. The noise of money thrown down, he says, three of his daughters also heard at a different time. He adds that figures were seen by different members of the family, as of a rabbit or badger, but indistinct. In John Wesley's own memoranda, he says, that the noise was frequently attended by a rising of the wind, and its whistling round the house. It moved nothing, even when it made the whole house jar, except the latches of the doors. Whatever noise of any other kind was made, its dead hollow note would be clearly heard above all, and none of them could imitate it. It seems not to have been a bad spirit; for it ceased to knock when Mr. Wesley, fearing his son Samuel was dead, asked it to knock three times if it were his spirit; and after Mrs. Wesley desired it never to disturb her at her devotions, it never did. Mr. Wesley did not know, as is well known now, that it is very difficult for a spirit to speak audibly to those in the body, and that knocking is the easiest mode by which spirits can communicate. Had he hit on the method of questioning it by the alphabet, he might soon have learnt the object of its visits.

In Mrs. Wesley's letter to her son John, she says that she at first thought the noises proceeded from rats, and, as a neighbour had frightened rats away by blowing a horn, she had one blown for half a day; but from that time the noises, which had been only heard at night, were heard night and day all over the premises. When she stamped, it repeated the exact number of strokes under her feet; when little Kezzy, only six or seven years old, stamped, it did the same.

It may well be imagined what a sensation these strange occurrences made on the minds of the boys at school. There are letters from nearly all the family to John, and also to the eldest brother Samuel at Westminster. Though his father wrote him out the whole account, he insisted that all his sisters should send him their own accounts. In fact, Samuel, who afterwards so stoutly opposed the religious reforms of his brothers, was perhaps the most curious of them all on this subject. And here it may be observed, that, though this visitation continued only two months, we are assured by John Wesley that these knockings had been heard by his mother long before in the same house, and that they had never failed to come before any signal misfortune, or illness of any of the family. No particular calamity appears to have followed this manifestation.

John Wesley, having had such unquestionable proof of supernatural agency in his own family in his youth, held fast his faith in it through his whole remarkable career, and has recorded numerous instances of such direct agency both in his Journals and in the Arminian Magazine. It is not necessary here to trace the grand progress of John and Charles Wesley, and their contemporaries, in the wonderful revival of religion in the eighteenth century, not only in Great Britain, but in the most distant quarters of the world. The whole of that great history stands recorded by ablest pens, and in the millions of men and women who now walk in the pleasant light and in the happy feeling which they spread abroad. I shall only remark that, like all other revivals, it met with the devil's tempest, which beats on the heads of God's emissaries, only to drive them and their opinions the farther and wider, and to fix them deeper in the battered and storm-drenched earth. From the church to which these devoted men of God belonged, and within which they would fain have relit the sacred fire on the altar, they experienced the most savage and insulting treatment. The little knot of undergraduates who met in the University of Oxford for the purpose of religious improvement—who lived by rule, and took the sacrament weekly—were speedily marked out for ridicule and persecution. They were dubbed Sacramentarians, Bible-bigots, Bible-moths, the Holy, or the Godly Club. Amongst the leading members of this Godly Club, which began with two or three, and soon grew to seven, and then to fifteen, were John and Charles Wesley, George Whitefield, and Hervey, afterwards author of the 'Meditations.' When Whitefield joined them, he says that he was set upon by all the students, and treated as a very odd fellow. The lives and manners of the students at that time were such as Butler, in his 'Analogy,' had described them, gross and vicious; and as Cowper had just then described them,

> A dissolution of all bonds ensued :
> The curbs invented for the mulish mouth
> Of headstrong youth were broken ; bolts and bars
> Grew rusty by disuse ; and massy gates
> Forgot their office, opening with a touch ;
> Till gowns at length are found mere masquerade ;
> The tasselled cap, and the spruce band, a jest,
> A mockery of the world.

CONDITION OF THE CHURCH.

Such was the condition of the embryo prophets of the nation. That such sons of Belial should insult and abuse the Methodist revivalists, was natural; but the authorities of the university were equally hostile to them. An appearance of real religion within the university was so odd and out of place, that they held meetings to consult how it was to be put down. On Whitefield, after quitting the university, returning to Oxford to preach, he found all the churches shut against him. The vice-chancellor came in person to the house where he was exhorting, and accosted him thus: 'Have you, sir, a name in any book here?' 'Yes, sir,' said I; 'but I intend to take it out soon.' He replied, 'Yes, and you had better take yourself out too, or otherwise I will lay you by the *heels!* What do you mean by going about, and alienating the people's affections from their proper pastors? Your works are full of vanity and nonsense! You pretend to inspiration! If ever you come again in this manner among these people, I will lay you first by the heels, and these shall follow' ('Life of Whitefield,' by Philip, p. 106).

Both the Wesleys and Whitefield, though regularly ordained ministers of the Church, soon found all pulpits shut against them; even that of his native place and parish, which his father had occupied so many years, was refused to John Wesley. The Bishop of Bristol desired Wesley to go out of his diocese, where he was not commissioned to preach, and where, consequently, Southey says, 'he had no business.' But both the Wesleys and Whitefield held that they had a commission from the Head of the Church to preach anywhere in the world. They asked, like the apostles, whether they were to obey God or man? When the churches were closed against them, they were told that it was irregular to preach either in the open air or in a private house. The chancellor of the diocese of Bristol showed Whitefield the canons prohibiting it. Such irregularities were not becoming a minister of the Established Church; they were only fit for Christ and His apostles, who preached both in private houses and out of doors, anywhere where they could save souls. Driven to follow the practice of the Founder of the Christian church, and of Him who said, 'Go into the highways and hedges and compel them to come in,' the success was wonderful and the fury of clergy, bishops, magistrates and mobs unbounded. The days of the Quakers came again. The leaders and the ministers of the Methodists were hooted, stoned, spit upon, cursed, and thrown into horse-ponds, for endeavouring to rekindle religion again in the country. They were denounced as Papists, Jesuits, seducers, and bringers in of the Pretender. At Chelsea the mob threw wildfire and crackers into the meeting; at Long Lane they broke in the roof with large stones; John Nelson, one of the preachers, was forced to go for a soldier, and, refusing to comply, was thrown into prison; mobs were collected by the sound of horn; windows were demolished; houses broken open; goods destroyed; men, women, and children beaten, pelted and dragged in the kennels; and even pregnant women outraged to the imminent danger of their lives, and the disgrace of humanity. John Wesley had a narrow escape for his life at Birmingham, Charles in another place, and Whitefield at Oxminton Green in Ireland. Some of the preachers did not escape at all, but, like poor Thomas Beard, the fellow-prisoner of Nelson, they perished in prison, or from their cruel treatment.

But persecution only produced its usual effects. The success of the Methodists became stupendous. The fire of God seemed to accompany them, and people were converted by thousands and tens of thousands. There were wide differences in the natural geniuses of these men. Whitefield was all impulse and oratory; he took no pains, probably he possessed no talent, necessary to organise a great religious body. He preached as with energies of heaven, as with flashes of lightning, and the people rushed after him in millions, and were struck down and converted by thousands. But what he lacked in constructive power was soon presented in the Countess of Huntingdon, who shaped into organic form the Whitefieldian or Calvinistic-Methodist church, which still exists, and especially throughout Wales. As for John Wesley, who was of the same original stock as the Duke of Wellington (see Southey's 'Life of Wesley,' i. 40) he possessed many of the qualities of that great general. He was eminently calm, firm, and full of constructive genius. He perfected a scheme of church government most remarkable for comprehending all the qualities which can draw men to it, and keep them there when attracted. He seized upon material necessary for such an organisation wherever he could find it; and one of his earliest connections was with the society of the Moravians, from whom he drew his Love-feasts, and Class-meetings, and all those agencies which make every man and woman something in his system, in exact opposition to the system of the Church of England, where the clergy are everything and the laity nothing. He not only consulted Count Zinzendorff on these points, but he personally visited the chief settlement of the Moravians at Herrnhut in Saxony, and studied their religious institutions there. At the same time his brother Charles, who was not only an able preacher, and a sound and good counsellor, but an excellent poet, wrote many admirable hymns for the society. Thus arose Methodism, Arminian and Calvinistic, which have done such mighty service for religion in many regions of the world; and what concerns us to know is that they did it by spiritualism of the most marked and avowed kind.

I have said that the Wesleys always retained the faith in spiritual apparitions, which they learned under the paternal roof so startingly. As to direct belief in miracles and interferences of Providence, they found this in William Law, the great disciple of Jacob Böhme, with whom they entered into close communion, and in the Moravians, who were full of it. The 'Life of Wesley' by Southey, in connection with this and other particulars, is one of the most amusing of books, at least in the third edition; for he had sent a copy of the work to Coleridge, who made marginal notes as he went along, and then left the volume, at his death, to Southey. These notes are introduced by Southey's son into the third edition.

Coleridge, who is himself sometimes inclined to sneer at the supernatural, wont allow Southey to do it, but on all occasions when the laureate's High-churchism breaks out, pulls him up, asking continually, 'Does not Robert Southey know this?' and 'Does not Robert Southey know that?' In all such cases he becomes the staunchest champion of the truth of the views of Wesley. In the course of my reading I imagined that I had made a great discovery—namely, that Protestantism only, of all churches, Christian or Pagan, rejected the supernatural; but Coleridge had made the discovery before me, and, in a note to Southey's 'Wesley,' introduces it. 'I cannot forget that this opinion of an essential difference, of the diversity of these (the miracles of the Gospels) from the miracles of the two or three first centuries, and that of the withdrawing of the miraculous power from the church at the death of the apostles, *are confined to Protestants*, and even among these *are but modern*' (vol. i. 253). Southey complains of certain words of Wesley's being fanatical, 'and yet,' asks Coleridge, 'does not Robert Southey see that they are the very words of the apostles?' In another place, 'Did Robert Southey remember that the words in italics are faithfully quoted from the Articles of the Church?' (vol. i. 245.) When Southey thinks a woman, who appeared to Wesley to be possessed, was acting a part, Coleridge quotes numerous authorities on such cases, and what Treviranus said to himself when in London: 'I have seen what I am certain I would not believe on *your* telling, and in all reason, therefore, I can neither expect nor wish that you should believe it on mine' (vol. i. 258). When Wesley asserts the wonderful powers of real faith, Coleridge adds, 'Faith is as *real* as life; as actual as force; as effectual as volition. It is the physics of the moral being, no less than it is the physics or morale of the zoo-physical' (vol. ii. 82). When Southey treats the physical phenomena of Methodism as proceeding from bodily disease (for he was very ignorant of mesmeric science), Coleridge exclaims, 'Alas, what more, or worse, could a young infidel spitaller, fresh from the lectures of some facetious anatomist or physiologist wish, than to have the "love of God and the strong desire for salvation" represented as so many symptoms and causes of a *bodily* disease? Oh, I am almost inclined to send this, my copy of his work, to R. Southey, with the notes, for my heart bears him witness that he offendeth not willingly' (vol. ii. 165). And he did send it.

The preaching of both the Wesleys and Whitefield produced those symptoms of violent agitation, convulsion and the like, which have appeared in the late revivals, and which, in fact, have been common to all great revivals in every age since the people in the Apostles' days cried out ' What shall we do to be saved?' and since the devils threw their victims on the earth and tore them, before they would leave them. If we regard the convulsions and prostrations, the foamings and outcries, as the sufferings of nature under the operations of God's omnipotent Spirit, and the resistance of the devil, loth to relinquish his hold on the souls of men, there appears nothing anomalous or extraordinary in these phenomena, which have so often been treated with ridicule or reprehension. Such were the effects of the preaching of the Friends of God in the middle ages, of the Lollards, the Puritans, the Covenanters, the Camisards, the first Friends, and so on till our own day, and no doubt such will recur again and again to the end of the world.

In Gillie's 'Historical Collections' we find precisely such phenomena occurring at the same period, 1750, in Scotland and Holland, as have been so much wondered at amongst the early Methodists and since.

'Few Sabbaths did pass away without some evidently converted, or some crowning proofs of the power of God accompanying his word: yea, that many were so taken by the heart that, through terror, the spirit in such a measure convincing them of sin, in hearing of the word, they have been made to fall over, and were carried out of the church; who after proved the most solid and lively Christians' (' Religious Movements in Scotland,' 1750.)

'In this way was ushered in that uncommon dispensation of the Spirit, which they looked not for; for at last, the preaching of the gospel began to be attended with such awful power, that several were made to cry out aloud with many tears, under a painful sense of their distress and misery. The troubled and broken-hearted were brought to Mr. Kuyper's house, who, upon conversing with them, soon discovered that the Holy Spirit, by the word, had begun a work of conviction in them. Mr. Kuyper, finding things thus with them, began to conceive some hope; yet he stood astonished, conflicting with doubts and fears, to see so many persons so strangely affected. His doubts and fears had this good effect; they made him very careful and circumspect in examining all these appearances, and comparing them with the Lord's word. The next day there was an almost universal dejection and astonishment among the inhabitants of the town. Mr. Kuyper went early in the morning to the houses of such as were awakened and distressed as were best known to him, and the work being great, he got some private Christians to go to others; they were busy the whole day going to innumerable houses. From that day the work increased beyond description; there is no painting it to the life, it was a perfect commentary on the second chapter of the Acts. Mockers ridiculed, but multitudes were pricked at heart, and cried, "What shall we do?"' (*Ibid.*, Affairs in Holland, 1750).

On Whitefield's visit to Cambuslang, in 1742, amid the most numerous and rapid conversions, it is stated, 'the visible convulsive agitations which accompanied them exceeded everything of the kind which had yet been observed.'

Wesley healed the sick by prayer and laying on of hands. He and some others joined in prayer over a man who was not expected to live till morning; he was speechless, senseless, and his pulse was gone. Before they ceased, his senses and speech returned. He recovered; and Wesley says they who choose to account for the fact by natural causes have his free leave : *he* says, it was the power of God (vol. ii. 385). He believed in dreams and impressions of a vivid and peculiar character. John Nelson dreamed that Wesley came and sate down at his fireside, and spake certain words. Four months after he did come, for the first time, sate down as he had seen him in his dream, and pronounced the very words. Nelson seems to have experienced the inner breathing described by Swedenborg and Harris. 'His soul,' he said, 'seemed to breathe its life in God, as naturally as his body breathed life in the common air.' Wesley believed, with Luther, that the devils produced disease, bodily hurts, storms, earthquakes, and nightmare. That epilepsy and insanity often proceeded from demon influence. He declared that, if he gave up faith in witchcraft, he must give up the Bible. When asked whether he had himself ever seen a ghost, he replied, ' No ; nor have I ever seen a murder; but unfortunately I am compelled to believe that murders take place almost every day, in one place or another.' Warburton attacked Wesley's belief in miraculous cures and expulsion of evil spirits; but Wesley replied that what he had seen with his own eyes he was bound to believe; the bishop could believe or not as he pleased. Wesley records the instantaneous cure of a woman named Mary Special, of cancer in both breasts. Southey quotes the relations regarding Thomas Walsh, one of the Wesleyan preachers, which very much resemble those of Catholic saints. He was sometimes found in so deep a reverie that he appeared to have ceased to breathe; there was something resembling splendour on his countenance, and other circumstances seemed to attest his communion with the spiritual world.

But the fact for which Southey decries Wesley the most, is his faith in apparitions. On this point, Mr. Watson ably defends him; and, with his remarks, I may close mine on Wesley: ' To Mr. Wesley's learning, and various and great talents, Mr. Southey is just ; but an attack is made upon what he calls his " voracious credulity." He accredited and repeated stories of apparitions, and witchcraft, and possession, so silly, as well as monstrous, that they might have nauseated the coarsest appetite for wonder; this, too, when the belief on his part was purely gratuitous, and no motive can be assigned, except the pleasure of believing.

'On the general question of supernatural appearances, it may be remarked, that Mr. Wesley might at least plead authorities for his faith as high, as numerous, and as learned, as any of our modern sceptics for their doubts. *It is in modern times only that this species of infidelity has appeared*, with the exception of the sophists of the atheistical sects in Greece and Rome, and the Sadducees amongst the Jews. The unbelief, so common in the present day among free-thinkers and half-thinkers on such subjects, places itself, therefore, with only these exceptions, in opposition to the belief of the learned and unlearned of every age and every nation, polished, semi-civilised, and savage, in every quarter of the globe. It does more: it places itself in opposition to the Scriptures, from which all the criticism, bold, subtle, profane, or absurd, which has been resorted to, can never expunge either apparitions, possessions, or witchcrafts. It opposes itself to testimony, which, if feeble and unsatisfactory in many instances, is such in others that no man in any other case would refuse assent to it; or, so refusing, he would make himself the subject of a just ridicule. That there have been many impostures is allowed; that many have been deceived is certain; and that all such accounts should be subjected to rigorous scrutiny before they can have any title to our belief, ought to be insisted upon. But even imposture and error presuppose a previous opinion in favour of what is pretended or mistaken; and if but one account in twenty, or a hundred, stands upon credible evidence, and is corroborated by circumstances in which, from their nature, there can be no mistake, there is sufficient to disturb the quiet, and confound the system of the whole body of infidels.

'Every age has its dangers. In former times, the danger lay in believing too much; in our own time, the propensity is in believing too little. The only ground which a Christian can safely take on these questions is, that the *à priori* arguments of philosophic unbelievers as to the "*absurdity*" and "*impossibility*" of these things, go for nothing, since the Scriptures have settled the fact that they have occurred, and have afforded not the least intimation that they should at any time cease to occur. Such supernatural visitations are therefore possible; and where they are reported, ought to be carefully examined, and neither too promptly admitted, nor too harshly rejected. An acute and excellent philosopher of modern times has come to the same conclusion (Mr. Andrew Baxter, in his "Enquiry into the Nature of the Human Soul," in the Essay on the Philosophy of Dreaming). Although Δεισιδαιμονία, or a fear of spirits, hath been abused by vain or weak people, and carried to extremes, perhaps, by crafty and designing men, the most rigorous philosophy will not justify its being entirely rejected. That subordinate beings are never permitted or commissioned to be the ministers of the will of God, is a hard point to be proved' (Watson's 'Observations on Southey's Life of Wesley,' p. 189-193).

I have already introduced proofs of Whitefield's spiritualism. He had a profound belief in the immediate and miraculous operation of the Divine Spirit. When Bishop Warburton ridiculed his belief in immediate inspiration, and declared 'all influence exceeding the *power of humanity* miraculous, and, therefore, not now to be believed in, the church being perfectly established,' Whitefield referred him to the Catechism, where it tells the child that it is not able to do what is required of it except by God's *special grace*; and asked him whether, when he ordained ministers, he did not say, 'Dost thou trust that thou art inwardly moved by the Holy Ghost? Then receive thou the Holy Ghost.' Though these might, to the bishop, as to Essayists and Reviewers now, have become a mere form of words, to Whitefield they were living and sacred truths. He saw wonderful effects produced by his preaching, and he attributed these to divine power. 'He found,' says his biographer, 'that the divine presence might be calculated upon whenever the divine glory was consulted' ('Life' by G. Philips, p. 76). 'How often have we been filled as with new wine; how often have I seen them overwhelmed with the divine presence!' (p. 78.) 'Vile teachers who say that we are not to receive the Holy Ghost!' (p. 85.) 'We do not mean that God's Spirit does manifest itself to our *senses*, but that it may be perceived by the soul, as really as any sensible impression made upon the body' (p. 88). 'In my prayer the power of God came down and was greatly felt. In my two sermons there was yet more power' (p. 295). 'I felt a divine life *distinct* from my animal life' (p. 321). This was when he was suffering agonies of bodily pain; and he declares that this divine life suspended all his pains, and enabled him to go out and preach. 'A gale of divine influence everywhere attended his preaching' (p. 408). It was only such a power that could produce the effects which followed Whitefield.

In America, Whitefield went with William Tennant, who had once lain in a trance for three days, and was only saved from being buried alive by his physician. For the wonders of this trance see Howitt's Translation of 'Ennemoser's History of Magic,' ii. 429. Tennant totally lost his memory for a long time after this trance. When the agitations attending his preaching were, like spiritualism to-day, attributed by the clergy to the devil, Whitefield replied, 'Is it not amazing *rashness*, without enquiry and trial, to pronounce that a work of the devil which, for anything *you* know, may be the work of the infinitely good and Holy Spirit' (p. 300). For some time, Whitefield says, he was constrained, whether he would or not, when praying for the king, to say 'Lord, cover Thou his head in the day of battle.' He adds that he did not know that the king was gone to Germany, till he heard of the battle of Dettingen, and the king being in it. He then saw why he had been forced to pray thus. In what light such doctrine of prayer must have been held by the church at that time is evident from six students, in 1763, being expelled from St. Edmund's Hall, Oxford, for praying and reading the Scriptures. They were, some of them, charged with the additional offence of having followed *trades* before they entered the University. They were taken into Lady Huntingdon's College, at Trevecca, in Wales: Whitefield and Lady Huntingdon not having forgotten that 'the carpenter's Son' was the head of *their* religion.

A noble fellow-worker with both Wesley and Whitefield was Fletcher, of Madeley. Mr. Fletcher was a Swiss by birth, and his real name was Jean Guillaume de la Flechere; but, on coming to England, he anglicised it into plain John Fletcher. He was descended from a noble family in the Pays de Vaud, and was educated for the ministry; but, as he could not subscribe to the doctrine of predestination, he resolved to seek preferment as a soldier of fortune. Various circumstances prevented this, and he came to England and became tutor in the family of Mr. Hill, of Fern Hall, in Shropshire. He there received ordination as a minister of the Church of England, and was presented with the living of Madeley, in Shropshire, through Mr. Hill's influence. The income was small, and the people, chiefly colliers and iron-workers, exceedingly rude and ignorant. For some time his attempts at religious reform met with much violence and persecution from them, as well as from the neighbouring magistrates and clergy; but the mild and truly Christian spirit of Mr. Fletcher, and his warm benevolence, won for him the affection and veneration of the whole country. Never did the religion of Christ show itself in a more beautiful and amiable form than in the practice and teaching of John Fletcher, of Madeley. He married Miss Bosanquet, a lady of a distinguished London family, and who, having had similar religious and spiritual experiences to his own, went hand in hand with him in all his religious and benevolent exertions; so that their names have become household words, not only in their own neighbourhood, but with the public at large. When the followers of Wesley and Whitefield separated on account of the great doctrines of Calvin and

Arminius, as well as on some minor points, John Fletcher went of necessity, as he could not accept predestination, with Mr. Wesley; but he also entertained a warm friendship for Whitefield and Lady Huntingdon. As Wesley's spiritualism was of a many-sided character, and Whitefield's more concentrated on the immediate power of the Holy Ghost in preaching; so Fletcher's combined the faith of Whitefield with a more marked reliance on divine providences. His life records many striking instances of such. As I have said, he was bent on being a soldier in his youth. He went to Lisbon and became a captain of volunteers of his own countrymen, bound for Brazil, contrary to the injunctions of his parents. But the morning that the ship sailed, the maid let the kettle fall and so scalded his leg that he could not go. The ship sailed without him, and was never heard of again ('Life,' p. 10).

He was addicted, like too many, to reading in bed till very sleepy. One night he dreamed that his curtain, pillow and cap were all on fire, but went out without doing him any harm. In the morning he found his curtain, pillow, and part of his cap all destroyed by fire. His hymn-book, too, was partly burnt, and in this state was preserved by Mrs. Fletcher. Not a hair of his head was singed. He attributed the extinction of the flame to a messenger from God (p. 26). On another occasion, he was intending one Sunday evening to proceed to Madeley Wood to catechize, but he was suddenly called to bury a child, and the delay thus created prevented a villainous design of the colliers. They had brought a bull to the place of preaching, and had agreed to pull the parson off his horse, when he came, and set the dogs on him, as they said, 'to bait the parson'; but owing to the long time before Fletcher appeared, the bull had broken loose, and dispersed the drunken colliers, and the preaching went on in peace (p. 73).

He relates, that a man having vowed never to come into the church whilst he was minister, he bade him prepare to come on his neighbour's shoulders, if he would not come on his own feet; and he was astonished to learn that from that time the man, though then perfectly well, wasted away, and he soon had to bury him in the very spot where this conversation took place (p. 79).

He gave to John Wesley an account of his once bathing in the Rhine, and being carried away by the current, and drawn under a mill. That he struck against one of the piles, and lost all consciousness, and when he recovered it, found himself on the shore, five miles below the spot at which he had entered, but free from any soreness or weariness. A gentleman, amongst others, who had seen him disappear under the mill, said that he was under the water twenty minutes. But some will say, 'Why, this was a miracle!' 'Undoubtedly,' observes Mr. Wesley. 'It was not a natural event, but a work wrought above the power of nature, probably by the ministry of angels' (p. 7).

Whilst Mr. Fletcher presided over the college at Trevecca, he had many journeys to make. One day, as he was riding over a wooden bridge, just as he got to the middle of it, it broke in. The mare's fore-legs sank into the river, but the body was kept up by the bridge. In that position she lay as still as if she had been dead, till he got over her neck, and took off his bags, in which were several manuscripts, the spoiling of which would have occasioned him much trouble. He then endeavoured to raise her up; but she would not stir till he went over to the other side of the bridge. But no sooner did he set his foot upon the ground, than she began to plunge. Immediately the remaining part of the bridge broke down, and sank with her into the river. But presently she rose up again, swam out, and came to him (p. 83).

Incidents like these the cold, logical professor of a traditionary Christianity, always struggling against the vitality of the gospel, will reason quietly away as mere curious occurrences; but the early leaders of Methodism, in my opinion, more truly set them down as providential acts in the case of God's servants. There are many other passages in all the lives of the early Methodists which relate spiritual revelations and impressions which mere theoretic professors would smile at as fancies and enthusiasm. All vital Christians, however, of whatever church, have found them as real as any other circumstances of their lives. The language of the early Methodists is strikingly like that of the early Quakers in many particulars. They continually say they are 'impressed' so and so.

Mr. Fletcher says, that on one occasion, when quite awake, he had a very clear and palpable vision of Christ on His cross. On another occasion, he heard a divine voice speaking to him 'in an inexpressibly awful sound.' At another time he had, like Moses, a supernatural discovery of the glory of God, and had an ineffable converse with Him; whether in the body or out of the body, he could not tell. Many impressions of the presence of the Holy Spirit were felt by him in an extraordinary manner.

One dark and wet night, he being in the country on a preaching journey, Mrs. Fletcher had a sudden vision of her husband being thrown over the head of his horse, which had fallen. The scene was clear to her eyes. She commended him to God, and immediately peace flowed into her soul. When he at length arrived, he called for water to wash, proceeding to relate exactly what she had seen (p. 338).

One morning Mr. Fletcher had set out into the country to visit an eminently pious clergyman. When he had walked several miles, he saw a great crowd collected at the door of a house, and found that a poor woman and child were dying. The woman had been only recently confined; she appeared very near death; and little better was the case of the infant, which was convulsed from head to foot. The room was filled with people. He spoke with them of the power of God to forgive sins and raise the dead: and he then prayed that He would save both the sufferers and the spectators. Whilst he prayed, the child's convulsions ceased, and the mother became easy, then cheerful, then strong. The people were amazed, and stood speechless, and almost senseless!

Whilst they were in this state, he silently withdrew. When they came to themselves, he was gone. Many of them asked, 'What could it be?' Some said, 'Certainly it was an angel' (p. 290).

On one occasion Mr. Fletcher was seized with a strange confusion. As he ascended the pulpit, his sermon and the very text vanished from his memory, and he thought he should have to descend without saying anything. But on reading the first lesson, the third chapter of Daniel, containing the account of the three worthies being cast into the fiery furnace, his mouth was opened, and he preached on the subject in a manner extraordinary to himself. He believed there was some cause for it, and desired that, if it applied in any way to anyone present, they would let him know. On the following Wednesday he was informed that a butcher had threatened to cut his wife's throat if she persisted in going to Mr. Fletcher's church. That Sunday she had been in great terror, but resolved, notwithstanding, to go. Her husband said that, if she did go, he would not cut her throat, but that he would heat the oven, and throw her in the moment she came home. The sermon was singularly applicable to her case; she gathered courage, and firmly believed that she too should be delivered from the savage wrath of her husband. When she opened the door, to her astonishment, her husband was sitting in a remarkably subdued mood, and the very next Sunday he himself accompanied her to church, and received the sacrament. Mr. Fletcher adds that the man's good impressions did not remain, but that he himself saw why his sermon had been taken from him (p. 336).

Like many good men, this eminent servant of God had a clear announcement of his approaching death by impression. His wife writes, 'About two months ago he came to me and said, "My dear love, I know not how it is, but I have a strange impression that death is near us, as if it were in some sudden stroke upon one of us, and it draws all my soul in prayer, that we may be ready." The intimation was not long in being fulfilled. He was contemplating a journey to London, but during prayer, when seeking light upon the subject, the answer was, " Not to London, but to thy grave." He was seized with a shivering in his pulpit, and remarked on returning home that he had taken cold. It was the commencement of his last illness.'

Such were the first founders of Methodism. Men who restored religion in a most remarkable manner, and to a most splendid extent, by boldly asserting the present and eternal vitality of the power and divine gifts of the church. Their success was a proof of the truth of their doctrine. Obeying that doctrine, they became the witnesses of it to the modern world as the apostles had been to the ancient one. In this fact lies a great subject of reflection; a warning to the professors of all phases of Christianity to let its ancient spirit work.

CHAPTER XIX.

BÖHME, SWEDENBORG, AND IRVING.

I am acquainted with holy mysteries, which the Lord Himself hath discovered and explained to me; and which I have read in the tablets of heaven.—*The Book of Enoch*, p. 164.

I ALLOCATE these three spiritualists together merely for convenience. Böhme and Swedenborg have features in common, but vaster differences; Irving is rather a frank admitter of spiritualism and mediumship than a medium himself. All have alike excited the wonder and ridicule of those indoctrinated to stand still, and all have left traces more or less deep, more or less extensive in the substance of human life. 'Seul Dieu,' says Michelet, 'est assez Dieu pour protéger ce qui n'est autre que la pensée de Dieu même.' The eloquent Vinet says too, 'No experiences prevent all such truths from being combated, and their first witnesses from passing for madmen. At the head of each of those movements which have promoted the elevation of the human race, what do we see? In the estimation of the world, madmen. And the contempt they have attracted by their folly has always been proportioned to the grandeur of their enterprise, and the generosity of their intentions. The true heroes of humanity have always been crowned by that insulting epithet. And the man who to-day, in a pious enthusiasm, or yet more to please the world, celebrates those men whose glory lies in having dared to despise the world, would, during their lives, have, perhaps, been associated with their persecutors. He honours them, not because they are worthy of honour, but because he sees them honoured. His fathers have killed the prophets, and he, their son, subdued by universal admiration, builds the tombs of the prophets' (Vinet's 'Vital Christianity').

'There is a small market-town in the Upper Lusatia, called Old Seidenburg, distant from Görlitz about a mile and a half, in which lived a man whose name was Jacob, and his wife's name was Ursula. People they were of the poorest sort, yet of sober and honest behaviour. In the year 1575 they had a son, whom they called Jacob. This was the divinely illuminated Jacob Behmen, the Teutonic philosopher, whom God raised up in the most proper period, both as to the chiliad and century, to show the ground of the mystery of nature and grace, and open the wonders of His wisdom. His education was suitable to their wealth; his first employment being the care of the common cattle, amongst the rest of the youths of the town. But when grown older, he was placed at school, where he learned to read and write, and was from thence put apprentice to a shoemaker in Görlitz. Having served his time, in the year 1594 he took to wife Catherine, the daughter of John Hunshman, a citizen of Görlitz, and had by her four sons, living in the state of matrimony thirty years. His sons he placed in his lifetime to several honest trades. He fell sick in Silesia of a hot burning ague, contracted by too much drinking of water, and was at his desire brought to Görlitz, and died there in 1624, being near fifty years of age, and was buried in the churchyard.'

Such is the summary of the life of Jacob Böhme, prefixed to his works, the works themselves consisting of four ponderous volumes in quarto. A few other particulars follow, which show Jacob to have been a great spiritual medium. 'When he had been for a time an apprentice, his master and mistress being abroad, there came a stranger to the shop, of a reverend and grave countenance, yet in mean apparel, and taking up a pair of shoes desired to buy them. The boy, being scarce got higher than sweeping the shop, would not presume to set a price on them; but told him his master and mistress were not at home, and himself durst not venture the sale of anything without their order. But the stranger, being very importunate, he offered them at a price which, if he got, he was certain would save him harmless in parting from them, supposing also thereby to be rid of the importunate chapman. But the old man paid down the money, took the shoes, and departed from the shop a little way, where, standing still, with a loud and an earnest voice, he called, "Jacob, Jacob, come forth." The boy within, hearing the voice, came out in a great fright, at first amazed at the stranger's familiar calling him by his Christian name; but, recollecting himself, he went to him. The man, with a severe but friendly countenance, fixing his eyes upon him, which were bright and sparkling, took him by his right hand, and said to him, "Jacob, thou art little, but shalt be great, and become another man, such a one as at whom the world shall wonder. Therefore, be pious, fear God, and reverence His word. Read diligently the Holy Scriptures, wherein you have comfort and instruction. For thou must endure much misery and poverty, and suffer persecution; but be courageous and persevere, for God loves and is gracious to thee." And therewith, pressing his hand, he looked with a bright sparkling eye fixed on his face, and departed.'

This prediction made a deep impression on Jacob's mind, and continued the subject of his constant thoughts. Some time after, as he was with his master in the country about their business, he was, according to his own expression, 'surrounded with a divine light for seven days, and stood in the highest contemplation and kingdom of joys.' He became so serious in his conduct, and so reproved both those about him and his master himself for scurrilous and blasphemous words, that he became a scorn and derision to them; and his master was glad to set him at liberty, to be free from his reproofs. In his twenty-fifth year he was again 'surrounded by the divine light, and replenished with the heavenly knowledge, insomuch that, going abroad into the field, to a green before Neys-gate at Görlitz, he there sate down; and, viewing the herbs and grass of the field, in his inward light, he saw into their essences, use, and properties, which were discovered to him by their lineaments, figures and signatures.'

The reader will here be reminded of the similar experiences of George Fox and Swedenborg, as well as of the chapter of Henry More in his 'Antidote against Atheism,' on the signatures of plants. Böhme afterwards wrote a book on this subject, called 'Signatura Rerum; or, the Signature of All Things; showing the sign and signification of the several forms, figures, and shapes of things in the creation; and what the beginning, ruin, and cure of everything is; comprising all mysteries.' We are told that whilst these mysteries were passing through him, he lived in great peace and stillness, scarcely mentioning what had happened to him till 1610, when he was again taken into the light, and the mysteries passed through him as a stream; and he then wrote his 'Aurora, or the Morning Redness,' a voluminous work, which is a description of the beginning of creation, the introduction of evil, and the condition of men under it; 'all,' he says, 'set down from a true ground in the knowledge of the Spirit, and by the impulse of God.' He describes the mode of writing 'coming and going as a sudden shower,' and then his pen was impelled with such haste that in many words letters would be wanting, and sometimes only a capital letter for a word. He says, 'I can write nothing of myself, but as a child which neither knows nor understands anything, which neither has ever been learnt, but only that which the Lord vouchsafes to know in me, according to the measure as He Himself manifests in me.'

But, in this state, he says, 'I saw and knew the Being of all Beings, the Byss and the Abyss, and the eternal generation of the Holy Trinity, the descent and original of the world, and of all creatures through the divine wisdom. I knew and saw in myself all the three worlds—namely, the divine, angelical, and paradisiacal; and *the dark world*, the original of the nature of the fire; and then, thirdly, the external and visible world, being a procreation or external birth from the inner and spiritual world. And I saw and knew the whole working essence, in the evil and the good, and the original and existence of each of them; and likewise how the fruitful-bearing womb of Eternity brought forth.' He had, he says, a thorough view of the universe, as in a chaos, wherein all things are couched and wrapped up; but it was impossible for him to explain what he saw, till this was by degrees opened in him as in a young plant; and this process, he says, was going on in him for twelve years. The books which he wrote are, principally, the 'Aurora,' 'The Three Principles of the Divine Essence,' 'The Treatise of the Incarnation,' 'The Signatura Rerum,' 'The Six Great Points of the Great Mystery,' 'The Magnum Mysterium, an explanation of Genesis,' with numerous minor treatises, letters, &c., amounting altogether to thirty-two volumes.

The reader may wonder where a man of the most scanty education in his native tongue picks up those Latin and Greek phrases which are continually occurring; but we are told that he gathered them from the learned men, and particularly from chemists, who flocked to him from all parts after the publication of his 'Aurora.' But this could not be wholly the case; for we find such terms as Mercurius, in ternario sancto, and the like, in the 'Aurora' itself. These phrases, however, increase with the successive dates of his works, and it may be said that his obscurity increases equally with them. None of his works are, though he himself thought it his most imperfect one, perhaps, so intelligible as the 'Aurora.' This work, immediately on its publication, brought down a storm of persecution upon him. Richter, the principal clergyman of Görlitz, attacked it from the pulpit; and stirred up the magistrates so vehemently against him that he was banished the place, and cited to Dresden, where he was examined by a number of doctors of divinity and professors of mathematics in the presence of the Elector of Saxony, and honestly dismissed. It does not appear that he ever returned to Görlitz except to die; for we are told that soon after Böhme's return to Görlitz died his adversary, the pastor primarius Gregory Richter, and Böhme himself survived him only three months and a half. When the hour of his departure was at hand, he called his son Tobias and asked him whether he heard that delightful music? The son said, 'No.' 'Open,' he then said, 'the door, that you may hear it the better.' Asking what time it was, he was told it was two o'clock. 'My time,' he said, 'is not yet; three hours hence is my time.' When that time had arrived he took leave of his wife and son, and, blessing them, said, 'Now I go home to Paradise.' He then requested his son to turn him, which being done, he gave a deep sigh and departed.

The new primarius would not bury him, but his colleague, Magister Elias Theodore, was compelled by the magistrates to preach his funeral sermon, and the clergy were also compelled by the magistrates to attend. Theodore said he would rather have walked a hundred miles than preach Böhme's funeral sermon. Such was the hostility of the clergy to the theological shoemaker, who seemed to have far eclipsed them in their own science. His friends erected a cross on his grave; his enemies pelted it with mud and broke it to pieces. But all this time the learned and other professions had flocked from all parts of Germany to converse with Böhme, and his writings were reprinted and extensively read in Russia, Sweden, Poland, Denmark, the Netherlands, England, France, Spain, Italy, and even in Rome itself, as well as in Germany. A learned physician of Silesia, Balthasar Walter, had travelled through Egypt, Syria, and Arabia, to collect original information on the ancient magical learning; but he returned with little fruits of his expedition, and with much consequent disappointment. He became inspector of the chemical laboratory of Dresden. He visited Böhme, and, after conversing with him, declared that he had found, in a poor cottage in Germany, that which he had sought vainly in the East. It was Walter who gave the name of 'Philosophus Teutonicus' to Böhme, and to him and the writings of Paracelsus, which he had, it is likely, heard discussed (though he says he never read other men's writings), we may probably attribute the communication of the principal Greek and Latin terms used by Böhme. Walter also collected, from the different universities, forty questions on the nature of the soul, being such as were deemed impossible to answer. These he submitted to Böhme, who answered them in his work, 'Answer to Forty Questions concerning the Soul.' In the answer to the first question is the philosophic globe, or Wonder-Eye of Eternity, or Looking-glass of Wisdom, in itself containing all mysteries, with an explanation of it.

The writings of Böhme have found enthusiastic admirers in all times since. The younger Richter, son of his persecutor, intending to write a defence of his father, read Böhme, and was so struck with the truth of his ideas that he exclaimed, 'O father, what hast thou done?' and became a zealous editor and champion of Böhme's writings. George Fox read and commended them; there have been numerous editions of them in various languages, some of these extending to ten volumes. Pordage wrote much in explanation of them. Charles I. praised them; Charles Hotham, fellow of Peter House, was an ardent worshipper of Böhme, and in 1646 published a treatise on his philosophy, for which he was expelled the university. Extracts from them were found amongst the papers of Sir Isaac Newton, and Law supposes that he drew some of his theories from them. But none of his disciples have equalled the zeal and industry of the Rev. William Law, author of 'The Serious Call,' in explaining and recommending the theology of Böhme. And now, what is this theology? I fear that few persons of this time will wade through the four huge quartos in which it is contained, or rather buried, in order to dig it out. It is a mine, no doubt, of great and valuable truths; but these are so overwhelmed with masses of chaotic rubbish, of rubble, and earth, and drosses, that the farther you penetrate, the greater becomes your confusion and despair. Jacob Böhme appears to me like a man with a lantern wandering in a mighty mist. He certainly has light with him, but it is so steeped in the fog that it seems generally only to show that there is a light in the heart of the vapour, and no more. We can discern this, however, that he teaches that the outer world is an emanation from the inner or spiritual world. Thus he anticipated Swedenborg in the doctrine of correspondences, as St. Paul anticipated them both by declaring that everything on earth is made after the pattern of things in the heavens. Böhme holds that Adam, before the Fall, was in Paradise, or the middle state; that in that condition his body was little removed in quality from spirit. That, had he continued in that state, men would have descended from him alone without woman, who would have been a superfluity; his descendants proceeding from each other in succession, just as men's thoughts flow from them. He contends that it was only after the fall that Adam and Eve's bones became solid, and their flesh gross and corruptible. His theory is, that man, withdrawing himself from God, had lost the divine life in his soul, and that all communication between him and his Maker was nearly lost. In order to reopen the intercourse between the Deity and the soul of man, the second person in the Trinity became man. This, he affirms, is declared by the apostle when he says, 'God was in Christ reconciling the world unto Himself,' and this he argues gives the true view of the atonement. It would be a service to theologic literature for some advocate of Böhme to give us a clear abstract of his doctrines, divested of their alchemic language, and stripped of their endless verbiage. Dr. Hamberger has attempted this in German, and a brief synopsis of Böhme's teaching is drawn from Hamberger by Ennemoser in the second volume of his 'History of Magic,' commencing p. 297 of Howitt's translation. In his theory of creation Böhme gives a very different origin to the angels to that of Swedenborg. Swedenborg says that all angels and spirits were originally men, or incarnated beings in some world or other. Böhme, on the contrary, says they were created *at once* as purely of spiritually essences. 'God in His moving created the holy angels, *at once*, not out of strange *matter*, but out of Himself, out of His own power and eternal wisdom' ('Aurora,' p. 44. See also p. 237). Both Böhme and Swedenborg profess to write from the inspiration of God, but both here cannot be right. These discrepancies teach us that, whilst we admit the divine illumination of such men as Böhme and Swedenborg, we must remember that they were men, and liable to the intrusion of lesser spirits, even when they thought they were only under the influence of the Highest. Modern spiritualism has shown how eager and ambitious departed spirits are to communicate their favourite theories; and, using the salutary right of private judgement, we may believe that what these and other mediums present to us is derived, frequently, from sources which they, at the time, little suspected. Certainly a great deal of Böhme's writing would seem to have been dictated by the spirits of old alchemists and schoolmen. His theories of the production of worlds and creatures, by what he calls Salitter, or Sal Nitrun—that is, nitre—and by sulphur and mercurius, and of the entrance of such substances into the nature of God Himself, are too revolting and absurd to need the present advanced state of analytical chemistry to show their nonsense. He tells us, indeed, that there is really no sulphur in God; but that it is generated from Him ('Aurora,' p. 14). The inexactness of Böhme's terms is as great as their strangeness. He describes a thing at one time as one thing, at another as quite a different thing. He dilates vastly on the *qualities* or principles which exist in God, and, proceeding from Him, influence all nature—the cold, the hot, the bitter, the sweet, the sour, the astringent, the saltish, &c. A quality he describes as 'the mobility, boiling, springing, and driving of a thing.' This word quality he derives from the German word *Qual*, pain, and this again from *Quelle*, a well or spring. But on the subject of derivations we may obtain a very good notion of Böhme's style, and this may suffice in extract from him. Mercurius, he tells us, is sound or the tone of all the qualities in nature, and this is his analysis of the word:—' Understand rightly the manner of the existence of this Mercurius. The word MER is first the strong, tart, harsh attraction ; for in that word or syllable MER, expressed by the tongue, you understand that it jars, proceeding from the harshness, and you understand also that the bitter sting or prickle is in it; for the word MER is harsh and trembling, and every word is formed or framed from its power or virtue, and expresses whatsoever the power or virtue does or suffers. You understand that the word or syllable CU is the rubbing or unquietness of the sting or prickle, which makes that the harshness is not at peace, but heaves and rises up ; for that syllable presses forth with the virtue from the heart out of the mouth. It is done thus also in the virtue or power of the Prima Materia, or first matter, in the spirit ; but the syllable CU having so strong a pressure from the heart, and yet is so presently snatched up by the syllable RI, and the whole understanding is changed into it. This signifies, and is the bitter prickly wheel in the generating, which rises and whirls itself as swiftly as a thought. The syllable US is, or signifies the fire-flash, that the Materia or matter kindles in the fierce whirling between the harshness and the bitterness in the swift whirl, where you may very plainly understand in the word how the harshness is terrified, and how the power or virtue sinks down, or falls back again upon the heart, and becomes very feeble and thin; yet the sting or prickle with the whirling wheel continues in the flash, and goes forth through the teeth out of the mouth, where then the spirit hisses like a fire in its kindling, and returning back again strengthens itself in the word' ('Aurora,' c. i. 11).

Just similar is the analysis of the word sulphur, from SUL, which, he says, is the soul of a thing, and PHUR, which is the beauty or welfare of a thing. Phur is also, according to him, the Prima Materia. There is a fierce conflict in the issue of these syllables from the spirit to the heart, from the heart to the mouth, like the very battle of chaos, but it is too long for quotation; take a small portion of it :—' For the harshness is as hard as a stone, and the bitterness rushes and rages like a breaking wheel, which breaks the hardness and stirs up the fire, so that all comes to be a terrible crack of fire, and flies up ; and the harshness or astringency breaks in pieces, whereby the dark tartness is terrified and sinks back, and becomes, as it were, feeble and weak, or as if it were killed and dead, and runs out, becomes thin, and yields itself to be overcome. But when the strong flash of fire shines back into the tartness, and finds the harshness so thin and overcome, then it is much more terrified; for it is as if water were thrown into the fire, which makes a crack. . . . . And the harshness kindles and shrieks, &c. Here observe, the shriek or crack of the fire is kindled in the anguish in the brimstone-spirit, and then the shriek flies up triumphantly, and the aching or anxious harshness or brimstone-spirit is made thin and sweet by the light,' &c., &c., &c. ('Aurora,' c. ii. 14).

Such are examples of Böhme's analyses or *explanations* of words. And if thus of words, it may be supposed what are his descriptions of things through four huge quartos. These certainly do not much resemble the relations of truth in the New Testament, which are the essence of lucidity, brevity, and simplicity. They are the great volumes of fog which cloudy and vapoury spirits cast about that lantern of truth which we see him carrying along with him. Yet, ever and anon, the fog breaks, and we see clear or clearish facts. He finds no distance in spirit-nature. ' The feet signify near and far off, for things near and far off are all one to God; but man, be where he will, he is in nature neither near nor far off; for in God these are one thing.' He warns us that his language is figurative. ' It is with Mercurius in this manner or form also. Thou must not think that there is any hard beating, striking, toning, or sounding, or whistling, and turning in the Deity, as when one takes a great trumpet, and blows in it, and makes it to sound. Oh, no, dear man, thou half-dead angel, that is not so, but all is done and consists in power.'

Böhme tells us that, when the inspiration left him, he could not understand his own writings. He is not likely to be any better understood by the generality of readers. In his highest and truest clairvoyance, he has seen and left gems of truth, which, in his lower mediumistic conditions, he overwhelmed with his enormous fog-spirit, and they can only be found and picked out by those who, in the love of truth, are willing to penetrate those dense fogs, and gather them for the general benefit. That he had great and genuine spiritual illuminations is unquestionable; that he had great and bewildering fog seasons is equally apparent, and no one is called upon to value his mists at the same rate as his sunshine.

Emanuel Swedenborg, who appeared in Sweden in 1688, the year of our political revolution, and sixty-four years after the death of Böhme, was a man in very different conditions of seership to Böhme. Böhme was a poor, diminutive shoemaker, destitute of education, and having to draw all his intelligence from his inspiration. Under these circumstances it was no wonder that his communications became laboured, cloudy, and verbose in passing through a mind naturally ill furnished with language. Yet, under much persecution, he had shown the meekness and gentleness of a great Christian, whilst his learned enemies had shown the opposite qualities of insolence and vengeful pride. Swedenborg came to his task as a seer furnished with all the advantages of academical education. The tools of language and idea were prepared for his spiritual use by long practice on scientific and philosophical subjects. We see the effect of this in the much simpler style of Swedenborg. While Böhme is laboured and cloudy, Swedenborg is perspicuous and, as it were, mechanical. Though he deals with the most interior topics and scenes from the invisible world, he seems to build up his work, as it were, brick by brick, line upon line, stroke upon stroke, as if he were dealing with the most outward and substantial of things. He is essentially matter-of-fact in presenting the reader with the most unearthly subjects. Hence the astonishment of people who have been accustomed to a theology which leaves everything in the future world vague and impalpable, which leaves our future home 'a land of darkness, and of the shadow of death, without any order, and where the light is as darkness' (Job x. 22), to find Swedenborg representing this unknown world so very much like our own. To find it a world of seas and mountains, of cities and of men and women with all the habits, aspirations, and affections of humanity; where everyone is still busy in some pursuit for the general good, and where all are at once learning and teaching—learning from those who have gone before or have risen into higher wisdom, and teaching those who newly arrive, or have come in a condition of great spiritual ignorance and poverty. And yet this must be the case if this world be an emanation of that; if the things here are made after the patterns in the heavens. Swedenborg, from his previous education (which he regarded as entirely preparatory to his seership and teachership), became, therefore, a more effectual instrument in the divine hand, and, in his numerous writings (in which, though difficult enough in places, from the very nature of their topics, are clear as diamond compared to the writings of Böhme), has laid down a system of theology which is gradually new modelling the old systems; and from pulpits, and books, both prose and poetry, where the reader least suspects it, is giving form and substance to the popular views on the condition and world of the disembodied. How many of our most popular preachers of different denominations are now actually promulgating Swedenborgianism! how many of our philosophical writers and philosophical poets are doing the same, and it passes in them for originality! What an amount of Swedenborgianism exists in 'In Memoriam.'

> How pure at heart and sound in head,
> With what divine affections hold
> Should be the man whose thoughts would hold
> An hour's communion with the dead!

But they are Swedenborgianism and spiritualism in all modern theologies which teach the practicability of such intercourse, and encourage it. What a mass of Swedenborgian truths are swallowed down by the poetical public in 'Aurora Leigh,' and imagined to be the original ideas of Mrs. Browning, much to the amusement of the American gentleman who lent her his works, and thus indoctrinated her in their philosophy. How Swedenborg again peeps forth in the following lines :—

> O God, take care of me !
> Pardon and swathe me in an infinite love,
> Pervading and inspiring me thy child,
> And let thy own design in me work on
> Unfolding *the ideal man in me;*
> *Which, being greater far than I have grown,*
> *I cannot comprehend.* I am thine not mine.
> One day completed unto thine intent,
> I shall be able to discourse with thee ;
> For thy idea, gifted with a self,
> Must be of one with the mind whence it sprung,
> And fit to talk with thee about thy thoughts.
> Lead me, O Father, holding by thy hand.
> I ask not whither, for it must be on.
> GEORGE MACDONALD.

It is thus that the mind of Swedenborg, either by direct inhaustion or by reflex action from those who drink of him secretly, is giving substance, form, strength, and colour to the soul-world. Men are no longer taught to imagine the spirit of man a something hidden somewhere in the physical frame, perched, birdlike, in the brain, or seated simply in the pineal gland; a thing to be buried in the rotting body for some thousands of years hence till the general resurrection — a vapour, a spark, a life-germ, an idea, a something next to nothing, going into a long darkness and oblivion ere it should come to the light. They are coming to know from Swedenborg and spiritualism that the spirit is the real man, the body but a mere temporary wrapping. That heaven, till his time so far off, is found to be just at hand. The body falls, and we are in the midst of the spirit-world, there and in that condition which our purification or impurification here has

prepared for us. Once more, freed from the figments and
selfish frauds of papal purgatory, rises the intermediate state
between us and highest heaven, and the Jacob's ladder of
progressive perfectment ascends into the loftiest empyreum,
framed in the assurance of infinite advancement towards the
glory and beatitude of God. Once more the spirits of the
departed 'enter at the open door,' and assert the deathless
nature of love; and show us that they are waiting for us,
and caring for us; and the legions of guardian angels whom
Christians read of and believe in a poetic figure, beam out
from their concealment, and stand round our tables, and cast
their celestial warmth through our homes. By the silently,
almost unconsciously diffused revelations of Swedenborg,
death has lost his terrors; for he has ceased really to exist,
and doubt, that horrible rack of modern souls, is vanishing
in a positive knowledge of man's immortal nature. And all
this is done not by teaching new truths, but by bringing us
back to the simple and matter-of-fact truths of the Bible,
which spurious theories had treated as mere phrases, instead
of substantial things. And all this is going on not by the
means of the sect of Swedenborgians, which, like all other
sects, is endeavouring to shut up the door that their apostle
opened. They tell us that Swedenborg alone trod the invisible realms, and no one must dare to follow him there.
And this they say in the face of Swedenborg himself.
'Man was so created that during his life on earth amongst
men he might, at the same time, also live in heaven amongst
angels, and during his life amongst angels he might, at the
same time, also live on earth amongst men; so that heaven
and earth might be together, and might form one; men
knowing what is in heaven, and angels what is in the world'
('Arcana Cœlestia', 1880). This, Swedenborg says, is the
condition of man at large, not of himself solely or of any
other individual. The doctrines of Swedenborg, in fact,
like those of Fox, were never meant for the narrow region
of a sect, but for all mankind; and amongst mankind they
are doing more to restore the substance and similitude of

Christianity than those of any teacher who has appeared since the apostolic ages.

The proofs of Swedenborg's seership I have already given in the second chapter, when quoting the testimony of Kant. Little more need be said of him here. He was born at Stockholm, in Sweden, being the second son of Dr. Jasper Swedberg, Bishop of Skara, who was a voluminous author on various subjects, and a man of great talent and influence, descended from a mining family of the Stora Kopparberg, or great copper mountain. His mother was also the daughter of Albrecht Behm, the Assessor of the Royal Board of Mines. Thus he was born and brought up amongst mining affairs, and he himself in after years became also Royal Assessor of Mines. He altered his name from Swedberg to Swedenborg, as Burns, the poet, altered his name from Burness. He was very completely educated at the Great University at Upsala, and he became so intimate with the Latin language that he wrote all his works in it. He accomplished himself by extensive travel, and everywhere made acquaintance with celebrated men, especially those distinguished in mathematics, astronomy, and mechanics. Charles XII. appointed him Extraordinary Assessor of Mines. He went on writing numerous works on science and the arts. On 'Algebra,' the 'Decimal System;' on the 'Motion and Position of the Earth and Planets;' on 'Docks, Sluices, and Salt Works;' on the 'Principles of Natural Philosophy;' 'The Principia, First Principles of Natural Things,' which, in fact, had no less design than to trace out a true system of the world. Next followed 'Outlines of a Philosophical Argument on the Infinite;' 'Dissertations on the Nervous Fibre and the Nervous Fluid,' then a great work on the 'Economy of the Animal Kingdom.' He then set about to study anatomy and the whole system of the human frame.

But this was only as an introduction and qualification for the object of investigating the soul. Having done this, he wrote a work on the Worship and Love of God, as the result of his studies, and the completion of his other works.

The second part of this included an enquiry into the nature of the soul and the intellect; but here, when he seemed to think this portion of his work concluded, he found that it was only beginning. All his labours and enquiries had been tending to a developement of which he had no intimation. Suddenly, whilst he was in London, engaged in the publication of this work, he had a vision of the Lord, and his eyes were opened to see into the spiritual world. This, he says, occurred in 1743; consequently, when he was fifty-five years of age. He had devoted himself to writing on the natural sciences, he says, about thirty years, and from this time he gave them all up, and devoted himself to supernatural enquiry, and the explanation of the Scriptures, through these, for nearly thirty years more, or till the age of eighty-four. He says, at this time ' God opened my sight to the view of the spiritual world, and granted me the privilege of conversing with spirits and angels.' The Lord, he was informed, had prepared him for elucidating the spiritual sense of the word. For many years before his mind was thus opened, and he was enabled to speak with spirits, he had dreams informing him of the subjects on which he was writing, changes of state whilst he was writing, and a peculiar light in the writings. Afterwards, many visions when his eyes were shut; light miraculously given, spirits influencing him sensibly as if they appealed to the bodily sense, temptations from evil spirits almost overwhelming him with horror, fiery lights, words spoken in early morning, and many similar events ('Diary,' 2951). He says, that an inward spiritual breathing was opened up in him, and his spirit breathed the divine atmosphere directly from the Holy Spirit. This he considers as essential to a perfectly spiritual state, and to occur in all apostles and holy persons who live and act under immediate inspiration. We have seen that persons in the old pagan world occasionally entered the spirit world, as Epimenides and Hermotimus, who, returning, related what they had seen; but Swedenborg's condition was different and superior to theirs. During the absence of their spirits, their bodies lay as dead, but Swedenborg could enter the spirit world, yet appear to be present and acting in this. He did not, however, arrive at the perfect enjoyment of these two states, and the power of voluntarily passing from one to the other, for some time. He now poured forth rapidly, considering the colossal nature of the works themselves, his spiritual productions. First came his 'Arcana Cœlestia,' or exposition of the spiritual sense of the books of Genesis and Exodus. This consisted of eight volumes quarto. Then followed a whole library of volumes, the chief amongst which are the 'Last Judgement and Destruction of Babylon;' 'Heaven and Hell;' the 'White Horse of the Apocalypse;' the 'Planets of the Solar System, and their Inhabitants;' the 'New Jerusalem and its Heavenly Doctrine;' several other volumes on the 'New Jerusalem;' on the 'Divine Love and Divine Wisdom;' on the 'Divine Providence;' his 'Diary,' published after his death; the 'Delight of Wisdom;' 'Concerning Conjugial Love,' &c., on the 'Intercourse between the Soul and Body;' the 'Apocalypse Revealed, and Apocalypse Explained;' the 'True Christian Religion,' &c. In these spiritual works he frequently announces great scientific truths, which are now, from time to time, proving themselves such.

It is now regarded as a surprising discovery of Professors Kirchoff and Bunsen, that they have found iron to exist in the body of the sun, by tracing its effects in the solar rays. That this was a fact, Swedenborg asserted a century ago. The scientific men are continually asking for the spiritualists to announce beforehand unknown natural facts. This is one instance out of many in which Swedenborg did it, and long before Swedenborg, Anaxagoras announced that the sun was a great mass of mineral.

Many of these works have been translated into French and German as well as into English, which latter are published by the Swedenborgian Society. They may be read, and they are now extensively read, and their truths taught, as I have said, by men who are little suspected of it. The pulpits of both Church and Dissent are invaded by Swedenborg. There are also excellent and concise lives of him in English by Dr. Wilkinson and Mr. William White. I shall conclude by quoting a passage or two from the former. 'A visitant of the spiritual world, Swedenborg has described it in lively colours, and it would appear that it is not at all like what modern ages have deemed. According to some, it is a speck of abstraction, intense with saving faith, and other things of terms. Only a few of the oldest poets— always excepting the Bible—have shadowed it forth with any degree of reality, as spacious for mankind. There Swedenborg is at one with them, only that he is more sublimely homely regarding our future dwelling-place. The spiritual world is the same old world of God in a higher sphere. Hill and valley, plain and mountain, are as apparent there as here. The evident difference lies in the multiplicity and perfection of objects. The spiritual world is essential nature, and spirit besides. Its inhabitants are men and women, and their circumstances are societies, houses, and lands, and whatever belongs thereto. The commonplace foundation needs no moving to support the things which eye hath not seen, nor ear heard, nor heart of man conceived. . . . Stone and wood, bird and animal, sea and sky, are acquaintances which we meet with in the spiritual sphere, in our latest manhood or angelhood, equally as in the dawn of the senses, before the grave is gained' (p. 96).

Again, 'Our crotchet of the abstract nobleness of spirits receives there a rude shock. Our fathers' souls are no better than ourselves; no less mean, and no less bodily, and their occupations are often more unworthy than our own. A large part of their doings read like police reports. Even the angels are but good men in a favouring sphere; we may not worship them, for they do not deserve it; at best they are of our brethren the prophets. It is very matter-of-fact, death is no change of substantials. The same problems recur after it, and man is left to solve them. Nothing but goodness and truth are thriving. There is no rest beyond the tomb, but in the peace of God, which was rest before it' (p. 146).

Spiritualism uniformly confirms these views, especially of the intermediate regions. And also, that 'the earthly soul cleaves to the ground and gravitates earthwards, dragging the chain of the impure affections contracted in the world; spirits haunt their old remembered places attached by undying ideas. Hatred and revenge, pride and lust, persist in their cancerous spreading, and wear away the incurable heart-strings. Infidelity denies God most in spirit and the spiritual world; nay, staked on death, it ignores eternity in the eternal state with gnashing teeth and hideous clenches, and the proof of spirit and immortal life is farther off than ever.' An awful lesson. On the other hand, in the better regions, ' noble offices are assigned to finite beings, as of attending the birth of the newly dead into the spiritual state, of educating departed infants and simple spirits, of governing sleep and infusing dreams, and of indefinite other things besides, which constitute a department of the duties of the human race translated into the sphere of spiritual industry. For heaven is the grand workman; the moments of the eternal Sabbath are strokes of deeds, and the more of these can be given to be done by men and angels, the more is the creation real, because cooperating with God' (p. 157).

A serious truth is stated by Swedenborg in his ' Diary'—namely, that ' all confirmations in matters pertaining to theology are, as it were, *glued fast into the brains*, and can with difficulty be removed; and, while they remain, genuine truths can find no place.' This is what I have so often noticed in this work—the difficulty of erasing educational dogmas and modes of thinking, however erroneous. He states also the great fact so constantly shown by spiritualism, that in spiritual intercourse, like seeks like, and the spiritual condition of a man may be known by the spirits which seek to him — that is, habitually; for bad spirits will seek to deceive and confound the good too, and more especially in their first entrance into spiritual conditions, in order to drive them out of them. These are repelled by prayer and faith. As to the seeing and communing with spirits, Swedenborg says it is the natural condition of man, which has been lost only by his gross and degraded state. The review of the history of Swedenborg draws from his biographer remarks which thousands are now making:—

'Nothing is more evident to-day than that men of facts are afraid of a large number of important facts. All the spiritual facts, of which there are plenty in every age, are denounced as superstitions. The best-attested spirit-stories are not well received by that scientific courtesy which takes off its grave hat to a new beetle, or fresh vegetable alkaloid. Large-wigged science behaves worse to our ancestors than to our vermin. Evidence on spiritual subjects is regarded as impertinence by the learned; so timorous are they, and so morbidly fearful of ghosts. If they were not afraid, they would investigate; but nature is to them a churchyard, in which they must whistle their dry tunes to keep up their courage. They should come to Swedenborg, who has made ghosts themselves a science. As the matter stands, we are bold to say that there is no class that so little follows its own rules of uncaring experiment and induction, or has so little respect for facts, as the hard-headed scientific men. They are attentive enough to a class of facts that nobody values— to beetles, spiders, and fossils; but to those clear facts that common men and women, in all time and place, have found full of interest, wonder, or importance, they show them a deaf ear and a callous heart. Science in this neglects its mission, which is to give us in knowledge a transcript of the world, and primarily of that in the world which is nearest and dearest to the soul' (p. 258).

Edward Irving, who produced so much excitement and so much ridicule just about thirty years ago, by permitting apostolic manifestations in his congregation—namely, speaking tongues, and curing otherwise incurable diseases by prayer and faith in Christ—presents a wholly different phase of character to either Böhme or Swedenborg. He was not the seer or medium, but simply a gospel minister recognising, where they occurred, gospel facts. In this he was the more meritorious, because, not experiencing in himself, but only seeing in others those gifts, he embraced them without any difficulty as genuine. He had been educated, in his native country of Scotland, in the strictest sect of Caledonian Pharisaism; but he was, nevertheless, so Christianly liberal that he found it difficult to obtain a call to exercise his ministry. Dr. Chalmers at length perceived his extraordinary talents and great spiritual powers, and he became his assistant minister in his church of St. John in Glasgow. From Glasgow he was called to become the minister of the Caledonian Asylum in Cross Street, Hatton Garden. The popularity of his preaching became such that the church was crowded Sunday after Sunday to overflowing by people of every class, from the Royal Family downwards. Judges, ministers of state, nobles, and ladies of highest rank and fashion, literary men, and noted theologians, elbowed each other in growing throngs, and thrust out in their rush of admiring attendance his regular congregation. It was found necessary to build a large church, and this arose in Regent Square, at a cost of 15,000*l*., in the year 1827. Mr. Drummond and what were called the Albury Prophets, from meeting at Mr. Drummond's seat at Albury, in Surrey, had now joined his congregation and brought wealth into it. These gentlemen had been nicknamed prophets because, some twenty or thirty in number, they had united to study the Scriptures, and especially as they related to the spiritual gifts of Christianity. Three years after the erection of the new church in Regent Square, Mr. Irving and his friends were startled by the news that, at Port Glasgow in Scotland, there had occurred an outbreak of speaking in an unknown tongue. Religious women were said to speak in the manner of the apostles at Pentecost. He sent down an elder to judge of the nature of the phenomenon, who reported well of it; and on his return, his wife and daughter were found influenced in this manner. The matter was treated with much care and in private; and the utterance was found to be no senseless jargon, but orderly and harmonious, though unknown in its meaning to anyone. Yet, according to the order of the primitive church, it was found that what one spoke in the unknown tongue, another uttered the interpretation of in plain English, though he or she did not understand the unknown tongue, but received the same matter collaterally from the spirit. In October of 1830, however, a female of the congregation broke forth in the midst of it, but was quickly led away into the vestry, where she delivered her burden. From this time these manifestations became public and frequent, exciting a wonderful sensation in the public mind, and all sorts of people flocking to the church to witness them.

Contrary to the misrepresentations which on all extraordinary occasions are made, these manifestations are declared by Irving himself in 'Fraser's Magazine;' by Mr. Wilks, his earliest biographer; and by the 'Morning Watch,' a quarterly magazine established to record and explain this dispensation, to have been not only orderly, but full of eloquence as interpreted, and though delivered frequently in a high key, they were marked by a grandeur and music of intonation that resembled more a noble chant than oratorical speaking. Irving said they recalled to his mind the old cathedral chants traced up to the days of St. Ambrose. All those who spoke represented themselves as incited and carried on by a supernatural power. Irving says, ' He who spake with tongues in the church did nothing else than utter words unknown alike to himself and to all the people, and there was needed therefore another with the gift of interpretation. As the speaker spoke the unknown words, the meaning of them rose upon the interpreter's heart, and the proper native words came upon his lips. But he was all the while as ignorant of the foreign words as the utterers and hearers of them. It was a spiritual gift, and not an act of translation from one tongue into another.'

But not only unknown tongues, but known tongues

(Hebrew, Greek, Spanish, and Italian, amongst others), were spoken correctly by persons who naturally knew nothing of them. The spirit of prophecy was manifested, and the first visit of the cholera was distinctly predicted, and arrived in the following summer. Still more, many persons were healed by prayer and laying on of hands. Many cases are recorded. Miss Fancourt, the daughter of a clergyman, had been a hopeless cripple for eight years. She had curvature of the spine, an enlargement of one collar bone, disease in nearly every joint, and was utterly incapable of walking. The medical men had tried every possible remedy upon her. She had truly 'suffered many things of many physicians'— blisters, leeching, setons, bleeding, caustics, sea and warm baths; but all in vain, and the doctors declared her case so thoroughly organic that it was hopeless. Through the prayer of Mr. Greaves, one of Irving's congregation, she was suddenly and perfectly healed. Her father publicly attested the perfect cure; she did the same in the 'Christian Observer,' and that she was become quite straight, her collar bones quite equal in size, and she altogether healthy and well. A Mrs. Maxwell, who had been lame twenty-four years, and whose case was pronounced equally hopeless, became suddenly quite sound. A little girl of about eleven years of age, with curved spine, diseased knee, and also pronounced incurable by the faculty, was perfectly cured by earnest prayer. These and like cases were attested by the parties, by medical men and clergymen, and in the usual way were recklessly denied, or declared otherwise curable, in spite of the doctors themselves.

These circumstances were only such as the Catholic Church has recorded in all ages, and continues to record. They were the same as had occurred to Gassner, to Valentine Greatrakes, to the people at the tomb of the Abbé Paris, to the Cevennois, to Swedenborg, to the Seeress of Prevorst, and to thousands of others. Swedenborg declared that there was a spiritual language; the Seeress not only asserted the same, but spoke and wrote it. What astonished the people in

Irving's time is just in its varied phases what has been occurring since in every place where spiritualism has appeared. The records of this volume show that in America, in Germany, France, England, and other countries, people have spoken under spiritual influence both known and unknown tongues. (See Judge Edwards' 'Letters.') Every spiritualist has seen spiritual writing, which only certain mediums can read, but which is so peculiar and marked by such characteristics that, once seen, it is instantly recognised let it come from whence it may. I have seen such sent from India bearing an unmistakable relationship to what I had seen written by mediums here, and to the writing of the Seeress of Prevorst. The same law attaches to spirit-drawing. Wherever or by whomsoever done, however varying in each particular example from all others, to the eye familiar with spirit-drawing it at once identifies itself. I have seen spirit-drawings done by a person in Australia who had never heard of spiritualism or spirit-influence, but who, wholly ignorant of the art of drawing, had followed the impulse in his hand, and executed what every spiritualist who saw them at once pronounced spirit-drawing and no other.

The laws of spirit-life and action are now so well known, that all the movements amongst the Irvingites present themselves to the initiated as simple and natural. There were those even of Irving's congregation who thought some of the inspirations satanic, and Irving himself was thrown into doubt and anxiety by some of them. They were quite right; no divine inspiration can occur without the satanic endeavouring to insinuate itself to confound and, if possible, to destroy the true influence. This ought not to have surprised them. This is why the apostle cautioned the primitive church not to believe all spirits, but to try them. The false are soon known by their fruits, but those fruits may prove bitter; they are soon felt by the light of divine guidance and experience, but that experience implies foregone mischief, and people suffer from the ignorance perpetuated on the subject by Protestant fallacy. The great error of the Irvingites, or, as they now call themselves, the Catholic Apostolic Church, was in supposing, like the Swedenborgians, that these manifestations were sent exclusively to them, and therefore immediately to enclose them in a community. This, however, was their misfortune, the result of this enforced Protestant ignorance. They did not know that they are the divine gifts of the church at large, and which must be left to wander at large through the universal church of universal man. The wind and the Spirit blow where they list, and are not to be hedged in as the wise men of Gotham hoped to hedge in the cuckoo. From the time that the Saviour sent them down to earth, they have appeared, now here, now there, wherever the human heart craved after the Comforter; wherever the dragon of infidelity sought to swallow up faith; wherever man, freeing himself from the cordage and scaffolding of mere ecclesiastical theories, opened his soul to their reception. And if man, petrified by the Protestant spiritual education, could believe anything spiritual, the existence of these same phenomena, in a nearly two thousand years' sequence, in every church but their own, and amongst the most illustrious men in the annals of religion and philosophy, would present to them a mass of evidence which, for depth of foundation, for breadth of base, for a solidity of piled superstructure of facts, transcends that of any other human question. Yet Edward Irving was expelled from his pulpit amid jeers and laughter, and his life cut short in sorrow, for simply having received a legitimate dowry of the Christian church as became a minister of the church.

CHAPTER XX.

THE MORAVIAN BRETHREN OR UNITAS FRATRUM.

A band of brothers in the wilderness.
JAMES MONTGOMERY.

A religion which should appear reasonable to the whole world, could not be the true one. The true religion must, at its first appearance amongst men, be saluted from all sides with that accusation of folly which Christianity has so loftily braved.— VINET.

THIS religious body, with which Wesley was originally much connected, is most preeminently a spiritual church. Like the Friends, all their institutions are based on the belief of the continuous and immediate influence of the Divine Spirit. They cast lots on the most important occasions in life, in full faith that they will be spiritually decided for the best. Their history abounds with special providences, and with instances of their faith in the perpetuation of the supernatural power of Christianity. They have their descent from the primitive church, and from the Waldenses, and number John Huss and Jerome of Prague amongst their martyrs. Their bishops, so early as 680, were expected at the sixth council at Constantinople, but would not attend because they objected to image-worship. Some of the Waldenses made their appearance in Bohemia, in 1176, and joined them in resisting the attempts to reduce them to the yoke of the Church of Rome. The most terrible persecutions and extirpations of them both in Bohemia and Moravia were carried on against them by the Catholic powers, and being joined by other brethren in the like faith, they altered their name from Fratres, as at first adopted, to Unitas Fratrum, or the Unity of the Brethren. So early as 1467 they elected their ministers by lot. After many troubles and dispersions into Poland, Prussia, and other countries, an emigration from Moravia, under the guidance of Christian David, a carpenter, descended from a noble race of martyrs, was received by the Count Zinzendorf upon a newly-purchased estate of his in Upper Lusatia. They settled on an elevated and wild spot called the Hutberg, near the villages of Upper and Lower Bertholdsdorf, on the high road from Löbau to Zittau. At this spot Christian David struck his axe into a tree, and exclaimed, 'Here hath the sparrow found a home, and the swallow a nest for herself; even thine altars, O Lord of hosts!' There they commenced their settlement and called it Herrnhut, or the Lord's Watch. Numbers of their brethren flocked after them from Moravia and Bohemia, and Herrnhut became thenceforward their chief settlement. It was not without difficulty that the brethren escaped from their tyrants in Moravia. Such as sought to secretly dispose of their property or to carry their effects with them in wagons, were mostly stopped, plundered, and carried back; but such as 'sought nothing but the salvation of their souls, and, on that account, forsook their possessions, parents, or children, friends and relatives, were favoured with such success that they were often able to free themselves from their chains in a wonderful manner, to leap from a high prison without hurt, to pass through the guards undiscovered in the open day, or to run away and hide themselves from them' ('Crantz, History of the Brethren' p. 108).

Christian David held that he had a divine call to bring away his oppressed brethren from Moravia, and made many journeys for the purpose, at the peril of both liberty and life; but, says Crantz, he succeeded, 'amid amazing instances of the divine protection.' During one of these visits of Christian David and Melchior Nitschmann, the brethren at Herrnhut on a particular day fell on their knees and prayed for their safety. At that moment the two absent elders felt themselves so strongly and peculiarly affected that they fell on their knees, and with a flood of tears prayed earnestly. Feeling persuaded that something had occurred at home, they enquired on their return what had happened at Herrnhut on August 13, when they learned not only of this prayer for them, but also that their own prayer at the same moment had been almost in the same words (Crantz, p. 117). From Herrnhut they soon spread to different parts of Germany, to England, and Denmark, and their missions to Greenland, the West Indies, Labrador, and the Cape of Good Hope, Guinea, North and South America, the East Indies, and in almost every quarter of the world.

The Count Zinzendorf endeavoured to persuade them to unite with the Lutheran Church, but they put the question to the lot, and the text was drawn, 'Therefore, brethren, stand fast, and hold the traditions which ye have been taught' (2 Thess. ii. 15). So thorough was the faith of the United Brethren in Count Zinzendorf's time, that Crantz mentions the following fact as a proof of it: ' I have heard of a very particular circumstance, evidently directed by Providence, which happened on this occasion. The count, having thrown some papers which were of no farther use, into the fire, they were all consumed, excepting one small billet, on which was written the daily word for February 14, " He chooses us for His inheritance the excellency of Jacob whom he loveth" (Psalm xlvii. 4—Luther's version), under which stood the old Lutheran verse:—

> O let us in thy nail-prints see
> Our pardon and election free.

'All the brethren and sisters who saw this billet, the only one which remained unconsumed amongst the cinders, were filled with a childlike joy' (p. 180).

They preserved, indeed, a perfectly apostolic faith in miracles, spiritual gifts, spiritual impressions, and special acts of Providence on behalf of His servants. Zinzendorf himself says, 'I owe this testimony to our beloved church, that apostolic powers are there manifested. We have had undeniable proofs thereof in the unequivocal discovery of things, persons, and circumstances, which could not humanly have been discovered; in the healing of maladies, in themselves incurable, such as cancers, consumptions, when the patient was in the agonies of death—all by means of prayer or by a single word.' What is to be said when churches and persons of all persuasions agree in asserting these facts ? He enumerates various other supernatural circumstances, and says that the brethren and sisters entirely relied on Christ to do what He had graciously promised, when they earnestly entreated Him in prayer to do so. Their missionaries, like Brainerd and Hans Egede, relate many wonderful providences on their behalf amongst the savage peoples amid whom they lived; and not only from wild men, but wild beasts. On one occasion, a huge serpent fell upon one of them as he slept under a tree, and coiling itself twice round his head and neck, drew itself as tightly as possible. Remembering, however, the promise of the Lord that His disciples should take up serpents, and that they should not hurt them, he found himself strengthened to tear the serpent from its hold and fling it away.

During the wars in Germany, they were often plundered, and sometimes their houses burnt by the contending armies; but their lives were wonderfully preserved, and often their property too. Instances of this are given at Neusalz in Silesia, in 1759, when they were marvellously saved from the Russians, and again at Rücksdorf, in 1760, from the same enemy. On one occasion, as Count Zinzendorf was on a journey, he was about to retire to rest at a friend's house, when an irresistible impression seized him to proceed on his way, and scarcely had he set out when the ceiling of the room where he was to have slept fell in. David Nitschmann, one of a family highly distinguished amongst the brethren, and David Schneider, being in prison in Moravia, one night had it impressed on their minds that they were to escape. Wondering how it was to be done, they suddenly found the fetters on their hands loose, and the two doors between them and the street open. They escaped into Silesia. Both

Count Zinzendorf and Lady Zinzendorf, in that spiritual clairvoyance which is but another name for prophecy, foresaw and distinctly foretold important passages in their lives. In the lives of the Nitschmanns, of Spangenberg, Dober, Steinmetz, and others, numerous such extraordinary events are recorded as matters at which Christians ought not to be astonished.

Perhaps no innocent people ever went through such an amount of base calumniation from their fellow-Protestants on account of their simple faith; perhaps none so few in numbers have sent forth so many devoted missionaries. Most of their congregations are Pilgrim congregations, ready to a man to offer themselves for the most distant and dangerous services for the conversion of souls. Perhaps no people have so thoroughly renounced the pursuits and love of the world. Their settlements are places of a wonderful silence and repose. On a visit to Herrnhut, in 1841, we found the settlement lying in a high cold region, the woods which once covered it now extirpated by industrious hands, and singular groups of rocks starting from the cultured plains in a strange pyramidal form. The horizon on different sides is bounded by the Riesengebirge, or Giant Mountains, and the hills of the Saxon Switzerland. But it was not till we had made a progress quite through the place that we began to discover its great pleasantness. As we came to its yet remaining woods, its wood-walks, its gardens, its charming though formal cemetery, its Hutberg or Hill of the Watch, and saw all round the smiling fields and the busy people in them, and the bounding glen, in which lie, amid their crofts and orchards, the populous and picturesque villages of Great Hennersdorf, Hennersdorf, and Bertholdsdorf, we began to feel that it was still more in the spirit and institutions of the place than in its external aspect, that its singular character lies.

It was a singular pleasure to tread the ground where this noble and united band of Christians had first created themselves into a people devoted to the great cause of Christian civilisation; where they asserted the great Christian truth, that we are not to live only for ourselves, but for God and our neighbour; where they lived and loved, grew and prospered;—whence they sent out to every quarter of the globe the most patient and successful labourers; and where, their day's work gloriously done, they laid down their weary bodies, and departed to the eternal Unitas Fratrum.

But what a silence lay in the place, even amid all its active industry! It is wonderful that, from amid that brooding stillness, so many energetic persons should have gone, and do still go forth, to all parts of the world; that from a centre which seems the very centre of the realms of repose, so much life should stream forth to the ends of the earth. They call it themselves Life in Stillness. The whole manner and bearing of the people are such as have nothing to do with the passions and agitations of this world, but are already wrapt in the spirit and consciousness of another. A worthy old officer, Major von Aderkas, whom we found there, said, smiling, 'I have had a stormy and troubled existence, and longed for a quieter haven; and, thank God, I have found it, and enjoy it from my soul; and here I shall end my days with thankfulness. But many come here who at first are struck with the repose of the place, and, thinking nothing could be so agreeable as to spend their lives here, they try it, and generally think a month long enough. No, Herrnhut is not the place for those who have not weaned themselves thoroughly from the world, nor have arrived, through troubles and treacheries, at an abiding weariness of it.' To the Herrnhuters themselves, however, their daily labour, their religious and social meetings, their prayer and singing hours, and their discharge of their duties to the community, are enjoyments sufficient. Every now and then, too, they have meetings for the reading of letters from their different missionary stations all over the world; and these are times of much interest. We were conducted by the venerable Bishop Reichel over the various departments of the institution, over the house of the brethren, the house of the sisters, the church, the rooms for dining, for social assemblage, for music, which they greatly cultivate, and through the bishop's abode at Bertholdsdorf. We attended one of their singing meetings in the room where they hold their love-feasts — the Agapai of the early Christians — and visited their schools for boys and girls. We learned that, in 1823, they had sixteen settlements in Germany, seventeen in England, one in Scotland, four in Ireland, five in Sweden, one at Zeist in the Netherlands, one in Russia, and upwards of twenty in North America. The inhabitants of these settlements then amounted to about 17,000, and yet this little quiet body in their various missionary stations—in Greenland, Labrador, North America, amongst the Indians, in the West Indies, South America, South Africa, and amongst the Calmucks in the steppes of Asiatic Russia, had no less a number of converts than 30,000.

We sought out with much interest the spot where Christian David cut down the first tree. This is now marked by a monument of granite bearing this inscription, 'Am 17 Januar 1722 wurde an diese Stelle zum Anbau von Herrnhut der erste Baum gefället' (Ps. lxxxiv. 3). 'On the 17th of January, 1722, was, on this spot, for the building of Herrnhut, the first tree felled.' The quotation from the Psalms is 'Well for them who dwell in thy house; who praise thee for evermore.' But the whole Psalm is singularly adapted to the conditions, faith, and feelings of the little band at the mount. The monument is near the highway, and is still in the wood, which is purposely spared. Here the temporary huts only were erected, the village itself was located a few hundred yards from the place. Here, then, you are as much immersed in the forest as the first settlers were. Pleasant walks with the best taste are carried in all directions through these woods from Herrnhut; so that visitors as well as the inhabitants can still please themselves with a very lively impression of the scene as it first appeared to the settlers.

Equally full of interest is the Friedhof or Cemetery. This lies on an elevated slope above the village, and is very

conspicuous by its extent and form. It contains several acres, is square, and fenced by a lofty hedge, or rather trimmed green wall of hornbeam. Over the entrance is inscribed:—
Christus ist auferstanden von den Todten;
Er ist der Erstling worden unter denen die da schlafen.

Within the Friedhof or Court of Peace, as the Germans commonly call their burial-grounds, or as frequently Gottes Acker, God's Field, is intersected with avenues also of hornbeam trees, and at each corner and at the end of each avenue is an arbour of the same. The whole place is wonderfully neat. No separate family burying-place is allotted; all are buried in regular rows, as they die, and on each grave lies a simple slab with an inscription, having a much better effect than that of ordinary cemeteries, which are loaded with heaps of cumbrous and, notwithstanding all contrivances to the contrary, unsightly stone. The only exception to this rule is made in the case of the family of the founder. In the centre of the four principal crossing avenues stands a row of eight massy altar-tombs. These are the tombs of Count Zinzendorf and his immediate family and friends, the first founders and champions of the Herrnhut community. The two centre ones are those of the Count and Countess Zinzendorf. On the right lie Sophia Theodora, Gräfin Reuss, the beloved cousin of Count Zinzendorf, and wife of his friend Count Reuss, who ended her days here; Elizabeth von Watteville, the Count Zinzendorf's daughter, and Frederick Rudolph, Freiherr von Watteville, her husband. On his left Anna Nitschmann, the count's second wife, Frederick von Watteville, his old friend and first civil senior here; and, last, Benigna Justina von Watteville, the count's daughter, married to Johannes, the adopted son of Baron Watteville, one of the count's most attached and active friends. Many old servants and contemporaries, well known to the readers of the history of the founding of the settlement, lie around, and amongst them that fine old patriarch, Christian David.

Just above the Friedhof, and on the crown of the eminence, stands, on one of the singular groups of rocks which so particularly mark this landscape, a sort of temple or watch-house. This is the Hut-berg, or Watch-Hill. From this building, the whole country round to a vast extent is seen, with various mountains rearing themselves in different directions, amongst them the lofty remarkable peak, called Die Sächsische Krone—the Crown of Saxony. Here, too, lies sloping down on all sides from this point around you, the noble estate conferred by Count Zinzendorf on the community, with Herrnhut in its whiteness, amid its gardens, its original woods, its pleasant glen and string of villages, Bertholdsdorf with its direction-house, and the fine avenue of trees connecting Bertholdsdorf and Herrnhut.

Such is Herrnhut, the quiet but active head-colony of one of the most remarkable communities, whether regarded on account of their thorough renouncement of the world and its desires, their sober but unshaken faith in the communion with the spirit-world, or for the miracles of civilisation, which, by such spiritual concentration and in its power, they have effected from pole to pole by a mere handful of simple, pious, and indefatigable people.

Like Swedenborg, Count Zinzendorf spent much time in England. He made four or five journeys hither, and made long abodes here, having successive residences in Red Lion Square, Bloomsbury Square, London; Lindsey House, Chelsea, formerly belonging to the Duke of Lancaster, which he bought; and a country-house, Ingatestone Hall, four-and-twenty miles from London. His only son, who lived to manhood, Christian Renatus Zinzendorf, an excellent youth, died in London, and his remains lie in Chelsea. The attention excited to this primitive body brought over many base calumnies from their German enemies. A Herr Rimius, Aulic Counsellor to the King of Prussia, published a basely calumnious attack on them, which he was at the pains to dedicate to the Archbishop of Canterbury. This led to enquiry, and enquiry to a knowledge of the real Christian worth of the Brethren.

CHAPTER XXI.

A CHAPTER OF POETS.

> 'Ch' è quel, dolce padre, a che non posso
> Schermar lo viso, tanto che mi vaglia,'
> Diss' io ; ' e pare inver noi esser mosso ? '
> 'Non ti maravigliar s' ancor t' abbaglia
> La famiglia del cielo,' a me ripose.
> ' Messo è che viene ad invitar c' uom saglia.
> Tosto sarà c' a veder queste cose
> Non ti fia grave ; ma fieti diletto
> Quanto natura a sentir ti dispose.'
> *La Divina Commedia di Dante, Purgatorio*, canto xv.

ALL genuine poetry is, of its own nature, spiritual: all genuine poets write under inspiration. With the ancients, vates and poet were synonymous. If it be replied, that what poets have written under invocation to the Muses, or to other powers, has been to themselves most commonly consciously and avowedly fable and fiction, it may be responded that, in this form of fable, they have endeavoured to lay down eternal truths, and, in the very machinery of supernatural agencies adopted, have recognised the faith of their predecessors. Campbell defined poetry on this principle :—

> For song is but the eloquence of truth.

In their closets, and under their truest influences, all authors, prose or poetic, are spiritualists. Nothing would be easier than to establish this position, from the pages of every man and woman who have written with sufficient energy to seize on the spirit of their age. I have shown the genuine spiritualism of the ancient classical poets: if we pass through the literature of any modern country, we find the best authors asserting spiritual impressions on their minds in the hours of composition. I have noticed the confession of Schiller; and in the conversations of Eckermann with Goethe, and in Goethe's autobiography, we have repeated declarations of that poet's belief in supernatural agency. He relates the constant prescience of his grandfather, who knew long beforehand what would come to pass, and when current events ran apparently counter to his internal intimations. So we might go through the great writers of both Germany, Scandinavia, France, and every other country. Rousseau was full of such convictions; and perhaps no man was ever more under direct spirit-influence. My space allows me only to notice the spiritualism of a few of the leading poets of Italy and our own country as examples, and when I say poets, the same applies to all prose writers and to artists. I have already quoted the 'Confessions of Raphael,' and to him might be added Michael Angelo and other great artists of Italy. There are most amazing facts of the kind in the life of Benvenuto Cellini. In our own country, and that even in our own time, the involuntary confessions of our novelists, even of those who profess to scoff at spiritualism, are extraordinary. Amongst these, Charles Dickens has played with spiritualism as a cat with a mouse; it has a wonderful fascination for him. All his literary life through he has been introducing the marvellous and the ghostly into his novels, and has of late years, in his periodicals, been alternately attacking spiritualism, and giving you most accredited instances of it. He has printed accounts of apparitions, assuring you that he knows the persons who have seen them, and that they are not only perfectly sane, but thoroughly trustworthy. To him we owe the first publication of the extraordinary experiences of Mr. Heaphy, the artist. When he forgets the critical and sceptical world, the bugbear of literary men, in the power of his closet convictions, we hear him using this language:—'It is an exquisite and beautiful thing in our nature that, when the heart is touched and softened by some tranquil happiness or affectionate feeling, the memory of the dead comes over it most powerfully and irresistibly. It would seem almost as though our better thoughts and sympathies were charms, in virtue of which the soul is enabled to hold some vague and mysterious intercourse with the spirits of those we loved in life. Alas! how often and how long may these patient angels hover around us, watching for the spell which is so seldom uttered and so soon forgotten!' Miss Brontë is still more decided:—' Besides this earth, and besides the race of men, there is an invisible world and a kingdom of spirits. *That world is round us, for it is everywhere;* and those spirits watch us, for they are commissioned to guard us,' &c. She makes a voice to be heard from an impossible distance according to natural acoustics, and asserts that, though strange, it *is true*. Miss Mulock describes her spiritualistic friends as people with good warm hearts, but with little head, and then she goes and embellishes her volumes with all sorts of spiritualism. Such are the inconsistencies of minds in a woful dilemma betwixt their education and the ineradicable force of nature. The deep interest which Sir Edward Bulwer Lytton has always taken in spiritual phenomena he has himself made familiar to everyone. But, from these general remarks, I revert to my immediate object.

The great poets of Italy are, from their religion, necessarily spiritualists. They are taught by the Catholic and Infallible Church full faith in the agency on earth of spiritual powers, sacred and infernal, and that exhibited in every form of divine interposition, and of magic. Dante makes himself be conducted through hell, purgatory and paradise by departed spirits—by Virgil, through the two former regions; by Beatrice through the latter. The whole frame and substance of his great poem, the ' Divina Commedia,' is spiritual, and had we not had other evidence of Dante's more poetical belief, we might safely have pronounced his knowledge of spiritual subjects spiritually communicated, the laws of spiritual life as communicated by him being so perfectly, for the most part, in accordance with still more modern revelations. It would be a good work of some one well acquainted with the poetry of Dante, to give us an elaborate demonstration of this, to which I can merely allude. He pronounces the great law of spirit intercourse, however, in his Paradise, most positively not as a poetical idea, but as a philosophical truth.

> High functions to pure substances were given,
> When first created ; these with powers were graced
> To execute on earth the will of heaven.
> To matter lowest station was assigned,
> Compounded natures in the middle placed,
> Subject to bonds which no one may unbind.
> WRIGHT'S *Translation, Paradise,* c. xxix.

This is strikingly borne out by all the experiences of modern spiritualism. The doctrine of guardian angels is not more fully confirmed than that direct communication betwixt embodied and disembodied spirits can only take place under fixed and jealously guarded laws. It is these laws that present spiritual experiences are rendering every day clearer, to the ignorance of which sceptical minds owe their constant self-exposures, and many well-meaning persons their disappointments. In the prose works of Dante, the 'Convito' and the 'Monarchia,' are numerous avowals of his faith in, and knowledge of, spiritualism. In the 'Monarchia,' he says: 'To the first kind of happiness we arrive by means of philosophical studies, following them up by the practice of moral and intellectual virtue; the second we reach by means of spiritual writings, which surpass human reason.' And again, 'God does, and will do, many things by means of angels, which the Vicar of God, the successor of St. Peter cannot do' (Book iii.). In the 'Convito' he says, 'Oh, happy those few who sit at that table where the bread of angels is eaten.' (Trat. i. c. 1.) And again, 'The life of my heart—i. e. of my inner man—is wont to be a secret thought, a thought which ascends to God — i.e. I contemplate in thought the kingdom of heaven.' (Trat. c. ii. 8.)

But in the 'Vita Nuova' we find Dante having visions illustrative of his coming life. This faculty he appears to have inherited from his mother. Boccaccio in his life of him says, ' A little while before Dante's birth, his mother saw in a dream what her future child was to be, which was then unknown both to her and to others, but is now manifest to all from the result. The gentle lady in her sleep fancied she was under a very high laurel tree, which grew in a green meadow by the side of a copious fountain: and there she gave birth to a son, who being maintained only by the berries that fell from the laurel tree, and with the waters of the clear fountain, seemed ·in a very short time to grow up into a shepherd, who endeavoured with his utmost powers to seize the leaves of the tree with whose fruit he had been fed. In the midst of these endeavours, he seemed to fall down, and on rising up again, he was no longer a man, but had become a peacock. At this change, she was struck with so much wonder that she awoke, and little time elapsed before she gave birth to a son, who, with the consent of the father, was called Dante, and deservedly so; Dante being an abbreviation of Durante, which means, lasting, enduring.'

In the ʳ Vita Nuova,' he tells us that, having received a pleasant salutation from Beatrice Portinari, the young lady of his love, ' I quitted the company, as it were, in a state of intoxication: and retiring to my chamber, I sate down to meditate on this most courteous lady. During my meditation, a sweet sleep came over me, in which appeared a wonderful vision. I seemed to see in my chamber a cloud as red as fire, in the midst of which I discerned the figure of a man whose aspect struck fear into the beholder, whilst, wonderful to say, he appeared all joy. He spoke of many things, few of which I understood; but amongst them was this, " Ego dominus tuus," " I am thy master." In his arms I seemed to see a sleeping figure, naked, except a slight covering of a blood-red coloured drapery —but looking more attentively, I saw that it was my lady of happiness, who had condescended to address me on the day before. In one of his hands he seemed to hold something which was all in flames, and to say these words, " Vide cor tuum," " Behold thy heart."—And after a short time he seemed to me to awaken her who slept, and to exert his skill in such wise that he forced her to eat that which was burning in his hand —and this she did with hesitation and fear. He stayed but a short time after this, but his joy was changed into a most bitter lamentation. Weeping, he folded her in his arms, and, with her, directed his course to heaven.'

Dante asked his friends what could be the meaning of this life-like vision, and several of them wrote him explanations according to their several fancies—amongst them his dearest friend Guido Cavalcanti, in a sonnet commencing, ' Vedesti al mio parere ogni valore'—but time was the only true interpreter, and that quickly, for Beatrice died at the age of twenty-four.

As Dante believed in spirit communication, so it seems that, after his death, he had to make one himself. Boccaccio relates the circumstance in his Life of Dante, and it has been reprinted in various memoirs of him; amongst others, in one prefixed to his edition of the ' Divina Commedia,' by Palma of Naples, in 1827. The thirteen last cantos of the ' Commedia' were missing, and all efforts to discover them by the family and friends of Dante proved vain. Boccaccio says— ' Jacopo and Piero, sons of Dante, who were themselves accustomed to write verses, were much importuned by their friends to do their best to finish their father's work, in order that it might not remain in an imperfect state, when Jacopo was surprised by an extraordinary vision (he being far more zealous in the matter than his brother), which not only took the presumptious notion out of his head, but showed him where the thirteen cantos were which they had hitherto vainly endeavoured to find. A worthy citizen of Ravenna, named Pietro Giardino, who had long been a disciple of Dante, related that about eight months after the death of his master, one night a little before dawn, Jacopo, Dante's son, came to his house and told him that he had, a little before that time, seen Dante, his father, in a dream, clothed in shining garments, and with an unusual light shining in his countenance, and that when he enquired of the apparition if it yet lived, he was answered, " Yes, real life, not such as yours." Upon which he further enquired if he had finished his poem before passing into real life, and if so, where was the remainder, which none of them had been able to find. In reply to which he received the following answer, " Yes, I did finish it; " and then it seemed to him that the spirit took him by the hand and led him to the chamber in which he generally slept when alive, and touching one of the partitions, said, " What you have so much sought for is here," and with that Dante and his dream vanished. He then stated that he had not been able to rest any longer till he had come to tell him what he had seen, in order that they might go together and search the place pointed out—which was firmly imprinted on his mind—in order to see whether the information came from a genuine spirit, or was a delusion. On this account, although the night was not yet spent, he arose, and they both went to the place indicated, and there found some hangings fixed on the wall, and having slightly raised them, they saw in the wall an opening which none of them had ever seen before, or known to be there, and in it they found some manuscripts, nearly moulded and corrupted by the dampness of the wall; and having gently cleansed them from the mould and read them, they found them to be the thirteen cantos so much sought for by them. They then placed them in the hands of Messer Cane della Scala, as the author himself was wont to do, who joined them to the rest of the work, and the work which had taken so many years to prepare was at length finished.'

Boccaccio was himself a profound believer in spiritualism. The stories of the Decameron abound with proofs of the love of the marvellous, and where that love exists there is sure to be more or less faith. He drew these stories, however, not from romance, but from the chronicle of Helinandus, published in 1212, as facts, only changing the names of persons and places. He could, therefore, believe and relate the apparition of Dante as a reality. The change of his own life had been occasioned by a prophetic message. In 1359, Boccaccio went to meet Petrarch in Milan, and on his return he stated that Petrarch had seriously advised him to abandon worldly pleasures, and fix his affections on those above. In 1361, Petrarch wrote to him, that he was commissioned by Pietro Petroni of Certosa—a man celebrated for his piety, and for the miracles done by him, who had died in May of that year—to tell him, that amongst the things impressed on his mind on his death-bed were, that not many years of life remained to Boccaccio, and that he would do well to abandon poetry. This fact, more fully stated by Manni, and by the Abbé de Sade, had such an effect on the mind of Boccaccio, that he determined not only to abandon poetry, but to part with all his books, and to abandon every profane study. Petrarch wisely counselled him that it was by no means necessary to relinquish all polite literature, much less to strip himself of all his books, but to make a good use of them, as the most holy fathers and doctors of the church had done in all ages. Neither the life nor the writings of Boccaccio, up to this moment, had been very commendable, as the Decameron is sufficient evidence; but he now adopted the clerical habit, and commenced the study of sacred literature, in which, however, he made so little progress that he again relinquished the pursuit. In this passage we see a proof of Petrarch's spiritual faith, as well as of Boccaccio's. In fact, Petrarch was profoundly penetrated by faith in the spiritual powers of the church.

In the great poems of both Ariosto and Tasso, the elements of supernaturalism run to perfect riot. Angels and archangels, prophets, magicians, and devils, are the active agents of the events celebrated. These were all founded on history, both sacred and profane, and were not only used as machinery, but believed in by these master poets.

The very first words of Tasso, in the 'Gerusalemme Liberata,' are spiritualistic—

Manda a Tortosa Dio l'Angelo.

In the words of Wiffen's translation—

> God to Tortosa sends his angel down;

a fit opening to one of the most exuberant specimens of supernaturalism in any language. Scarcely in Milton—who was an ardent admirer of Tasso, and the friend of Tasso's best friend, the Marquis Manso—are the conflicts of Deity and Demonism, of archangels and arch-fiends, more largely, boldly, and vigorously introduced. As Jupiter from Olympus looks down to earth in Homer, so the Eternal Father in Tasso. As the one sends down Mercury, so the God of Christians sends down the Archangel Gabriel to their aid. The Prince of Darkness musters his powers below to resist the hosts of the Cross; Beelzebub appears, like the ancient gods, in arms in the field; the fury, Alecto, fans the infernal flame of strife; and then the Archangel Michael is commissioned to rout the diabolic powers. But these powers reappear in the shape of magic. The enchanted gardens of Armida, the spectral forest where demon serpents and fierce beasts prowl, and where every tree is animated by its spirit, are familiar to the reader. Let us pass this as fable, and view the poet in his own life and experience. What he sung, he there acts and believes. He saw and conversed with spirits, and the world pronounced him mad. He was mad in the same fashion as millions are mad now, as the prophets and apostles were mad.

It is now fully admitted, by all those who have carefully examined the matter, that Tasso was as sane, and more so, than those who condemned him to the hospital of Santa Anna at Ferrara. It was the policy of that most vindictive and implacable of tyrants, Alphonso, the petty duke of Ferrara, to brand Tasso as mad, because he had *presumed* to fall in love with his sister, Leonora D'Este. That sister might have married some wealthy duke or prince, the dull and gilded grub of the place and the hour, and have been no more heard of. But for a man to love her whose princedom was to extend over all time, and was to cast a blazon on even the meanest thing of state that came near it, was an offence only to be expiated by the most shameful and detestable treatment that ever genius suffered from the hands of pampered insignificance. Those men of intelligence who gained admittance to the great poet—where, amid howling maniacs, and in the vilest squalor and contemptuous neglect, he passed his days, whilst publishers far and near were enriching themselves by his plundered copyrights, and torturing him with barbarous issues of his noblest poem — declared unanimously that he was perfectly sane; but that, though he was not mad, he had suffered enough to have driven him so. Manso, his most generous and faithful of friends, who knew him intimately at and after this time, declares him perfectly sound of intellect; and during the short remaining time which he lived after his seven years' detention in the mad-house, and which he spent in honour amid popes, cardinals, princes, nobles, and men of genius of all kinds, no man showed himself more sane. That he was restless and nervous was the consequence of his long cruel treatment from many causes and many men, acting on such a finely-strung temperament as could only have produced the 'Jerusalem Delivered.' It was the business of the venal Serassi—the tool of the Estes, and who, as has been pointed out by my old schoolfellow, Jeremiah Wiffen, the elegant translator of the 'Jerusalem,' dedicated his work to that Maria Beatrice D'Este who would not even permit the name of Tasso to remain attached to an opera of his performed before her, but obliged the manager to substitute for it that of Lope de Vega!—it was his business to endeavour to perpetuate the stigma of insanity which the little despot of Ferrara had stamped on him. Manso, and later Italian biographers—in England, Milman and Wiffen—have sufficiently exposed the base endeavour.

In his 'Ambassador,' Tasso introduces a dialogue betwixt himself and a spirit, which, however, he represents as merely imagined; but in his cell at Santa Anna he assures us that he was visited, pestered, and plundered by mischievous spirits, and especially by one that he calls the Folletto, or Sprite. That he was robbed by his keepers, in his absence from his room, he also tells us; but he makes as positive statement that he was robbed by the spirits when he was present. Flames, he says, wreathed and twined themselves across the dark walls of his prison; sparks of fire seemed to flash from his own eyes; shadowy forms of rats and other obscure animals glided over the vault of his room, where they could not possibly be. Strange noises, whistlings, ringing and tolling of bells, and striking of clocks, beset him. Horses trampled on him, monsters butted him in his bed. All these things were, of course, set down to his frenzy, but were, no doubt, the result of his having, by his tortures of mind from his scandalous treatment, been raised into the condition in which the spirit puts forth its powers energumenically, and takes hold on the spiritual world, and comes into startling *rapport* with it. His letters, and gloves, and money, were drawn out of locked boxes when no one was there but himself, and flung about the place. To secure his money, he sent it out of the prison to a friend. His books were flung down from the shelves, a loaf was snatched out of his own hands, and a plate of fruit, which he was offering to a Polish youth. 'God knows,' he says, 'that I am neither a magician nor a Lutheran, that I never read heretical books, nor those which treat of necromancy, nor any prohibited art; yet I can neither defend myself from thievish men when I am absent, nor the devil when I am present.' To comfort him, however, he says that he had a vision of the Blessed Virgin, and that when he was so reduced by illness that he could not bear medicine any longer, he prayed most fervently to her, and was instantly cured. He has recorded this miraculous cure in a sonnet, commencing,

Egro Io languina, e d'alto sonno avinta.

After his release from the mad-house, and when living with Manso at his country estate near Bisaccio, he joined in all the sports and pursuits of those around him. Manso, in a letter, says—'The Signior Torquato is become a mighty hunter, and triumphs over all the asperity of the season and of the country. When the days are bad, we spend them, and the long hours of evening, in hearing music and songs; for one of his principal enjoyments is to listen to the improvvissatori, whose facility for versification he envies. Sometimes, too, we dance with the girls here, a thing which affords him much pleasure; but we chiefly sit conversing by the fire, and often we have fallen into discourse of that spirit which, he says, appears to him.'

Whether grave or gay, this spirit often came to him, and he often held long discourses with it. Manso endeavoured to persuade him that it was a fancy, but Tasso maintained that it was as real as themselves, a Christian spirit, and which Manso admits gave him great comfort and consolation. Tasso, to convince Manso of the reality of this spirit, begged him to be present at an interview. Manso says that he saw Tasso address himself to some invisible object, listen in return, and then reply to what it appeared to have said. He says that the discourses of Tasso 'were so lofty and marvellous, both by the sublimity of their topics and a certain unwonted manner of talking, that, exalted above myself into a certain kind of ecstasy, I did not dare to interrupt them.' Tasso was disappointed, however, that Manso did not see or hear the spirit—which he ought not to have been, after what he himself tells us, that to see spirits the human eye must be purified, or the spirits must array themselves in matter. This is the present acknowledged law in such cases of apparitions. They who see them must be mediums—that is, have their spiritual eyes open—or the spirits must envelope themselves in matter obvious to the outer eye. Tasso did not recollect that Manso might not be in the clairvoyant condition in which he himself was; and Manso, wholly ignorant of these psychological laws, could only suppose Tasso dealing with a subjective idea. Yet Manso evidently *felt* the presence of the spirit, for he was raised by it 'into a kind of ecstasy,' and he confesses that Tasso's spiritual interviews 'were more likely to affect his own mind than that he should dissipate Tasso's true or imaginary opinion.'

To the tens of thousands of to-day who have practically studied these phases of physchology, the whole of Tasso's experience is simple and agreeable to familiar fact, and place the great poet in the numerous class of those who have been treated as visionaries, because they really were more clear-sighted and more matter-of-fact than their horney-eyed neighbours. Perhaps Tasso himself did not comprehend the real condition of those improvvissatori, at whose facility of poetic declamation he so much wondered. Improvisation is but one mode of mediumship. This class of extempore poets, who at a moment break forth often into very sublime and wonderful strains, are frequently noted in their ordinary moods for their very dull and common-place minds. They are but the flutes and trumpets through which spiritual poets pour the music and eloquence of other spheres for the occasion.

Turning to our own poets, we might collect evidences from Chaucer to Shakespeare, but in Milton we come on an avowal that has been a thousand times quoted, of the millions of spiritual beings that walk the air both when we wake and when we sleep. In his 'Paradise Lost,' he teaches doctrines since taught by Swedenborg, and now accepted by thousands—of the soul growing so gross, in the indulgence of sensual tastes in this life, that it cannot well rise from it. He thinks that a period may arrive when men, by growing spiritual purity, may refine the body almost wholly away. Raphael speaks:—

> Time may come when man
> With angels may participate, and find
> No inconvenient diet, nor too light fare;
> And from these corporal nutriments, perhaps,
> Your bodies may at last turn all to spirit,
> Improved by tract of time, and winged, ascend
> Ethereal as we; or may, at choice,
> Here or in heavenly paradises dwell.

Through long ages, however, a different condition was to follow the fall:—

> But when lust,
> By unchaste looks, loose gestures, and foul talk,
> But most by lewd and lavish act of sin,
> Lets in defilement to the inward parts,
> That soul grows clotted by contagion;
> Imbodies and imbrutes till she quite lose
> The divine property of her first being.
> Such are those thick and gloomy shadows damp,
> Or seen in charnel vaults and sepulchres :
> Lingering and sitting by a new-made grave,
> As loath to leave the body that it loved,
> And linked itself by carnal sensuality
> To a degenerate and degraded state.

In his prose, Milton holds the same language. They are not the Muses, he says, but ' the Eternal Spirit, which assists with all utterance and knowledge, and *sends out his Seraphim* with the hallowed fire of his altar to touch and purify the lips of whom he pleases.'

I must leave to some other hand to collect from the long line of our religious poets, Quarles, Herrick, Herbert, Cowper, Keble, as well as from Tennyson, Mrs. Browning, Philip Bailey, and others, the numerous spiritualisms that are scattered through their works. There are abundance of such in Young's ' Night Thoughts.' We may take one:—

> Smitten friends
> Are angels sent as messengers of love;
> For us they languish, and for us they die·
> And shall they languish, shall they die in vain ?
> Ungrateful, shall we grieve their hovering shades
> Which wait the revolution in our hearts ?
> Shall we disdain their silent, soft address —
> Their posthumous advice and pious prayer ?

From the many like admissions in Mrs. Hemans, take also one:—

> Hast thou been told that from the viewless bourne
> The dark way never hath allowed return?
> That all which tears can move with life is fled —
> That earthly love is powerless on the dead?
> Believe it not.

I have already quoted the candid avowal of Southey, of his belief in ghosts; the evidences of the spiritualism of Byron and Shelley ; and as to Coleridge, though in one place he says he has seen too many ghosts to believe in them, in another we find him gravely telling a ghost-story in his 'Table-Talk,' which is given in the second volume of the 'Spiritual Magazine,' p. 229. As for their contemporary, Rogers, he pronounces spiritualism 'a new mode of sense,' 'that mysterious guide,'—

> That oracle to man in mercy given,
> Whose voice is truth, whose wisdom is from heaven.
> ROGERS'S *Poems*, ' *The Voyage of Columbus*.'

Sir Walter Scott, independent of his large use of apparition lore in both his prose and poetry, condemns the narrow prejudice which cannot accept it. He says:—'We talk of a credulous vulgar without recollecting that there is a vulgar incredulity, which, in historical matters, as well as in those of religion, finds it easier to doubt than to examine, and endeavours to assume the credit of an *esprit fort*, by decrying whatever happens to be beyond the very limited comprehension of the sceptic' (*Introduction to 'The Fair Maid of Perth'*).

In the opening chapter of this work, I gave some specimens of the spiritualism of Wordsworth, and as his inculcations of it are both bold and extraordinary, I close this chapter with him.

He opens the third part of 'Peter Bell' with these remarkable stanzas:—

> I've heard of one, a gentle soul,
>   Though given to sadness and to gloom,
> And for the fact will vouch. One night
> It chanced that by a taper's light
>   This man was reading in his room:
>
> Bending as you or I might bend
>   At night o'er any pious book,
> When sudden blackness overspread
> The snow-white page on which he read,
>   And made the good man round him look.
>
> The chamber walls were dark all round,—
>   And to his book he turned again;
> The light had left the good man's taper,
> And formed itself upon the paper
>   Into large letters, bright and plain!

The godly book was in his hand,
　And on the page, more black than coal,
Appeared, set forth in strange array,
A *word* — which to his dying day
　Perplexed the good man's gentle soul.

The ghostly word, full plainly seen,
　Did never from his lips depart;
But he hath said, poor gentle wight!
It brought full many a sin to light
　Out of the bottom of his heart.

Dread spirits! to torment the good
　Why wander from your course so far,
Disordering colour, form, and stature!
Let good men feel the soul of nature,
　And see things as they are.

I know you, potent spirits! well.
　How, with the feeling and the sense
Playing, ye govern foes and friends,
Yoked to your will for fearful ends —
　And this I speak in reverence!

But might I give advice to you,
　Whom in my fear I love so well,
From men of pensive virtue go,
Dread beings; and your empire show
　On hearts like that of Peter Bell.

Your presence I have often felt
　In darkness and the stormy night;
And well I know, if need there be,
Ye can put forth your agency
　When earth is calm and heaven is bright.

Then coming from the wayward world,
　That powerful world in which ye dwell
Come Spirits of the Mind! and try
To-night, beneath the moonlight sky,
　What may be done with Peter Bell.

He adds—

There was a time when *all mankind*
Did listen with a faith sincere
To tuneful tongues in mystery versed.

In his 'Ecclesiastical Sketches,' sonnet xviii., he says :— -

Death, darkness, danger, are our natural lot,
And evil spirits may our walk attend
For aught the wisest know, or comprehend.
Then be *good* spirits, free to breathe a note
Of elevation; let their odours float

> Around these converts; and their glories blend,
> Outshining nightly tapers, or the blaze
> Of the noon-day. Nor doubt that golden cords
> Of good works, mingling with the visions, raise
> The soul to purer worlds.

What Wordsworth taught in song, he asserted also in actual life. Mr. and Mrs. Wordsworth returning once from Cambridge, where they had been paying a visit to the poet's brother, Dr. Wordsworth, Master of Trinity College, they related to us this occurrence. A young man having just come to enter himself a student at Trinity, brought a letter of introduction to Dr. Wordsworth, and on presenting it, asked if the master could recommend to him comfortable chambers. Dr. Wordsworth mentioned to him some then vacant, and the young man took them. In a few days seeing him, Dr. Wordsworth asked him how he liked them. He replied that the chambers themselves were very convenient, but that he should be obliged to leave them. Dr. Wordsworth asking for what reason, the young man replied, that he might think him fanciful, but the rooms were haunted. That he had been woke each night by a child that wandered about the rooms, moaning, and strange to say, with the palms of its hands turned outwards. That he had searched his rooms, found them on each occasion securely locked, and that nothing but an apparition could thus traverse them. Dr. Wordsworth said, he would now be candid with him; that these rooms had been repeatedly abandoned by students who asserted the same thing, but having perfect reliance on his veracity and judgement, from what he had heard of him, he was desirous to see whether he would confirm the story, having had no intimation of it beforehand. I relate the account from memory, after the lapse of a good many years, but I believe it to be substantially correct. Whether the young man thanked the doctor for his recommendation of such lodgings does not appear.

CHAPTER XXII.

MISCELLANEOUS MATTERS.

Gather up the fragments that remain, that nothing be lost.
St. John's Gospel, vi. 12.

WE have now traversed all ages and all countries, and everywhere we have found the faith and the facts of supernaturalism existing in all classes of men—in the highest philosophers as in the simplest individuals; nay, they are the highest philosophers, and the most illustrious apostles of religion, who have been the boldest and firmest asserters of them. It is in the Jewish history, whence we draw our spiritual faith, that supernaturalism reigns supreme. From the heights of Ararat, of Carmel, and of Sinai, it streams down upon us in dazzling glory; it irradiates the tents and the palm-shades of the ancient patriarchs; from the Wilderness of Arabia, from all the cities and plains and streams of Judea, it comes to us in the shape of imperishable manna, and is spread before us with the clusters of the vine, with the piled baskets of figs and pomegranates. The history of our Saviour is one great blaze of the miraculous; it is the promised heritage of his apostles and disciples to the end of time. All Christian churches claim it, all revivers of the faded glories of our faith are reinvested with it. Derided and spurned at by the *Terræ Filii* in every age, it still lives on regardless of them. Wherever literature extends it stamps the page in the face of all opposition: wherever man lives with instructed or uninstructed nature, it lives with him. With the Platos, the Socrateses, the Aristotles, the Senecas, Tacituses, and Ciceros of Antiquity—with those men worshipped for their mighty intellects by the learned of all succeeding ages, it was itself a worshipped guest and power. In our enquiry after it, we have not had to pry into obscure thickets and corners for it, to peer after it as for some minute object in deep grass; we have met it coming as legion and in battalia on all the highways; found it enthroned in all temples; seated at the door of every hall of state, every cottage, and every tent of the nomade. It has been forced on our attention rather than sought after, and so prolific are its perennial harvests, that we have been compelled to lay up but a meagre tithe of it in our historic barns. This volume is but the result of an ear plucked here, a grain picked up there; to have fairly stated its facts would have been to write libraries. And yet is this the thing that we are now-a-days doubting of and denying! We are come to the proof of the proverb, that we cannot see the wood for trees! If we cannot see it, it must be because it is too colossal in its bulk to enter our petty vision. We are in the case of the fly on St. Paul's, that could not comprehend the totality of a single stone, much less of the whole structure. If it be not visible to us, it must be that this country of ours is truly that dusky Cimmeria which the ancients believed it.

Yet along all the course of our progress, there have lain stones and timbers of truth, not easily reducible to our plan; of a shape or character that did not work up in immediate keeping with our line of wall; yet true fragments and commodities for Truth's other temples—in other words, series and classes of facts which demanded an arrangement of their own. Those in the past ages must lie till some mightier builder passes and gathers them; but there are some of our own time, or of that just past, which must at least have an allusion here. Though these traits and facts did not fall fully into my plan of history, they may be here catalogued, though they cannot be fairly detailed.

The department of apparitions alone is a most voluminous one, and that on evidence that has resisted all efforts, however violent, to dislodge it. Amongst those of recent times which have fixed themselves with an invincible pertinacity in popular faith is that which warned Lord Lyttleton, in a dream, of the day and hour of his death, the truth of which has been assailed in vain. Equally well attested is that of the predecessor in a church living of the Königsberg Professor, as related by Count Falkesheim to Sir Nathaniel Wraxall, which revealed a double murder by the pastor of the living. That which appeared to Dr. Scott in Broad Street, London, and sent him to discover the title-deeds of a gentleman in Somersetshire, who would otherwise have lost his estate in a lawsuit with two cousins. That which drove Lady Pennyman and her family out of a house in Lisle, at the commencement of the French Revolution, is well authenticated and well known. That which announced to Sir Charles Lee's daughter, at Waltham in Essex, three miles from Chelmsford, her death that day at twelve o'clock, and which took place then, is related by a Bishop of Gloucester. That of Dorothy Dingle, related by the Rev. Mr. Ruddle, a clergyman of Launceston in Cornwall, occurring in 1665, is well known. Still more celebrated is that of Lord Tyrone to Lady Beresford, to warn her against a most miserable marriage, and to predict the marriage of his (Lord Tyrone's) daughter with Lady Beresford's son, and her own death at the age of forty-seven. In proof of the reality of this ghostly visit, the spirit took hold of her ladyship's wrist, which became marked indelibly, so that she always wore a black ribbon over it. This black ribbon was formerly in the possession of Lady Betty Cobb, Marlborough Buildings, Bath, who during her long life was ever ready to attest the truth of the narration, as are said to be, to this hour, the whole of the Tyrone and Beresford families. The story of Old Booty, from the log-book of Captain Spinks, master of a merchant-ship, and which was confirmed by Captains Spinks and Barnaby and their men, in court at Westminster, in 1687, reign of James II., before Chief Justice

Herbert and three other judges, is familiar to everyone. Scarcely less so is the relation of an apparition by Sir John Sherbrooke and General Wynyard abroad, the apparition being that of a brother of General Wynyard, then in England. The brother, it was learnt in due course of the post, died at that very time; and Sir John Sherbrooke afterwards accosted a gentleman in Piccadilly, from his strong likeness to the apparition, who is said to have been a twin brother of the deceased. In some narratives of this affair the gentleman is stated not to have been a twin brother, but one who strikingly resembled him. The leading facts in every account are the same. The apparition to Dr. Donne of his living wife, when he was in Paris, representing the death of his child, is related by Izaak Walton, in his 'Life of Donne,' as narrated by Dr. Donne himself. The apparition of the father of the Duke of Buckingham, warning his son of his approaching fate, is well known and well attested. Baxter relates several cases as communicated to him at first hand. All these are published in a variety of works, but most of them may be found collected in Bohn's edition of Ennemoser's 'History of Magic.' Mr. Dale Owen has recorded several well-proved cases of apparition in his 'Footfalls on the Boundary of Another World;' amongst others one occurring to my own mother, furnished by myself, and well known in the family. In the 'Spiritual Magazine' will be found a number of cases of recent occurrence, amongst them one occurring to a lady in Yorkshire, confirmed, on application, by herself; and in the same number, the saving of a ship by a dream of the captain, also confirmed, on application, by himself (vol. i. 551). In the second volume of the 'Spiritual Magazine' are also two cases occurring to Hugh Miller, extracted from his autobiography.

But of all the cases of apparition of ancient or modern times, none are better authenticated than that of Captain Wheatcroft, who fell at the storming of Lucknow in 1847, as related by Mr. Owen in his 'Footfalls,' and in an earlier page of this work.

Colonel Swift, late Keeper of the Crown Jewels in the Tower, relates, in 'Notes and Queries' of September 8, 1860, a singular apparition witnessed by himself and family in October 1817, in his room in that ancient fortress, famous for so many royal murders and royal and aristocratic executions; and adds, that soon afterwards, a sentinel on duty before the door of the jewel-office was so frightened by an apparition, that he died.

In the third volume of the 'Spiritual Magazine' will be found an account by me of the appearance of lights and spirits in a cottage near Ilam, Staffordshire, called Clamps-in-the-Wood, for upwards of fifty years, and down to the present year, when the family living in it have deserted it. The phenomena were familiar to the whole neighbourhood. Clamps himself lived there fifty years, was fond of the appearances, and called them his glorious lights. His successors saw them the same.

These are here noted, in addition to various cases already related in this work. In fact, nothing is more universal than apparitions. The Cambridge Association for Spiritual Enquiry, familiarly called the Ghost Club, consisting of eminent members of the university, have stated that their carefully-conducted researches on the subject of apparitions have led them to regard such appearances as a settled fact. A member of this association informed Mr. Dale Owen that he had collected 2,000 cases of apparitions: and Dr. Garth Wilkinson says truly, in his 'Life of Swedenborg:' 'The lowest *experience* of all time is rife in spiritual intercourse already; man believes it in his fears and hopes, even when his education is against it; almost every family has its legends; and nothing but the wanting courage to divulge them keeps back this supernaturalism from forming a library of itself.' This was also the candid confession of Kant; and I am bound to say, that I never yet met with a family which, when its members came to open their hearts on the subject, was not found to have its facts or knowledge of this kind. Even while declaring that they do not believe them, what numbers of individuals oddly assure you that the facts are as they relate them. Believed by nature, disbelieved by education, and yet true notwithstanding! Such is the pitiable see-saw of mind induced by fashionable theory and the terror of imputed superstition.

The positive statements, by most creditable people, of hauntings, are equally numerous. Besides those extraordinary cases, already noticed as witnessed by Dr. Kerner in Germany, and others, given in Mr. Owen's 'Footfalls,' those of the celebrated Cock-lane Ghost and the Drummer of Tedworth, though often declared to be delusions or impositions, have never been proved so. Dr. Johnson has been much ridiculed for believing in this ghost; but he appears to have had excellent reasons for his belief. He made a thorough investigation of the matter; floors and wainscots were pulled up, but no trick discovered, though the search was made under the supervision of Dr. Johnson, Bishop Percy, and other gentlemen. The ghost is declared to have appeared to three different persons; and the poor girl through whom it made the raps—a child of only thirteen—was tried in all sorts of ways, and with tied-up hands and feet, from the supposition that she made the noises herself; but in vain: the noises went on, and that in different rooms, and even different houses. That such a deception should be carried on by a family, on which it only brought persecution, the pillory, and ruin, was too absurd for the belief of any except the so-called incredulous. The girl was simply a medium; and all the phenomena were in accordance with laws now perfectly familiar. An able analysis of the case is given in the 'Spiritual Magazine,' ii. 73.

The drummer of Tedworth is equally celebrated, and equally clear, by the light of modern experience, to have been a *bonâ fide* case of spiritual agency. It was carried on in the house of Mr. Mompesson, a gentleman and magistrate of Tedworth, in Wilts, vastly to his annoyance and injury, but too plainly to him anything but imposture. In fact, all the phenomena were precisely such as have, at the present day, occurred in scores and hundreds of cases in England and America — lights, knockings, moving of furniture, answering to raps by counter-raps, and abundance of such things, which are become now the sheerest commonplaces. The whole narrative may be seen in Glanville's 'Sadducismus Triumphatus,' and a good summary of it in the second volume of the 'Spiritual Magazine,' p. 18, by Truth-Seeker.

As for knockings, there seem to have been no age and no country without them. Aubrey says that he heard knocks in his bed—heard them a few days before his father died—and he relates other instances. Melancthon says Luther was visited by a spirit which announced itself by knocking at his door. A burgess of Oppenheim having died, noises and knockings were in the house, and being asked if it were he, to make three distinct raps; this was done. It was twelve months before the occupants of the house got to comprehend and satisfy his demands, when he went away; a close approach to the discovery of communication with spirits by raps, in 1620, which was not fully made in America till 1846. Calmet, in his 'Phantom World,' says that M. de St. Maur was haunted by knocks, as well as other manifestations, and. at last, by a distinct voice. Mr. Sargent found rappings and similar manifestations amongst the Indians of the Rocky Mountains, and over extensive countries, where they had been witnessed for ages. Many of the natives declared the answers to be those of 'lying spirits,' a fact only too well recognised in Europe, and wherever spiritualism exists. Beaumont, in his 'Gleanings of Antiquities,' published in 1724, avows his belief in the supernatural in all its powers, and mentions *rappings* there (p. 202). There is a house in London in which, for three years last past, have been heard and still are, almost continual knockings against the wainscot overhead, and sometimes a noise like telling money, and of men sawing, to the great disturbance of the inhabitants, and often lights have been seen like flashes of lightning; and the person who rents this house has told me that when she has removed eighteen miles from London, the knockings have followed her. Glanville, that staunch champion of spiritual action, gives earlier accounts of knockings. He says there were such, and *a hand seen* at old Gast's House, in Little Burton, in 1677. The knockings were on a bed's head, and the hand was seen holding a hammer, which made the strokes. Little Burton is near Leigh, in Somersetshire. In 1679 knockings were also heard at the house of a Mr. Lawrence, in the Little Minories, London. Our times have not the exclusive experience of even knockings; and Bishop Heber says the evidences of such things which Glanville gives are easier to ridicule than disprove.

An Italian physician assured Mr. Elihu Rich that he was an eye-witness to the following circumstance, which took place at a camp fire, where one of the ponderous saddles used by the horsemen of the prairies was brought forward, and the owner of it, by the contact only of his fingers, caused it to bound like an India-rubber ball from the ground, till it finally sprang to twice the height of a man. This took place in the open field, to the astonishment of the spectators, of a saddle galloping without a horse. But not only on the American continent are spirit influences so readily excited; a Mr. Wolf, of Athens, United States, writes: ' I have seen spirits, talked with them and shaken hands with them as really and *substantially* as one man shakes hands with another'—a fact which numbers now-a-days can confirm. The same gentleman says, that he has not only seen direct spirit-writing done, but seen the hand doing it.

In our own day no hauntings have been more remarkable than those of the house at Willington Mill, between Newcastle-on-Tyne and North Shields. Between the railway running betwixt those places and the River Tyne there lie, in a hollow, some few cottages, a parsonage, and a steam flour-mill and miller's house; these constitute the hamlet of Willington. This mill belonged to Messrs. Unthank and Procter, and Mr. Joseph Procter resided in the house by the mill. He is a member of the Society of Friends, and, when these events came to my knowledge, was a gentleman in the prime of life, and his wife was an intelligent lady of the family of the Carrs, the celebrated biscuit-bakers of Carlisle. I learned that this very respectable and well-informed family, belonging to a sect of all others most accustomed to control, to regulate, and even to put down the imagination—the last people in the world, as it would appear, to be affected by mere imaginary terrors—had for years been persecuted by the most extraordinary noises and apparitions. It was said that the figures seen were of a man in the dress of a priest and of a woman in grey, and having no eyes. That these figures frequently went about the house, and that the man would sometimes be seen gliding backward and forward, about three feet from the floor, level with the bottom of the second story window; sometimes in the window itself, partly within and partly without the glass, quite luminous, and diffusing a radiance all around it. This figure, which went by the name of Old Jeffery, the same as the ghost at the Wesleys, was seen by various persons, and under circumstances which precluded all possibility of its being produced, as had been suggested, by a magic lantern. Besides this, it was said that various noises were heard at times, and glasses and other articles at table would be lifted up and put down again without any visible cause. I was moreover informed that Dr. Drury, of North Shields, had volunteered to sit up in the house, in order to satisfy himself of the truth of these reports; that he had done so, in company with a friend, and had been so terribly frightened by the appearance of the female apparition as to faint away, and to become, for a considerable time, extremely ill. It was added that a narrative of these events and circumstances had been published by Mr. Richardson, of Newcastle, in a pamphlet, and afterwards repeated in the 'Local Historian's Table Book.'

Being on a tour in the north in 1845, I called at the shop of Mr. Richardson for the pamphlet. On receiving it, I made some jocose remark about the ghost; but I was gravely assured by him that it was no joking matter, but one which had been amply proved to be perfectly true by many most intelligent people of that town and neighbourhood, and had proved a serious cause of annoyance to Mr. Procter and his family, who had done all they could to check the circulation of the report, as it brought them so many curious enquirers.

On reading the pamphlet, I found it to contain a letter from Dr. Drury to Mr. Procter, detailing the particulars of his awful, and, as it proved to him, serious visit. My room does not permit my giving all these particulars: they may be read in the Table-Book just mentioned; in 'Howitt's Journal' of 1847; and in Mrs. Crowe's 'Nightside of Nature.' One thing, however, must be noticed, which is, that one of the first announcements of the presence of the ghost was a 'rapping, as of one knocking with his knuckles amongst their feet.' This had frequently been heard by the family, and also a heavy pounding, as with a paviour's rammer. Dr. Drury says, in his letter to Mr. Procter, that no one ever went to the house more disbelieving than he was: and Mr. Procter, in the correspondence, says that he has 'thirty witnesses to various things, which cannot be satisfactorily accounted for on any other principle than that of spiritual agency.'

I was myself extremely desirous to spend a night in the house, and, if possible, see the ghost, notwithstanding Dr. Drury's catastrophe. For this purpose I called, but found the family gone to Carlisle. The foreman and his wife, however, showed me over the house, and confirmed all that I had heard from their own personal knowledge, as matters too palpable and positive to be questioned, any more than that the house stood and the mill ground. I afterwards saw Mrs. Procter, her friends, brothers, and sisters at Carlisle, who all confirmed the story in every particular; some of them having had very serious experience of the apparition, and one of the ladies having in consequence, during her stay, removed to the foreman's house to sleep, refusing to pass another night in the house itself. All these particulars may be read in the 'Nightside of Nature,' as copied from my account by Mrs. Crowe; and as again confirmed to her by Mr. Procter himself.

After enduring these annoyances from the apparitions for many years, Mr. Procter, apprehensive of the effect of the many strange phenomena on the minds of his children, quitted the house, and removed to North Shields, and subsequently to Tynemouth. By a correspondence betwixt him and a Catholic gentleman enquiring into these matters, only a year or two ago, it appears, that the hauntings never followed him to either of his new abodes. That, though they still appeared occasionally at the old house, now turned into dwellings for the mill-people, they don't mind them. Mr. Procter adds, that a lady, a clairvoyant, a stranger to the neighbourhood, being thrown into the clairvoyant state, and being asked to go to this mill, described the priest and the grey lady; and added, that the priest refused to allow the female ghost to confess a deadly crime committed in that spot many years ago, and that this was the troubling cause of the poor woman; representations quite agreeing with the impressions of those who had repeatedly seen the ghosts. The publication of these occurrences brought Mr. Procter an extraordinary number of letters from different parts of the country, and from persons of different ranks, some of them of much property, informing him that they and their residences were, and had been for years, subject to visitations of precisely a similar character. Similar ones were taking place about the same time at Windsor, Dublin, Liverpool, Carlisle, and Sunderland.

In Mrs. Crowe's 'Nightside of Nature,' will also be found the account of the hauntings of an old house at Cheshunt, belonging to Sir Henry Meux. This account was taken down from the relation of Mr. and Mrs. Charles Kean by a well-known publisher, and I myself heard the same particulars from the same popular actor. This house had been taken by Mr. Chapman, the brother-in-law of Mrs. Kean. It was large, and had a considerable quantity of land attached to it. The unusually low rent at which it was offered induced Mr. Chapman to take a lease of it. From causes fully detailed by Mrs. Crowe, they were soon, however, compelled to quit it, and then learned that many others had been under the same necessity before. They kept the cause of their removal still, and managed to sell their lease to a clergyman who kept a school. He, in his turn, was compelled to give up the house for the same causes, and for years it stood empty. It has recently been partly pulled down and rebuilt, and it would seem that this alteration has broken the spiritual spell, for it is now inhabited and reported free from haunting.

A case of modern possession was published something more than thirty years ago by the Rev. James Heaton, Wesleyan minister. The subject was a boy, who, under the influence supposed to be demoniac, would run about in the surbase of the room with the utmost rapidity, where in his ordinary state he could not find standing room for a moment. The Wesleyan ministers used many prayers to exorcise the demon; with what success I do not remember; for, having presented the volume to Sir Walter Scott for use in a proposed second edition of his Demonology, I have never since seen a copy of it. It is still, I understand, in the Abbotsford library.

Cases of sudden prophetic inspiration occur, here and there, at the present day.

When Miss Bremer was in Rome in 1858, before the Italian Revolution had broken out, she went to reside for some weeks in the Convent of the Sacré Cœur, in Rome, in order to have a living idea of conventual life. She gives this scene:—' Last evening the prophetic spirit fell upon Sœur Genevieve, under the influence of which, drawing herself up to her full height, she, with upraised arms, foretold the fall of the temporal power of the Pope, war, bloodshed, and great revolutions, but out of which the Catholic Church shall come forth renovated, victorious, poor. but holy and powerful as in the earliest times ' (' Switzerland and Italy,' p. 220).

A singular prophecy for a nun, since, in a great measure fulfilled, and probably to be so wholly.

A very remarkable prophecy by an American Friend, Joseph Hoag, of the successive schisms in that and other religious societies; of the strange outbreak of the Freemasons; and, lastly, of the American civil war, has for many years been printed and in circulation amongst the Friends. The 'Life of Joseph Hoag,' containing these prophecies, may be obtained of Mr. Alfred Bennett, 5 Bishopsgate Without.

SECOND-SIGHT.

The curious book of ninety-seven pages called the 'Secret Commonwealth,' written by the Rev. Robert Kirk, minister of Aberfoil, in 1691, and of which a hundred copies only were published by Messrs. Longmans in 1815, gives much the same account of what are called the Highland superstitions as we find in various other Scotch works, and especially in Martin's 'Western Isles' and 'Voyage to St. Kilda.' He tells us that the creatures called fauns, elves, fairies, brownies, and the like, are the forms under which the ancestors of the people of different countries appear occasionally. 'Their apparel and speech is like that of the people and country where they lived; so are they seen to wear plaids and variegated garments in the Highlands of Scotland and suanocks in Ireland. The very devils conjured in any country do answer in the language of the place.'

The author thinks that the fact of people, on leaving the Highlands, generally losing the faculty of second-sight, proves that these spirits, wherever they are found, and under whatever form they appear, are *Demones Loci*, and never quit their proper countries. As it is mentioned in Daniel that the Prince or Angel of Persia had withstood the angel who came to that prophet, so it is possible that all nations have their spiritual princes, overseers, and attendants upon them. So the lares, and lemures, and penates of Greece and Rome; the nymphs and fauns, the satyrs and various spirits, of the classical times and countries; the necks and alves of Northern Europe; the cobolds and spirits of the mines in Germany; the genii and peri of the East—are all of this class, and probably ancestral spirits. This is a kindred idea to that of nearly all the nations of the world, which have universally based their mythologies on the worship of the dead, and has a very curious coincidence with the experience of modern spiritualism, where the ancestral spirits are always coming forward to notice.

In this volume and its appendix, by Theophilus Insulanus, there are numerous recitals of Doubles, or Co-Walkers, of wraiths or apparitions, of funeral processions, troops, and battles, wrecks and murders, seen beforehand. Some of the seers inherit the faculty; others acquire it by particular ceremonies. The gift is generally a melancholy one; and they who possess it would gladly be rid of it. Some possess it young, and lose it as they grow up; others acquire it only when of mature age. Mr. Kirk, though a minister, was of opinion that the seership is by no means evil. When they are first made participant of this curious knowledge, he says, they are put into a transport, rapture, and sort of death—as divested of their bodies and all their senses; but it occasions 'no wramp or strain in the understanding;' and he testifies that they are, 'for the most part, candid, honest, and sociable people.'

How exactly are these the conditions of clairvoyance! The faculty of second-sight is, in truth, clairvoyance produced by the conditions of the mountains and isles. They are the results of electric and magnetic influences prevailing there preeminently, as they prevail in the Swabian Alps, in Germany, and in many other hill regions. They are remarkable amongst the Druses of Lebanon. Mr. Kirk adds, that the goodness of the lives of the seers, like that of the ancient seers and prophets, is the best proof of their mission. One of the modes of the seers of the Highlands and Western Isles, he says, in divining the future, was to look steadily at the shoulder-blade of a sheep, goat, &c. This is the same class of operations as that of looking into mirrors, or upon a black surface, or into ink, as the Egyptians, and akin to crystalography; or seeing images in a boy's nail.

The treatise of Theophilus Insulanus, which is published separately, as well as appended to the 'Secret Commonwealth,' consists of 119 sections, every section of which includes a fact in second-sight. These facts are supported by names of all the places and persons introduced, and furnish a remarkable collection of instances of seership. Amongst these is one announcing the death of George II., with its attendant circumstances, by John Macleod, of the Isle of Skye, and the remarkable vision of the death of Archbishop Sharpe, by Robert Barclay, of Urie, in Scotland, already given under the head 'George Fox and his Friends.' Insulanus zealously defends the faculty of second-sight on moral, religious, and historic grounds, with abundance of proofs from both Scripture and classic literature; and he, in 1762, arrived at the same conclusion as the spiritualists of the present day, that the seers do not see the objects observed with the *outer*, but with the *inner* eye: and this, he says, is the more certain, because seers, after becoming blind, saw by second-sight quite as clearly as before. He argues, that everyone who denies this power of spiritual vision and prescience, not only denies the truth of the greatest men of all countries and ages, but weakens the very foundations of scriptural revelation. 'As to those uncommon, fanciful gentlemen,' he says, 'who neither believe a future state of rewards and punishments, nor that they are of the rank they hold in creation, they are truly to be pitied, and to be allowed to be what they choose. Under this category we must always include those adepts in science who refine themselves into infidelity; are the nuisances of society, and the disgrace of human nature; who bring themselves to the level of the brute-beasts that perish! Happy, indeed, were it for them, could they succeed in that boasted metamorphosis!'

But the most valuable portion of the 'Secret Commonwealth' is the letter of Lord Tarbot to the Hon. Robert Boyle, the philosopher, because it contains relations of his personal knowledge and experience. He says, 'I had heard much, but believed very little of the second sight; yet its being assumed by several of great veracity, I was induced to make enquiry after it in the year 1652, being then confined to abide in the north of Scotland by the English usurpers.' Amongst the different phases of the phenomenon which he gives, is one agreeing remarkably with the experience of the spiritualists of to-day—namely, that the seers could not easily tell what space of time would intervene betwixt the apparition and the event predicted. All spirits appear to have little idea of time. Yet he says the seers by habit acquire an impression of the probable nearness or distance of the foreboded event. In cases of prefigured death, the person seen will die sooner or later, according as the winding-sheet in which he appears shrouds more or less of his body. If it closes over the head, the death will take place at once, or has taken place already at a distance.

The facts of second-sight seen by Lord Tarbot are too bulky for my space, but they were such as must have convinced any reasonable man. One of his own train who was a seer, on entering a house where they were to stay all night, suddenly retreated with a loud cry, saying he saw a corpse being carried from the house, and that somebody would die there very soon, and entreated his lordship not to lodge there. Lord Tarbot went in, and, finding no one ill there, determined to remain. Before he left the next day, however, the landlord, a healthy Highlander, died of apoplexy. In all cases he found the seer perfectly correct, though often under the most unlikely circumstances.

Besides the works of Martin, already mentioned, the reader will find many extraordinary facts of second-sight in the works of Stewart and Grant, on the 'Highlands,' and in the literature of Germany and Denmark, where it also prevails.

What is called the Preaching Epidemic in Sweden, which

broke out in 1842, particularly in the provinces of Kalmar, Wexio, and Jön Kopping, was, in fact, a Revival, presenting very much the same symptoms as were displayed in the American Revivals, and since then in this country and Ireland, and for a complete view of which Mr. William Wilkinson's excellent work on that subject may be studied. It resembled the demonstrations amongst the early Friends, the early Methodists, those of the Cevennois, and strong religious excitement in different ages and countries from the first revival at the day of Pentecost until now — strong convulsions, outcries under a sense of sin, prostration, tremblings, and often trance. The full account of it, as translated by Mrs. Howitt, from the statement of the Bishop of Skara to the Archbishop of Upsala may be read in the second volume of 'Ennemoser's History of Magic,' p. 503, and a good *resumé* of it in the 'Spiritual Magazine,' iv. 544. The Swedish clergy treated it as a disease, and snubbed and physicked it, and at length had the pleasure of seeing it pass away. The good bishop asks himself the question whether the religious impressions produced were in accordance with the established notions of the operations of grace in the heart, and thinks they were not, because the excited person, immediately after he began to quake, experienced 'an unspeakable peace, joy and blessedness.' It might have been supposed that peace and joy in the Holy Ghost *were* signs of Christian conviction, but the bishop holds that these ought to spring from a sense 'of new-born faith through atoning grace,' and they were, on the contrary, from 'a certain immediate and miraculous influence from God.' What the notions of atoning grace may be in Sweden I do not pretend to understand, but an immediate and miraculous influence from God producing 'peace, joy, and blessedness' would have been undoubtedly understood as the effects of divine grace in the time of Christ and the apostles. The bishop admits, too, that in this state the people were endowed with a wonderful eloquence, and a purity of language far above their ordinary condition and knowledge.

There was a grace in their manner, a holy beauty in their countenances that astonished him. Even children spoke, he says, in language which, in a normal state, would have been impossible to them. Under the ministry of one of these inspired children, the whole assembly sate in the deepest silence, and many wept. The young people went about singing what are called Zion's hymns; and, what is most important, the bishop admits that it always produced a religious state of mind, strengthened by the apparently miraculous operations within; that no disorder or impropriety of any kind took place, and that it sent multitudes to church who never went there before, reclaimed many from the error of their ways, and produced lasting effects on the minds of many a hardened sinner. The oddity of calling such a dispensation a 'disease' makes one startlingly conscious of the strange, factitious sort of thing modern Christianity must have become, when it stares at the aspect of its own mother and calls her a mad woman. What difference is there betwixt the ideas of such school-bred bishops and clergy who assiduously put down this movement, and those of the people who thought the apostles drunk at Pentecost?

BEALINGS BELLS.

On Tuesday, February 2, 1834, the bells in Major Moor's house at Great Bealings, near Woodbridge, commenced an unaccountable ringing without any visible agency, which they continued almost every day, more or less, till March 27, in all fifty-three days. On returning from church on Sunday afternoon, on the aforesaid February 2, he was told by the two only servants left in the house, a man and a woman, that the bell of the dining-room, in which nobody was, had rung three several times. The next day the same bell rang several times, the last time in the major's hearing, and though no one was within reach of the bell-pull. In the afternoon, all the bells in the kitchen, a row of nine, rang violently. Whilst the major was watching the bells, five of them rang again so violently that he says he should not have wondered to see them broken from their fastenings. To make a short story, these ringings continued, all the time mentioned, at intervals, though every means were used to discover the cause. Sometimes all nine rang together, sometimes five, sometimes only one. On one occasion one of them was knocked against the ceiling, and struck off the whitewash. All the bells were rang at one time or other except the front-door bell, which hung in the row betwixt the five which often rang together and the nine. Some other odd bells, making up twelve, also rang. Major Moor had all his servants collected together to make sure that none of them rang the bells, and the bells rang in their faces as merrily as ever. On publishing an account of the annoyance in the 'Ipswich Journal,' he received a number of letters suggesting that there were mice or rats in the walls, or mischievous servants, or somebody in concert with the servants; but he took measures to ascertain if any such causes existed, and satisfied himself that they did not.

His letter, however, brought in a number of accounts of similar ringings and other hauntings. Like Mr. Procter, of Willington, he had touched on a tender place, and found that he was not by any means alone in his persecution. He was informed of ringings and other strange occurrences at a house in Kent; at Chesterfield in Derbyshire; at Earl Street, Westminster; at Ramsgate; at Aldborough in Suffolk; at Cambridge; at Chelmsford; at Greenwich Hospital; at Lark Hall, Burrowdown, Northumberland; at Oxford; at Prestbury near Cheltenham; at Sevenoaks; at Sydersterne Rectory, Norfolk; at Stapleton Grove, Gloucestershire; at Clewer, near Windsor; in Ipswich, and at other places, the names of which the parties haunted declined to have published. Almost all of these were reported to him as confirmed on application by gentlemen and ladies of fortune, by clergymen and officers. A lady in Suffolk, living at a country hall, gave him repeated accounts of their bells ringing previous to her father's death, though every means were taken to detect any person concerned in a trick, and to decide that it could not be rats in the walls. Mr. William Felkin, since Mayor of Nottingham, sent the major word of the ringing of the bells at Rose House, Chesterfield; and Mr. Ashwell, the inhabitant, a literary and scientific gentleman, confirmed the report on direct application to him. He said that he had had the wires cut, and yet the bells rang as fast as ever. He fixed a bell up in front of a wall without a wire, and it commenced ringing immediately. At Earl Street, Westminster, the servant-maid went into convulsions at the mysterious ringing. One of the most extraordinary cases was that at Greenwich Hospital, in the room of Lieutenant Rivers. Major Moor put himself in communication with Lieutenant Rivers, and in his little book called 'Bealings Bells' he has published the lieutenant's own account. These bells were watched night and day; all persons were excluded from the apartments where the bell-pulls were, except the bell-hanger and his assistants, who watched. They still rang, but in this instance when the bell-hanger cut the wires they ceased to ring, but, as soon as he reunited them, they rang again. The neighbours were admitted to see the ringing, and exercise their ingenuity in the discovery of the cause, but in vain. All the bells rang but the front-door bell, and, to prevent this occurring, Lieutenant Rivers tied up the bell-pull. While observing to some friends that that never rang, it immediately set up a good peal, and with that the ringing ceased altogether. The bells in another officer's apartments were similarly rung for a week. The ringing in Mr. Rivers' apartments continued only four days. Major Moor visited the hospital, and went over the rooms with Lieutenant and Mrs. Rivers, who declared the ringing still inexplicable. In all these cases, except where the wires were cut and the bells still continued ringing, rats or servants, or other mischievous persons might be still suspected, but the bells in various cases still ringing in the faces of the owners of the houses, without any wires, put these suspicions out of court. One gentleman told the major that in his father's house, the bells ringing thus without apparent cause, his father fixed a bell without wire to a wall and it rang, and the piano in the parlour began to play of itself. Nor were the ringings all: in many cases there were knockings, and other mysterious noises. The Rev. Mr. Stewart, the Incumbent of Sydersterne, near Fakenham, Norfolk, says in a letter to the major — ' Our noises are of a graver character. Smart successions of tappings, groanings, cryings, sobbings, disgusting scratchings, heavy trampings, and thundering knocks in all the rooms and passages, have distressed us here for a period of nearly *nine* years, during the occupancy of my cure. They *still* continue, to the annoyance of my family, the alarm of my servants, and the occasional flight of some of them; and I am enabled clearly to trace their existence in this parsonage to a period of sixty years past.' Mr. Stewart adds that he has no doubt that, could he have the evidence of his predecessors, he could trace the nuisance very much farther back. In 1833 and 1834, he says, they kept open house to enable respectable people known to them, or introduced to them, to satisfy their curiosity; but their kindness, he says, was abused, their motives misinterpreted, and even their characters maligned. 'We therefore,' he says, 'closed our doors, and they remain hermetically sealed.'

There are various other cases given in Major Moor's little volume, which I have already referred to. The major is anxious, throughout, to disclaim any belief in the causes being supernatural, though he thinks them *præternatural*; and with this fine distinction he leaves himself in that curious poise of mind, induced by modern education, in which a man, professing not to know what to make of it, hopes to escape the charge of superstition.

Amongst the MEDIUMS who appeared before spiritualism was much or at all talked of in England, there are two who ought not to be unnoticed in this history: they are Mary Jobson and Elizabeth Squirrel.

MARY JOBSON, OF SUNDERLAND.

The case of this little girl, of thirteen years of age, the daughter of John and Elizabeth Jobson, of Sunderland, was made known by Dr. Reid Clanny, F.R.S., Physician in Ordinary to the late Duke of Sussex, and Senior Physician of the Sunderland Infirmary. It occurred in 1839, and Dr. Clanny only became aware of it by accident, having to go to the house on other business. The little girl was then in the latter stage of her illness; but Dr. Clanny saw and heard various striking phenomena in her presence, and had the candour to enquire thoroughly into all the extraordinary circumstances of the case, the fairness to believe the unimpeachable evidence of numerous other witnesses, as well as of his senses, and the boldness to publish them. One of the most remarkable facts of the case is, that so many medical men admitted full conviction of the truth of the manifestations—namely, two physicians and three surgeons. The witnesses altogether amount to sixteen. Doctor after doctor was called in; the child was suffering from pain and pressure on the back of the head, and dimness of sight. She was leeched, blistered, purged, but all without producing any relief; convulsions ensued; fresh doctors were called in; fresh blisters and medicines applied. For three-and-twenty weeks this went on; the successive doctors pronounced her complaint water on the brain, an abscess, a contraction—in short, the doctors were totally confounded, and the poor child became blind, deaf, and dumb. Still a Mr. Ward was for another blister and fresh medicine, when strange knocks at the head of the bed began to be heard, a voice, coming from the bed's head or from the child, in a tone and manner totally different from her own, bade them dismiss the doctors, who could do her no good, and that the cure would be performed by a miracle. We have the direct statement of the father, who heard the knocks and the voice, but put more faith in the doctors than them. He would insist on putting on the blister, but the knocks and other noises became so violent that they were compelled to take it off again, when they ceased. The father says, as he used to watch by her, he heard loud knocks, clashings of arms, stamping of footsteps—though no person could be seen—and the sweetest music at times. The voice often commanded water to be thrown on the floor, and it was thrown there in splashes by invisible hands. The mother and another sister and many neighbours saw and heard the like things—doors opening and shutting, steps coming up the stairs, but nobody visible, and the doors all found fast. The Messrs. Embleton, surgeons, and their assistant, Mr. Beattie, heard the same things, and Mr. R. B. Embleton took down a message from the voice. A beautifully represented sun and moon were painted on the ceiling, after the manner of Pordage's scenes: they all saw it, the doctors as well as the neighbours. The father, who was not then convinced, washed them over with whitewash, but they reappeared through it, and Dr. Clanny saw them still there after the recovery of the child—for she did recover, and suddenly, on June 22, 1840, after an illness of nearly eight months. She continued well, but frequently continued to hear sweet music at times, and Dr. Drury, who visited her several times after her wonderful recovery, heard it too. Many other phenomena, as the removal of mugs and other articles, took place; but we may close this notice with the evidence of Mr. Torbock : ' I have had, at different times and places, lengthened and very serious conversations with nearly all the persons who have borne testimony to this miraculous case, and I am well assured that they are persons who are known to be religious and trustworthy; and moreover, that they have faithfully discharged their duty in this important affair between God and man.' Dr. Clanny did not escape the inevitable amount of ridicule and persecution for his publication of this case; but he reprinted it in a second edition, and asserted that his views remained unchanged, and that nothing had shaken the proofs of any of these extraordinary facts.

HEALING BY SPIRITUAL MEANS.

In the preamble to a statute of Henry VIII. of England, in the year 1511, is stated, that 'smiths, weavers, and women, boldly and accustomably take upon them *great cures*, and things of great difficulty, in which they partly use sorcery and witchcraft.'

SLEEPING PREACHERS.

A particular class of such clairvoyants are sleeping preachers. There have been many such. In the reign of James I. one Richard Haddock, of New College, Oxford, who practised medicine there, and was equally ignorant of Latin and Greek, as well as of divinity, had fallen into the habit of preaching in his sleep, during which he not only astonished his hearers by the depth and eloquence of his discourses, but by his accurate quotations of the learned languages. When awake—which is almost invariably the case with clairvoyants—he knew nothing of what he had said or done in his sleep, and could not pronounce a word of the classical tongues. The man was sent for to court, and first heard in his sleep, and then examined by the king, who dealt with him in his usual way of imagined shrewdness, till he had satisfied himself that the man had assumed this peculiarity to attract attention; and he badgered and cross-examined the poor man till he prevailed on him to confess that this was so. The king's profundity, however, did not attempt to solve the mystery of a man's speaking Greek and Latin who knew none: and it is probable that, with his subtle questionings, he mingled more persuasive promises, so as to give himself credit for unusual sagacity, for he sent the man back to Oxford, and soon after gave him preferment in the Church, having him ordained for the purpose— a singular mode, certainly, of punishing religious imposture.

The 'Republican,' a newspaper of Cadiz, Ohio, United States of America, states that Mrs. Burney, a highly respectable member of the Presbyterian Church, has preached a sermon in a sleep-state, half an hour long, every other Sunday, at ten o'clock, for eighteen years. It adds that her sermons are excellent and abound in scriptural quotations; and that when she wakes she knows nothing whatever of what she has said. Medical men have watched her case and have decided that there is no deception about it, but that it surpasses their comprehension.

In Barber's 'History and Antiquities of the Northern States of America,' there is an account of another lady, Miss Rachel Baker, of the State of New York, who from 1812 to 1816 almost every night, on retiring to rest fell into a peculiar sleep, in which she went through a regular course of religious exercises, commencing with prayer, then giving a sermon, and again concluding with prayer. During this time the body had no more motion than a statue. Her discourses were pronounced excellent, and were sometimes embellished with fine metaphors, vivid descriptions, and poetical quotations. During all this period her health was extremely good; her friends, however, were not at ease about it, and got the medical men to destroy this spiritual lucidity by means of opium and other narcotics.

Southey, in his 'Life of Wesley,' speaks of similar manifestations, and, from his ignorance of mesmeric science, treats them as assumed. He says, one man in this condition could make himself as stiff as an iron bar, so that no force could possibly bend him. No man *could* make himself so, but catalepsy does it regularly; but of this Southey had no knowledge. These hasty conclusions of the learned, who yet do not know everything, reminds us of some excellent remarks of a writer in 'Blackwood's Magazine' for June, 1850:—'It would really seem as if we required some new apostle of charity, for, practically, it has disappeared among us. Why is it that almost invariably we put the worse constructions on the conduct of our neighbours? Why should we seek, with such amazing avidity, to infer guilt from equivocal circumstances, and reject, with a certain fiendishness of purpose, all extenuating matter? This is a very common, but a very bad feature of the age we live in.' Men speak in a proud contempt of phenomena which they do not understand, and the progress of science throws back that contempt on themselves.

Amongst instances of hearing music on the approach of death, none are more affecting than that of the unfortunate Dauphin of France, the son of Louis XVI. Everyone is familiar with the atrocious treatment of this poor child by the revolutionists. In his last hours, Gomin, one of his attendants, seeing him calm, motionless, and mute, said to him, 'I hope you are not in pain just now?' 'Oh, yes, I am still in pain, but not nearly so much — the music is so delightful.' Now, there was no music to be heard; no sound from without could penetrate the room where the young martyr lay expiring. Gomin, astonished, said to him, 'From what direction do you hear this music?' 'From above.'—'Is it long that you have heard it?' 'Since you knelt down. Do *you* not hear it? Listen! listen!' And the child, with a nervous motion, raised his faltering hand, as he opened his large eyes, illumined by ecstatic delight. His poor keeper, unwilling to destroy the last sweet illusion, appeared to listen. After a few minutes of attention, the child again started, his eyes sparkled, and he cried out in intense rapture, 'From amongst all the voices I have distinguished that of my mother.'

Lasne, one of the other guardians, came up to relieve Gomin. He sat down near the bed, and the prince looked at him long and with a fixed and dreamy eye. On his making a slight movement, Lasne asked him how he felt, and what he would like. 'Do you think my sister could have heard the music?' said the child. 'How much good it would have done her!' Lasne could not answer. The anguished glance of the dying boy turned eagerly and peeringly towards the window. An exclamation of joy escaped his lips. Then he said, looking at his keeper, 'I have something to tell you.' Lasne came close to him, and took his hand. The little prisoner leaned on the keeper's breast, who listened—but in vain! All was said. God had spared the young martyr his last mortal convulsion of anguish. God had kept to Himself the knowledge of his last thought. Lasne put his hand upon the child's heart. The heart of Louis XVII. had ceased to beat. The time was a quarter past two P.M.

This account of the last moments of the Dauphin was taken from the lips of these, his guardians, when they were old men, each eighty years of age. From Lasne in 1837, and from Gomin in 1840. ('The Life, Sufferings, and Death of Louis XVII.,' by A. de Beauchesne.)

Direct Spirit-Writings.

One of the most surprising spiritual manifestations of the present day is that of direct spirit-writing. Many mediums have written, as well as drawn, under the influence of spiritual agency in their hands; but numbers, also, have witnessed paper and pencil laid at a distance from everyone in the company, and writing being then and there done by invisible intelligence. The Baron Guldenstubbe, a Swedish nobleman living in Paris, has published a work on this subject, 'Pneumatologie Positive.' In that work he gives sixty-seven facsimiles of writings made on paper, before witnesses of high reputation, without any person approaching them. They are in various languages, ancient and modern. Amongst the persons who witnessed these astounding operations were the Prince Leonide de Galitzin of Moscow; Prince S. Metschersky; M. Ravené, senior of Berlin; Dr. Georgii, a disciple of Ling, the Swedish poet and physiologist, at that time living in London; Colonel Toutcheff; Dr. Bowron of Paris; M. Kiorboé, a distinguished artist of Paris, residing 43 Rue de Chemin de Versailles; Colonel Kollman of Paris; Baron de Vorgts-Rhetz; and Baron de Uexkull. Count d'Ourches, who witnessed similar writings being done, laid paper himself in his own room, in churches, on tombs, and on the banks above the monuments of Pascal and Racine in the cemetery of Montmartre, and obtained direct communications in writing of the most striking character. Since then Baron Guldenstubbe is said to have increased his collection of such specimens to many hundreds, all done under such observation as prevented any collusion. Mr. Dale Owen paid two visits to Paris to be an eye-witness of this phenomenon, and called at my house, before his return to America, to show me the results. As I was not at home, he left a note saying he was extremely successful.

This manifestation is another confirmation of the ancient occurrence of such things. Having myself witnessed some of the recent manifestations, I am bound to credit those of the past. The first of these on record is the writing of the Mosaic Law, by the finger of God, on Mount Sinai. The second, I believe, is the writing on the wall of the banquetting hall of Belteshazzar at Babylon, when the hand that wrote was visible to the whole court. But both profane and church history have assertions of the same fact. In the fifth century Synesius, the good Bishop of Cyrene, is related to have been accused of embezzling three hundred pounds of gold intrusted to him by Evagrius, the philosopher, for the poor. In a dream Evagrius appeared to the bishop, and assured him that he had written an acquittal, and that it would be found in his hand in his tomb. Synesius, fully believing the dream, called on the sons of Evagrius and told it to them. They then, in astonishment, confessed that their father had commanded them to put the bill for the money in his tomb, and bury it with him. They all proceeded to the tomb, broke it open, and found the bill, fully receipted, in the hand of the philosopher, also adding, that Jesus Christ had repaid him, as the bishop had promised.

Similar cases are recorded by the old ecclesiastical historians, but we must pass them to come to more modern times. In 'News from the Invisible World,' p. 119, the following account is quoted from Dr. Moore:—'In the northern part of England, I think Lancashire (for I had the story from a clergyman of that county), the minister, before he began to read prayers at church, saw a paper lying on his book, which he supposed to be the banns of marriage. He opened it, and saw written, in a fair and distinct hand, words to the following purport: "John P. and James D. have murdered a travelling man, have robbed him of his effects, and buried him in ——'s orchard." The minister, extremely startled, asked his clerk hastily if he had placed any paper in the prayer-book. The clerk declared that he had not; but the minister prudently concealed the contents of the paper, for the two men's names therein contained were those of the clerk and the sexton of the church.

'The minister then went directly to a magistrate, told him what had happened, and took out the paper to read it, when, to his great surprise, nothing appeared therein; it was a blank piece of white paper! The justice on that accused the minister of whim and fancy, and said that his head must certainly have been distempered when he imagined such strange contents upon a plain piece of paper. The good clergyman plainly saw the hand of God in this matter, and by earnest entreaty prevailed with the justice to grant his warrant against the clerk and sexton, who were taken up on suspicion, and separately confined and examined; when many contradictions appeared in their examinations, for the sexton, who kept an alehouse, owned the having lodged such a man at his house, and the clerk said he was that evening at the sexton's, and no such man was there. It was thought proper to search their houses, in which were found several pieces of gold, and goods belonging to men who travelled the country; yet they gave so tolerable an account of them that no positive proof could be made out, till the clergyman, recollecting that the paper mentioned the dead body to be buried in such an orchard—a circumstance which before slipped his memory. The place was searched, and the body was found; on hearing which the sexton confessed the fact, accusing the clerk as his accomplice, and they were both accordingly executed.'

A still more curious case was in my possession some time

ago, and which I understand is likely to be published in full in the expected work of Mr. Dale Owen. I can only give a brief outline from memory. The account was derived from direct authority, having been written down at the time by the minister of the place, an eye-witness of the circumstance. In the reign of Charles II.—I do not recollect the precise date—a laird of Redcastle, in the Highlands of Scotland, was astonished by the receipt of letters, written in a hand quite unknown to anyone in that part of the country, and without signature, yet detailing the most private affairs of all his neighbours round. Next, these letters were dropped in his house, or put into desks under lock and key, and, when the laird would not pay attention to them, they were hung on trees in the garden—containing the most secret conversation of himself and wife in their private room. He was thus obliged to look well after them, and take care of them. On one occasion he was told that the next day he should find a document nearly concerning himself in the secret drawer of his cabinet where he kept his most private papers. He immediately searched the cabinet, took out all the papers from the secret drawer, and convinced himself that no such document was there then. He immediately placed a guard on the cabinet to prevent anyone approaching it; but the next morning a paper was hung on a tree in the garden, saying he would find the promised document in the cabinet. He opened it, and found the document amongst the papers in the secret drawer. More than this— his son being strangely affected, and supposed to be bewitched by the spirits, was sent to some distant watering-place. In his absence, one of these mysterious letters informed the laird of his son's improvement in health, announced his speedy recovery through the aid of themselves—the spirits—and when he would return home. On the journey, the son and his tutor had been haunted by these spirits, who at night, in their inn had poured out all the money from their pockets upon the table, and hung their clothes up at the top of the room. All endeavours to exorcise these spirits being found useless, a shrewd friend advised the laird not to read the letters, but to put them at once into the fire, saying that spirits were as sensible to contempt as men, and if thus treated they would soon desist, which proved to be the case.

We may close this chapter with a fact related in the life of George Washington Walker, a member of the Society of Friends, who some years ago visited South Africa with James Backhouse, and another friend. At Clumber in Albany they were at the house of a pious settler named Richard Hulley. He told them that, going on one occasion to seek honey for a sick friend, he fell from a tree, had two ribs broken, and was seized with locked jaw. His life was despaired of, and not being at all at peace in his conscience, he fell into great agony, and prayed intensely for forgiveness and restoration. Whilst doing this, he felt a strong assurance that he was healed. This was confirmed by a spirit-voice; he rose, found his broken ribs quite reset and sound. To his astonishment he was perfectly well, and the effect of this had been a permanent condition of gratitude and piety—another proof of the continued faith of Friends in spiritual help, and of its operations in every quarter of the globe.

CHAPTER XXIII.

CONCLUSION.

This is your hour and the power of darkness.
St. Luke xxii. 53.

I MAY now finally remind the reader, of what, indeed, the whole progress of this history has shown him, that the evidence on this subject is so voluminous, that no one work, no, nor a dozen large volumes, could contain it. The farther I have gone, the more, as I have often had to avow, I have been compelled to select and reject. On all sides came pouring in facts. Men of all nations, and all religions, of all grades of education, and every rank of intellect, pressed on to put in their claims as witnesses. In the heart and soul of mankind the great truth is found to be rooted inextricably with the roots of life, and of all consciousness. It has proved itself, what I started with calling *Lex Magna*, a great law of creation. It is no longer what the incapables, I mean those become incapable of judging of and admitting evidence, would fain call it, the belief of a few weak or visionary individuals; we may boldly pronounce it the faith of all the race, the contrary being only the exceptions. The greatest names in the history of intellect and of human achievement are the prominent names in this cardinal faith. The list of these names, and the proofs of the fact *in extenso*, would make a large volume of itself. We must go on numbering the princes and chieftains of mind through all time. Like Scott's clans, they come thronging over the hills —

> Still gathering as they pour along,
> A voice more loud, a tide more strong.

But it must be admitted that in no age have the deadening effects of a materialistic education been so prominent as in the present. It is a curious coincidence that, as I sit down to put the last words to this work, a circumstance has occurred which most singularly demonstrates this; showing that the scientific mind is fast losing the power of accepting even the most physical facts, if they have anything of the wonderful in them.

In the Eastern Annexe to the Great Exhibition Building there is a specimen of coal, containing a cavity, from which a frog is stated to have been taken, and the frog also is exhibited. The frog and coal are from the collieries of Mr. John Russell, Newport, Monmouthshire, and have excited great curiosity in the visitors.

In the 'Times' of this present month, September, 1862, Captain Buckland, the son of the late Dean of Westminster, the well-known geologist, accused in a letter the directors of the Exhibition of allowing the display of a gross imposition, and recommending that this frog and piece of coal should be expelled the Exhibition. He contended that it was utterly impossible that any toad or frog could have borne the heat and enormous pressure attending the formation of coal strata, at the depth of more than one hundred yards, to say nothing of the thousands, possibly millions of years, during which it must have continued to live enclosed in the coal. Not only did Captain Buckland declare the whole a gross imposition; he quoted the settled opinion of his father on the subject, and Professor Owen, in a note to him, positively backed him up in the assertion that such a thing was impossible. Buckland and Owen, his great authority in Natural History, made very merry about 'Froggy' having tumbled into the pit, or gone down in the machinery, and so having crawled into a hole in the coal. The 'Times' reporter, with that avidity with which the press of to-day always jumps at an opportunity of denying the marvellous, also pronounced it 'an enormous humbug.'

Now, whatever might be the merits of the individual case at the Exhibition, all this was so utterly in the face of scores of recorded cases of frogs and toads found in stone, coal, and in the heart of solid trees, with the dates, names, and places of the persons witnessing the facts given at the time, that one was curious to see if no one would contradict this new *ex cathedrâ* doctrine. On September 20 appeared a note from Mr. John Scott, Lilleshall Coal Depôt, Great Western Railway, Paddington, giving two such cases from living witnesses. One was his own wife, who was prepared to state that she saw one of her father's workmen, many years ago, split open a piece of coal, and discover in the middle of it a moderate-sized frog or toad, she was not sure which, alive and still able to move, and she remembered distinctly the oval shape and smooth surface where the animal had lain.

Secondly, he stated that Samuel Goodwin, a stonemason, whom he had known five-and-twenty years, and who is very trustworthy, deposes as follows: — 'When I worked in the quarry at Kettlebrook with Charles Alldridge, we sawed a stone through about four feet thick, quite solid, and in the middle was a toad about the size of my fist, and a hole about twice the size. We took it out, and it lived about half an hour and then died. We worked the stone, and it was used as a plinth in Birmingham Town-Hall.'

Another correspondent stated that he knew a stonemason who had found a toad in what is called Rowley-rag, a hard stone with which Birmingham streets are paved; and a third, that a toad was known to have been ejected from a large lump of coal actually laid on the fire, and which burst open with a loud explosion, no doubt from the expansion of the air in the cavity where the toad was. Another correspondent stated that he was informed at Chillingham that a toad had been found enclosed in the solid marble of a chimney-piece in the castle there, the seat of Lord Tankerville.

Immediately after these letters in the 'Times,' a friend cut the following paragraph from the 'Stamford Mercury.' The exact date of the paper I do not know, but it was presented to me on October 31, 1862.

'TOAD FOUND IN STONE. — On Monday morning last, as the workmen of Mr. Wm. Wartnaby, of Little Gonerby, were engaged in excavating the ground in the Brewery-yard at Spittlegate, of Mr. J. B. Burbidge and Co., brewers, for the purpose of making a cellar, one of the men, who was using the pickaxe in a bed or layer of stone, at the depth of between seven and eight feet from the surface, broke into a stone in which was embedded a live toad, in rather a shallow cavity. Mr. Wartnaby and three of his workmen were in the excavation at the time, and he took the toad out of its cavity. It was injured in one of its hind legs, near to the juncture with the body, by the blow of the pickaxe which opened the stone, but it lived and moved till the following morning. Both stone and toad are preserved. Further particulars may be given hereafter, as a very rigid examination has been made into the circumstances; but no fact can be more fully or certainly established by human evidence than the above, let sceptics on this subject say what they will. One can only suppose this very ancient inhabitant of the earth has come on purpose to revive the recent discussion about him and his stony habitation.'

On September 23, another correspondent reminded the editor of the 'Times' that the preceding ones had not informed the public of what had already been done on the other side of the channel on this very subject, namely, to test the assertions made for ages, that toads can live in a cavity shut in from light and air. He said that M. Seguin had been trying for some years to verify it, and, going to work as all practical men should do, had imprisoned twenty toads, each in a separate block of plaster of Paris, and after twelve years had broken open the blocks, and found four of the toads alive. He then repeated the experiment, and it is proposed that the second series of blocks shall be broken open in the presence of the Academy.

Four toads had survived twelve years in this enclosure. We are not told at what period of the year M. Seguin enclosed them. Probably, if this was done at the moment they were about to hybernate, when their physical condition is prepared by nature for such cessation of breathing, more, perhaps all the twenty, would have been found living. Humboldt notices the fact that frogs, just at coming out of their winter sleep, can remain eight times longer under water without drowning than they can later on in spring: and there is little doubt but at the moment of going into the sleep they could be enclosed hermetically without much damage to their vital power. How many perished on being buried in coal and other strata, in proportion to those that survived, we have no means of ascertaining, but probably the greater proportion perished. In M. Seguin's experiment one-fifth of the number survived twelve years, and if twelve years, why not twelve thousand, where there could be no decomposing influence?

I have heard of a stone which had stood probably for some hundreds of years as a ball on the gate-post of an old mansion falling and breaking, and in the centre, thus laid open, a live toad in its hole. Now all naturalists, and thousands of other persons, know that toads and frogs, like tortoises, serpents, dormice, and the whole tribe of insects which bury themselves in the earth, or conceal themselves in secret places, where they live through the winter without food,— sink themselves into the ground, or in the mud at the bottom of pools and ditches to pass the winter. For six months they are, as it were, hermetically sealed up, many of them in cases of solid mud, preventing all possibility of breathing, and come out at spring fresh and active. Vipers, when young, have been shut up, excluded from all but air, and have grown and thriven on that apparently meagre aliment; nay, two cerastes, a sort of Egyptian serpent mentioned by Dr. Shaw, lived five years in a bottle closely corked, without anything in the bottle except a small quantity of sand. When he saw them, they had just cast their skins, and appeared as brisk and lively as ever.

Some years ago, I saw at Farnsfield in Nottinghamshire, a ditch which was undergoing a thorough digging out and cleaning. It appeared to have grown full of earth and stiff mud from years of neglect. At the bottom of more than a foot's depth of mud as stiff as butter, on the firm earth below it, lay a regular stratum of frogs. It was a wonderful sight! Scores of frogs, which, as they were thrown out with the stiff mud, such only excepted as were cut in two by the spade, speedily woke up, and hopped away to seek fresh quarters. If these frogs could live six months in this nearly solid casing of viscous mud, why not six or any number of years?

In my 'Two Years in Victoria,' I relate that Dr. Valentine of Campbell-Town, Tasmania, an experienced naturalist, and a man of undoubted veracity, told me that, having collected some hair-worms in a saucer in water, he kept them some time in his laboratory; that he then put them in a cupboard and forgot them. Three years afterwards, wanting a saucer for some purpose, and seeing this in the cupboard, he took it out. Observing at the bottom what appeared a cake of dried mud, he drew his finger once or twice across it, and it appearing to be dried mud, he poured water upon it, and left it to dissolve. On his return to the room he was astonished to see a number of hair-worms in the saucer in active life and motion, and he then recollected the circumstance of his putting them there three years before.

This fact is supported by Dr. Braid, who says there are creatures which have not the power of migrating, which, in the intense summers of torrid climates, are preserved through a state of torpor, superinduced by a want of sufficient moisture, their bodies being dried up by excessive heat. This is the case with snails, which are said to have been revived by a little water thrown upon them, after having remained in a dry and torpid state for fifteen years. The *vibris tritici* has also been restored, after perfect torpitude and apparent death for five years and eight months, by merely soaking in water. Some small microscopic animals have been apparently killed and revived again a dozen times, by drying and then applying moisture to them. This is remarkably verified in the case of the wheel-animalculi; and Spallanzani states that some animalculi have been recovered by moisture after a torpor of twenty-four years. According to Humboldt, a host of microscopic insects are lifted by the winds from the evaporating waters below. Motionless, and to all appearance dead, they float on the breeze, until the dew bears them back to the nourishing earth, and bursting the tissue which encloses their transparent bodies, instils new life and motion into all their organs. Humboldt also adds, that some large animals are thrown into apparent death by want of moisture. Such he states to be the case with the alligator and boa-constrictor during the dry season in the plains of Venezuela, and with other animals elsewhere. (See Humboldt's ' Views of Nature,' and Braid's ' Human Hybernation'). In the latter work proofs are given that this vital power exists even in man, and amongst other proofs, the great Lahore case, of the burial and revival of the Fakir, is given on the authority of Sir Claude Wade, an eye-witness.

All these facts point to the great inference that, if animals can live for years excluded from the air, in solid substances, why may not this be done in the bowels of the earth for any number of years? So long as the organisation of such creatures is preserved from injury by external action, why should they not continue to retain the vital principle for any term of years, however immense? The undoubted facts already given prove that they do, and perhaps the most extraordinary of such facts remains yet to be produced.

The Rev. Richard Cobbold, when attending the lectures of the celebrated geologist, Dr. Edward Daniel Clarke, wrote the following letter, since published, to his mother, the late accomplished Mrs. Elizabeth Cobbold of Holy Wells, near

LIVE LIZARDS IN CHALK-STONE.

Ipswich. The letter is dated Caius College, Cambridge, Feb. 14, 1818:—

'I must here mention one of the most interesting specimens placed before us to-day. What think you, mother, of an animal now living upon the face of the earth, that in all probability was antediluvian? Your first expression will be "Oh! such a thing is impossible!" and I should certainly have thought the same. But if you had heard Dr. Clarke express his belief in such a case, in as firm and animated terms as I have this day done, you would have come away with the same impression of confidence in that fact as I now have.

'A clergyman, a friend of Dr. Clarke's, was digging a chalk-pit upon his estate. He visited the workmen with him one day and gave orders that if they dug up any fossils they should preserve them. Whilst he was there, he saw them dig out several fossil remains of the echina and of the lizard species called newts.

'Now, mind, a mass of chalk-stone was brought up from a depth of forty-five fathoms from the surface of the earth, which, upon being broken to pieces, presented the curious phenomena of three whole creatures, which, upon being extracted from the chalk and placed upon a piece of brown paper, were laid down upon the earth, whilst the doctor and his friend went to look upon the workmen. The sun was shining fully upon them. When they returned to these specimens, they found, to their astonishment, that they were exhibiting symptoms of life. By the warmth of the sun they were actually reanimated.

'The gentlemen took them home, thinking it would be of the utmost consequence if they could be preserved alive. Two of them died, which two were placed before us, but one, which was placed in tepid water, was perfectly restored to activity. It skipped and twisted itself about, and was as well as if it had never been torpid. So active did it become that it skipped out of the vessel in which it was placed upon the garden lawn, and made its escape, so that, in all possibility, *there is an animal now living upon the face of the earth which was before the flood*!

'That no cavil might be made, Dr. Clarke and his friend were at great expense in collecting newts from various parts of the kingdom, but not one resembled these. They are of an entirely extinct species, never before known. Dr. Clarke took particular delight in mentioning this, as he hoped to extend the information of it into all countries.'

That newts, like frogs, are amphibious animals, may, perhaps, furnish a reason for their power of retaining life in this extraordinary manner. If anyone, however, desires to see this question completely set at rest by unquestionable facts, he has only to refer to the works of the eminent naturalist, Gosse.

That men like Professor Owen, famous as physiological naturalists, should, with facts like these in abundance before them, and on such evidence as Dr. Clarke and M. Seguin, to say nothing of hundreds of other respectable people, deny these powers in nature—a nature crowded with marvels, when we look into it, in the instincts, modes of life, and transformations of insects, in the habits and functions of birds and larger animals, in the growth, the properties, deadly or beneficent, the glories and essences of plants—is a melancholy proof of the progress of that paralysis of faith, in the operations of God in creation, which is fast ruining the human mind. If this spirit go on, the soul of man will soon have suffered a deadly gangrene in all its finer endowments, and cease to be anything but mechanical. Its triumphs in that direction seem to be at the expense of every finer power or perception. Nature itself is a congeries of miracles, yet, every day, those whose business it is to develope and demonstrate them are denying even these. Dr. Garth Wilkinson, in his 'Human Body in connection with Man,' has well said:—' In no science does the present state of knowledge appear so manifestly as in physiology; in none is the handwriting on the wall so plain. Great is the feast of professors here; but *Mene, mene, Tehel, Upharsin*, is brighter than their chandeliers.' The professors themselves acknowledge how vast is the province they have to traverse, even in their own department. Dr. Carpenter says:—' Of by far the larger part of the organised creation, little is certainly known. Of no single species—of none of our commonest native animals—*not even of man himself*—can our knowledge be regarded as anything but imperfect. Yet, in pursuing this species of knowledge, men of science delight to obliterate the old landmarks as they go. If they cannot now grasp such facts as the tenacity of life in reptiles, how far must they be from a capacity to comprehend the facts of spirit-life?

Scarcely was the denial of the existence of toads and frogs in stone, coal, &c., rebutted by facts, when a writer, signing himself ' Y,' stoutly denied, in the ' Times,' the evidence of the phenomenon called ' Will-o'-the-Wisp'—the *ignis fatuus*. Proofs, however, of its frequent occurrence, were speedily adduced; especially by Dr. Phipson, the author of ' Phosphorescence, or Emission of Light by Minerals, Plants and Animals,' who, on the 4th of November, not only showed that he had seen them himself, but quoted Beccaria, Humboldt, and other great naturalists and natural philosophers, for well-authenticated cases of this light, which appears to be merely carburetted hydrogen gas, produced from the decomposition of vegetable matter in marshy places, in a state of ignition. What next? Will the contracting spirit of faith of this age next expect us to believe that there is no sun or moon?—that they are mere popular delusions?

But we are not yet at the end of this process of mental petrifaction. Christ said, ' When I come shall I find faith on the earth?' The obvious inference from his words is, that he should find little; and the prophecy, in its hastening fulfilment, is one of the most luminous proofs of the truth of his religion. Whatever happened to Christ, in his divine mission, undoubtedly typified what must happen to his church. He was ' driven into the wilderness to be tempted of the devil:' and every follower of him, and his whole church, have to pass through this ordinance of temptation. As he was rejected of the great and learned, so must his church be. As he had to acknowledge 'the hour and power of darkness,' and undergo the agony and bloody sweat, so must his church. As he was tried and condemned by the authorities of this world, so must his church be, the *scribes* and pharisees shrieking all the time, ' Crucify him!' As he was executed in ignominy, and amid the desertion even of his few remaining friends, so must his church be. But, at the moment of that consummation, the satanic spell will be broken, the earth will be darkened, but the rocks of indurated intellectual pride will be rent asunder, and the veil torn wide which prevents the human eye seeing the spiritual life beyond.

As Christ walked the earth in his open mission for three years, so it may be three thousand before he has walked through the earth in his church, and fulfilled in it the cycle of his prefigured dispensations. But no man can avoid seeing the determined tendency of the world's career towards this fulfilment. The pulpit, growing less and less spiritual, will find itself wholly unable to cope with a press growing more and more infidelized. Nay, the pulpit and the prelatical throne are already, in this country, outstripping the press in infidelity. At this moment, the Bishop of Natal publishes a book, declaring his abandonment of Biblical history, and prognosticating that, in five years, no young man in the Church of England will retain faith in it. This bishop is not ashamed to own that he has been brought to this humiliating condition by the questions put to him by African savages. Was not this to be foreseen, when the Church of England, at its establishment, abandoned the Gospel assurance that miracles should everywhere attend the true ministers of Christ. How is it possible that any missionaries can convert the heathen, who go to them unfurnished with the celestial credentials, the miracle-working powers, by which the early apostles convinced and converted the heathen? A church in such a condition is an ecclesiastical

Samson shorn of his locks. In vain do we expect from a church thus devirilized the life which must convert a world. And where, indeed, is now the favourite boast of the Anglican church, that Christianity once proved by miracle, that proof is sufficient for all time? Here we have the answer from Bishop Colenso: he has found that it is not sufficient for sharp-witted Kaffirs. They refuse to accept Christianity, except on the same conditions that the ancient world accepted it, accompanied by those supernatural evidences which pronounced its divinity. They are right, and Protestantism is wrong, and must go to school to the spiritualists if it is not to go to utter ruin.

The hour and the power of darkness advance portentously. The triumph of unbelief, generated by an unnatural union between unspiritual Protestantism and demon-spirited philosophy, will become terrible beyond conception. The great battle of Armageddon *must* be fought. Those horrors now feebly typified in the frightful conflict in America—the abandonment of a youth of concord; the brother's hand dyed in brother's blood; the lust of dominion grown monstrous; the vaunt of liberty no longer heard; the most hideous despotism will rage over the unchristianized earth. Men, having achieved their grand hope of treading out the life of Christ, will, like Jean Paul in his dream, find themselves in a ' horror of great darkness,' searching through the universe for a divine fraternal and paternal Power; seeking for a Saviour, every man from his own woe-haunted soul, and from the lawless ferocity of his own neighbour. That will be the hour of darkness following our Saviour's final crucifixion in his church. Let us pray that this hour, and that the forerunning reign of infidelity, may be short, for, as the Saviour has foretold, unless it be shortened, ' no flesh shall be saved.' The triumph of infidelity alone can work its own cure, in the dreary horror and frightful chaos of its own experience. Let us pray, then, that this second chaos may speedily feel the great spirit brooding over it, and recalling it to light and order. That the spiritual proofs of the Gospel may be sent down to us more palpably and abundantly; seeing that the lack of miracles has blunted all the logical weapons of the Protestant church in its voluntary renunciation of the spiritual gifts of Christ. In the return of this spirit and manifestation of life lies the sole hope, the sole resource of the Christian church.

Let us all pray, then, that the healthy balance of the human mind may be restored. That we may be endowed with the vigour of judgement necessary to weigh and distinguish the false from the true — to recognise natural and spiritual facts, each in their places; and thus to avoid superstition on the one hand, and the far worse error of infidelity on the other. In a word, that man may recover from the paralysis of his intellect in its more spiritual regions, and once more, like the great minds of all past times, repossess the whole compass of his nature, exercising the natural and spiritual faculties in the perfection of his being.

Jurieu, in his 'Pastoral Letters,' has well said, 'There are times in which men believe everything; in this wherein we now are, they believe nothing.' He thinks there is a mean to be struck, and that men at least ought to believe *something*. That to be superstitious is weak, but to be sceptical is weaker, and is the worst and most fatal disposition in the world. That because historians have not been all infallible, is no reason that we should treat them as all liars; and if they are not so, then abundance of facts recorded by them prove the truth of revelation. Since Jurieu's day the sceptics have pushed their historic doubts right through the Scriptures; and we now see these materialistic teredines, in the garb of established clergy, and furnished with a national sanction, and sustained on the national wealth, boring their joyous way through the old timbers of the Church of England. At such a sight one is strongly reminded of the severe rebuke of the great sceptic, Lord Bolingbroke, to the Vicar of Battersea—'Let me tell you, seriously, that the greatest miracle in the world is the subsistence of Christianity, and its preservation as a religion, when the preaching of it is committed to the care of such unchristian wretches as you.'

Thus out of the extreme of infidelity bursts forth the voice of a better conviction, and the faith of all true men is justified. The vigorous and noble-minded American poet, Whittier, has said it already —' The supernaturalism of all countries is but the exaggeration and extortion of actual fact. A great truth underlies it. It is nature herself, repelling the slanders of the materialist, and vindicating her claims to an informing and all-directing spirit—the confused and incoherent utterance of her everlasting protest against "the fool" who hath said in his heart " there is no God."' That balance of the human mind which so urgently demands restoration Isaac Taylor, in his ' Physical Theory of Another Life,' tells us must come as a moral necessity. He says, ' Notwithstanding prejudices of all sorts, vulgar and philosophic, facts of whatever class, and of whatever tendency, will, at length, receive their due regard as the materials of science —and the era may be predicted, in which a complete reaction shall take its course, and the true principles of reasoning be made to embrace a vastly wider field than that which may be measured by the human hand and eye' (p. 257). Therefore, whatever may be the depths of disbelief to which the age may have yet to go, in the words of that spiritual poet, and spiritual sufferer, William Cowper—

> Thus heavenward all things tend. For all were once
> Perfect, and all must be at length restored.
> So God hath greatly purposed ; who would else,
> In his dishonoured works himself endure
> Dishonour, and be wronged without redress.

THE END.

LONDON
PRINTED BY SPOTTISWOODE AND CO.
NEW-STREET SQUARE

www.ingramcontent.com/pod-product-compliance
Lightning Source LLC
Chambersburg PA
CBHW021425300426
44114CB00010B/658